I0289754

Ghanshyam Sharma, Rajesh Bhatt (Eds.)
Trends in Hindi Linguistics

Trends in Linguistics
Studies and Monographs

Editor
Volker Gast

Editorial Board
Walter Bisang
Hans Henrich Hock
Natalia Levshina
Heiko Narrog
Matthias Schlesewsky
Amir Zeldes
Niina Ning Zhang

Editor responsible for this volume
Hans Henrich Hock

Volume 325

Trends in Hindi Linguistics

Edited by
Ghanshyam Sharma
Rajesh Bhatt

DE GRUYTER
MOUTON

ISBN 978-3-11-070805-9
e-ISBN (PDF) 978-3-11-061079-6
e-ISBN (EPUB) 978-3-11-060806-9
ISSN 1861-4302

Library of Congress Control Number: 2018955059

Bibliographic information published by the Deutsche Nationalbibliothek
The Deutsche Nationalbibliothek lists this publication in the Deutsche Nationalbibliografie; detailed bibliographic data are available on the Internet at http://dnb.dnb.de.

© 2020 Walter de Gruyter GmbH, Berlin/Boston
This volume is text- and page-identical with the hardback published in 2018.
Printing and binding: CPI books GmbH, Leck

www.degruyter.com

To Annie Montaut

Preface

This volume grows out of a very unique gathering of linguists working on Hindi that was organized by the first editor at INALCO, Paris, from September 14–16, 2016. The conference brought together linguists with a wide range of interests, backgrounds and methodologies and we hope that this volume will give the reader a taste of the depth, diversity, and progress that characterize contemporary work on Hindi and South Asian languages more generally. The bulk of the papers engage with questions in syntax and semantics but they do so with quite different research programs and they do so with different tools. What is beautiful is that this does not lead to conceptual incoherence; rather in the best argumentative tradition of the subcontinent, we have research that is deepened by the multiplicity of vantage points. To point out just a few of these dimensions, we have arguments from historical change (Montaut), detailed analysis of corpora (Kostina, Zakharyin), cross-linguistic variation (Hook & Koul), stylistic variation (Khoklova), and computational analysis of texts (Fatma).

The complex verbal structures of Hindi, their syntax and their semantics, have drawn the attention of linguists through the years and we are happy to report that they have not lost their allure. The papers by Manetta, Montaut, Kostina, Das, Fatma, and Drocco all deal with various aspects of Hindi verbal structures. Manetta's paper introduces a new line of attack by using arguments from Verb Phrase Ellipsis to argue for particular structures and in doing so it also establishes a place for Verb Phrase Ellipsis in the grammar of Hindi. The question of participial relative clauses receives attention from Zakharyin and Mahajan. Zakharyin discusses pragmatic restrictions on the availability of participial relativization while Mahajan presents us with a case based analysis of participle relatives in Hindi.

In addition to new approaches to the classic phenomena of Hindi grammar, several authors introduce new questions. The paper by Dayal which kicks off the volume examines the semantics of bare nominal expressions in Hindi and provides us with a set of diagnostics that tell us that the naive idea that they are just underdetermined with respect to definiteness is incorrect. Instead we are given a picture where indefiniteness has structural correlates but definiteness may not. The paper sets up a program of research in cross-linguistic semantics and has implications for second language acquisition. Another new angle is brought up by the Hook & Koul contribution which gives us a way forward on a mystery of Hindi syntax—predicates which behave intransitively despite the presence of transitive verb *kar* 'to do'. In the best traditions of cross-linguistic work, they note that the corresponding structures in Kashmiri have an expletive exponent; an

https://doi.org/10.1515/9783110610796-201

observation that makes the exceptional behavior of the Hindi cases less mysterious. We would like to thank Professor Hans Heinrich Hock for his help in editing the volume. We would also like this occasion to note with sorrow the death of two eminent Hindi linguists: Professor Alice Davison and Professor Omkar Koul. Professor Davison was looking forward to attending the meeting in Paris and anonymously reviewed two of the articles in this volume. Unfortunately, she could not make it to the conference. Professor Koul passed away while this volume was being completed. Their passing is a big loss to the field. We feel grateful that they were both involved in this volume, Professor Davison through her reviewing and Professor Koul through his co-authored paper.

Ghanshyam Sharma
Rajesh Bhatt

Contents

Preface —— vii

Acknowledgements —— xi

Transliteration —— xiii

Veneeta Dayal
(In)definiteness without articles: diagnosis, analysis, implications —— 1

Rajesh Bhatt, Vincent Homer
Differential comparatives in Hindi-Urdu —— 27

Emily Manetta
The structure of complex predicates in Hindi-Urdu: evidence from verb-phrase ellipsis —— 47

Anoop Mahajan
Case licensing in Hindi prenominal relative clauses —— 85

Boris Zakharyin
Constraints on attributive functions of Hindi perfect participles manifesting the resultant state —— 107

Annie Montaut
On the nature of the Hindi infinitive: History as an answer to its syntactic behavior? —— 115

Ekaterina Kostina
Main verb form in structures of ability/possibility in Hindi —— 147

Pradeep Kumar Das
Agreement in conjunct verb construction: let's solve the problem —— 187

Shamim Fatma
Conjunct verbs in Hindi —— 217

Peter Edwin Hook, Omkar N. Koul
Impersonal expressions in Hindi-Urdu and phantom valents in Kashmiri — 245

Andrea Drocco
An attempt to understand the encoding of reduced transitivity in Hindi: the case of compound verbs with *jānā* — 265

Liudmila Khokhlova
Syntactic constraints in modern Hindi — 287

Ghanshyam Sharma
A pragmatic account of directive strategies in Hindi — 303

Tej Krishan Bhatia
Discovering the Hindi grammatical tradition: Historicity and second language acquisition — 333

List of contributors — 355

Index — 359

Acknowledgements

The present volume contains some of the peer-reviewed papers presented at the International conference on Hindi studies organized by Ghanshyam Sharma at the Institut national des langues et civilisations orientales (INALCO) in Paris on September 14–16, 2016. The conference was organized under the auspices of the Indian Ministry of Foreign Affairs, Delhi and the Embassy of India in Paris. We would like to thank all the authorities in Delhi and Paris who lent their full support to the organization of the conference.

We are also grateful to the authorities at the following institution who provided generous financial support to organize the Hindi conference in Paris.

- Institut national des langues et civilisations orientales (INALCO), Paris
- Mondes iranien et indien (UMR-7528), Paris
- Laboratoire d'excellence – Empirical Foundation of Linguistics, Paris

Last but not least, we are deeply indebted to Professor Hans Henrich Hock for his personal interest in the project of bringing out the present volume in the Mouton de Gruyter's series TiLSM. Not only did he welcome our proposal to publish the volume with Mouton, he has been supportive at every stage of this project: Thank you!

https://doi.org/10.1515/9783110610796-202

Transliteration

In order to ensure consistency in transliteration, a slightly modified version of the Sanskrit method is used to transliterate the Hindi examples used in this volume.

Tab. 1: Devanagari transliteration method used in the book

Vowels		Vowel nasalization	
अ	a	अँ	ã
आ	ā	आँ	ā̃
इ	i	इँ	ĩ
ई	ī	ईं	ī̃
उ	u	उँ	ũ
ऊ	ū	ऊँ	ū̃
ऋ	r̥	---	---
ए	e	एँ	ẽ
ऐ	ɛ	ऐं	ɛ̃
ओ	o	ओं	õ
औ	ɔ	औं	ɔ̃

Consonants					
क	ka	ट	ṭa	प	pa
ख	kha	ठ	ṭha	फ	pha
ग	ga	ड	ḍa	ब	ba
घ	gha	ढ	ḍha	भ	bha
ङ	ṅa	ण	ṇa	म	ma
क़	qa	ड़	ṛa	फ़	fa
ख़	xa	ढ़	ṛha	य	ya
ग़	ġa	त	ta	र	ra
च	ča	थ	tha	ल	la
छ	čha	द	da	व	va
ज	ja	ध	dha	श	śa
झ	jha	न	na	ष	ṣa
ञ	ña			स	sa
ज़	za			ह	ha

https://doi.org/10.1515/9783110610796-203

Veneeta Dayal
(In)definiteness without articles: diagnosis, analysis, implications

Abstract: This paper addresses the view that bare nominals in languages without articles can be definites as well as indefinites. In particular, it challenges the status of bare nominals as indefinites, providing contexts in which English uses the indefinite article but an article-less language like Hindi must resort to a numeral construction. The empirical generalization based on Hindi is that bare nominals are ambiguous between definites and kind terms and that bare plurals, but not bare singulars, can have kind derived indefinite readings. The indefinite readings available to bare singulars must be traced to external factors. The paper then provides an explanation for these facts within a Neo-Carlsonian approach to bare nominals, addressing the issue of null determiners vs covert type shifts. The last section of the paper extends the insights gained from the case study of Hindi bare nominals to other languages, highlighting empirical and theoretical issues of relevance in determining whether bare nominals in a given language are definites or indefinites. It also comments on the well-established fact that adult learners of a language like English have trouble with the determiner system if their L1 does not have articles, from the vantage point of the findings about Hindi bare nominals.[1]

Keywords: Indefiniteness, Cross-linguistic variation, L2 Acquisition

1 The definite-indefinite dichotomy

In this section we introduce two perspectives on the (in)definiteness of bare nominals in article-less languages, one which holds them to be ambiguous between definite and indefinite and one which takes them to be indefinites with a wider distribution. I argue against both perspectives by looking closely at bare

1 I would like to thank the audiences at the Workshop on Semantic Universals (University of Pennsylvania), TripleA 3 (University of Tuebingen), the International conference on Hindi studies (INALCO, Paris), and University College London for helpful comments. All errors and omissions remain my responsibility. Parts of this paper were included in the *Proceedings of Triple A*.

Veneeta Dayal, Rutgers University, Department of Linguistics, 18 Seminary Place, NJ 08901, USA, phone: (848)-932-0477. Email: dayal@linguistics.rutgers.edu

https://doi.org/10.1515/9783110610796-001

nominals in Hindi. On the basis of explicit diagnostics, it is established that bare nominals can be definites as well as kind terms. Bare plurals, but not bare singulars, can also have narrow scope indefinite readings that can be ascribed to their status as kind terms. Other possible sources for indefinite readings, available to both bare singulars and bare plurals, are derivative on properties of the constructions they appear in.

1.1 The ambiguity of bare nominals

That bare nominals in languages without articles can function as definites as well as indefinites is a reasonable assumption when viewed from the perspective of languages with articles. The following comment from Löbner (1985: 320) is representative of this view: "as for languages which do not have a definite article, it is plausible to assume that they just do not explicitly express the way nouns are to be interpreted." I take this to imply that bare nominals in such languages are ambiguous between definite and indefinite.

A more nuanced view is presented in Heim (2011): "in languages without definiteness marking, the relevant 'ambiguous' DPs may simply be indefinites. They are semantically equivalent to English indefinites. But they have a wider range of felicitous uses than English indefinites, precisely because they do not compete with definites and therefore do not get strengthened to carry the implicatures that would show up if they were uniformly translated as indefinites into English". To put this in context, consider the following meanings for the definite and indefinite articles. (1a) encodes the uniqueness of singular definites, while (1a') gives an extension that is applicable to both singular and plural definites.[2]

(1a) $[\![\text{the}]\!] = \lambda P{:}\ \exists x\ \forall y\ [P(y) \leftrightarrow y = x].\ \iota x[P(x)]$

(1a') $[\![\text{the}]\!] = \lambda P{:}\ \exists x\ \forall y\ [(MAX(P))(y) \leftrightarrow y = x].\ \iota x[(MAX(P))(x)]$
Where $MAX(P) = \lambda x\ [P(x)\ \&\ \neg\exists y\ [P(y)\ \&\ x < y]]$

(1b) $[\![\text{a/an}]\!] = \lambda P.\ \lambda Q.\ \exists x\ [P(x)\ \&\ Q(x)]$

2 For present purposes we work with the simpler version in (1a). The version in (1a') includes plural individuals and imposes uniqueness on maximal individuals, those that are not individual parts of bigger individuals. In the case of singular common nouns P = MAX(P), but in the case of plural individuals MAX(P) is a set with only one individual, the one that is the sum of all the singular individuals in P. This facilitates the shift from the perceived uniqueness of singular terms (*the man is tall*) to the perceived universality of plural terms (*the men are tall*).

(1c)

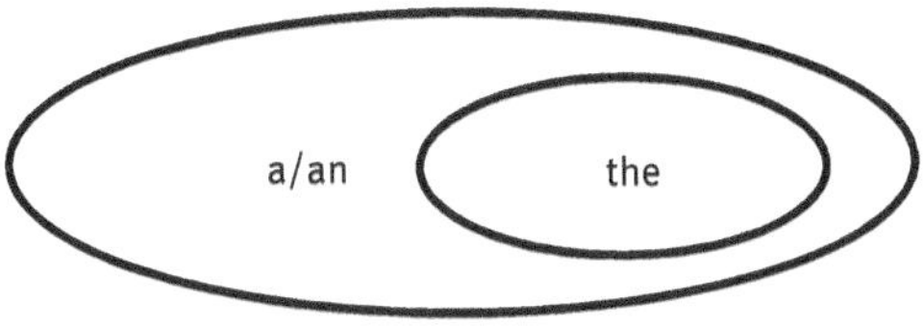

Fig. 1: Relation between the definite and the indefinite articles

The definite and indefinite articles differ in two respects. The former presupposes uniqueness – it can be used felicitously only in contexts where there is exactly one individual that satisfies the common noun predicate – and it picks out that unique individual as its referent. The latter imposes no requirements on how many individuals must satisfy the common noun predicate. It denotes a generalized quantifier, namely the set of properties such that at least one individual who has the common noun property also has that property. Focusing on the first difference, we see that it sets up an entailment relationship between the definite and the indefinite. Every context in which a statement with *the N* is felicitous and true is a context in which the corresponding statement with *a/an N* is also felicitous and true, but not the other way around.

Consider from this perspective a context in which it is known that there is exactly one cat who may or may not be sitting on the mat.

(2a) The cat/ #A cat is on the mat.
(2b) The sun/ #A sun is shining.

Both sentences in (2a) are defined in this context – whether they are true or false would depend on what that cat is doing. The version with the indefinite has an implicature that there should be more than one cat in the context. This is due to competition with the definite since Gricean principles of conversation require a speaker to use the strongest statement compatible with the known facts. The perceived infelicity of the indefinite in (2a) is thus accounted for. This is illustrated even more dramatically in (2b) where world knowledge entails the existence of a single sun.

Heim's statement, that the so-called ambiguity of bare NPs in languages without articles arises simply from lack of competition, can be schematically represented in (3a). The more standard view is represented in (3b):

(3a)

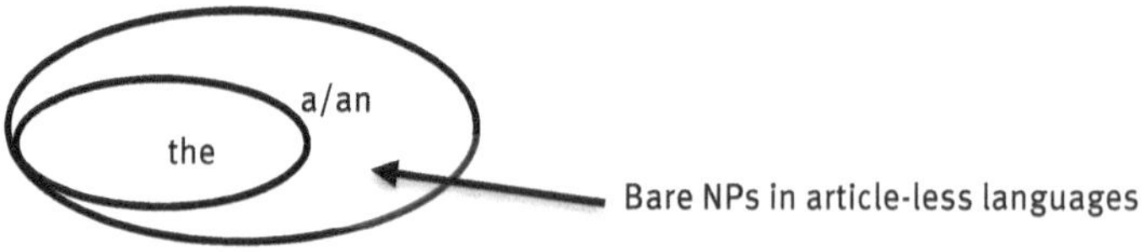

(3b)

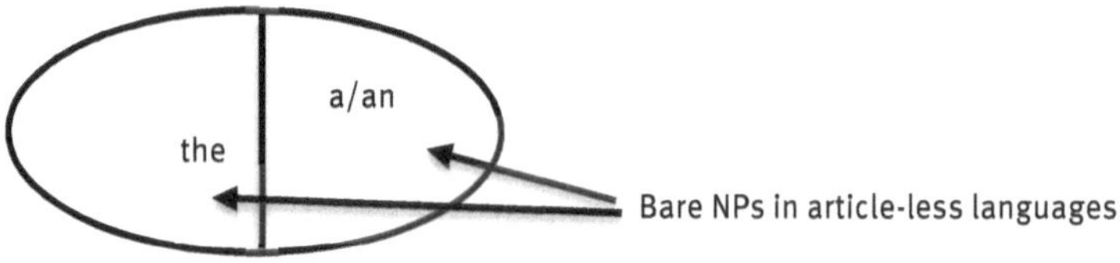

Fig. 2: Bare NPs in article-less languages

These two views about the interpretation of bare nominals in articleless languages are echoed in the literature on Hindi, which we will take as our primary example of this type of language. They have been taken to be ambiguous between definite and indefinite (Mahajan 1990, Mohanan 1994, for example), and as indefinites whose definite interpretation is pragmatically derived (Kidwai 2000 and Thakur 2015). The next subsections will show that Hindi bare nominals are indeed definites but will provide evidence to challenge the claim that they are indefinites. In effect, then, we will be arguing also against the view that Hindi bare nominals are ambiguous between specific and definite meanings (Verma 1971, Masica 1991), and asserting the claim in Kachru (1980) and Dayal (2004, and previous work) that they are ambiguous between definites and generics only.[3]

1.2 The definiteness of bare nominals

There are two clear diagnostics that together determine whether a bare noun phrase is definite: anaphoricity and homogeneity. Let us consider the anaphoricity test first:

(4a) A boy and a girl came into the room. The girl sat down.

3 Thanks to Deepak Alok (p.c) for these references.

(4b) एक लड़का और एक लड़की कमरे में आए। लड़की बैठ गयी।
ek laṛkā ɔr ek laṛkī kamre-mẽ āe. laṛkī bɛṭh-gayī.
one boy and one girl room-in came. girl sit-go-PFV.F.SG
'A boy and a girl came into the room. The girl sat down.'

As we see in (4a), a definite is required in the second sentence to refer back to a discourse referent introduced in the first sentence. An indefinite would not be felicitous. When we translate the discourse into Hindi in (4b), we see that the bare NP *laṛkī* 'girl' is quite felicitous.[4] Thus the bare NP passes the first test for definiteness.

The homogeneity test, due to Löbner (1985), differentiates definites from demonstratives as well as indefinites, and aligns it with proper names. This is in keeping with the semantics of the definite determiner given above:

(5a) A dog is sleeping and a dog is barking.
(5b) That dog is sleeping and that dog is barking.
(5c) #The dog is sleeping and the dog is barking.
(5d) #Fido is sleeping and Fido is barking.

Given the analysis of definites as denoting a single individual, it follows that one cannot predicate incompatible properties of a definite. That is, they behave in this respect like proper names. The test also applies to plural definites (*#the dogs are sleeping and the dogs are barking*), though the test has to be administered with some care.[5] Turning to Hindi, we see that a bare NP in this context is unacceptable:

(6) #कुत्ता सो रहा है और कुत्ता भौंक रहा है।
#kuttā so-rahā-hɛ ɔr kuttā bhɔ̃k-rahā-hɛ.
dog sleep-PROG-PRS and dog bark-PROG-PRS
'The dog is sleeping and the dog is barking.'

4 Using two distinct noun phrases in the first sentence makes the use of a full DP in the second sentence more natural by making a null or overt pronoun either unavailable or less preferred.
5 Briefly, plural definites do not require that every member of the set be actively involved. For example, the statement *the reporters asked questions* may be considered true even in contexts where only some of them did. However, it is still the case that the predication applies to the group as a whole so that *the reporters asked questions but the reporters kept quiet* or *the reporters asked questions but some of them kept quiet* would be deemed contradictory (see Dayal 2013 and references cited there).

Based on these two tests, then, we can safely classify the Hindi bare NP as a definite.

1.3 The non-indefiniteness of bare nominals

The fact that bare NPs in languages without articles can be definites is not controversial. But we will now look at diagnostics that call their status as indefinites into question. In fact, the example in (6) is already suggestive. If the bare NP *kuttā* 'dog' could be interpreted as an indefinite in (6), the sentence would have been acceptable under the reading that the English (5a) has. The next three diagnostics drive home this point: partitive specificity, referential specificity, scopal inertness, all show the Hindi bare NP diverging from the English indefinite.[6]

Consider the test of partitive specificity, discussed in Enç (1991), where the boy and girl referred to in the second sentence are understood as belonging to the set mentioned in the first:

(7a) There were several kids in the room. A boy and a girl were playing cards
(7b) कमरे में कई बच्चे थे। लड़का और लड़की ताश खेल रहे थे।
kamre-mẽ kaī bačče the. #laṛkā ɔr laṛkī tāś khel-rahe-the.
room-in several kids were #boy and girl cards play-PROG-PAST
'There were several children in the room. #The boy and the girl were playing cards."

No matter how we set up the context, if there were several kids in the room, there must be a plurality of girls or boys or both. If the bare NPs were indefinites, there would be no problem in getting a partitive specific reading, in analogy with (7a). But what we see in (7b) is the infelicity that is predicted of NPs that encode uniqueness. Given that both NPs have singular morphology, the context has to be one with a unique boy and a unique girl. In the given context, the numeral *ek* 'one' would have to be added to the NPs to convey the intended meaning.

Next consider referential specificity, brought into the public discussion by Fodor and Sag (1982). The important point here is that the speaker has a particular individual in mind, one that the hearer does not necessarily know about. Had the intended referent been identifiable to both the speaker and the hearer, the

6 See von Heusinger (2011), among others, for a survey of issues related to indefiniteness and specificity.

plain definite *my relative* instead of *a relative of mine* would have been used in (8a).

(8a) If a relative of mine dies, I will inherit a fortune.
(8b) अगर मेरे रिश्तेदार की मौत हो जाए तो मुझे बहुत पैसा मिलेगा।

agar	*mere*	*riśtedār*	*kī*	*mɔt*	*ho jāe*	*to*	*mujhe*	*bahut*	*pɛsā*	*milegā.*
if	my	relative	of	death	happen	then	I-DAT	lot	money	get-FUT

'If my relative dies, I will get a lot of money.'

The bare NP in (8b) denotes a unique referent identifiable to both speaker and hearer. The addition of a numeral *ek*, as in *mere ek riśtedār* 'my one relative' is needed to make it parallel to (8a). It should be noted that this diagnostic is known to be a delicate one. The difference between a definite and specific indefinite with respect to referential specificity is slight, riding crucially on a gap between a speaker's presupposition of uniqueness vs. common ground knowledge.[7]

The distinction between bare NPs and indefinites becomes clearer when we look at cases of intermediate scope, by now a well-established fact in the literature on specific indefinites (Farkas 1981, among others). The intermediate scope reading in (9a) allows the choice of topic to vary with students. Thus, (9a) can be continued with *Mary has read every article on fake news and Sue has read every article on the Affordable Care Act.* This reading is distinct from the wide scope reading we saw in (8) as well as a narrow scope reading. A narrow scope reading for the indefinite would require every student to have read every paper on any current topic – that is every student would have read every paper on every current topic:[8]

(9a) Every student has read every article on a current topic.

7 One may argue, quite rightly, that the definiteness in this example is due to the possessive construction. The absence of the relevant reading can be ascertained by translating examples like *if a tall dark-haired student comes, tell her to wait* which do not involve possessives. See von Heusinger (2011) for the types of modification that facilitate this reading.

8 It is unclear to me why some form of modification facilitates the relevant reading in (9a) with the indefinite article *a*, but is not needed with *some*. In the interest of space I am setting aside many important differences between different indefinite articles (see Farkas and Brasoveanu *forthcoming*, among others, for relevant discussion). Hindi (9b) is not fully acceptable without modification. To get the definite reading without modification, a demonstrative *us viṣay* 'that topic' seems to be required. At this point, I must content myself with simply noting this fact.

(9b) हर विद्यार्थी ने मौजूदा विषय पर हर लेख पढ़ा ।
har vidyārthī-ne mɔjūdā viṣay-par har lekh paṛhā.
every student-ERG current topic-on every article read
'Every student read every article on the current topic.'

(9c) हर विद्यार्थी ने एक/ किसी-एक विषय पर हर लेख पढ़ा।
har vidyārthī-ne ek/ kisī-ek viṣay-par har lekh paṛhā.
every student-ERG one/ some-one topic-on every article read
'Every student read every article on one topic/some topic.'

We see from (9b)–(9c) that Hindi needs an overt marker of indefiniteness to get the relevant reading, one that allows a follow-up with different students paired with different topics. Other examples can be constructed along the same lines to show that the surviving reading of a bare nominal is that of a definite:

(10a) Every teacher wrote two articles which he gave to a student of his.
(10b) हर अध्यापक ने दो लेख लिखे जो उसने अपने विद्यार्थी को दिए।
har adhyāpak-ne do lekh likhe
every teacher-ERG two articles wrote
jo us-ne apne vidyārthī-ko diye.
that he-ERG self's student-DAT gave
'Every teacher wrote two articles which he gave to his student.'

While (10b) allows students to vary with teachers, a reading that is forced by the anaphoric possessive in the relative clause, the presupposition of uniqueness projects. Each teacher is assumed to have a single student who is contextually relevant. What we do not get is the specific indefinite reading. In order to get that reading, we would need to add the overt marker of indefiniteness *apne ek vidyārthī-ko* 'self's one student-DAT'. With this addition, each professor could have multiple students but only one of whom would be referred to as the recipient of the articles.[9]

It turns out that the inability to take intermediate scope is simply a reflex of an apparently indefinite bare nominal's inability to take scope over any clause-mate operator. In this respect Hindi bare nominals behave like English bare nominals:

9 Again, we may want to steer clear of the possessive construction to ensure that it is not the locus of definiteness (see footnote 6). However, in this case, having the bare *vidyārthī* 'student' shifts the interpretation to one where there is exactly one student assumed to be salient in the discourse. The reason for the missing narrow scope reading will be taken up in section 1.4.

(11a) John didn't read a book/books.
(11b) Rabbits/ #A rabbit kept dying.
(11c) Dogs have evolved from wolves.

As originally pointed out by Carlson (1977), a sentence like (11a) with a singular indefinite has two readings, one where there is a particular book John didn't read while he may have read others (∃ >¬); and another in which he read no books at all (¬ >∃). The bare plural has only the latter reading. This may suggest that bare plurals are a sub-type of indefinites but the example in (11b) shows that this is not the case. The indefinite has the implausible reading where the same rabbit died several times (∃ > Duration) while the bare plural has a plausible differentiated reading that allows for different rabbits to die at different times (Duration > ∃). Carlson's account of bare plurals is that they are not indefinites at all but rather kind terms and that they can be arguments of kind level predicates, as in (11c). When they occur as arguments of individual and stage level predicates, semantic operations make their instantiations available for semantic composition. We will come back to details of the theory in section 2. For now it is important to note that there is a correlation between scopal inertness and kind terms, a correlation that is also present in Hindi:

(12a) शेर विलुप्त हो जा सकता है।/ शेर विलुप्त हो जा सकते हैं।
śer vilupt ho-jā saktā hɛ./ śer vilupt ho jā sakte hɛ̃.
tiger extinct become can/ tigers extinct become can
'The tiger can become extinct.'/ 'Tigers can become extinct.'
(12b) तीन दिन तक
tīn din tak
three days till
'For three days'
खरगोश मरते रहे। /#खरगोश मरता रहा। /#एक खरगोश मरता रहा।
khargoś marte-rahe./#khargoś martā rahā./#ek khargoś martā-rahā.
rabbits die-PROG/ rabbit die-PROG/ #one rabbit die-PROG
'Rabbits kept dying.' / 'The rabbit kept dying'/'A rabbit kept dying.'

In (12a) we have a kind-level statement with a bare singular and a bare plural. In (12b) we see the differentiated scope behavior of bare plurals, where different rabbits can be understood to die during the interval referred to. We note that the same is not true of the bare singular or the indefinite.[10] We will return to this difference between bare plurals and bare singulars, both of which are bona fide kind terms, in the next subsection.

What we have established here is that Hindi bare nominals are not like English indefinites. In particular, they cannot be classified as specific or partitive indefinites. We have also noted that they are scopally inert and related it to their being kind terms. Interestingly, this scopal inertness results in readings, at least in the case of bare plurals, that are unavailable to regular indefinites. We will now turn to a consideration of the evidence that has formed the basis of the commonly held view that bare nominals in languages like Hindi are indefinites.

1.4 The pseudo-indefiniteness of bare nominals

One of the strongest motivations for taking bare nominals to be indefinites comes from examples like (13a). A background question like *What were you doing yesterday afternoon?* removes the likelihood of there being a salient book in the common ground. And answers like (13a) in such a context are most naturally translated with an indefinite determiner. However, this does not necessarily mean that the indefiniteness is inherent to the bare nominal, as (13b)–(13c) show:

(13a) मैं किताब पढ़ रही थी।
mɛ̃ kitāb paṛh-rahī-thī.
I book read-PROG-PAST
'I was reading a book.'

(13b) मैं बच्चे को खाना खिला रही थी।
mɛ̃ bačče ko khānā khilā-rahī-thī.
I child-DAT food feed-PROG-PAST
'I was feeding the child.'

(13c) मैं बच्चों को खाना खिला रही थी।
mɛ̃ baččõ-ko khānā khilā-rahī-thī.
I children-DAT food feed-PROG-PAST
'I was feeding children/the children.'

10 Note that a bare singular does not lend itself to a narrow scope reading in conditionals. The Hindi translation of *if a student filed a complaint, she will be reprimanded* would need *koi vidyārthī* 'some student'. The bare singular would suggest the existence of a single contextually salient student, as mentioned in footnote 8.

If the person answering the question with (13b) or (13c) works in a daycare or any situation with multiple children in it, there is no reason why the bare singular indirect object should not have an indefinite reading. The fact that (13c) can have a non-specific indefinite reading establishes that there is no pragmatic obstacle involved. What we can conclude from this paradigm is that the indefinite readings we see in (13) come from two distinct sources. One is the indefiniteness associated with plural kind terms (13c), the other is the indefiniteness associated with incorporation and/or complex predicate formation, a process that targets direct objects (13a). If indefiniteness were inherent to the bare nominal, changing from direct to indirect object position in (13b) would not make the difference it does.

A second case where indefiniteness is perceived is the existential construction. The position of arguments in relation to locative phrases has been noted to correlate with (in)definiteness. While there is clearly validity to this generalization, it is worth noting that it does not readily extend to all bare nominals, especially singular bare nominals:

(14a) चूहा कमरे में है।
čūhā kamre-mẽ hɛ.
mouse room-in is
'The mouse is in the room.'

(14b) कमरे में चूहा है।
kamre-mẽ čūhā hɛ.
room-in mouse is
'There's a mouse in the room.'

(14c) #कमरे में बूढ़ी औरत है।
#kamre-mẽ būṛhī ɔrat hɛ.
room-in one old woman is
'There's an old woman in the room.'

Why should the switch from *čūhā* 'mouse' to *būṛhī ɔrat* 'old woman' make a difference to indefiniteness? The bare plural counterpart of (14c) would be quite acceptable. This suggests again that bare singulars in existential contexts are dependent on factors independent of quantificational properties of the noun phrase, factors that are not very well understood currently.

Let me end this section with a canonical property associated with indefinites, namely the ability to introduce discourse referents. We can test this by setting up a presentational context, ruling out the possibility of reference to familiar entities. Neither of the following seem acceptable without the addition of the unstressed numeral *ek* 'one', especially if the story is expected to elaborate on the relevant individuals:

(15a) बहुत साल पहले इस घर में एक बूढ़ी औरत रहती थी।
bahut sāl pahle is ghar-mẽ ek būṛhī ɔrat rahtī thī.
Many year back this house-in one old woman live-HAB-PAST
'Many years ago, an old woman used to live in this house.'

(15b) बहुत साल पहले इस घर में एक विद्यार्थी की मौत हो गयी थी।
bahut sāl pahle is ghar mẽ ek vidyārthī kī
Many year back this house in one student-GEN
mɔt ho gayī thī.
death happen-PAST
'Many years ago, a student had died in this house.'

Though there is some speaker variation regarding the ability of bare singulars to introduce novel discourse referents, I believe it can be safely claimed that for most speakers there are at least some contexts in which bare singulars cannot introduce new entities into the discourse. And for no speaker is it the case that bare NPs are preferred over the corresponding indefinite. Substituting bare plurals in (15a)–(15b) leads to marked improvement, making them perhaps even fully acceptable.

1.5 A snapshot of the empirical landscape

In the previous subsections, I have collected together the evidence in the literature establishing that bare nominals in an article-less language like Hindi are definites but not specific or non-specific indefinites and that their apparent indefiniteness is construction specific and/or restricted to bare plurals. I summarize the findings for indefiniteness in the following table:

(16)

	ENGLISH INDF NP	HINDI NUM NP	HINDI BARE SG	HINDI BARE PL	ENGLISH BARE PL
Partitive specificity	√	√	X	X	X
Referential specificity	√	√	X	X	X
Wide intermediate scope	√	√	X	X	X
Narrow scope/ Universal & Neg	√	√/X	√	√	√
Differentiated scope under ADV	X	X	X	√	√
Presentational context	√	√	X	√	√

There are a couple of points worth noting in the above. We have not discussed the inability of the numeral NPs *ek N* in Hindi to take scope under negation. This will be taken up in section 3. I have also idealized the data for bare singulars in presentational contexts. As noted in section 1.4 this may well be contextually sensitive and subject to speaker variation. The point to note though is that bare nominals are not specific indefinites. And it is not at all clear that their non-specific indefinite behavior can be delinked from their life as kind terms. The fact that singular and plural terms behave differently with respect to differentiated scope and presentational contexts is significant in this connection. I therefore take the relevant generalization to be that bare nominals in Hindi are ambiguous between definites and kind terms. In section 2 I provide a theoretical account for this generalization. Those not particularly interested in the theory or already familiar with it should feel free to skip to skip to section 3 where I discuss how the empirical landscape outlined above could be used to study the (in)definiteness of bare nominals in other languages as well as the acquisition of the determiner system by adult learners whose first language does not include determiners.

2 A neo-Carlsonian account of bare nominals

This section presents an account of the facts discussed in section 1. It recognizes the universality of operations that yield kind, definite and indefinite readings, allowing for these operations to have lexical exponents or be available as covert type shifts. The theory also includes constraints on type shifts, in relation to overt determiners and in relation to each other. Finally, a formal distinction between singular and plural kind terms is drawn with respect to individuals that at the intuitive level are instantiations of the kind. Together they account for the core generalization that bare nominals in article-less languages are bona fide definites but not bona fide indefinites. The section ends by addressing the implications of treating bare nominals as DPs with a null determiner versus NPs that undergo covert type-shift in argument positions.

2.1 Bare plurals as kinds and definites

The basic premise of the neo-Carlsonian approach is that bare plurals in argument position refer to kinds, not only in the case of kind-level predication but also in the case of object-level predication, as originally proposed in Carlson (1977). Their quantificational force, however, is governed by the same principles that have been established for the variable quantificational force of regular indefinites (see Dayal 2011a and references cited there for background).

Chierchia (1998) extends the kind-based view of English bare plurals to a cross-linguistic theory of noun phrase variation. Within the general perspective of flexible types (Partee 1987), he admits three basic operations for turning an NP with a predicative meaning (type <*e,t*>) into an argument (type e or <<*e,t*>*t*>), *nom*, *iota* and *∃*:

(17a) iota: $\lambda P\ \iota Ps$, if there exists a unique maximal entity in P, undefined otherwise.
(17b) nom: For any property P and world/situation s, $^{\cap}P = \lambda s\ \iota P_s$, if $\lambda s\ \iota Ps$ is in K[IND] undefined otherwise, where Ps is the extension of P in s.
(17c) ∃: $\lambda P\ \lambda Q\ \exists x\ [P(x)\ \&\ Q(x)]$

Of these, he considers the first two meaning preserving in the sense that they map a predicate into an entity without introducing quantificational complexity. *Iota* picks out the unique maximal entity in the extension of the predicate at the relevant situation, if there is one, and is undefined otherwise. As indicated in section 1, this is the lexical meaning of the definite article in English, but in languages without a definite article it operates as a covert type shift. *Nom*, the kind forming operator, is a function from indices to the maximal entity that is in the extension of the predicate at that index – that is, it yields the unique maximal entity that instantiates the kind at the index. *Nom*, which is not lexically encoded in English, is a partial function because it is undefined for predicates that do not fit the concept of a kind. It also only operates on plural predicates. The third type-shift ∃ not only turns a predicative expression into an argument, it also introduces ∃ quantification. This is the meaning of the determiner *a/an* in English. Since this yields a generalized quantifier, it can interact with other scopal expressions. Unlike the first two operations, ∃ is a total function. These possibilities are constrained by two principles specific to type shifts:

(18a) Ranking: nom > {iota, ∃} *to be revised – cf. 23*
(18b) Blocking Principle ('Type Shifting as Last Resort'): For any type shifting operation π and any X: * $\pi(X)$ if there is a determiner D such that for any set X in its domain, $D(X) = \pi(X)$.

Finally, the rule of DKP mediates between a kind denoting term and a predicate of objects, a repair operation on sorts. Essentially, it existentially binds instantiations of the kind at the relevant index. Since this ∃ is introduced at the point where the sort adjustment is required, it ensures obligatory narrow scope for its operand:

(19a) DKP: If P applies to objects and k denotes a kind, then $P(k) = \exists x\,[{}^{\cup}k(x) \wedge P(x)]$

(19b) PRED ($^{\cup}$): $\lambda d_{<s,e>}$ {$\lambda x\,[x \leq d_s]$ if ds is defined, λx[FALSE] otherwise}, where d_s is the plural individual that comprises all of the atomic members of the kind.

A simple demonstration of the system can be given for English:

(20a) Dogs have evolved from wolves.

(20b) evolve-from($^{\cap}$dogs, $^{\cap}$wolves)

(21a) Dogs are barking.

(21b) $\exists$[are-barking (s) ($^{\cap}$dogs(s)(x))] =*DKP*⇒ $\exists$s x [$^{\cup\cap}$dogs(s)(x) $\wedge$ are-barking (s)(x)]

Since *evolve* in (20a) is a kind level predicate, and the predicates *dogs* and *wolves* have the requisite intensionality, *nom* turns them into arguments which can be fed into the verb meaning directly. Since *bark* in (21a) is an object-level predicate, it cannot hold of the kind, only of its instantiations and DKP comes into play. The truth conditions associated with (21b) are identical to those of a corresponding statement with an indefinite but there is a difference that shows up in scopal contexts. Even when a bare plural outscopes negation, for example, it ends up having narrow scope:

(22a) Dogs are not barking.

(22b) [dogs$_i$ [not [t$_i$ are barking]]]

(22c) λx_i ⟦[not [t$_i$ are barking]]⟧ (⟦$^{\cap}$dogs⟧)
⇒ ¬are-barking (s) ($^{\cap}$dogs) =DKP⇒ ¬ $\exists$x[$^{\cup\cap}$dogs(s)(x) $\wedge$ are-barking(s)(x)]

Since the bare plural is individual denoting (type <*s*, *e*>), it gets lowered into the argument position of the negative predicate. When DKP adjusts the mismatch between *barking* and $^{\cap}$*dogs*, $\exists$ enters into the derivation, necessarily below negation. The regular indefinite instead is a generalized quantifier, which means that it enters into an operator-variable relation with its trace and can therefore have scope over negation. Appealing to reference to kinds for bare plurals and to a generalized quantifier meaning for indefinites thus yields radically different scopal properties for them. This difference, we saw, is particularly striking in the case of differentiated scope readings in which bare plurals have readings unavailable to indefinites.[11]

The ranking proposed by Chierchia requires revision since it does not capture the facts that he wants to capture, namely that bare nominals in languages without articles can be definite as well as indefinite. The ranking in (18a) predicts that both *iota* and *∃* would be outranked by *nom*, making both definite and indefinite readings unavailable. We have argued against the (in)definiteness of bare nominals in Hindi. As such, the ranking of type shifts that is needed is the one in (23) from Dayal (1999, 2004):

(23) Ranking: {nom, iota} > ∃

The ambiguity of Hindi bare nominals as definites and kinds, but not indefinites, now follows straightforwardly. The only indefinite readings possible are derivative on their kind reading or due to properties specific to certain syntactic positions or constructions. Hindi and English bare plurals differ, of course, in the possibility of the definite reading because *iota* is available in Hindi as a covert type shift but is lexically blocked in English by the definite determiner.

2.2 Singular vs. plural bare nominals

The revised ranking of type shifts explains the properties of Hindi bare plurals. We now need to account for differences between Hindi bare plurals and Hindi bare singulars. Let us focus on the differentiated scope reading, illustrated in (12b) and repeated below:

(24) तीन दिन तक खरगोश मरते रहे।/ #खरगोश मरता रहा।
tīn din tak khargoś marte rahe./ #khargoś martā rahā.
three days till rabbits die-PROG/ #rabbit die-PROG
'For three days rabbits kept dying.'/ 'For three days, the rabbit kept dying'

To recap, the bare plural names a kind and is of type <s,e>. It can therefore function as a direct argument of the verb. If the verb is not a kind-level predicate, as in this case, there is a sort mismatch which DKP repairs. We get the narrowest

11 The unavailability of differentiated scope readings for indefinites is one of the strongest arguments for adopting the neo-Carlsonian approach over an approach that treats bare plurals as ambiguous between kinds and indefinites (see Dayal 2011a for a survey).

scope reading in cases like these where the adverbial operator takes scope immediately above the verb and below the position at which a generalized quantifier is interpreted. Thus the existential associated with the bare plural kind term takes scope at a position unavailable to the indefinite. But if bare singulars are also kind terms but do not have DKP-based indefinite readings, an explanation is called for.

The account of singular kind terms proposed in Dayal (2004) takes them to be semantically plural but grammatically atomic, in analogy with collective nouns like *committee* or *team*. Briefly, it is proposed that *nom* is not responsible for singular kind terms. Rather, they are formed by the application of *iota* to a property of taxonomic/sub kinds. In languages in which *iota* is lexicalized, we get the definite singular generic, in languages in which it operates as a covert type-shift we get bare singular kinds, as in the singular variant of Hindi (12a):

(25a) The lion is an endangered species
(25b) endangered-species(ιx [LION(x)])

The relevant point here is that such terms do not allow access to their instantiations for purposes of predication. Any indefinite reading of bare singulars, then, must be based on its predicative meaning interacting with construction-specific factors. For example, in direct object position a bare singular can be treated as a predicative term of type <*e*,*t*>, which feeds into the meaning of an incorporating verb and ends up having existential force. Thus a non case-marked bare singular in object position, but not in subject position, can show differentiated scope. I refer the reader to Dayal (2004) for the full picture on singular kind terms and to Dayal (2011b) for their indefinite reading in direct object position. Similar reasoning applies to the existential construction in (14b).

Let me end the discussion of kind terms by making two points. The first is that Hindi bare singulars and English definite singulars can both function as kind terms but Hindi bare singulars can also function as predicates. This explains why bare singulars seem to have a wider range of readings than definite singular generics. It still leaves open why it is possible, to whatever extent, to use at least some bare singulars in presentational contexts. Note that we cannot appeal to a generalized quantifier interpretation for those cases as it would incorrectly predict that they would behave like indefinites more generally. The second point is that in languages in which plural kind terms must occur with a definite determiner, such as the Romance languages, kind terms do not have DKP based indefinite readings. This suggests that the presuppositions associated with a lexical exponent of *nom* or *iota* cannot be overridden by DKP while those that rely on covert type shifts can. Due to constraints of space, however, I must leave further discussion of these issues for another occasion.

2.3 Syntactic issues

The neo-Carlsonian explanation for the Hindi facts was couched in a view of bare nominals as syntactic NPs. But it is also conceivable that such nominals are syntactic DPs. Let us see whether making this move has consequences for the theory discussed above, where a bare nominal with a basic predicative meaning must resort to covert type shift to achieve semantic status as an argument. As such, the principles of *Blocking* and *Ranking*, crucial to a cross-linguistically valid theory of meaning, are defined in terms relevant to covert type shifts. However, the issues at the heart of the account would not be affected by a shift from an NP analysis to a DP analysis for bare nominals. Let us see why by considering two possible implementations of such an approach:

(26a) [DP ø [NP dogs]]
(26b) [DP $dogs_i$ [NP t_i]]

There is a null determiner in (26a), while the N head moves from inside NP to D in (26b). Such proposals have been made in the literature and I will briefly mention a few instances in the course of the discussion, without any claim to giving an exhaustive list. The goal here is to demonstrate the relationship between these syntactic options and the issue of indefinite vs. definite interpretation.

Let us assume, then, that everything we have said about Hindi bare NPs holds true but that the structure of the bare nominals involves a null determiner. Based on what we have seen in section 1, we would have to say that this null determiner encodes two type shifts, *iota* and *nom*. Crucially, it does not encode the ∃ type shift. If we wanted to derive this in a principled way and to make cross-linguistic predictions we would have to say that null determiners are subject to the same *Ranking* that was proposed for covert type shifts, namely {nom, iota} > ∃. Moreover, we would have to say that the *Blocking Principle* applies to null determiners in the same way that Chierchia claimed for covert type shifts. Only then could we explain why bare plurals in languages like English do not have definite readings while bare nominals in languages like Hindi do. In other words, positing a null determiner does not provide any substantive advantage as far as interpretation is concerned, as Carlson had already pointed out in (1977). In this case, it simply changes the terms of the discussion from talking about covert type shifts to covert determiners but leaves untouched the essence of the claims.

One final consideration has to do with a possible requirement that the null determiner be syntactically licensed. While clearly some kind of licensing requirement holds for bare plurals in Italian (Longobardi 1994, Chierchia 1998), which are generally acceptable in direct object position but not in subject position, it does not transfer over to English bare plurals or Hindi bare plurals which do not show any subject-object asymmetries. And even for Italian the claim of a null determiner is not enough to settle the semantic question. Chierchia has argued that the null determiner encodes *nom* and under that view it follows that the indefinite readings associated with Italian bare plurals can only have narrow scope readings. Longobardi, among others, have argued that Italian bare plurals unlike English bare plurals are not kind terms. But on that view, there is no explanation for the fact that they have obligatorily narrow scope readings. It would seem then that if they are not kind terms and they are restricted to object position, they may well be cases of NPs pseudo-incorporated by the verb.[12]

Now let us turn to the second option, given in (26b). Note that such structures typically have an effect on word order, as shown for Italian by Longobardi (1994). Such structures have also been claimed for articleless languages such as Bangla (Bhattacharya 1999). The base order of Bangla numeral constructions is the one given in (27a) and the derived order in (27b), with N→D being semantically triggered by definiteness/specificity:

(27a) $[_{\text{NumP}}$du $[_{\text{CL-P}}$ To $[_{\text{NP}}$ boii]]]
two CL book
"Two books"

(27b) $[_{\text{DP}}$ boii$_i$ $[_{\text{NumP}}$ du $[_{\text{CL-P}}$ To t_i]]]]
Book two CL
"The two books"

I have argued in Dayal (2012, 2014) that (27a) has an indefinite reading, specific as well as non-specific, while (27b) has only a definite reading. Setting aside several important details, the relevant point from the present perspective is that N→D movement is not enough to provide an account of available meanings. *Ranking* has to be included in the theory to predict the definiteness of such structures and the absence of indefiniteness, specific and non-specific.

12 Thanks to Ivano Caponigro and Gennaro Chierchia for discussions related to this issue. Note that for Chierchia's kind-based account of this to work, he has to exempt the null determiner from competition with the overt plural definite determiner or give a somewhat different semantics to the definite determiner. He inclines to the latter.

The more general point is that positing a DP structure with a null D or a DP structure with N→D movement does not replace the task of semantic explanations. Absent a fully worked out compositional account, there is no particular advantage in making the move from the theory given in 2.2 which is based on bare nominals as NPs undergoing type shift. I should clarify, however, that there is no inherent incompatibility between the neo-Carlsonian account and a DP based account. I simply want to highlight the need for an independently defensible semantics to go with whatever syntactic option one proposes.

3 Further implications

In this section we take up two areas where the findings for Hindi proposed in sections 1 and 2 have significant implications. We first consider the possibility of cross-linguistic variation by exploring whether the theory allows for article-less languages in which bare nominals are indeed ambiguous between definite and indefinite readings. We then consider the well-known fact that L2 learners of articled languages coming from an article-less L1 face problems with the determiner system. Here we look at recent experimental work in this area and draw out the implications of the proposal forwarded here that bare nominals in article-less languages are not truly ambiguous between definite and indefinite.

3.1 (In)definiteness in other article-less languages

Let us start by briefly considering the extent to which the insights gleaned from our study of Hindi bare nominals can inform investigation into the semantic properties of bare nominals in other article-less languages. The first issue to settle for any language is whether it has definite and indefinite lexical determiners. We know that definite determiners develop from demonstratives and indefinite determiners from the numeral *one*. Demonstratives and numerals are attested in most, perhaps all languages, so we need diagnostics to identify lexical determiners. We have already seen diagnostics for identifying definite determiners, namely anaphoricity and homogeneity (cf. section 1.2). Note though that anaphoricity may also be possible with demonstratives. It is, therefore, important to probe the uniqueness inherent to definites in a different way, using the homogeneity test. One possibility is to take a context in which there are several children and see whether a singular bare nominal can be used felicitously. If it can, perhaps with a pointing gesture, we have evidence that the determiner is a demonstrative not a definite:

(28a) That child is standing and that child is sitting.
(28b) #The child is standing and the child is sitting.

Related to this is the fact that demonstratives have a non-uniqueness implicature (Robinson 2005). If there is only one student in the context, it is a bit odd to say *that child is sitting.*

There are two diagnostics for separating indefinite determiners from the numeral, discussed in Chierchia (1998). Indefinite determiners lend themselves to generic statements and are able to take scope under negation:

(29a) A student works hard.
(29b) John didn't buy a book.

The Hindi translation of (29a) with *ek vidyārthī* 'one student', for example, lacks the reading that working hard is the property of students generally. And the Hindi translation of (29b) with *ek kitāb* 'one book' does not have a neutral narrow scope reading, conveying instead a wide scope reading for the indefinite or an emphatic narrow scope reading. In this respect it is similar to *John didn't read one book.* We can say with some confidence, then, that any language that aligns with Hindi in these respects lacks both the definite and the indefinite articles.

It is worth noting, though, that while the presence or absence of a definite determiner makes a clear difference in the possibility of definite readings for bare nominals, the presence or absence of an indefinite determiner may not have an impact on indefinite readings. Recall that we have proposed two constraints on covert type shifts: *blocking* and *ranking* (cf. 18). Although *blocking* is not without its complexities (see Dayal 2013), it is still a good predictor of the availability of definite readings for bare nominals. But if *nom* and *iota* outrank *∃*, it is predicted that bare nominals will not have a genuine indefinite interpretation regardless of the presence or absence of an indefinite determiner in the language. Therefore, whether the language has an indefinite determiner or not, the theory as currently stated will predict the absence of genuine indefinite readings for bare nominals in articleless languages.

Of course, it is entirely possible that *ranking* is subject to cross-linguistic variation, and if so, bare nominals in a language that does not follow this principle would have all three readings: kind, definite and indefinite. While this is a possibility, one of the lessons from the case study of Hindi in section 1 is the importance of going beyond intuitions regarding the novelty-familiarity of the referent in determining the status of a bare nominal as indefinite. Tests probing specificity and scope were shown to be significant in this connection. If a bare nominal seems to take obligatory narrow scope, even in contexts where an indefinite would not, we can be relatively sure that it is not a bona fide indefinite.[13] The source of the perceived indefiniteness would then have to be constructional or derivative on a kind level meaning. Direct objects, we saw, can be targets of incorporation and/or complex predicate formation. Similarly, subjects may involve topichood and therefore lean towards a definite interpretation. It is thus important to check for indefinite readings in a variety of syntactic positions. The indirect object position, which has neither of these biases, proved to be revealing in the case of Hindi bare singulars.

As mentioned above, kind terms are one source for narrow scope indefinite readings of bare nominals. It may be worth highlighting that their status as kind terms needs to be established on the basis of kind-level predicates rather than on the basis of generic statements. As observed by Carlson (1977), this test separates English indefinites, which are compatible with generic statements, from bare plurals which are genuine kind terms. (30b) is only acceptable under a taxonomic reading, referring to a subtype of dinosaur:

(30a) Dinosaurs are extinct.
(30b) *A dinosaur is extinct.

Note in this connection that Hindi and English both mark number inside the nominal and that singular and plural kind terms differ in two respects. Languages with articles typically disallow bare singulars and do not typically admit indefinite readings for singular kind terms.[14] In languages that do not make a similar distinction but allow bare nominals to refer to kinds, bare nominals typically behave like bare plurals rather than bare singulars. This holds for languages like Chinese that require the obligatory use of classifiers for counting as well as for languages like Haitian Creole that do not. So far I have not come across languages

13 The crucial contrasts were demonstrated in (12b). Unfortunately, these cases have been generally neglected in the literature leading to the erroneous view that bare plurals are simply a subtype of indefinites.

14 The definite singular generic lends itself to representative object interpretations, as in *We photographed the lion on our trip* or *The rat reached Australia in 1770* (see Dayal 2011a for a survey).

in which bare nominals are bona fide indefinites, displaying the full range of readings associated with indefinites.

3.2 From article-less L1 to articled L2

The statement that adult learners of a language with articles never quite master the system if their L1 lacks articles is almost a truism. This observation has recently been validated with systematic tests using modern methods of statistical experimentation and analysis. In this final section I would like to briefly consider this issue from the perspective of the view espoused in this paper about bare nominals in article-less languages. In particular, it makes claims about the types of errors adult learners are likely to make: errors of misuse versus errors of omission. To get a sense of what is at issue, consider the following paradigm:

(31)

		Hindi L1	English L2
a.	There were ten children in the room. __ girl was playing ...	*ek* 'one'/*Ø	no error
b.	Our rules say that if ___ student registers for a class, it will not be canceled.	*koī* 'some'/*Ø	no error
c.	A boy and a girl came in. ___ girl sat down.	Ø	omission

The paradigm is modeled on Ionin (2003), where subjects are given forced-choice tasks in which they are asked to choose between THE, A or Ø to fill in the blank. The target for the above, would be *A*, *A* and *The*, respectively. The prediction that the current theory of Hindi bare nominals makes is that adult learners would not make errors in (31a) and (31b) since transfer from their L1 would suggest the need for a lexical exponent which is the closest correspondent to *ek* or *koī*. In the case of (31c) the prediction would be that there would be errors of omission as the bare nominal would be fully accepted in their L1.

As would be obvious, the paradigm in (31) targets contexts where the L1 situation is unambiguous. No Hindi speaker would use a bare nominal for the first two cases, and no Hindi speaker would use the numeral or the indefinite determiner in the third case. We know, of course, that had we chosen examples which targeted the direct object position, the L1 situation could be construed as favoring the definite or the indefinite. This is particularly so in the case of written tasks that do not have the benefit of prosody to disambiguate. One general question this raises, of course, is whether interference from L1 is sensitive to specific constructions or is more global. Is it the case that if a bare nominal can be construed as definite or indefinite in some constructions, the ambiguity becomes a factor in L2 learning regardless of the particular construction? Or is it the case that interference from L1 will be context dependent, as shown above?

Although there are fairly extensive studies on L2 acquisition of determiner systems at this point (Ionin 2003, Ko et al 2010, Schönenberger 2014, among others), they do not target this particular question.[15] The basic premise of most such studies is that bare nominals in article-less languages are ambiguous. In fact, the following quote from Schönenberger (2014: 84) about the experimental design being reported on is telling, "to ensure that word order would not influence article choice, all the test items contained transitive verbs and article choice always concerned nominals in the object position. These nominals were singular count nouns, which always require an article." Now, as we have seen, the direct object position is precisely the context where bare singular count nouns in the L1 articleless languages are prone to ambiguity. It would be worthwhile for further studies in this domain to control for syntactic position and interpretation as a way to probe more deeply and compare the results with those for direct object position. A second comment, also from Schönenberger (2014: 99–100), is interesting in the context of our findings in sections 1 and 2, "article omission is significantly higher with definites than with indefinites." This is exactly what one would expect if bare nominals in L1 are definite rather than indefinite.

4 Conclusion

In this paper I have collected together various tests that I have used in the past to determine the semantic properties of bare nominals. In the process, I have emphasized the need for precision and clarity in making claims about their interpretation. Although much more is known about the semantics of bare nominals today than even twenty years ago, we still need to flesh out an empirically adequate picture of noun phrase interpretation in order to refine our current understanding of cross-linguistic variation. Shifting our attention from languages with overt exponents of (in)definiteness to those without articles can help us gain a deeper

15 The L1 in the studies I have looked at are not Hindi. Although I do not want to make claims here for other languages, as I have already indicated, I have not found bare nominals in the L1 referred to in these studies (Russian, Korean, for example) to have bona fide indefinite readings.

understanding of what constitutes definiteness and indefiniteness. And making headway in this domain can also shape the way in which we probe issues related to the acquisition of the determiner systems by bilinguals and add to our understanding of how (in)definiteness is encoded in the human brain.

References

Bhattacharya, T. 1999. Structure of the Bangla DP. University College, London. PhD dissertation.
Carlson, G. 1977. Reference to kinds in English. PhD dissertation, University of Massachusetts, Amherst.
Chierchia, G. 1998. Reference to kinds across language. *Natural language semantics* 6.4, 339–405.
Dayal, V. 1999. Bare NP's, reference to kinds, and incorporation. In *Proceedings of SALT*, vol. 9, 34–51.
Dayal, V. 2004. Number marking and (in)definiteness in kind terms. *Linguistics and Philosophy* 27, 393–450.
Dayal, V. 2011a. Bare noun phrases. In K. von Heusinger, C. Maienborn & P. Portner (eds.) *Semantics. An International Handbook of Natural Language Meaning*. Vol. 2. Berlin: de Gruyter, 1088–1109.
Dayal, V. 2011b. Hindi pseudo-incorporation. *Natural Language & Linguistic Theory* 29.1, 123–167.
Dayal, V. 2012. Bangla Classifiers: Mediating between Kinds and Objects. *Rivista di Linguistica/Italian Journal of Linguistics* 24.2. 195–226.
Dayal, V. 2013. On the existential force of bare plurals across languages. In I. Caponigro and C. Cechetto (eds.), *From grammar to meaning: the spontaneous logicality of language*. Cambridge: Cambridge University Press, 49–80.
Dayal, V. 2014. Bangla Plural Classifiers. *Language and Linguistics* 15.1. 47–87.
Enç, M. 1991.The Semantics of Specificity, *Linguistic Inquiry* 22.1, 1–25.
Farkas, D. 1981. Quantifier scope and syntactic islands. In: R. Hendrick et al. (eds.). *Papers from the Seventeenth Regional Meeting Chicago Linguistics Society* (= CLS) 17. University of Chicago, 59–66.
Farkas, D. and A. Brasoveanu. 2016. In M. Aloni and P. Dekker (eds.) *Cambridge Handbook for Formal Semantics*, Cambridge: Cambridge University Press, 246–283.
Fodor, J. D. and I. Sag. 1982. Referential and quantificational indefinites. *Linguistics and Philosophy* 5, 355–398.
Heim, I. 2011. Definiteness and indefiniteness. In K. von Heusinger & C. Maienborn & P. Portner (eds.) *Semantics. An International Handbook of Natural Language Meaning*. Vol. 2. Berlin: de Gruyter, 996–1025.
von Heusinger, K. 2011. Specificity. In K. von Heusinger & C. Maienborn & P. Portner (eds.) *Semantics. An International Handbook of Natural Language Meaning*. Vol. 2. Berlin: de Gruyter, 1025–1058.

Ionin, Tania. 2003. Article semantics in second language acquisition. PhD thesis, MIT dissertation.
Kachru, Y. 1980. *Aspects of Hindi Grammar*. New Delhi: Manohar Publications.
Kidwai, A. 2000. XP adjunction in universal grammar: scrambling and binding in Hindi-Urdu. New York: Oxford University Press.
Ko, H, T. Ionin, & K. Wexler. 2010. The Role of Presuppositionality in the Second Language Acquisition of English Articles. *Linguistic Inquiry* 41.
Löbner, S. 1985. Definites. *Journal of Semantics* 4, 279–326.
Longobardi, G. 1994. Reference and Proper Names. *Linguistic Inquiry* 25.
Mahajan, A. 1990.The A/A-bar distinction and movement theory. Doctoral dissertation, MIT, Cambridge, Mass.
Masica, C. 1991. *The Indo-Aryan Languages*. [Cambridge Language Surveys], Cambridge: Cambridge University Press.
Mohanan, T. 1994. *Argument Structure in Hindi*. [Dissertations in Linguistics] CSLI Publications, Stanford, California..
Partee, B. 1987. Noun phrase interpretation and type-shifting principles. In: J. Groenendijk, D. de Jongh & M. Stokhof (eds.). *Studies in Discourse Representation Theory and the Theory of Generalizd Quantifiers*. Dordrecht: Foris, 115–144.
Schönenberger, M. 2014. Article use in L2 English by L1 Russian and L1 German speakers. *Zeitschrift fur Sprachwissenschaft* 33.
Thakur, A. 2015. *Theory of Nouns: The Hindi Noun Phrase*. Partridge India.
Verma, M. K. 1971. *The Structure of the Noun Phrase in Hindi and English*. New Delhi: Motilal Banarasidass.

Rajesh Bhatt, Vincent Homer

Differential comparatives in Hindi-Urdu

Abstract: We provide an analysis of nominal comparatives with differentials in Hindi-Urdu. Nominal comparatives in Hindi-Urdu pattern (‘*zyādā kitābẽ*’) with nominal comparatives in English (‘more books’). However, once we introduce differentials, we see an asymmetry. While English allows for both ‘two more books’ as well as ‘two books more’, Hindi-Urdu only allows for the latter option as ‘*do zyādā kitābẽ*’ is ungrammatical. We demonstrate, however, that the asymmetry goes further. While it superficially seems that ‘*Ram-ne Ramesh-se do kitābẽ zyādā paṛhī*’ is parallel to ‘Ram read two books more than Ramesh’, we show that the Hindi-Urdu differential comparatives have an entirely different analysis. In fact, ‘*do kitābẽ*’ (two books) and ‘*zyādā*’ (more) do not even form a surface constituent. This can be seen by the fact that postposition cannot combine with the sequence ‘*do kitābẽ zyādā*’. Hence the string ‘**do kitābẽ zyādā ko*’ is ungrammatical. Instead, we argue that Hindi-Urdu differential comparatives pattern with Differential Verbal Comparatives in Mandarin as analyzed in Li (2014). Following Li’s analysis, we give a compositional treatment where ‘*zyādā*’ (more) operates on the main verb as a result of which its first argument is interpreted as a differential. A surprising aspect of our analysis is that differentials can only be expressed with nominal comparatives that appear as bare direct objects or as subjects of unaccusatives. Differentials in all other positions are simply ineffable. This claim is borne out by a search of the 200 million word Corpus of Spoken Hindi developed by the University of Osaka.

Keywords: Differential comparatives, Hindi-Urdu

1 Introduction

We show that in Hindi-Urdu, the syntax of comparatives with differentials is quite strikingly different from the syntax of comparatives without differentials. The latter are not substantially different from their counterparts in English while the

Rajesh Bhatt, Department of Linguistics, University of Massachusetts, Amherst, USA. Email: bhatt@linguist.umass.edu
Vincent Homer, Department of Linguistics, University of Massachusetts, Amherst, USA. Email: vincent.homer@gmail.com

https://doi.org/10.1515/9783110610796-002

former are. Hindi-Urdu differential comparatives resemble in some ways the differential verbal comparatives described and analyzed by Li (2015). We show that differential comparatives in Hindi-Urdu are subject to severe argument structure and adjacency restrictions as a result of which they have a limited distribution. They are only available with bare objects of transitives and bare subjects of unaccusative verbs. We provide a compositional semantics for them that has *zyādā* 'more' combining directly with the verbal route.

2 Simple comparatives in Hindi-Urdu

We start with a quick introduction to comparatives without differentials in Hindi-Urdu. Such comparatives can be phrasal or clausal. Clausal comparatives have the syntax of correlatives.

(1a) Phrasal:
रीना मीना से (ज़्यादा) लंबी है।
Rīnā Mīnā-se (zyādā) lambī hɛ.
Rīnā.F Mīnā-than more tall.F be.PRS.SG
'Rīnā is taller than Mīnā.'

(1b) Clausal:
मीना जितनी लंबी है रीना उससे ज़्यादा लंबी है।
[Mīnā jitnī lambī hɛ] [Rīnā us-se
Mīnā.F REL.much.F tall.F be.PRS.SG Rīnā that-than
(zyādā) lambī hɛ].
more tall.F be.PRS.SG
'Rīnā is taller than Mīnā.'
(Literally: 'How tall Mīnā is, Rīnā is taller than that')

The above comparatives are comparatives on adjectives – it is also possible to have comparatives on nominals. The degree quantified nominal can appear in a range of syntactic positions – it can be a direct object, an indirect object, an adjunct, or a subject (of a transitive, an unergative, or an unaccusative).

(2a) Bare Direct Object:
रीना ने मीना से ज़्यादा किताबें पढ़ीं।
Rīnā-ne Mīnā-se zyādā kitābẽ paṛhī̃.
Rīnā-ERG Mīnā-than more books.F.PL read.PFV.F.PL
'Rīnā read more books than Mīnā.'

(2b) Differential Object Marked (DOM) direct object:
रीना ने मीना से ज़्यादा लोगों को डाँटा।
Rīnā-ne Mīnā-se zyādā logõ-ko ḍā̃ṭā.
Rīnā-ERG Mīnā-than more people-DOM scold-PFV.DEF
'Rīnā scolded more people than Mīnā.'

(2c) Indirect Object:
रीना ने मीना से ज़्यादा लोगों को तोहफे दिए।
Rīnā-ne Mīnā-se zyādā logõ-ko tohfe diye.
Rīnā-ERG Mīnā-than more people-DAT present.M.PL give.PFV.M.PL
'Rīnā gave presents to more people than Mīnā.'

(2d) Adjunct:
रीना मीना से ज़्यादा बार दिल्ली गयी।
Rīnā Mīnā-se zyādā bār Dillī gayī.
Rīnā.F Mīnā-than more times Delhi go.PFV.F.SG
'Rīnā went to Delhi more times than Mīnā.'

(3) Subjects of:

(3a) Transitives:
LGB MP-से ज़्यादा लोगों ने पढ़ी।
LGB MP-*se zyādā logõ-ne paṛh-ī.*
LGB.F MP-than more people read-PFV.F.SG
'More people read LGB than MP.'

(3b) Unergatives:
कल आज से ज़्यादा तीर्थ यात्री नहाएँगे।
kal āj-se zyādā tīrth-yātrī nahā-ẽge.
tomorrow today-then more pilgrim bathe-FUT.M.PL
'More pilgrims will bathe tomorrow than did today.'

(3c) Unaccusatives:
कल आज से ज़्यादा पेड़ कटेंगे।
kal āj-se zyādā peṛ kaṭ-ẽge.
tomorrow today-then more tree.PL cut.UNACC.FUT.M.PL
'More trees will be cut tomorrow than were today.'

These examples reveal that the *zyādā* 'more' forms a constituent with the NP that it degree quantifies over. The degree quantified NP can appear in a range of syntactic positions, it can appear with overtly case-marked NPST, and does not need to be adjacent to the verb. Finally a comparison with the English translations shows that the Hindi-Urdu comparatives are not structurally substantially different from their English counterparts, modulo the location of the -se/than phrase. For further details we refer the reader to Bhatt and Takahashi (2011) where we have discussed the syntax and semantics of Hindi-Urdu comparative have been discussed.

3 Differential comparatives

Let's start with looking at what happens to English comparatives if we add a differential.

(4a) Adjectival comparative:
Mīnā is 1cm. taller than Rīnā.
(4b) Nomina comparative:
Mīnā read 2 more books than Rīnā.

This all looks very well-behaved. If we think of the comparative head -er/more as denoting a greater than statement, then handling the differential only requires adding an additional differential argument.

(5a) Variant without differential:
$[[\text{-er}]] = \lambda P_{dt}\, \lambda Q_{dt}\, .[\iota d.Q(d) > \iota d.P\,(d)]$
(5b) Variant with differential:
$[[\text{-er}]] = \lambda d_{d}\, \lambda P_{dt}\, \lambda Q_{dt}\, .[\iota d.Q(d) = \iota d.P\,(d) + d]$

The above semantics sits well with the syntax – the differential argument appears structurally adjacent to the comparative degree head. With nominal comparatives in English, we find one additional option where the more appears after the NP.

(6a) Mīnā read 2 books more than Rīnā.
(6b) Mīnā met with two students more than Rīnā.

In Bhatt and Homer (2018), we analyze cases like (6). We treat '2 books more' as a constituent and propose that the '2 books' functions as a differential of more and that more degree quantifies over a covert NP.

Turning now to Hindi-Urdu, we find that adjectival comparatives with differentials and nominal comparatives with differentials part ways. The former are not substantially different from their English counterparts modulo the independent difference that in Hindi-Urdu adjectival comparatives, the comparative degree head can be covert. The differential, which is expressed by a measure phrase, appears adjacent to the comparative degree head.

(7) Adjectival comparative with differential:
रीना मीना से दो इंच ज़्यादा लंबी है।
Rīnā Mīnā-se do inč (zyādā) lambī hɛ.
Rīnā.F Mīnā-than two inch more tall.F be.PRS.SG
'Rīnā is 2 inches taller than Mīnā.'

But nominal comparatives with differentials are quite different. The English order 2 more books is simply ungrammatical; the only option is the 2 books more order.[1]

(8) Nominal comparatives with differentials:

(8a) '2 more books':
*रीना ने मीना से दो ज़्यादा किताबें पढ़ीं।
**Rīnā-ne Mīnā-se do zyādā kitābẽ paṛhī.*
Rīnā-ERG Mīnā-than two more book.F.PL read-pfv.F.PL
Intended: 'Rīnā read 2 more books than Mīnā.'
(8b) '2 books more': OK
रीना ने मीना से दो किताबें ज़्यादा पढीं।
Rīnā-ne Mīnā-se do kitābẽ zyādā paṛhī.
Rīnā-ERG Mīnā-than two book.F.PL more read-pfv.F.PL
Intended: 'Rīnā read 2 more books than Mīnā.'

1 The reader might think at this point of the additive aur. English uses more for both the additive and the comparative but Hindi- Urdu has aur for the additive meaning and *zyādā* for the comparative meaning. Curiously *ɔr* allows for both orders.
i. मेरे पास दो किताबें हैं। उसके पास तीन और किताबें / किताबें और हैं।
mere pās do kitābẽ hɛ̃. uske pās tīn
me.GEN near two books be.PRS.PL s/he-GEN near three
ɔr kitābẽ hɛ̃.
more$_{add}$ books/books more$_{add}$ be.PRS.PL
'I have two books. He has three more$_{add}$ books.' (he has 3 book, not 5)
Thus, *ɔr* in *tīn ɔr kitābẽ* 'three more$_{add}$ books' is like English more in allowing for a numeral argument. But the 'tīn kitābẽ *ɔr*' order ends up patterning with the Hindi-Urdu *tīn kitābẽ zyādā* 'three books more$_{comparative}$' in its syntactic properties and not with the English 'three books more$_{add}$' – the evidence against treating *tīn kitābẽ zyādā* 'three books more$_{comparative}$' as a surface constituent extends to the *tīn kitābẽ ɔr* order. Neither sequence can be followed by a postposition.

At this point it could be the case that Hindi-Urdu only permits nominal comparatives with differentials in '2 books more' order but is otherwise like English i.e. we can use our treatment for '2 books more' in English to handle (8). In lacking the '2 more books' order and only having the '2 books more', Hindi-Urdu would not be unique. In Bhatt and Homer (2018), we document that there are many languages which display exactly this pattern. However further investigation shows that the analysis of '2 books more' in Hindi-Urdu has to be quite different from the analysis of the corresponding sequence in English. Unlike English, where '2 books more' forms a constituent, the Hindi-Urdu sequence is not in fact a constituent. Initial evidence against treating the counterpart of '2 books more' as a constituent comes from the fact that '2 books more' cannot combine with a postposition.

(9) '2 books more K':
*रीना ने मीना से दो किताबें ज़्यादा को पढ़ा।
**Rīnā-ne Mīnā-se do kitābõ zyādā-ko paṛhā.*
Rīnā-ERG Mīnā-than two book.F.PL.OBL more-DOM read-PFV.DEF
Intended: 'Rīnā read 2 more books than Mīnā.'

It should be noted that the closely related word order '2 books K more' is grammatical but it lacks the differential comparative reading.

(10) '2 books K more': OK with non-differential meaning; *with differential meaning
रीना ने मीना से दो किताबों को ज़्यादा पढ़ा।
Rīnā-ne Mīnā-se do kitābõ-ko zyādā paṛhā.
Rīnā-ERG Mīnā-than two book.F.PL.OBL-DOM more read-PFV.DEF
Available: 'There are two books such that Rīnā read them to greater extent than Mīnā.'
Unavailable: 'Rīnā read 2 more books than Mīnā.'

The meaning available is that of a simple adverbial comparative; two books does not measure out the difference.

In fact the restriction is more general. In a differential comparative in Hindi-Urdu, the *zyādā* can never appear in a 'Num N *zyādā* K' sequence. This leads to a summary ban on differential comparatives on a vast range of syntactic positions – differential comparatives simply cannot be formed on ergative subjects, indirect objects, locatives etc. for the simple reason that these are all obligatorily marked by an overt case marker.

(11a) Ergative subject:
LGB MP-से दो लड़कों ने ज़्यादा/ *ज़्यादा ने पढ़ी।
LGB-f MP-*se* *do* *laṛkõ-ne* *zyādā/*zyādā-ne* *paṛh-ī.*
LGB MP-than two boys.OBL-ERG more/more-ERG read-PFV.F
Intended but unavailable: 'Two more boys read LGB than did MP.'
Adverbial comparative reading: 'Two boys read LGB to a greater extent than MP.'

(11b) Dative indirect object:
यह किताब राम ने रमेश से दो लड़कों को ज़्यादा/ *ज़्यादा को दी।
yeh kitāb *Ram-ne* *Ramesh-se* *do* *laṛkõ-ko*
this book.F Ram-ERG Ramesh-than two boys.OBL-DAT
*zyādā/*zyādā ko d-ī.*
more/ more -DAT give-PFV.F
Intended but unavailable: 'Ram gave this book to two more boys than Ramesh did.'
Adverbial comparative reading: 'Ram gave this book to two boys to a greater extent than Ramesh.'

As we have seen earlier, there is no ban on comparatives in these positions as long as they do not involve a differential. We can summarize what we have found concerning differential comparatives in Hindi-Urdu as follows:

(12a) Ordinary comparatives display a '*zyādā* NP' order while differential comparatives display the 'Num NP *zyādā*' order. The 'Num *zyādā* NP' order is ungrammatical.
(12b) The 'Num NP *zyādā* K' order is ungrammatical.
(12c) The 'Num NP K *zyādā*' is grammatical but it only has an adverbial comparative reading. There is no differential comparative reading.

4 An argument structure restriction

The ungrammaticality of the 'Num NP *zyādā* K' order means that differential comparatives cannot be formed on positions that are overtly case marked. We find a somewhat unusual situation of widespread ineffability. In fact the limitations on the distribution of differential comparatives go even further. If the only restriction on distribution was (12b), we would expect that all positions where NPST can appear without overt case marking would allow for differential comparatives. Such positions include subjects of non-perfective transitives, subjects of unergatives and unaccusatives, and direct objects without DOM-ko marking. But in fact only a subset of these positions allow for differential comparatives. We have already seen in (8b) that direct objects without DOM-ko allow for differential comparatives. Next we turn to subjects of unaccusatives and we find that these also permit differential comparatives.

(13) Unaccusatives:

(13a) Existential constructions:
इस कमरे में उस कमरे के दो खिड़कियाँ ज़्यादा हैं।
is kamre-mẽ us kamre-se do khiṛkiyā̃ zyādā hɛ̃.
this room-in that room-than two windows more be.PRS.PL
'There are two more windows in this room than in that room.'

(13b) Possessive constructions:
मेरे पास तुम से दो घोड़े ज़्यादा हैं।
mere pās tum-se do ghoṛe zyādā hɛ̃.
me.GEN near you-than two horses more be.PRS.PL
'I have two more horses than you.'

(13c) Change of state unaccusative:
इस साल पिछले साल से दो दुकानें ज़्यादा खुलीं।
is sāl pičhle sāl-se do dukānẽ zyādā khul-ī̃.
this year last year-than two shops more open-PFV.F.PL
'Two more shops opened this year than did last year.'

(13d) Verb of motion:
इस साल पिछले साल से पचास सैलानी ज़्यादा आए।
is sāl pičhle sāl-se pačās sɛlāni zyādā ā-e.
this year last year-than fifty tourists more come-PFV.F.PL
'Fifty more tourists came this year than did last year.'

(13e) 'DAT NOM' unaccusative:
मीना को टीना से दो धूमकेतु ज़्यादा दिखे।
Mīnā-ko Ṭīnā-se do dhūmketu zyādā dikh-e.
Mīnā-DAT Ṭīnā-than two comets more appear-PFV.M.PL
'Mīnā saw two more comets than Ṭīnā did.'

What about nominative subjects of transitives and unergatives? Given the absence of an overt case marker here, we might expect a differential comparative to be possible but this does not turn out to be the case. Differential comparatives on these positions are ungrammatical.

(14) Transitive:
(14a) ?/* लड्डू रसमलाई से तीन लोग ज़्यादा खाएँगे।
?/**laḍḍū rasmalāi-se tīn log zyādā khā-ẽge.*
laḍḍū rasmalāi-than three people more eat-FUT.3M.PL
Intended but unavailable:
'Three more people will eat *laddus* than will eat *rasmalāi.*'
Adverbial comparative reading is available: 'There are three people who will eat laddus to a greater extent than the extent to which they eat rasmalāi.'

(14b) * खाना इस कमरे में उस कमरे से तीन लोग ज़्यादा खाएँगे।
* *khānā is kamre-me us kamre-se tīn log*
food this room-in that room-than three people
zyādā khā-ẽge.
more eat-FUT.3M.PL
Intended but unavailable: 'Three more people will eat food in this room than will eat food in that room.'
Adverbial comparative reading is marginally available: 'There are three people who eat food to a greater extent in this room than in that room.'
With unergatives, the judgements are muddy.

(15) Unergative:
??इस कमरे में उस कमरे से तीन लोग ज़्यादा नहा सकते हैं।
is kamre-mẽ us kamre-se tīn log zyādā
this room-in that room-than three people more
nahā sakte hɛ̃.
bathe can.HAB.M.PL be.PRS.3PL
Intended but unavailable: 'Three more people can bathe in this room than in that room.'
Adverbial comparative reading is marginally available: 'There are three people who can bathe to a greater extent in this room than in that room.'

Finally we also consider temporal adverbials and path arguments which can be realized as bare NPST. These can be the locus of differential comparatives.

(16a) Temporal adverbial:
रवि ने मीना से यह किताब दो घंटे ज़्यादा पढ़ी।
Ravi-ne Mīnā-se yeh kitāb do ghanṭe zyādā paṛh-ī.
Ravi-ERG Mīnā-than this book.F 2 hours more read-PFV.F
'Ravi read this book for two hours more than Mīnā.'

(16b) Path argument:
वीना आज नीना से दो किलोमीटर ज़्यादा दौड़ेगी।
Vina āj Nina-se do kilomīṭar zyādā dɔṛ-egī.
Vina.F today Nina-than 2kms more run-FUT.F
'Vina will run two kilometres more than Nina today.'

We formulate a generalization based on the clear cases:[2]

(17) Differential comparatives can only be formed on the internal arguments of verbs – hence direct objects of transitive verbs and subjects of unaccusatives or on the event argument itself. A further condition is that the arguments cannot appear with overt case marking.

Our intuition is that the differential comparative specifies the difference between two events – we can measure out two events based on their theme argument or on the temporal properties of the event itself. Other theta roles cannot be used to measure out events. In our formal analysis we will implement this intuition by imposing a restriction on the attachment height of *zyādā*. We will require it to attach low, lower than the level at which agents and goals are introduced. At that level, only internal arguments and the event argument are available.

5 An adjacency restriction

We have seen so far that Hindi-Urdu allows for differential comparatives only with subjects of unaccusatives and direct objects of transitives. Moreover these arguments must not bear overt case marking.

(18a) Subject of unaccusative:
... Differential.Subject [=Num NP] ... *zyādā* ... $V_{unaccusative}$
(18b) Direct object of transitive:
... Differential.Direct.Object [=Num NP] ... *zyādā* ... $V_{transitive}$

2 If it turns out that subjects of unergatives can reliably be the locus of differential comparatives, then we will have to modify the generalization to refer to the first argument rather than to internal argument. But it is also possible that the 'unergatives' in question appear with unaccusative syntax in the construction at hand.

In the schematization above, it appears as if the differential argument can appear discontinuous from *zyādā* and that *zyādā* can appear discontinuous from the verb. It turns that this schematization is too liberal. In fact differential comparative interpretations are only available if the differential phrase immediately precedes the *zyādā* and the *zyādā* immediately precedes the verb. This adjacency restriction is specific to differential comparatives. In adverbial comparatives, *zyādā* can, but does not have to, im- mediately precede the verb.

(19) Adverbial Comparative:
(19a) *zyādā* XP Verb:
टीना मीना से इस साल ज़्यादा दिल्ली गयी।
Ṭīnā Mīnā-se is sāl zyādā Dillī gayī.
Ṭīnā.F Mīnā-than this year more Delhi go.PFV.F
'Ṭīnā went to Delhi to a greater extent than Mīnā.' (more times or greater duration)
(19b) XP *zyādā* Verb:
टीना मीना से इस साल दिल्ली ज़्यादा गयी।
Ṭīnā Mīnā-se is sāl Dillī zyādā gayī.
Ṭīnā.F Mīnā-than this year Delhi more go.PFV.F
'Ṭīnā went to Delhi to a greater extent than Mīnā.' (more times or greater duration)

Let us demonstrate the role of adjacency by taking a well formed differential comparative and then disrupting one at a time the adjacency between the differential and the *zyādā* and the adjacency between *zyādā* and the verb.

(20a) Control: [three boys] *zyādā* Verb: differential comparative reading is available
आज कल से तीन लड़के ज़्यादा आये थे
āj kal-se [tīn laṛke] zyādā ā-ye the
today yesterday-than three boys more come-PFV.M.PL be.PST.M.PL
'Three more boys had come today than yesterday.'
(20b) [three boys] *zyādā* XP Verb: differential comparative reading is unavailable
*आज कल से तीन लड़के ज़्यादा यहाँ आये थे।
**āj kal-se [tīn laṛke] zyādā yahā̃ ā-ye the*
today yesterday-than three boys more here come-PFV.M.PL be.PST.M.PL
Intended but unavailable: 'Three more boys had come here today than yesterday.' (An adverbial comparative reading is available marginally if we interpret three boys as referring to particular boys.)

(20c) [three boys] XP *zyādā* Verb: differential comparative reading is unavailable
*आज कल से [तीन लड़के] यहाँ ज़्यादा यहाँ आये थे।
**āj kal-se [tīn laṛke] yahā̃ zyādā*
today yesterday-than three boys here more
ā-ye the.
come.PFV.M.PL be.PST.M.PL
Intended but unavailable: 'Three more boys had come here today than yesterday.' (An adverbial comparative reading is available: 'three boys came here to a greater extent today than did yesterday'.)

We now have the final schematization for when the differential comparative reading is available. Assuming that direct objects of transitives and subjects of unaccusatives originate in the same location, the following structure characterizes the availability of differential comparatives in Hindi-Urdu:[3]

(21) ... [VP [Differential] *zyādā* Verb] (adjacency must be maintained)

6 A semantics for differential comparatives

6.1 Structural assumptions

The core idea behind our analysis is that in differential comparatives *zyādā* combines with the verbal projection in a way that is different from how the *zyādā* phrase combines with the verb in plain, differential-less, comparatives. In a plain comparative, *zyādā* is part of the syntactic projection of the noun phrase and the

---

3 The adjacency restriction that we report here might turn out to be an adjacency preference as the following case of non-adjacency seems acceptable.
(i) (Thanks to Veneeta Dayal for helping with this example)
मीना ने टीना से दो किताबें ज़्यादा कल पढ़ी थीं।
Mīnā ne Ṭīnā se do kitābe zyādā kal paṛhī thī̃.
Mīnā-ERG Ṭīnā-than two books more yesterday read-PFV.F be.PST.F.PL
'It was yesterday that Mīnā read two more books than Ṭīnā.'
This is a case of focus-motivated reordering which places the focused constituent kal 'yesterday' in the immediately pre-verbal posi- tion. We don't know why in this case we still retain the differential reading that gets lost in (20). Nevertheless we would like to note that there are no instances of adjacency violating differential comparatives in the two hundred million word Nishioka et al (2016-2017) Corpus of Spoken Hindi, which indicates that adjacency is, at the very least, a strong preference.

zyādā-modified NP appears as a syntactic argument of the verb. There is no restriction on the syntactic position of the *zyādā*-modified NP. The situation with differential comparatives is very different. Here the *zyādā* is not part of the syntactic projection of the noun phrase. Instead it combines directly with the verb. The differential argument (= [Num NP]) behaves syntactically like an argument of the verb. This can be seen in the examples below and the schematic representations associated with them.

(22a) Differential-Less Comparative: XP1 XP2 -than [more NP] V
ईला ने मीला से [ज़्यादा किताबें] पढ़ीं।
*Īlā-ne Mīlā-se [**zyādā kitābẽ**] paṛh-ī.*
Ila-ERG Mīlā-than more books.F read-PFV.F.PL
'Ila read more books than Mīlā.'

(22b) Differential Comparative: XP1 XP2 -than [Num NP] [more V]
ईला ने मीला से [दो किताबें] [ज़्यादा पढ़ीं]।
*Īlā-ne Mīlā-se [**do kitābẽ**] [**zyādā paṛh-ī**].*
Ila-ERG Mīlā-than two books.F [more read-PFV.F.PL]
'Ila read two more books than Mīlā.'

These structures make clear predictions. In the differential-less comparative, *zyādā* forms a constituent with the NP that follows it and the *zyādā*-NP (= [*zyādā* NP]) is an argument of the verb. It therefore appears with the appropriate case associated with its structural position. In the differential comparative, the differential phrase (= [Num NP]) and the *zyādā*]) do not form a constituent. Hence there is no way that a postposition can appear on the 'Num NP *zyādā*' sequence. The ungrammaticality of 'Num NP *zyādā* K' follows directly. A further point is that the differential NP in (22b) is syntactically the direct object of the verb.

(23) * [Num NP] more K
*ईला ने मीला से [दो किताबें] ज़्यादा को पढ़ा।
Īlā-ne Mīlā-se [do kitābẽ] zyādā ko paṛh-ā.
Ila-ERG Mīlā-than two books.F more DOM read-PFV.M.SG
Intended: 'Ila read two more books than Mīlā.'

We now have an explanation for why the sequence 'Num NP *zyādā* K' is ungrammatical. What blocks 'Num NP K *zyādā*'? Recall that this sequence is not actually ungrammatical – it just lacks the differential comparative reading. This sequence is exemplified below.

(24) [Num NP] K more
ईला ने मीला से [दो किताबों] को [ज़्यादा पढ़ा]।
Īlā-ne Mīlā-se [***do kitābõ***]*-ko* [***zyādā paṛh-ā***]
Ila-ERG Mīlā-than two books.F-ACC more read-PFV.M.SG
Intended but unavailable: 'Ila read two more books than Mīlā.'
Available: There are two books such that Ila read them more/to a greater extent than Mīnā did.

The reason the differential comparative reading disappears here is straightforward. A noun phrase like two books can be interpreted referentially as quantifying over two actual books or as a measure phrase. This systematic polysemy of noun phrase has received a considerable amount of attention in the semantic literature. (See Rett (2014) for an overview.) Now differential object marking (DOM) of two books forces a referential interpretation. Consequently 'two books' with DOM cannot actually be interpreted as a differential. This is sufficient to block the differential reading; an adverbial comparative reading is still available and that is what surfaces in (24).

Before we move on to the actual semantics, it is worth examining the case where the differential comparative is on a temporal adverbial.

(25) Temporal adverbial:
रवि ने मीना से यह किताब [दो घंटे] [ज़्यादा पढ़ी]।
Ravi-ne Mīnā-se yeh kitāb [*do ghanṭe*] [*zyādā paṛh-ī*].
Ravi-ERG Mīnā-than this book.F two hours more read-PFV.F.SG
'Ravi read this book for two hours more than Mīnā.'

Once again, *zyādā* combines with the verb and then the differential phrase combines with the verbal projection. In (22b), the differential was syntactically a direct object. In (25), the differential is syntactically an adverbial. But otherwise the two cases are the same. In both, *zyādā* combines with a verb and then the first element the verb plus *zyādā* combines with is the differential. The default adjacency between the differential phrase and *zyādā* and between *zyādā* and the verb that we discussed earlier follows from this aspect of the structure.

6.2 Semantics for differential comparatives with differential internal arguments

We consider direct objects here but the analysis generalizes to subjects of unaccusatives. Our analysis should be able to handle sentences like the following.

(26) Differential is direct object:
(26a) Standard of comparison is subject:
ईला ने मीला से [दो किताबों] को [ज़्यादा पढ़ा]।
Īlā-ne Mīlā-se [do kitābẽ] ko [zyādā paṛhā].
Ila-ERG Mīlā-than two books.F DOM more read-PFV.M.SG
'Ila read two more books than Mīlā.'
(26b) Standard of comparison is indirect object:
ईला ने शीला को मीला से [दो किताबें] को [ज़्यादा दीं]।
Īlā-ne Śīlā-ko Mīlā-se [do kitābẽ] [zyādā d-ī̃].
Ila-ERG Sheela-DAT Mīlā-than two books.F more give-PFV.F.PL
'Ila gave two more books to Sheela than to Mīlā.'
(26c) Standard of comparison is adjunct:
आज कल से ईला ने [दो किताबें] [ज़्यादा पढ़ीं]।
āj kal-se Īlā-ne [do kitābẽ] [zyādā paṛh-ī̃].
Today yesterday-than Ila-ERG two books.F more read-PFV.F.PL
'Ila read two more books today than yesterday.'

We can derive why subjects of transitives are not good locations for differentials:

(27) यह किताब उस किताब से [दो लड़के] [ज़्यादा पढ़ेंगे]।
Yeh kitāb us kitāb-se [do laṛke] [zyādā paṛh-ẽge].
This book that book-than two boys more read-FUT.3M.PL
Intended but unavailable: 'Two boys will read this book more than that book.'
Available: adverbial comparative reading: 'There are two boys who will read this book to a greater extent than that book.'

Our semantics has two major components. First, they *zyādā* takes a verb root and makes it a comparative verb root. The differential phrase combines with this comparative verb root and specifies the difference between the compared events.

(28) [two books] [more read]
(28a) ⟦read⟧ $= \lambda x \lambda e.[read(e) \wedge Th(e) = x]$
(28b) ⟦zyādā⟧ $= \lambda P\, \lambda d \lambda e_1\, \lambda e_2\, \exists y_1\, \exists y_2\, .[P\,(e_1, y_1) \wedge P\,(e_2\,, y_2) \wedge \#(y_1) - \#(y_2) = d]$
(28c) ⟦[2 books]⟧ = 2-book-degrees
⟦[two books][more read]⟧ $= \lambda e_1\, \lambda e_2\, \exists y_1\, \exists y_2\, .[\mathrm{read}(e_1) \wedge \mathrm{Th}(e_1) = y_1 \wedge \mathrm{read}(e_2) \wedge \mathrm{Th}(e_2) = y_2 \wedge \#(y_1) - \#(y_2) = \text{2-book-degrees}]$

Next we have to have a general way of introducing the constituents that are compared – the standard of comparison and its correlate. Note that the structure in (28) can appear in a structure where the correlate of the standard of comparison is a subject (26a), an indirect object (26b), or an adjunct (26c). Inspired by Schwarzschild (2002), we decompose the comparative into two parts: one part introduces the comparison and the other introduces the standard of comparison. We have already seen the first part – *zyādā*, which introduces the comparison – in (28). We will use an abstract morpheme CMPR to introduce the standard of comparison. Let's use the following example where the correlate of the standard of comparison is the subject.

(29) Subject Standard-than IO [DO two books] [more gave]
ईला ने शीला से मीला को [दो किताबें] [ज़्यादा दीं।]
Īlā-ne Śīlā-se Mīlā-ko [do kitābẽ] [zyādā d-ī̃].
Ila-ERG Sheela-than Mīlā-Dat two books.F more give-PFV.F.PL
'Ila gave two more books to Mīlā than Sheela did.'

We will use two modes for introducing arguments. The first will be a straightforward extension of event identification for comparative event descriptions like the one in (28).

(30) Introducing the Indirect Object:
(30a) $[\![v_{GOAL}]\!] = \lambda x \lambda e.Goal(e) = x$
(30b) Extended Event Identification:
combines a theta-role θ with a predicate like $\lambda e_1 \lambda e_2 .P(e_1, e_2)$
yields: $\lambda x \lambda e_1 \lambda e_2.[P(e_1, e_2) \wedge \theta(e_1) = x \wedge \theta(e_2) = x]$
$[\![$Mīlā-Dat v_{GOAL} [[two books] [more gave]]]$]\!] =$
$\lambda e_1 \lambda e_2 \exists y_1 \exists y_2.[\text{give}(e_1) \wedge \text{Th}(e_1) = y_1 \wedge \text{Goal}(e_1) = \text{mila}'$
$\wedge\ \text{give}(e_2) \wedge \text{Th}(e_2) = y_2 \wedge \text{Goal}(e_2) = \text{mila}'$
$\wedge\ \#(y_1) - \#(y_2) = \text{2-book-degrees}]$

The second mode will introduce the standard of comparison and its correlate. We can call this 'Comparative Event Identification'.

(31) Comparative Event Identification combines:
(31a) θ, the θ-role of the correlate of the standard of comparison
(31b) a comparative event predicate P ($[P] = \lambda e_1 \lambda e_2.P(e_1, e_2)$)

We notate comparative event identification using the abstract morpheme CMPR.

$$[\![[[\text{CMPR}\ \theta]\ P]]]\!] = \lambda y \lambda x \lambda e_1\, \lambda e_2\,.[P\,(e_1\,,\, e_2) \wedge \theta(e_1) = x \wedge \theta(e_2) = y]$$
$$[\![\text{CMPR}]\!] = \lambda\theta_{evt}\, \lambda P_{vvt}\, \lambda y_e\, \lambda x_e\, \lambda e1_v\, \lambda e2_v.[P(e_1,\, e_2) \wedge \theta(e_1) = x \wedge \theta(e_1) = y]$$

Applying this to our example, we get the following.

(32a) $[\![$[[CMPR v_{AG}][Mīlā-Dat v_{Goal} [[two books] [more gave]]]]$]\!]$ =
$\lambda x_2\, \lambda x_1\, \lambda e_1\, \lambda e_2\, \exists y_1\, \exists y_2\,.[\text{give}(e_1) \wedge \text{Th}(e_1) = y_1 \wedge \text{Goal}(e_1) = \text{mila}' \wedge \text{Ag}(e_1) = x_1$
$\wedge\ \text{give}(e_2) \wedge \text{Th}(e_2) = y_2 \wedge \text{Goal}(e_2) = \text{mila}' \wedge \text{Ag}(e_2) = x_2$
$\wedge\ \#(y_1) - \#(y_2) = \text{2-book-degrees}]$

(32b) $[\![$[Sheela-than [[CMPR v_{AG}][Mīlā-Dat v_{GOAL} [[two books] [more gave]]]]] $]\!]$ =
$\lambda x_1\, \lambda e_1\, \lambda e_2\, \exists y_1\, \exists y_2\,.[\text{give}(e_1) \wedge \text{Th}(e_1) = y_1 \wedge \text{Goal}(e_1) = \text{mila}' \wedge \text{Ag}(e_1) = x_1$
$\wedge\ \text{give}(e_2) \wedge \text{Th}(e_2) = y_2 \wedge \text{Goal}(e_2) = \text{mila} \wedge \text{Ag}(e_2) = \text{sheela}'$
$\wedge\ \#(y_1) - \#(y_2) = \text{2-book-degrees}]$

(32c) $[\![$[Ila [Sheela-than [[CMPR v_{AG}][Mīlā-Dat v_{GOAL} [[two books] [more gave]]]]]] = $\lambda e_1\, \lambda e_2\, \exists y_1\, \exists y_2\,.[\text{give}(e_1) \wedge \text{Th}(e_1) = y_1 \wedge \text{Goal}(e_1) = \text{mila} \wedge$
$\text{Ag}(e_1) = \text{ila}'$
$\wedge\ \text{give}(e_2) \wedge \text{Th}(e_2) = y_2 \wedge \text{Goal}(e_2) = \text{mila} \wedge \text{Ag}(e_2) = \text{sheela}'$
$\wedge\ \#(y_1) - \#(y_2) = \text{2-book-degrees}]$

With these tools in hand, we can handle all the examples in (26). We will need to assume that all elements – be they ‘arguments’ or ‘adjuncts’ – are introduced in a neo-Davidsonian fashion through dedicated heads.

6.3 Semantics for Differential Comparatives with differential adjuncts

We now have an analysis for the cases where the differential functions as the internal argument i.e. subject of an unaccusative or the direct object of a transitive. The semantics we have written for *zyādā* introduce the comparison and the differential by saturating the internal argument. So it’s not surprising that the analysis does not extend to cases where the differential corresponds to an adverbial and not an internal argument.

(33) Temporal adverbial:
रवि ने मीना से यह किताब [दो घंटे] [ज़्यादा पढ़ी]।
Ravi-ne Mīnā-se yeh kitāb [do ghanṭe] [zyādā paṛh-ī].
Ravi-ERG Mīnā-than this book.F 2hours more read-PFV.F
‘Ravi read this book for two hours more than Mīnā.’

To allow for these cases, we have to allow *zyādā* to directly operate on the event predicate before the theme argument has been introduced. We need to assume that there is a head τ that introduces the content of the adverbial – that it is measuring out the duration of the event.

(34a) Differential is direct object:
[Differential [zyādā [Theme Root]]]
(34b) Differential is an adverbial:
[Theme [Differential [zyādā [τ Root]]]]

In the case in hand, τ would map an event to its duration in a manner parallel to how a theta role maps an event to an event argument. With that in place, the semantics introduced for *zyādā* in the preceding section (repeated below) would operate without change.

(35) $[\![\text{zyādā}]\!] = \lambda P\, \lambda d \lambda e_1\, \lambda e_2\, \exists y_1\, \exists y_2.[P\,(e_1\,, y_1) \wedge P\,(e_2\,, y_2) \wedge \#(y_1) - \#(y_2) = d]$

7 Conclusion

We have shown that adding a differential to nominal comparatives in Hindi-Urdu has profound consequences for the syntax of the corresponding comparative. The differential-less comparative has the *zyādā* combining with the element that is being degree quantified. In terms of its syntax and in its distribution, such comparatives are not very different from the comparatives that we find in English. However, when we have a differential comparative, the *zyādā* combines not with the degree quantified element or the differential but directly with the verbal predicate. The modified verbal predicate then combines with the differential, which thus ends up playing double duty – it functions as an internal argument and it also functions as the differential. These differential comparatives end up resembling Mandarin differerential verbal comparatives analyzed in Li (2015). The distribution of these differential comparatives is severely restricted by a number of overlapping constraints. We derive these by requiring that the differential comparative *zyādā* directly combine with the verb root at which point we take only the theme theta role to have been introduced. This syntactic restriction derives a wide range of the properties that differential comparatives have. But we do not yet have an answer as to why this syntactic restriction holds. It does not, for example, hold for the superficially similar adverbial comparatives.

(36) Adverbial comparatives:

(36a) टीना मीना से इस साल ज़्यादा दिल्ली गयी।

Ṭīnā	*Mīnā-se*	*is*	*sāl*	*zyādā*	*Dillī*	*gayī.*
Ṭīnā.F	Mīnā-than	this	year	more	Delhi	go.PFV.F

'Ṭīnā went to Delhi to a greater extent than Mīnā.' (more times or greater duration)

(36b) आज कल से ज़्यादा रीना ने गाने गाए।

āj	*kal-se*	*zyādā*	*Rīnā-ne*	*gāne*	*gā-ye.*
today	yesterday-than	more	Rīnā-ERG	songs.M.PL	sing-PFV.M.PL

'Rīnā sang songs to a greater extent today than she did yesterday.'

We believe the similarity is only superficial though. It is plausible that *zyādā* here modifies an abstract EXTENT/TIMES nominal. These adverbial comparatives then are no different from ordinary nominal comparatives. Still we are left with the need to explain why the nominal *zyādā* is unable to combine with differentials unlike the English more, where two more books is acceptable. This, of course, is a wider cross-linguistic puzzle and a solution to that remains to be found.[4]

4 One other point of difference is that nominal *zyādā* does not require the decomposition into a difference introducing component and a standard introducing component that we introduced for the differential *zyādā*.

References

Bhatt, R. and V. Homer. 2018. "Differentials Cross-linguistically." In Daniel Altshuler and Jessica Rett (eds.), The Semantics of Focus, Plurals, Degrees and Times: Essays in honor of Roger Schwarzschild. (To appear)

Bhatt, R., and S. Takahashi. 2011. "Reduced and Unreduced Phrasal Comparatives", *Natural Language and Linguistic Theory* 29, 581–620.

Li, X. 2015. "Degreeless comparatives: The semantics of differential verbal comparatives in Mandarin Chinese", *Journal of Semantics* 32:1, 1–38.

Rett, J. 2014. "The polysemy of measurement", *Lingua* 143, 242–266.

Schwarzschild, R. 2002. "The Grammar of Measurement". In B. Jackson (ed.) *Proceedings of SALT* 12, Ithaca, NY: Cornell University Press, 225–245.

Schwarzschild, R. 2008. "The Semantics of Comparatives and Other Degree Constructions", *Language and Linguistics Compass* 2:2, 308–331.

Stavrou, M. 2003. "Semi-lexical nouns, classifiers, and the interpretation(s) of the pseudopartitive Construction". In M. Coene and Y. d'Hulst (eds.) *From NP to DP: The Syntax and Semantics of Noun Phrases*. Amsterdam/ Philadelphia: John Benjamins, 329–353.

Emily Manetta

The structure of complex predicates in Hindi-Urdu: evidence from verb-phrase ellipsis

Abstract: While complex predicates in Hindi-Urdu have received significant attention (Hook 1974; Mohanan 1994; Butt 1995, 2003, 2010; Butt and Ramchand 2005; Mahajan 2012), not yet addressed in the literature are the ways in which these constructions interact with verb phrase ellipsis (VPE). This is a significant lacuna, as VPE has famously revealed much about the features of the verbal domain (as early as Ross 1969). New evidence and careful testing (following Goldberg 2005; Simpson, Choudhury and Menon 2013; and Gribanova 2013a, b) demonstrates that Hindi-Urdu does indeed exhibit true verb-stranding verb phrase ellipsis (VVPE) and thus regular verb movement outside the vP-layer. This is an important discovery, since relatively little empirical evidence has been brought to bear on the question of verb movement in this head-final language. In a potentially surprising result, I show that unlike Persian (Toosarvandani 2009) Hindi-Urdu complex predicates resist VPE stranding the light verb (vVPE), indicating that the inflected light verb may not move out of the verb phrase independently of the main verb. I build on the approach to complex predicates featuring decomposed verbal structure found in Butt and Ramchand (2005) to develop an account of the verbal domain in Hindi-Urdu that captures the strong syntactic connectedness between the components of the complex predicate we find in VVPE, while also predicting a range of other properties of complex predicates.[1]

Keywords: Complex predicate, ellipsis, anaphora, island, Hindi-Urdu

1 This work has benefitted from the input of many, and I am grateful to all for their time and patience. In particular, thanks are due to Ayesha Kidwai, Rajesh Bhatt, Miriam Butt, Tafseer Ahmed, Anoop Mahajan, Vera Gribanova, Jim McCloskey, Peter Hook, and Asim Zia. I am grateful to audiences at the 2016 International Conference on Hindi Studies in Paris, France, for their excellent feedback and of course to Ghanshyam Sharma for his tireless work organizing the conference and editing the resulting volume. A special mention of thanks is due to the late Alice Davison, for her feedback on this paper, as well as for our many other productive conversations over the years; she will be missed.

Emily Manetta, Department of Anthropology, University of Vermont, 509 Williams Hall, 72 University Place, Burlington, VT 05405, USA. Email: Emily.Manetta@uvm.edu

https: //doi.org/10.1515/9783110610796-003

1 Introduction

Complex predicates are found in a diverse range of languages and feature multiple predicates which act as a single unit and map to a mono-clausal syntactic structure. While complex predicates in Hindi-Urdu have received significant descriptive and analytical attention (Hook 1974; Bashir 1989; Mohanan 1994; Butt 1995, 2003, 2010; Butt and Ramchand 2005; Mahajan 2012), not yet addressed in the literature are the ways in which these constructions interact with processes of verb phrase ellipsis (VPE). This is a significant lacuna, as VPE has famously revealed much about the features of the verbal domain (as early as Ross 1969). Complex predicates are important quite generally as they represent an instance of the systematic combination of syntactically and semantically independent elements to function as a single syntactic unit. Their cross-linguistic analysis remains a topic of much debate (e.g. the contributions to Alsina, Bresnan, and Sells (1996) and Amberer, Baker, and Harvey (2014)). The goal of this paper is twofold: first, to establish that VPE is indeed available in Hindi-Urdu, and second, to use VPE as a new tool for probing the structure and composition of the verb phrase in complex predicate constructions.

VPE in many languages has provided important information about the nature of head movement and the shape of the verbal domain (Sag 1976, 1981; Williams 1977; Hankamer and Sag 1976; Jayaseelan 1990; Hardt 1993; Fiengo and May 1994; Lobeck 1995; Kennedy 2008; Johnson 2001; *inter alia*). Hindi-Urdu does not permit the equivalent of classic VPE in English, in which the main verb and its internal arguments are omitted, leaving behind only an auxiliary verb.

(1) Meena bought a new car, and Manu did too.

(2) #मीना ने नयी गाड़ी खरीदी थी और मनु ने भी ___ थी।
   #Mīnā-ne nay-ī gāṛī kharīd-ī thī, ɔr Manu-ne bhī ___ thī.
   Mīna-ERG new.F car.F buy.PFV.F AUX.F and Manu-ERG also ___ AUX.F
   Intended: 'Meena bought a new car and Manu did also (bought a new car).'

However, I will argue here that Hindi-Urdu does exhibit a form of VPE in which the verb undergoes head movement to escape the vP and is thus stranded outside the ellipsis site-verb-stranding VPE or VVPE. In VVPE, all vP internal material is elided save the verb itself.

(3a) राम ने चॉम्स्की का नया लेख दो बार पढ़ा।
Rām-ne Čomskī-kā nayā lekh do bār paṛhā.
Ram-ERG Chomsky-GEN new paper two time read.PST.M.SG
'Ram read the new paper by Chomsky twice.'

(3b) राज ने भी ___ पढ़ा।
Rāj-ne bhī ___ paṛhā.
Raj-ERG also ___ read.PST.M.SG
'Raj also read (the paper twice).'
(Simpson, Choudhury, and Menon 2013: 112)

VVPE is known to occur in languages as diverse as Irish (McCloskey 1991), Hebrew (Doron 1991, Goldberg 2002), Portuguese (Martins 1994), and Russian (Gribanova 2013a, b), and is schematized in (4) for a head-final language.[2]

(4)

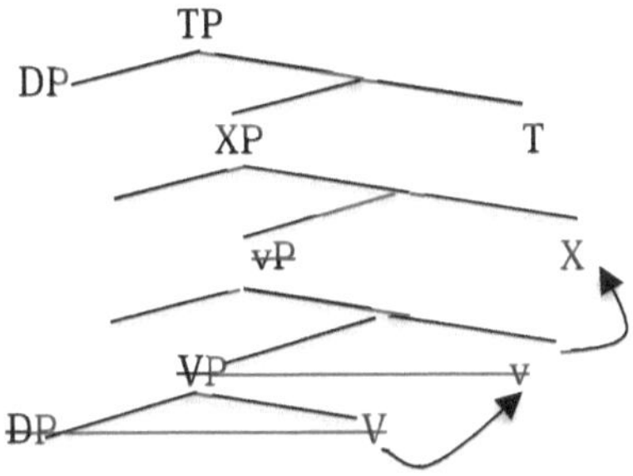

Positively identifying VVPE in Hindi-Urdu is complicated by the fact that there are other processes available which permit the internal arguments of a clause to go missing. Hindi-Urdu is known to exhibit null object pronominals (Davison 1999), and has been claimed to allow argument ellipsis (Simpson, Choudhury, and Menon 2013). In this paper I perform delicate testing along the lines pursued in Goldberg (2002), Gribanova (2013a,b), and Funakoshi (2016) in order to tease apart VVPE from these alternative processes; what emerges is that Hindi-Urdu does indeed exhibit true VVPE.

The syntax and semantics of complex predicate formation has been a key focus of research in Hindi-Urdu (Hook 1974; Mohanan 1994; Butt 1995, 1998, 2013; Butt and Geuder 2001; Butt and Lahiri 2003; Butt and Ramchand 2005; Butt, King, and Ramchand 2008; Mahajan 2012). The process in Hindi-Urdu is particularly rich, in that so-called light verbs may be combined with verbal, nominal, or

2 Also, for more controversial debate on VVPE in Chinese, Japanese, and Korean, see: Saito 1985; Kim 1999; Otani and Whitman 1991; and Hoji 1998.

adjectival components to create a single composed predicate with a single set of arguments.

(5) V-V complex predicate
मीना ने ख़त लिख लिया।
Amīnā-ne xat likh liy-ā.
Mina-ERG letter.M write take.PFV.M.SG
'Amina wrote a letter (completely).'

(6) N-V COMPLEX PREDICATE
अमीना ने कहानी याद की।
Amīnā-ne kahānī yād k-ī.
Amina-ERG story.F memory do.PFV.F
'Amina memorized the story.'

(7) A-V COMPLEX PREDICATE
अमीना ने मेज़ साफ की।
Amīnā-ne mez sāf k-ī.
Amina-ERG table.F clean do.PFV.F.SG
'Amina cleaned the room.'

Leading accounts of complex predicates in a number of languages have productively employed a decomposed verbal structure that presupposes a tight relation between the semantics of events and syntactic structure (as developed in Halle and Marantz 1993; Hale and Keyser 1993; Levin and Rappaport Hovav 1995; Hale and Keyser 2003; see also Ramchand 2008). This line of analysis is undertaken for Persian in Folli et al (2005) and Megerdoomian (2012), and for Hindi-Urdu by Butt and Ramchand (2005) and to a certain extent Davison (2005) (see also Davison (2014) and Butt (2014)). These diverse accounts share, among other things, the notion that the light verb component of the complex predicate originates at a point in the structure dominating the non-light-verb component, and that the light verb either originates in or combines via head movement/conflation with the v head (and thereby becomes associated with the meaning CAUSE).

On the other hand, there are a number of differences amongst various accounts of complex predicates in Hindi-Urdu, including the point at which the light verb is base generated, the nature of its movement to the v head and to higher, vP-external heads, and perhaps most importantly the degree of syntactic connectedness posited between the light verb and the non-light verb components of the complex predicate.

The investigation of VVPE in this article reveals that the Hindi-Urdu verb may regularly undergo head movement at least as high as the aspectual head (Asp^0).

This is an important discovery, since up to this point relatively little empirical evidence has been brought to bear on the question of verb movement in the language. As we will see below, because the verbal complex in Hindi-Urdu (including main verbs, light verbs, and a number of potential auxiliary verbs) is clause-final, any verb movement into higher heads would typically be string-vacuous. For this reason, although verb movement out of the vP has sometimes been assumed to take place (Kumar 2006, Bhatt and Dayal 2007, Bhatt 2008), it has been difficult to show that it must occur.

Further, in the case of V-V aspectual complex predicates, this article finds that the light verb may not undergo head movement independently of the main verb. Thus a string equivalent to vVPE, in which the light verb is stranded while the main verb is elided, seems unavailable for Hindi-Urdu.

(8a) अमीना ने ख़त पहली बार में लिख लिया।
Amīnā-ne xat pahlī bār me likh liy-ā.
Amīnā-ERG letter first time in write take.PFV.M
'Amīnā managed to write the letter on the first attempt.'

(8b) समीर ने भी ___ लिख लिया।
Samir-ne bhī ___ likh liy-ā.
Samir-ERG also ___ write take.PFV.M
'Samir also managed to write (the letter on the first attempt).'

(8c) ?*समीर ने भी ___ लिया।
?**Samir-ne bhī ___ liy-ā.*
Samir-ERG also ___ take.PFV.M
Intended: 'Samir also (wrote a letter on the first time).'

The article is organized as follows: section 2 works through a wide range of diagnostics intended to differentiate VVPE from null pronominals and argument ellipsis in Hindi-Urdu, ultimately arriving at least three configurations which can be identified unambiguously as VVPE. Section 3 examines complex predicates in Hindi-Urdu and provides new data revealing the ways in which complex predicates interact with VVPE. From this data emerges a discussion of the correct analysis of the syntactic structure of the verbal domain, verb movement, and complex predicates, presented in section 4. Section 5 concludes the article and presents directions for further research.

2 Identifying VVPE

Hindi-Urdu permits a string resembling those generated by verb-stranding verb-phrase ellipsis or VVPE, illustrated with a naturally occurring example in (9).

(9) KK: कभी किसी को दिल दिया।
kabhī kisī-ko dil di-yā?
ever someone-DAT heart.M give.PFV.M
'Have you ever given your heart to someone?'
Audience:
___ दिया।
___ *di-yā!*
___ give-PFV.M
'(I) have given (my heart to someone)!'
KK: मैंने भी ___ दिया।
mɛ̃-ne bhī ___ di-yā!
1SG-ERG also ___ give.PFV.M
'I have also given (my heart to someone)!'
[from "Om Shanti Om" by Anand Bakshi, performed by Kishore Kumar in the film Karz (1980)]

Under the widely accepted account of VVPE, the main verb is understood to move outside the vP, and the entire vP is then elided (for claims that it is indeed the vP that is elided in VPE, see Aelbrecht 2010, Merchant 2013). But as is mentioned above, Hindi-Urdu exhibits two other independent syntactic processes that permit internal arguments to go missing. Isolating VVPE in Hindi-Urdu thus represents a serious challenge. Similar to languages like Persian (Toosarvandani 2009) and Russian (Gribanova 2013a, b), Hindi-Urdu permits null pronominals in object position (see Davison 1999, 2013).

(10) मैंने (उसको) देखा।
mɛ̃-ne (us-ko) dekh-ā.
1-ERG 3-ACC see.PFV.M
'I saw him/her.'

(11) अलिआ (उससे) मिली।
Aliā (us-se) mil-ī.
Alia 3.with meet.PFV.F
'Alia met him/her.'

We must therefore exploit known properties of ellipsis that distinguish it from other kinds of anaphora in order to determine whether the construction of interest is truly VVPE. Hindi-Urdu has also recently been shown by Simpson, Choudhury, and Menon 2013 (henceforward SCM) to permit a more targeted ellipsis process called argument ellipsis. Argument ellipsis, also argued to take place in a number of East Asian languages (Oku 1998, Kim 1999; Takahashi 2006) is an ellipsis operation in which just the internal argument of a verb is elided. While I don't evaluate this analysis here, I mention it to illustrate that the analysis strings in which the internal argument alone is missing are far from straightforward.

(12a) अमित अपनी प्रेमिका को प्यार करता है।
Amit apnī premikā-ko pyār kar-tā hɛ.
Amit self's.F girlfriend-ACC love do.PRES.3MSG AUX.PRS.SG
'Amit$_i$ loves his$_i$ girlfriend.'

(12b) रवि भी ___ प्यार करता है।
Ravi bhī ___ pyār kartā hɛ.
Ravi also ___ love do.PRES.3MSG AUX.PRS.SG
'Ravi$_k$ also loves (his$_k$ girlfriend).'
(Simpson, Choudhury, and Menon 2013: 6)

The elliptical clause in (9b) above then has three potential analyses: one in which the missing object is a null pronominal, one in which it is an elided argument, and one in which it is contained in an elided vP out of which the verb has raised (VVPE).

In what follows I draw on a series of tests designed to tease apart argument ellipsis, null object pronominals, and VVPE drawing on a range of diagnostics developed for Hindi-Urdu in SCM (2013), for Russian in Gribanova (2013a,b), and for Japanese in Funakoshi (2016).

Tests designed to distinguish VVPE from other processes focus on the contents of the elided vP. The reasoning is as follows: for a given constituent XP that may go missing along with the internal arguments yet be interpreted within the ellipsis site, if that same constituent cannot otherwise be elided independently in the language, then it must have gone missing by virtue of VPE. Goldberg (2005) utilized this strategy in Hebrew with predicates that take both a DP and PP argument. Unfortunately, Hindi-Urdu permits both object DPs and argument PPs to go missing individually (Davison 2005), meaning that we will have to look to more complex VPs to isolate VVPE.

In the following section, I make use of a range of diagnostics to isolate VVPE form other processes that allow arguments to go missing. Unless the data is specifically cited otherwise, the judgments displayed were obtained from a group of nine native-speaker consultants who assessed sentences provided on a five-point scale. When native speakers judged the sentence anything but completely acceptable, a footnote explains the grammaticality marking.

2.1 Conjoined correlates

Gribanova 2013b proposes a second test that can isolate VVPE, differentiating this process from both null pronominals and argument ellipsis. If the correlate contains a disjunction, such as *yā* 'or', and given that there is no known independent process permitting disjunction drop (Payne 1985, Winter 1995, Gribanova 2013b), we can be fairly sure that ellipsis of the larger verb phrase (containing two disjuncts in this case) must be true VVPE. In other words, neither null pronominal objects nor argument ellipsis could explain the interpretation of the elliptical structure in (13b).

(13a) मुझे लगता है कि राम ने सीता को संतरा या मीना को अमरूद दिया होगा।
mujhe lagtā hɛ ki Rām-ne Sitā-ko
me-DAT seem.HAB.M AUX.PRS.SG that Ram-ERG Sitā-DAT
santarā yā Mina-ko amrūd diyā hogā.
orange or Mina-DAT guava give.PFV.M AUX.FUT
'It seems to me that Ram must have given an orange to Sita or a guava to Mina.'

(13b) नहीं, राम ने ___नहीं दिया होगा।
nahĩ, Rām-ne ___ nahĩ diy-ā hogā.
no Ram-ERG ___ NEG give.PFV.M AUX.FUT
'No, Ram must not have given (an orange to Sita or a guava to Mina)'
(Rajesh Bhatt, p.c.)

Thus the structure in (13b) must features the ellipsis of a larger vP containing two disjoined smaller VPs.

2.2 VP adverbs

SCM 2013 point out that under VVPE, temporal and manner adverbs that modify the VP can go missing and then may be interpreted in the ellipsis site (as in (14a) and (14b) below). I will call this reading of the elliptical structure the 'null adjunct' reading in what follows. The sentence in (14c) illustrates the fact that if the internal argument is not also missing, the null adjunct reading is not available. That is, there is not independent process by which adverbs alone may be elided.

(14a) राम ने चॉम्स्की का नया लेख दो बार पढ़ा।
Rām-ne Čomskī-kā nayā lekh do bār paṛhā.
Ram-ERG Chomsky-GEN new paper two time read.PST.M.SG
'Ram read the new paper by Chomsky twice.'

(14b) राज ने भी ___ पढ़ा।
Rāj-ne bhī ___ paṛhā.
Raj-ERG also ___ read.PST.M.SG
'Raj also read (the paper twice).'

(14c) राज ने भी वो लेख पढ़ा।
Rāj-ne bhī vo lekh paṛhā.
Raj-ERG also that paper read.PST.M.SG
'Raj also read the paper.' NOT communicated: 'twice' (SCM 2013: 112)

This is then our first piece of evidence that VVPE must be available in Hindi-Urdu, since there is no other clear explanation for the interpretation of the ellipsis in (14b).

We can further reinforce the conclusion that (14b) is indeed an instance of VVPE by checking another important property of VVPE. As Goldberg (2005) and McCloskey (1991) show for Hebrew and Irish respectively, in cases of VVPE the verb stem in the correlate and the verb stem in the ellipsis site must match. We will assume here that this is a general property of VVPE cross-linguistically. If (14b) above is in fact an instance of VVPE in Hindi-Urdu, attempting to change the verb following the ellipsis site should result in infelicity (provided that we restrict the interpretation to the null adjunct reading).

(15a) राम ने चॉम्स्की का नया लेख दो बार पढ़ा।
Rām-ne Čomskī-kā nayā lekh do bār paṛhā.
Ram-ERG Chomsky-GEN new paper two time read.PST.M.SG
'Ram read the new paper by Chomsky twice.'

(15b) #राज ने भी ___ भेजा।
#Rāj-ne bhī ___ bhej-ā.
Raj-ERG also ___ send.PST.M.SG
Intended: 'Raj also sent (the paper twice).'[3]

The infelicity of (15b) in the context of (15a) then confirms that this is a true instance of VVPE in Hindi-Urdu, since the verb following the ellipsis site must match the verb in the correlate.

An interesting wrinkle emerges when we consider pairs in which the elliptical clause includes negation. Consider (16b), in which the downward entailing environment means that the situations described by the reading which includes the adverbial are not a subset of the situations described when the adverbial is excluded.[4]

(16a) राम ने चॉम्स्की का नया लेख ध्यान से पढ़ा।
Rām-ne Čomskī-kā nayā lekh dhyān-se paṛh-ā.
Ram-ERG Chomsky-GEN new paper carefully read.PFV.M.SG
'Ram read the new paper by Chomsky carefully.'

(16b) राज ने ___ नहीं पढ़ा।
Rāj-ne ___ nahī̃ paṛh-ā.
Raj-ERG ___ NEG read.PFV.M.SG
'Raj did not read (the new paper by Chomsky (??carefully)).'

The sentence in (16a) asserts that Ram read the paper with care, but many speakers have difficulty obtaining the reading which includes the null adjunct in (16b). Thus (16b) has a dominant reading that Raj did not read the paper at all. If the null adjunct reading were indeed completely unavailable in these environments (as opposed to just strongly dispreferred), this would suggest that the process at work in (16) could not be VVPE.

To complicate the matter further, it seems that this same observation has been made in a number of unrelated languages (as early as Oku 1998 for Japanese) and that the judgements are not straightforward, even among native speaker linguists. In Persian, Rasekhi (2014) claims that the null adjunct reading is not available in downward entailing environments, though a footnote (ftnt 7) suggests that "some" speakers can obtain these readings with very strong

3 Out of nine native speaker informants, eight judged this sentence "unacceptable in this conversation" and one judged this sentence "barely acceptable, unnatural in this conversation".
4 I'm grateful to an anonymous reviewer for bringing this question to my attention.

contrastive stress on the equivalent of the adverb "carefully". On the other hand, Toosarvandani (to appear) states the null adverb interpretation is indeed available in these environments in Persian without any further discussion (Toosarvandani to appear, p. 18). Turning to Russian, Vera Gribanova (p.c.) observes that the null adjunct reading is relatively difficult to obtain in the Russian equivalent of (16b). In Japanese, Oku 1998 claims that the null adjunct reading is not present at all (though this claim is hedged in a footnote), while Funakoshi (2016) disagrees.

Helpfully, Funakoshi goes further, claiming we can facilitate the null adjunct reading (a) if the antecedent sentence is also negated (see also Takahashi 2008); (b) if the two clauses are disjoined (Funakoshi 2014); or (c) if rich context is provided. It seems that these strategies also facilitate the reading in Hindi-Urdu.[5]

(17a) राम ने चॉम्स्की का नया लेख ध्यान से नहीं पढ़ा।
Rām-ne Čomskī-kā nayā lekh dhyān-se nahī̃ paṛh-ā.
Ram-ERG Chomsky-GEN new paper carefully NEG read.PFV.M.SG
'Ram did not read the new paper by Chomsky carefully.'

(17b) राज ने भी नहीं पढ़ा।
Rāj-ne bhī nahī̃ paṛhā.
Raj-ERG also NEG read.PST.M.SG
'Raj also did not read (the new paper by Chomsky carefully).'

(18) राम ने चॉम्स्की का नया लेख ध्यान से पढ़ा मगर राज ने नहीं पढ़ा।
Rām-ne Čomskī-kā nayā lekh dhyān-se paṛh-ā
Ram-ERG Chomsky-GEN new paper carefully read.PST.M.S
magar Rāj-ne nahī̃ paṛhā.
but Raj-ERG NEG read.PST.M.SG
'Ram read the new paper by Chomsky carefully, but Raj did not read did not read (the new paper by Chomsky carefully).'

(19) Ram and Raj wash their parents' cars to get their allowance. Ram was thorough in his work, while Raj was not.

(19a) राम ने गाड़ी ध्यान से धोयी।
Rām-ne gāṛi dhyān-se dhoy-ī.
Ram-ERG car carefully wash.PFV.F.SG
'Ram washed the car carefully.'

5 Thanks to Ayesha Kidwai for her judgments and discussion of these examples. She reports that simply additional information about Raj's habitual carelessness facilitates the null adjunct reading in (16b).

(19b) राज ने नहीं धोयी। यह गाड़ी जिसको राज ने धोया अभी भी थोड़ी-थोड़ी गंदी रह गयी।
Rāj-ne nahī̃ dhoy-ī. Yah gāṛi jis-ko Rāj-ne
Raj-ERG NEG wash.PFV.FSG this car.M REL-ACC Raj-ERG
dhoy-ā abhī bhī thoṛī thoṛī gandī rah gay-ī.
wash.PFV.MSG now also little little dirty.F stay go.PFV.F.SG
'Raj did not wash (the car carefully). The car Raj washed still remained a bit dirty.'

Crucially, if the internal argument is not missing, the null adjunct reading cannot be drawn out by these means and remains unavailable (Funakoshi 2016).

(20) राम ने चॉम्स्की का नया लेख ध्यान से पढ़ा, मगर राज ने नया लेख नहीं पढ़ा।
Rām-ne Čomskī-kā nayā lekh dhyān-se paṛh-ā
Ram-ERG Chomsky-GEN new paper carefully read.PST.M.SG
magar Rāj-ne nayā lekh nahī̃ paṛh-ā.
but Raj-ERG new paper NEG read.PST.M.SG
'Ram read the new paper by Chomsky carefully, but Raj did not read the new paper (NOT included: 'carefully').'[6]

Since it is possible to make the null adjunct interpretation more accessible in Hindi-Urdu, we can conclude that the elliptical clauses in (17)–(19) also represent true instances of VVPE, in which the elided VP includes both the internal argument and an adverbial. Space constraints do not permit a detailed investigation of the pragmatics of the cross-linguistic phenomenon in which the downward entailing elliptical environment makes the null adjunct reading less accessible, but we can at the very least show here that these pairs don't provide an argument against VVPE analyses of elliptical strings altogether in these languages. This conclusion allows us to continue to use the adverbial test to isolate the VPE reading throughout the argumentation that follows.

6 An additional data point comes courtesy of Jim McCloskey (p.c.) who suggests that if the "low" (restitutive) reading (Johnson 2004) is available for an adverb like *again* (in Hindi-Urdu, *dubārā*) in a pair like (16), then that reading must be the one obtained from inclusion in the ellipsis site. As (i) illustrates, the restitutive reading does seem to be available. Thanks to Ayesha Kidwai and Rajesh Bhatt for their judgements.
(i) राम ने अपना दरवाज़ा दुबारा खोला, मगर राज ने नहीं खोला।
Rām-ne apnā darwazā dubārā khol-ā, magar Rāj-ne nahī̃ khol-ā.
Ram-ERG self's door again open-PRF.M but Raj-ERG NEG open-PRF.M
'Ram opened his door again, but Raj did not (open his door again)' = Raj did not return his door to the open state.

2.3 Deep and surface anaphora and islands

As Hankamer and Sag (1976) famously demonstrated, ellipsis generally is an instance of surface anaphora, requiring a linguistic antecedent, as shown here for English VPE.

(21a) [Hankamer attempts to stuff 9-inch ball through a 6-inch hoop]
Sag: #It's not clear that you'll be able to ___.
Sag: It's not clear that you'll be able to do it.
(21b) Hankamer: I'm going to stuff this ball through this hoop
Sag: It's not clear that you'll be able to ___.
Hankamer and Sag (1976: 392)

A second well-known property of VPE in English is that it is permitted within islands that exclude the antecedent.

(22a) Meena won't put the pig back in the barn.
(22b) Don't worry, Jorge knows [a student [who will ___]].

Gribanova (2013a) provides detailed discussion concerning the fact that in Russian, null object pronominals are relatively unacceptable inside of islands. Though space does not permit a thorough review of the equivalent evidence, the examples below in (23) and (24) illustrate that the same holds true for Hindi-Urdu (see also footnote 7).[7]

7 The fact that (23) and (24) are unacceptable indicates that VVPE, argument ellipsis, and null pronominals are all prohibited in these contexts. We can see from the improvement resulting from the provision of a linguistic antecedent in (25) and (26) below, that VVPE is certainly possible within islands. As we might expect, versions of (23) and (24) in which the gap is not embedded within an island are judged by the informants in this study to be significantly better (the ? label indicates that not all nine informants judged these to be fully acceptable).
(i) [Meena pulls up to the curb in a shiny vehicle while the two conversants watch]
Speaker: क्या मनु ने भी खरीदी थी?
?*Kyā Manu-ne bhī ___ kharīdī thī?*
Q Manu-ERG also ___ buy-PRF.F AUX.F
'Did Manu also buy (a new car)?'
(ii) [context: two conversants watch the salesman change a "for sale" sign on a car in the car dealership lot to a "sold" sign]

A test for VVPE laid out in detail for Russian in Gribanova 2013a exploits these two properties of VVPE (available in islands, requiring a linguistic antecedent) to create a context in which a felicitous sentence cannot be produced. If an alleged instance of VVPE in Hindi-Urdu is embedded within an island (ruling out a null pronominal analysis), but not provided with a linguistic antecedent (ruling out the ellipsis analysis), the result should be unacceptable. This is indeed the case, as illustrated in (23) and (24) below: [8]

(23) [Meena pulls up to the curb in a shiny vehicle while the two conversants watch]
Speaker:
आप जानते हैं यह बात कि मनु ने भी ___ खरीदी थी?
#āp jānte hẽ yah bāt ki Manu-ne
2PL know.HAB.PL AUX that fact that Manu-ERG
bhī ___ kharīdī thī?
also ___ buy.PFV.F AUX.F
'Do you know the fact that Manu also bought (a new car)?'

(24) [context: two conversants watch the salesman change a "for sale" sign on a car in the car dealership lot to a "sold" sign]
Speaker:
#मैं यह आदमी जिसने ___ खरीदा था जानता हूँ।
#mẽ yah ādmi jis-ne ___ kharīd-ā thā jāntā hũ.
1SG this man REL-ERG ___ buy.PFV.M AUX.M know.HAB.M AUX.1SG
'I know the man who bought (a new car).'

However, argument ellipsis is also an instance of ellipsis, and therefore should pattern with VVPE with respect to both the deep/surface distinction and

Speaker: उस आदमी ने खरीदी थी।
?us ādmi-ne ___ kharid-ī thī.
That man-ERG ___ buy-PRF.F AUX.M
'That man bought (the new car).'

I take this to mean that like in Russian, Hindi-Urdu does not permit null pronominal objects inside of islands, though space does not permit a detailed exploration of this claim here. For more on why this might be so, see Gribanova 2013a and references cited therein.

8 Out of nine native-speaker informants consulted, seven judged the contributions in (23) and (24) "unacceptable in this conversation" and two judged them "barely acceptable, unnatural in this conversation". When asked, all nine strongly preferred versions of these sentences with the full overt noun phrase (no gap). Of course, they also judged as fully grammatical versions with overt linguistic antecedents as in (25b) and (26b) in the main text.

islandhood, so this test alone does not rule out argument ellipsis as an analysis for (23)–(24). For our purposes in the case of Hindi-Urdu, we shall need to further complicate the structure by adding an adverbial in the correlate that is also interpreted to be within the ellipsis site. This will ensure that we are testing structures that are only potentially VVPE.

If we now provide a linguistic antecedent, as in (25a)–(26a), the resulting ellipsis in (25b)–(26b) is fully grammatical.

(25a) मीना ने नयी गाड़ी आज खरीदी थी।
Mīna-ne nayī gāṛī āj kharīd-ī thī.
Mīna-ERG new.F car.F today buy.PFV.F AUX.F
'Meena bought a new car today.'

(25b) क्या आप जानते हैं कि मनु ने भी ___ खरीदी थी?
kyā āp jānte hẽ ki Manu-ne
Q 2PL know.HAB.PL that Manu-ERG
bhī ___ kharīdī thī?
also ___ buy.PFV.F AUX.F
'Do you know the fact that Manu also bought (a new car today)?'

(26a) मनु ने उस नयी गाड़ी को आज खरीदा था।
Manu-ne us nayī gāṛī-ko āj kharīd-ā thā.
Manu-ERG that new.F car.F-ACC today buy.PFV.M AUX.M
'Manu bought that new car today.'

(26b) नहीं, मैं उस आदमी को जिसने ... खरीदा था जानता हूँ।
Nahī̃, mẽ us ādmi-ko jis-ne ___ kharīd-ā thā
No, 1SG this man-ACC REL-ERG ___ buy.PFV.M AUX.M
jān-tā hū̃.
know.HAB.M AUX.1SG
'No, I know the man who bought (that new car today).'

In sum, in comparing (23)–(24) with (25)–(26), we see that a pragmatic antecedent alone is not sufficient for this elliptical structure when embedded in an island. However, once a linguistic antecedent is provided, the sentence is markedly improved. Since this cannot be argument ellipsis due to the inclusion of the adverbial in the interpretation of the ellipsis site, nor can it be a null pronominal since it requires a linguistic antecedent, it must be understood as true VVPE.

2.4 Summary

In this section we have positively isolated at least three clear instances of true verb-stranding VPE in Hindi-Urdu. We can now confidently turn to using VPE as a diagnostic to learn more about the nature of verb movement and complex predicates in the language.

3 VPE and complex predicates

As in many Indic languages, Hindi-Urdu forms complex predicates in which a so-called light verb (a term attributed to Jespersen 1965) combines with a main verb, noun, adjective, or preposition to create a single composed predicate with a single set of arguments. In the case of complex predicates featuring two verbs, as in (27), the light verb typically contributes to the *aktionsart* of the overall predication. In noun-verb complex predicates as in (28), the light verb serves as a verbalizer. In each case, it is the light verb that carries inflection.

(27) V-V COMPLEX PREDICATE
अमीना ने ख़त लिख लिया।
Amīnā-ne xat likh liy-ā.
Amina-ERG letter.M write take.PFV.M
'Amina wrote a letter (completely).'

(28) N-V COMPLEX PREDICATE
अमीना ने कहानी याद की।
Amīnā-ne kahānī yād k-ī.
Amina-ERG story.F memory do.PFV.F
'Amina memorized the story'.

The semantic and syntactic properties of these complex predicates have been the subject of extensive research (Hook 1974; Mohanan 1994; Butt 1995; Butt and Lahiri 2003; Davison 2005; Butt and Ramchand 2005; Butt, King, and Ramchand 2008; Mahajan 2012).

In Hindi-Urdu, all light verbs are form-identical to a main verb in the language. As Butt 1995 reveals with careful testing, sentences with complex predicates are monoclausal. Yet it is clear from evidence including the potential for reduplication of the light verb and combinatory restrictions that light verbs are distinct from aspectual and tense auxiliaries (Butt and Geuder 2001; Butt 2003, 2010; Butt and Ramchand 2005). As these claims are uncontroversial and thoroughly reviewed elsewhere, I refer the reader to the cited literature for the detailed diagnostics.

A dominant analysis of light verbs within the Minimalist framework is that they are instantiations of the light verb v (Adger 2003, Butt and Ramchand 2005, Bhatt 2008, Mahajan 2012). However, there are some important differences in the way in which the light verb is treated across several of these approaches. These differences will be explored below, to determine whether the interaction of VVPE with complex predicates can provide new insights. For the purposes of this section, we will assume that the light verb is found in v prior to the verb movement that must precede VVPE. This is consistent with all of the leading accounts of complex predicates in Hindi-Urdu in the current framework.

To this point we have demonstrated that VVPE does occur in Hindi-Urdu with simplex main verbs. We might expect to see VVPE with V-V complex predicate constructions in which both main and light verb are stranded and the internal arguments and other vP-internal material are elided, though to my knowledge the interaction between VPE and complex predicates has not yet been addressed in the literature. VVPE is indeed available in these contexts in Hindi-Urdu, as in (29) below:

(29a) कबीर ने उस किताब को पहली बार में पढ़ लिया।
Kabir-ne us kitāb-ko pahlī bār me paṛh liy-ā.
Kabir-ERG this book-ACC first attempt in read take.PFV.M
'Kabir managed to read that book in his first attempt.'

(29b) मीना ने भी ___ पढ़ लिया।
Mīna-ne bhī ___ paṛh li-yā.
Mīna-ERG also ___ read take.PFV.M
'Meena also managed to read (that book in her first attempt).'

But we also might wonder whether both components of the V-V complex predicate need to be stranded for VPE to be licit. After all, the two components of the complex predicate are separate lexical items with distinct functional profiles. Only the light verb is inflected for tense and agreement. Further, in other languages with light verbs, such as Persian, researchers have identified VPE in which the light verb, understood to be in v, is stranded, and the lexical projection complement to v, VP, is elided (Toosarvandani 2009). Persian, like Hindi-Urdu, features N-V complex predicates, but does not have V-V complex predicates. Thus v-stranding VPE (or vVPE) in Persian occurs when the nominal component of the complex predicate remains within the vP and is elided, and only the light verb is stranded, as shown in (30).

(30) *Sohrāb piranha-ra otu na-zad vali rostam* [~~*piranha-ra otu*~~] *zad.*
Sohrab shirts-ACC iron NEG.do but Rostam shirts-ACC iron do
'Sohrab did not iron the shirts but Rostam did (iron the shirts).' (Toosarvandani: (4))

Toosarvandani provides the following tree illustrating the clausal structure that feeds vVPE in complex predicates in Persian (see also Folli et al 2005, Karimi 1999a,b).

(31)

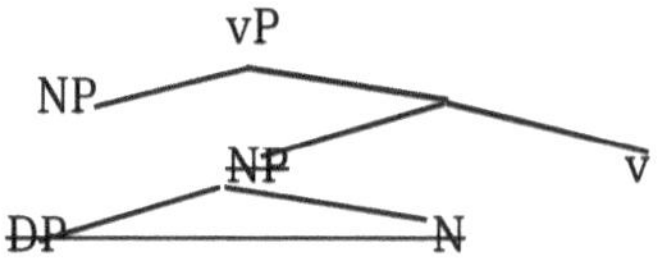

The question then becomes whether Hindi-Urdu also permits vVPE in V-V complex predicates. Ten native speakers of Hindi-Urdu were provided with VPE contexts in which the light verb in the complex predicate was stranded while the main verb component of the predicate and its internal arguments were elided. In the case of V-V complex predicates, speakers' judgments on these structures ranged from "barely acceptable, unnatural" (n=2) to "unacceptable" (n=8). I have marked these sentences (the (c) examples in (32)–(34)) with the symbol ?*. This is in sharp contrast to the VVPE versions of the same sentences in the (b) examples in which both main verb/nominal predicate and light verb were stranded. These were universally judged fully acceptable are thus unmarked below.[9]

v-v complex predicates

(32a) कबीर ने उस किताब को पहली बार पढ़ लिया।
Kabir-ne us kitāb-ko pahlī bār paṛh li-yā.
Kabir-ERG this book-ACC first time read take.PFV.M
'Kabir read this book for the first time.'

9 Note that adverbials were included in the correlate (and their potential for interpretation in the ellipsis site checked) in order to ensure that it is the properties of VPE that are being tested, and not other processes that allow internal arguments to go missing.

(32b) मीना ने भी ___ पढ़ लिया।
Mīna-ne bhī ___ paṛh li-yā.
Mīna-ERG also ___ read take.PFV.M
'Meena also read (this book for the first time).'

(32c) ?*मीना ने भी ___ लिया।
?**Mīna-ne bhī ___ li-yā.*
Mīna-ERG also ___ take.PFV.M

(33a) कबीर एक बात कल समझ गया।
Kabir ek bāt kal samajh gay-ā.
Kabir a fact yesterday understand go.PFV.M
'Kabir understood a fact yesterday.'

(33b) मीना भी ___ समझ गयी।
Mīna bhī ___ samajh gay-ī.
Mīna also ___ understand go.PFV.M
'Meena also understood (a fact yesterday).'

(33c) ?*मीना भी ___ गयी।
?**Mīna bhī ___ gayī.*
Mīna also ___ go.PFV.F

(34a) अमीना ने ख़त पहली बार में लिख लिया।
Amīnā-ne xat pahlī bār me likh liy-ā.
Amīnā-ERG letter first time in write take.PFV.M
'Amīnā managed to write the letter on the first attempt.'

(34b) समीर ने भी ___ लिख लिया।
Samir-ne bhī ___ likh liy-ā.
Samir-ERG also ___ write take.PFV.M
'Samir also managed to write (the letter on the first attempt).'

(34c) ?*समीर ने भी ___ लिया।
?**Samir-ne bhī ___ liy-ā.*
Samir-ERG also ___ take.PFV.M

In the case of N-V complex predicates, the larger picture is a bit more murky, but preliminarily we can observe that the N-V predicate *yād kar* 'to remember' patterns much like the V-V complex predicates above.

N-V COMPLEX PREDICATES

(35a) कबीर ने कहानी आसानी से याद की।
Kabir-ne kahānī āsāni se yād k-ī.
Kabir-ERG story.F easily memory do.PFV.F
'Kabir memorized a story easily.'

(35b) मीना ने भी ___ याद की।
Mīna-ne bhī ___ yād k-ī.
Mīna-ERG also ___ memory do.PFV.F
'Meena also memorized (a story easily).'

(35c) ??मीना ने भी ___ की।
??*Mīna-ne bhī ___ k-ī.*
Mīna-ERG also ___ do.PFV.F

Recent research suggests that there is in fact more than one class or type of N-V complex predicate that respond differently to a range of diagnostics (Ahmed and Butt 2011). Preliminarily, it seems that the predicates of different types also respond differently to VPE. This data is presented and discussed in greater detail in Manetta (in prep.), so I won't address it further at present.

What emerges clearly here is that in V-V complex predicates, Hindi-Urdu does not seem to permit the light verb to be stranded alone in the absence of the main verb. The novel data concerning VPE presented in this section raises a number of questions, but here we will limit our focus to the following:

(i) What does the potential for VVPE but not vVPE tell us about verb movement in Hindi-Urdu?
(ii) Does the availability of VVPE but not vVPE have any ramifications for existing approaches to the syntax of complex predicates in Hindi-Urdu and if so, does it favor one approach over others?

The following section explores the answers to these questions and outlines what we stand to learn from the interaction of VPE and complex predicates in Hindi-Urdu.

4 Verb movement in Hindi-Urdu

4.1 The verbal structure and the role of VVPE

The availability of VVPE and the unavailability of vVPE for V-V complex predicates reveal important properties of the verbal complex in Hindi-Urdu, including the potential for verb movement out of the verbal layer and the fine structure of complex predicates.

The Hindi-Urdu verbal complex is clause-final and rigidly ordered, and consists of a main verb potentially followed by the light verb and a number of auxiliaries.

(36) Main verb (light verb) (passive aux) (aspectual morphology/aux) (tense aux)

Following a range of previous work (Bhatt 2003, 2005; Kumar 2006; Butt and Ramchand 2005; Manetta 2011; among many others), I will adopt the widely-assumed basic structure below for a simple Hindi-Urdu clause as in (37).

(37)

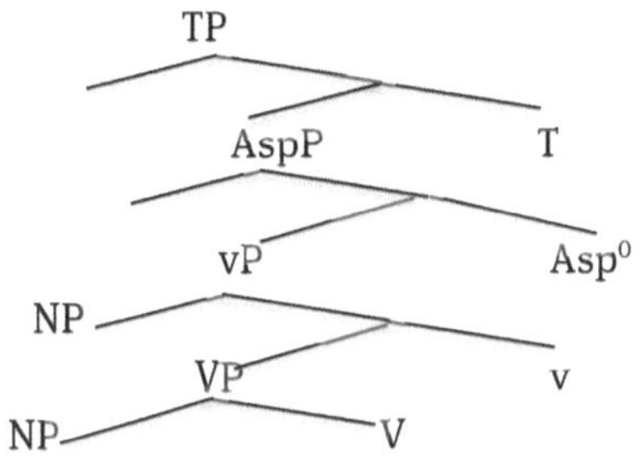

In a typical Hindi-Urdu sentence, any verb movement out of the vP would be string-vacuous, as all the heads of the verbal complex appear on the right. A number of researchers have assumed some degree of verb movement for various analytical reasons (e.g. Kumar 2006, Bhatt and Dayal 2007, Bhatt 2008). Kumar 2006, for instance, argues for obligatory successive head movement via adjunction for the purposes of better analyzing word order with respect to negation and the combination of aspectual morphology with the verb stem. Bhatt and Dayal 2007 assume optional verb movement to the head of the aspectual projection (over negation when present) in order to create VP-remnant structures that can subsequently be displaced. However, it is challenging to find direct evidence that verb movement has taken place, and tests for positioning of adverbs, post-verbal material, and subjects relative to the verb are unrevealing when the verb string is clause-final (Pollock 1989; McCloskey 1991; Depiante and Vincente 2012). The position of negation has the potential to be more useful, but as sentential negation can appear either immediately preceding or immediately following the inflected verb in the verbal string in Hindi-Urdu, these tests have not provided unambiguous information (Kumar 2006).

As a number of researchers working on head-final languages have suggested (Otani and Whitman 1991; Koizumi 2000; Simpson and Syed 2013), VVPE has the potential to provide just such evidence. The availability of VVPE in Hindi-Urdu demonstrates that at least the main verb and the light verb must be able to move out of the vP. VVPE is typically understood to be derived when the verb itself raises out of the verbal layer, and the verbal layer is then subject to ellipsis (indicated by strikethrough) (McCloskey 1991, Goldberg 2005).

In this article I have represented the constituent that goes missing in VVPE to be vP (as in Gribanova 2013a,b). A consensus has emerged in more recent work that the size of the constituent that is elided in English-style VPE is also vP (Merchant 2013; Aelbrecht 2010, 2013). We have already seen some evidence in Hindi-Urdu that VPE may elide a constituent as least as large as vP, since vP-adjoined manner adverbs such as *dhyān-se* 'carefully' are included in the ellipsis site (as in section 2; see Moulton 2008 and Sailor 2014 for discussion and Manetta (in prep) for more on the size of the constituent that goes missing in Hindi-Urdu VVPE). In the present article we will assume that closed-class functional head to which the verbal complex moves in Hindi-Urdu also possesses the [E] feature (Merchant 2001), meaning that its complement will go unpronounced. The complement vP is maximal and contains the verb root, verbalizer, verb arguments, and vP-adverbials–just the elements that go unpronounced in VVPE.

(38)

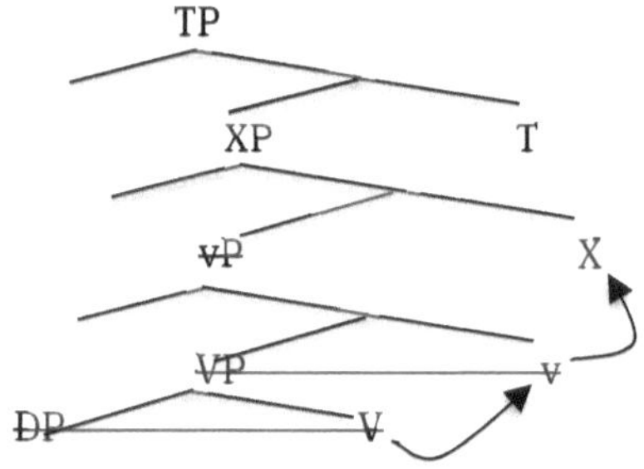

In section 3 above, we saw evidence that both a main verb and a light verb in a V-V complex predicate must escape the ellipsis site. If the light verb is indeed base generated or must combine with the v head, this means that both the main verb and the light verb must move to a functional head outside the vP prior to the point at which the vP then undergoes ellipsis. Since this movement is string vacuous, it is not entirely obvious to which functional head the V+v complex may move. Previous accounts of VVPE have posited that ellipsis is preceded by V-to-T movement (McCloskey 1991, Goldberg 2005). Gribanova (2013a) argues for Russian that the verb moves into the Aspect head located between V and T. There are at least two reasons to believe that V-to-Asp^0 movement might also be at work in Hindi-Urdu.

Hindi-Urdu has a number of dependent aspectual morphemes that combine with the verb root. The example in (39a) features the imperfective/ habitual suffix *-ta/ti/te* while the example in (39b) features the perfective suffix *-a/i/e*. Under the assumed framework, these components of verbal morphology are indeed syntactically independent, but are combined via head movement to produce a single morphophonological unit. In addition, the tense auxiliary *ho*, when present, follows the aspectually suffixed verb form as in (39a) and (39c).

(39a) खुशबू गाने गाती है।
Khuśbū gāne gā-tī hɛ.
Khuśbū songs sing.HAB.F AUX.PRS
'Khushboo sings songs.'

(39b) खुशबू कल आयी।
Khuśbū kal āy-ī.
Khuśbū yesterday come.PFV.F
'Khushboo came yesterday.'

(39c) खुशबू ने कई गाने गाये थे।
Khuśbū-ne kaī gāne gā-ye the.
Khuśbū-ERG many songs sing.PFV.PL AUX.PST.PL
'Khushboo had sung many songs.'

Once combined, the inflected verb and the auxiliaries of the verbal complex cannot be separated by any kind of displacement, though they can be displaced as a unit (see Butt 1995). The word order of these components would suggest that the composed verb form is located in Asp^0 while the independent tense auxiliary is in T. I will therefore propose, (along with others: Bhatt 2005, Bhatt and Dayal 2007) based on evidence from the availability of VVPE that in Hindi-Urdu the material in the V head, the v head, and the Asp^0 head combine via syntactic (string-vacuous) head movement.[10] Note that I have also assumed here that the subject will move to the specifier of TP (along with Bhatt 2003, 2005; Manetta 2011).

With this in place, we can now detail the head movement and ellipsis process required to create the VVPE in the complex predicate sentence in (40b) in the schematic in (41).

(40a) कबीर ने उस किताब को पहली बार पढ़ लिया।
Kabir-ne us kitāb-ko pahlī bār paṛh liy-ā
Kabir-ERG this book-ACC first time read take.PFV.M
'Kabir read this book for the first time.'

(40b) मीना ने भी ___ पढ़ लिया।
Mīna-ne bhī ___ paṛh liy-ā.
Mīna-ERG also ___ read take.PFV.M
'Meena also read (this book for the first time).'

(41)

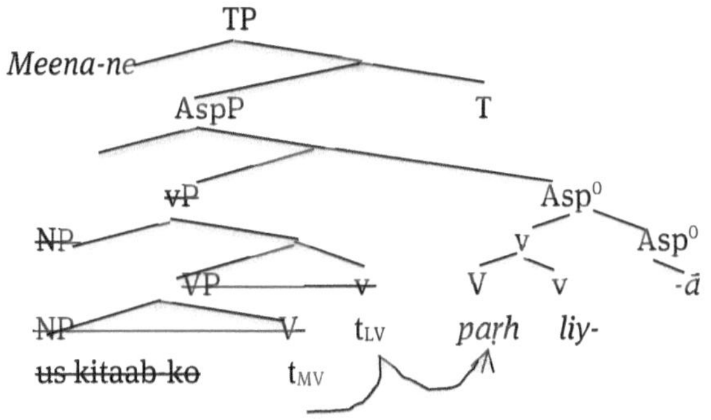

4.2 Blocking v-stranding VPE

We now must turn to ways to block the ungrammatical string in which the light verb is stranded in the absence of a main verb in a serial verb construction could be derived in one of two ways. Either the VP in (42A) below could be elided in the absence of any head movement (as in Toosarvandani's 2009 account of Persian),

10 Kumar claims (contra Mahajan 1990) that the head hosting negation is found below the aspectual head in Hindi-Urdu. I instead follow Dwivedi (1991) and Bhatt and Dayal (2007) in the claim that the verbs move to an aspectual head above vP, and that head dominates negation when present. Though space does not permit a detailed discussion of negation in Hindi-Urdu, the interaction of negation with some complex predicates is discussed in section 4.3.

or the entire vP could be elided after only the v head alone has moved out, as in (42B).

(42) ?*मीना ने भी ___ लिया।
?**Mīna-ne bhī ___ liy-ā.*
Mīna-ERG also ___ take.PFV.M
intended: 'Meena also read (this book for the first time).

(42a)

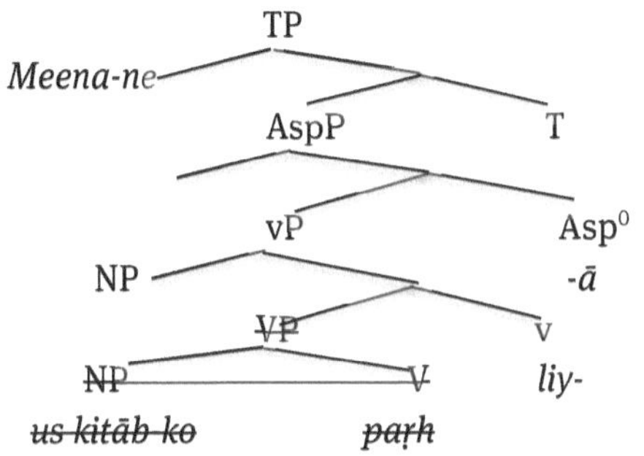

(42b)

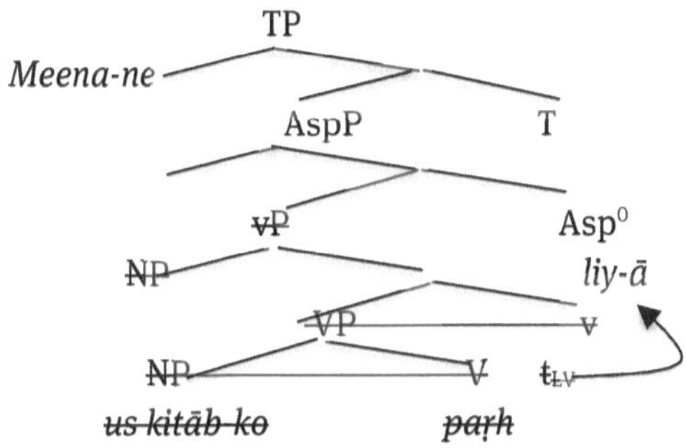

In Hindi-Urdu both of these derivations must be ruled out, as the resulting strings are ungrammatical. There are two clear ways to do this, detailed under option I and II below.

Option I is to claim that VPs cannot undergo ellipsis in Hindi-Urdu. That is, the smallest verbal layer that can be elided is the vP. Further, we must say that the verb movement feeding VVPE, though overall optional, must proceed from the bottom up (that is, the main verb must instigate verb movement, never the v head) (Brody 1997), and it must proceed to Asp⁰. These two stipulations, working in concert, would exclude the derivations in (42A) and (42B) above.

Option II would be to claim that V-to-Asp⁰ movement is obligatory in Hindi-Urdu. In this view it would be the case that in every clause, verb movement proceeded to a projection outside the verb layer, independent of the ellipsis process. There would then be no opportunity to strand the light verb alone, as it will always have formed a complex head with the main verb and (at least) the aspectual morphology/auxiliary. We would then no longer need stipulations about the size of the phrases that can undergo ellipsis, nor the nature of movement feeding specifically elliptical constructions. Further, movement of the verb into higher functional heads is assumed for many languages with a range of empirical motivations and consequences, and the theoretical mechanisms that drive it are relatively well elaborated (e.g. for Romance: Emonds 1978, Pollock 1989, Belletti 1990; for Germanic: den Besten 1983, Travis 1984, Zwart 1993, Roberts and Roussou 2002; for VSO order: Emonds 1980, Sproat 1985, Borsley and Roberts 1996; for Slavic Bailyn 1995, Gribanova 2013a). For this reason, I won't pursue a detailed account of the mechanics of head movement and ellipsis here (for an feature-based approach see Aelbrecht 2010, and also Merchant 2013). Instead I will turn to developing a more nuanced view of the composition of the syntax of complex predication in Hindi-Urdu.

4.3 Implications for previous approaches to the syntax of complex predicates: Butt and Ramchand (2005) and Mahajan (2012)

Though VVPE structures do not provide evidence that there is always verb movement to Asp^0 in Hindi-Urdu, they do show that it must always be available in order to produce licit ellipsis structures. This requirement is at odds with a recent account of complex predicates and case assignment proposed in Mahajan 2012.

Mahajan 2012 presents an approach to complex predicates in Hindi-Urdu intended to account for the pattern of ergative case assignment, which he shows depends on the properties of the light verb and not the main verb. His proposal is to split the vP into two distinct vP projections, each with a separate functional verbal head (v1 and v2). The lower v1 assigns accusative case to the internal argument, while the higher v2 introduces the external argument in its specifier and the light verb in its head.

Though I will not review the details of this account here, most important for our purposes is the way in which ergative case is assigned. Mahajan claims that whenever ergative case is assigned (whether in a simplex or complex predicate structure) it is assigned by the higher v2 head to the argument introduced in its specifier. When no overt light verb is present, the main verb in V must move into v2 (through v1) to provide v2 information with respect to its idiosyncratic case assignment properties. When an overt light verb is present, crucially the main verb in V must *not* move into v2, as its idiosyncratic case assignment properties do not contribute to the ergative case assignment potential of the predicate as a whole.

(43)

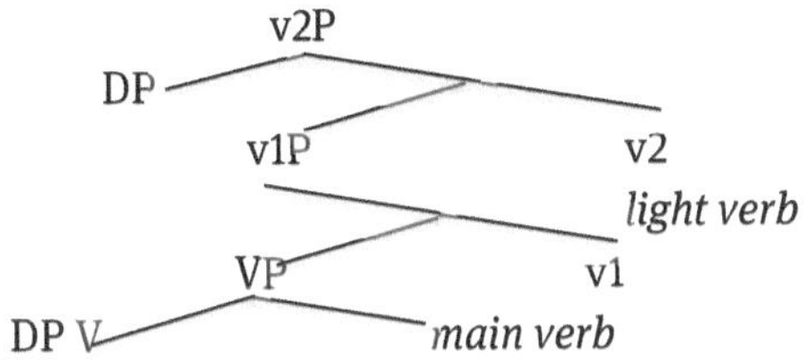

Though I will not review the details of this account here, most important for our purposes is the way in which ergative case is assigned. Mahajan claims that whenever ergative case is assigned (whether in a simplex or complex predicate structure) it is assigned by the higher v2 head to the argument introduced in its specifier. When no overt light verb is present, the main verb in V must move into v2 (through v1) to provide v2 information with respect to its idiosyncratic case assignment properties. When an overt light verb is present, crucially the main verb in V must *not* move into v2, as its idiosyncratic case assignment properties do not contribute to the ergative case assignment potential of the predicate as a whole.

In sum, this account would prohibit main verb movement into the head occupied by the overt light verb entirely, making it impossible to derive the VVPE cases discussed in section 3 above, in which the main verb and light verb are stranded together outside the vP and the vP itself is elided. In other words, the account of head movement for the purposes of ergative case assignment in Mahajan (2012) is incompatible with the nature of VVPE in Hindi-Urdu as investigated here. An alternative mechanism for accounting for ergative case in complex predicates is needed which does not rely on movement (see Manetta (in prep) for use of categorical feature-sharing in the extended projection as in Grimshaw (1991, 2005)).[11]

Another leading approach to complex predicates in Hindi Urdu in which independent movement of the light verb to the v head is already required is that found in Butt and Ramchand 2005. They propose the structure below for serial verb constructions of the type we have analyzed here (that is, those in which the

11 I am indebted to an NLLT reviewer for suggesting that this alternative approach to ergative case assignment be explored here.

main verb is in its stem form and the inflected light verb contributes to the *aktionsart* of the predicate as a whole).[12] This account is situated in a framework termed 'first phase syntax' (Ramchand 2008) which relies on event structure decomposition. Although the details of this approach are beyond the scope of this article, crucial to our work here is the notion that vP introduces the causation event (also licensing the subject/causer), VP specifies the nature of the change or process (and any entity undergoing the change/process), and the result phrase or RP introduces the 'result state' of the event (licensing the entity that holds the result state) (Butt and Ramchand 2005).

(44)

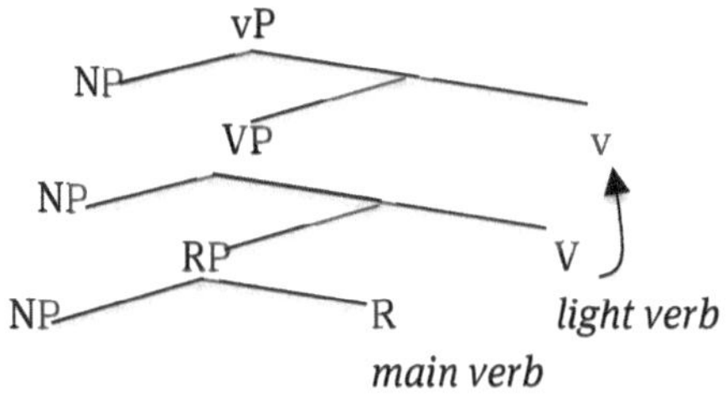

In Butt and Ramchand's approach to V-V complex predicates of this type, the main verb is hosted in Result (R) head, as it represents the result/final state of the predicate. The light verb originates in the V head (associated with the change in state). The light verb then moves independently to the v head to become associated with causation. In their view, then, V-V complex predicates of this type are accomplishment predicates that happen to be made up of two distinct lexical heads.

This final V-to-v movement of the light verb alone is not fully compatible with the account of VPE in the present article. Here I have proposed that movement from the position at which the main verb is introduced) (R in (44), otherwise V in the structures above) is obligatory in Hindi-Urdu, and composes the complex verbal structure. However, recall that permitting the light verb to move alone outside of the vP layer could potentially generate an ungrammatical structure in which VVPE stranded the light verb yet elided the main verb. It would require an outright stipulation against additional movement beyond v for the light verb in the

12 Butt and Ramchand (2005) also examine V-V constructions of the so-called 'let' type in which the main verb is in its infinitival form. I do not investigate these types of constructions here, though their interaction with verb phrase ellipsis should be part of a wider, more comprehensive approach to complex predication in the language.

structure in (44) above to prevent this outcome, since the light verb is already being permitted to move independently of the main verb.[13]

An alternative would be to adopt the structure proposed for these predicates by Butt and Ramchand (2005) and depicted in (44), but to replace their short light verb movement with the account of verb movement I have proposed here, in which V-to-Asp^0 (or indeed, R-to-Asp^0) is routine in Hindi-Urdu. This would then allow the light verb to pass through the v head and acquire the causal semantics Butt and Ramchand elaborate, while still deriving all and only the grammatical strings associated with VVPE.

4.4 v/VVPE: comparing Persian and Hindi-Urdu

As mentioned above, Persian permits vVPE in the context of N-V complex predicates in which the light verb/verbalizer is stranded but the nominal component of the complex predicate is elided along with any internal arguments. However, V-V complex predicates in Hindi-Urdu do not permit the equivalent string.

(45) *Sohrāb piranha-ra otu na-zad vali rostam [~~piranha-ra otu~~] zad*
Sohrab shirts-ACC iron NEG.do but Rostam shirts-ACC iron do
'Sohrab did not iron the shirts but Rostam did iron the shirts.'
(Persian; Toosarvandani: (4))

(46a) कबीर ने उस किताब को पहली बार पढ़ लिया।
Kabir-ne us kitāb-ko pahlī bār paṛh li-yā.
Kabir-ERG this book-ACC first time read take.PFV.M
'Kabir read this book for the first time.'

(46b) मीना ने भी ___ पढ़ लिया।
Mīna-ne bhī ___ paṛh li-yā.
Mīna-ERG also ___ read take.PFV.M
'Meena also read (this book for the first time).'

13 Another concern might involve the object created by head-adjoining movement. If the light verb moves into the v head, under standard Minimalist assumptions about head movement it will leave behind a trace/copy. The main verb in R would then need to adjoin to the trace/copy of movement. The complex head containing this adjunction would then move to adjoin to the v head, and that complex head in turn would move to adjoin to Asp^0/T. Adjoining to the trace left by previous head movement, like excorporation, is generally considered undesirable (and/or to create a morphologically illicit object), though there is relatively little empirical evidence available to support this position (for more discussion see Baker 1988, Kayne 1990, Hoekstra 1993, Zwart 1993).

(46c) ?*मीना ने भी ___ लिया।
?**Mīna-ne bhī ___ li-yā.*
Mīna-ERG also ___ take.PFV.M

The question then becomes whether the contrast between (44) and (45b) stems from a difference in the syntax of complex predicates in Persian and Hindi-Urdu. A number of proposals already exist in the literature for the structure of Persian complex predicates, including those found in Folli et al 2005, Toosarvandani 2009, and Megerdoomian 2012.

Folli et al 2005 propose the following syntax for a Persian complex predicate of the type we saw above (*otu zadan* = 'iron hit' = 'iron') in which the nominal component of the complex predicate is hosted in an NP complement to the main v containing the light verb. This is the structure employed by Toosarvandani 2009 in his approach to vVPE:

(47)

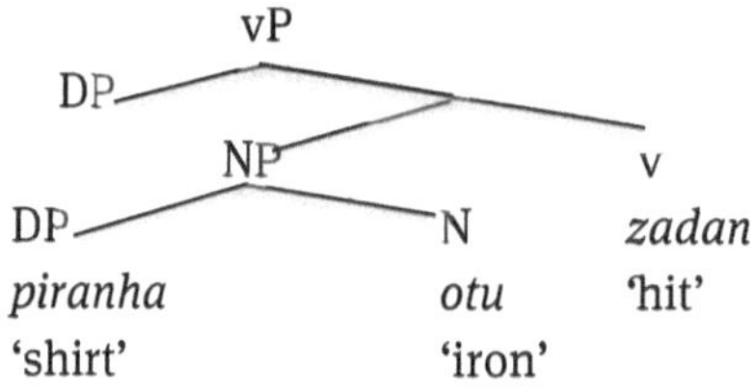

More recently, Megerdoomian 2012 has enhanced and refined this structure somewhat, based on evidence from a range of diagnostics including adjectival modification, degree of referentiality, and case assignment. She xpresents a structure that relies on verbal decomposition and conflation of empty functional heads with their overt complements via head incorporation (Hale and Keyser 2000). In this view a complex predicate like *šune zadan* 'to comb' will be comprised of the bare noun *šune* 'comb' and the verb *zadan* 'hit' conflated with an empty v head as in (47).

(48)

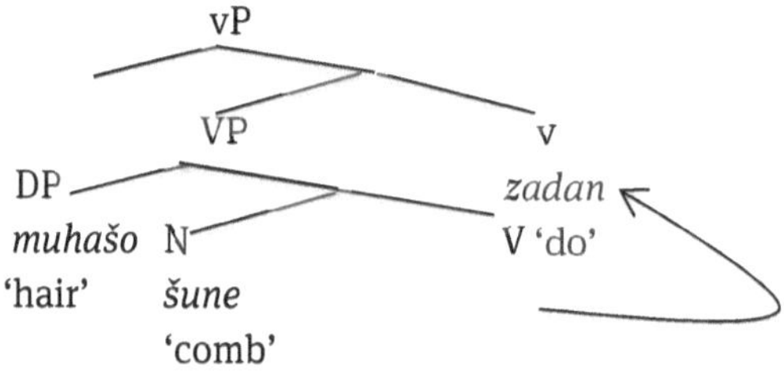

Crucially for our purposes here, Folli et al's proposal (as used by Toosarvandani 2009) and Megerdoomian's proposal have in common the fact that the light verb is ultimately found in v and that the nominal component remains in the head N. This means that in the case of vVPE, the nominal component of the complex predicate will be elided along with other VP-internal material, stranding the light verb alone.

Turning now to a comparison with the syntax developed here for Hindi-Urdu, the contrast is quite plain. The main verb in V-V complex predicates must become an integral part of the R head, which is an integral part of the verbal complex composed by obligatory head movement to Asp^0. The main verb can thus never be elided alongside other vP-internal material, and so no vVPE will result.

The interesting question now becomes: what about N-V complex predicates in Hindi-Urdu? As I mentioned above, some N-V complex predicates in Hindi-Urdu also resist VVPE, such as *yād kar* 'remember'

(49a) कबीर ने कहानी आसानी से याद की।
Kabīr-ne kahānī āsāni se yād k-ī.
Kabir-ERG story.F easily memory do.PFV.F
'Kabir memorized a story easily.'

(49b) मीना ने भी ___ याद की।
Mīna-ne bhī ___ yād k-ī.
Meena-ERG also ___ memory do.PFV.F
'Meena also memorized (a story easily).'

(49c) ?? मीना ने भी ___ की।
??*Mīna-ne bhī ___ k-ī.*
Meena-ERG also ___ do.PFV.F

Space does not permit a detailed investigation of N-V complex predicates here (though see Manetta (in prep)), but we might tentatively speculate that the syntax of N-V predicates like *yaad kar* 'remember' in Hindi-Urdu is more like that of V-V complex predicates in the language than like that of their Persian counterparts. Assuming the R head can host both nominal and verbal roots in Hindi-Urdu, a nominal root in R would also necessarily undergo R-to-Asp^0 movement. Though there is certainly ongoing empirical work to be done to better understand the nature of N-V complex predicates in Hindi-Urdu, VPE has the potential to serve as a useful diagnostic for the degree of connectedness between the components of complex predicates.

5 Conclusions and future directions

Complex predicates have the potential to provide an important insight into the way the syntax functions, as they represent an instance of syntactically and semantically distinct elements combining to predicate as a unit. Cross-linguistically, their structure and composition is a matter of ongoing debate (see, for instance, the contributions to Alsina, Bresnan, and Sells (1996) and Amberer, Baker, and Harvey (2014)). Verb-phrase ellipsis is a tool that has been used extensively to probe the shape of the verb phrase and the nature of head movement in a language. This article has introduced the use of VPE to better understand complex predicates, and establishing the relevance of VPE for assessing the tightness of the connection between the independent components of the complex.

To this point, the behavior of complex predicates under VPE in Hindi-Urdu had not been explored in the literature. The new empirical work in this article shows Hindi-Urdu V-V complex predicates permit VVPE, in which the verb is stranded outside of the elided vP. This provides evidence that Hindi-Urdu is a language with regular verb movement out of the verbal layer into the inflectional layer. While verb movement to the Tense or Aspect head had been assumed in some previous work, because Hindi-Urdu is verb final and the movement itself is thus string-vacuous, it was challenging to show that it must occur. I claim in this article that VVPE provides support for routineV-to-Asp^0 movement, forming the morphologically complex verb.

A second important finding is that Hindi-Urdu V-V complex predicates permit VVPE, but not vVPE, in contrast to complex predicates in Persian (Toosarvandani 2009). In other words, the light verb cannot be stranded independently of the main verb, suggesting that the two form a unit and that must vacate the verbal layer together. Employing the basic syntactic structure for complex predicates proposed in Butt and Ramchand (2005) based on a decomposed verbal structure, I claim that the main verb stem found in the R head moves through V and v, combining with the light verb and the meaning CAUSE. This complex then moves into the Aspect head to combine with aspectual morphology. This R-to-Asp^0 head movement is obligatory in Hindi-Urdu, meaning that only VVPE strings, but not vVPE strings, will be available for V-V complex predicates in the language. This analytical proposal (and the empirical observations which ground it) nicely capture the observation made by Butt and Ramchand (2005: 144) that V-V complex predicates have "properties that indicate integrity with respect to determining argument structure and event structure properties, just as one would expect from a single lexical item".

Certainly, V-V complex predicates are just one of many possible types of light verb constructions in Hindi-Urdu. Recent research suggests that there are multiple types or classes of N-V complex predicates in Hindi-Urdu (Mohanan 1994; Davison 2005; Ahmed 2011; Butt and Ahmed 2011; Ahmed et al 2012; Butt et al 2012; Sulger and Vaidya 2014) with distinct properties. Future research (pursued in Manetta (in prep)) asks whether evidence from the availability of vVPE might pattern in such a way as to support this distinction. Analytically, this would permit us to probe whether different basic structures might exist for different classes of N-V complex predicates, consistent with the differences in case-marking, agreement, adjectival modification, that were found to distinguish categories of N-V complex predicates in previous work.

This article reveals a number of open avenues for ongoing research. Within Hindi-Urdu, the rich inventory of N-V complex predicates and their properties is still under investigation, and complex predicates consisting of adjectives and prepositions have received very little attention. Research on A-V and P-V complex predicates is in its earliest stages, and data-gathering from naturally occurring speech is sorely needed. We would hope that a more comprehensive study of complex predicates and verb phrase ellipsis cross-linguistically would prove fruitful, ideally revealing a limited set of patterns conditioned by the availability of regular head movement of the verb into the inflectional layer and the tightness of the connection between the separate components of the complex predicate.

References

Adger, David. 2003. *Core Syntax: A Minimalist Approach*. Oxford: Oxford University Press.

Aelbrecht, Lobke. 2010. *The Syntactic Licensing of Ellipsis*. Amsterdam: John Benjamins.

Ahmed, Tafseer. 2011. Complex Predicates in Urdu. Presented at South Asian Languages: Formal Approaches and Computational Resources, LSA Summer School, Boulder, CO, 2011.

Ahmed, Tafseer and Miriam Butt. 2011. Discovering Semantic Classes for Urdu N-V Complex Predicates. In *Proceedings of the International Conference on Computational Semantics* (IWCS 2011), Oxford.

Ahmed, Tafseer, Miriam Butt, Annette Hautli and Sebastian Sulger. 2012. A Reference Dependency Bank for Analyzing Complex Predicates. *Proceedings of the Eight conference on International Language Resources and Evaluation* (*LREC'12*), Istanbul, 2012.

Alsina, Alex. 1993. Predicate Composition: A Theory of Syntactic Function Alternations. PhD thesis, Stanford University.

Alsina, Alex, Joan Bresnan, and Peter Sells. 1996. *Complex Predicates*. Chicago: CSLI.

Amberer, M., B. Baker, and M. Harvey. 2014. *Complex Predicates: Cross-linguistic Perspectives on Even Structure*. Cambridge: Cambridge University Press.

Bailyn, John Frederick. 1995. Underlying phrase structure and 'short' verb movement in Russian. *Journal of Slavic Linguistics* 3 (1): 13–58.

Baker, Mark. 1988. *Incorporation: A Theory of Grammatical Function Changing*. Chicago: University of Chicago Press.
Bashir, Elena. 1989. "Causal Chains and Compound Verbs." In: *Proceedings of the Symposium on Complex Predicates in South Asian Languages*. Ed. Manindra K. Verma and Usha Nilsson.
Belletti, Adriana. 1990. *Generalized Verb Movement*. Torino: Rosenberg & Sellier.
Bhatt, Rajesh. 2005. Long distance agreement in Hindi-Urdu. *Natural Language and Linguistic Theory* 23: 757–807.
Bhatt, Rajesh and Veneeta Dayal. 2007. "Rightward Scrambling as Rightward Remnant Movement" *Linguistic Inquiry* 38.2: 287–301.
Borsley, Robert, and Ian Roberts. 1996. *The syntax of the Celtic languages*. Cambridge: Cambridge University Press.
Butt, Miriam. 1995. *The Structure of Complex Predicates in Urdu*. Stanford, California: CSLI Publications.
Butt, Miriam. 1998. Constraining argument merger through aspect. In: Hinrichs E, Kathol A, Nakazawa T (eds.) *Complex Predicates in Nonderivational Syntax*. Cambridge: Academic Press, pp 73–113.
Butt, Miriam. 2003. The Light Verb Jungle. In Harvard Working Papers in Linguistics, ed. G. Aygen, C. Bowern, and C. Quinn. 1–49. Volume 9, *Papers from the GSAS/Dudley House Workshop on Light Verbs*.
Butt, Miriam. 2010. The Light Verb Jungle: Still Hacking Away, In M. Amberber, M. Harvey and B. Baker (eds.) *Complex Predicates in Cross-Linguistic Perspective*, 48–78. Cambridge: Cambridge University Press.
Butt, Miriam. 2013. Control vs. Complex Predication. Comment on Alice Davison. To Appear in a Special Issue of Natural Language and Linguistic Theory.
Butt, Miriam, and Wilhelm Geuder. 2001. On the (Semi)Lexical Status of Light Verbs. In *Semi-lexical Categories: On the content of function words and the function of content words*, ed. Norbert Corver and Henk van Riemsdijk. 323–370. Berlin: Mouton de Gruyter.
Butt, Miriam, Tracy H. King, and Gillian Ramchand. Complex Predication: Who made the child pinch the elephant? In Reality Exploration and Discovery: Pattern Interaction in Language and Life, ed. Linda Uyechi and Lian Hee Wee. Stanford, California: CSLI Publications.
Butt, Miriam, and Tracy Holloway King. 2006. Restriction for Morphological Valency Alternations: The Urdu Causative. In *Intelligent Linguistic Architectures: Variations on Themes*. by Ronald M. Kaplan, ed. Miriam Butt, Mary Dalrymple, and Tracy Holloway King. 235–258. CSLI Publications.
Butt, Miriam, and Aditi Lahiri. 2002. Historical Stability vs. Historical Change. Unpublished Ms. http: //ling.uni-konstanz.de/pages/home/butt/.
Butt, Miriam, and Gillian Ramchand. 2005. Complex Aspectual Structure in Hindi/Urdu. In *The Syntax of Aspect*. Nomi Ertishik-Shir and Tova Rappaport (eds). 117–153. Oxford: Oxford University Press.
Butt, Miriam, Tina Bögel, Annette Hautli, Sebastian Sulger and Tafseer Ahmed. 2012. Identifying Urdu Complex Predication via Bigram Extraction. In *Proceedings of the 24th International Conference on Computational Linguistics* (COLING), 409–424. Mumbai, India.
Butt, Miriam. 2014. Control vs. complex predication: Identifying non-finite complements. *Natural Language and Linguistic Theory* 32.1, 165–190.
Brody, Michael. 1997. Mirror theory. Ms. University College London.

Davison, Alice. 1999. Empty categories: anaphoric vs. pronominal coindexing, ms. University of Illinois.
Davison, Alice. 2005. "Phrasal predicates: How N combines with V in Hindi/Urdu." In Tanmoy Bhattacharya (ed.) *Yearbook of South Asian Languages and Linguistics*. Berlin: Mouton DeGruyter, pp. 83–116.
Davison, Alice. 2013. "Emtpy Categories in the Hindi-Urdu *binaa* participial clause". *Lingua Posnaniensis*, vol. LV (2)/2013. The Poznań Society for the Advancement of the Arts and Sciences. pp. 25–39.
Davison, Alice. 2014. Non-finite complements and modality in dee-naa 'allow' in Hindi-Urdu. *Natural Language and Linguistic Theory* 32.1, 137–154.
Dayal, Veneeta. 2003. "Bare Nominals: Non-specific and Contrastive Readings under Scrambling", in *Word Order and Scrambling*, Simin Karimi (ed.), London: Blackwell Publishers.
Dayal, Veneeta. 2011. "Bare Noun Phrases", Maeinborn, von Heusinger and Portner (eds), *Semantics: An International Handbook of Natural Language Meaning*, 33.2 1087–1108.
den Besten, Hans 1983, 'On the Interaction of Root Transformations and Lexical Deletive Rules.' in Werner Abraham (ed.) *On the Formal Syntax of the Westgermania*. Papers from the "3rd Groningen Grammar Talks" Groningen, January 1981. Amsterdam/Philadelphia: Benjamins. 1983. Linguistik Aktuell 3: 47–131.
Depiante, Marcela, and Luis Vicente. 2012. El movimiento y la morfología del verbo. In Brucart and Gallego (eds.) El movimiento de constituyentes, 95–106. Madrid: Visor Libros.
Doron, Edit. 1991. *V-movement and VP ellipsis*. Jerusalem: The Hebrew University of Jerusalem.
Dwivedi, Veena. 1994. Syntactic Dependencies in Relative Phrases in Hindi. PhD dissertation, University of Massachusetts, Amherst.
Emonds, J. 1978. 'The Verbal Complex V'-V in French.' *Linguistic Inquiry* 9: 151–175.
Emonds, J. 1980. 'Word Order in Generative Grammar." *Journal of Linguistic Research* 1.1, 33–54.
Fiengo, Robert, and Robert May. 1994. *Indices and identity*. Cambridge: MIT Press.
Folli, Raffaella, Heidi Harley, and Simin Karimi. 2005. Determinants of event type in Persian complex predicates. *Lingua* 115 (10): 1365–1401.
Funakoshi, Kenshi. 2014. Syntactic Head Movement and Its Consequences, PhD dissertation, University of Maryland.
Funakoshi, Kenshi. 2016. "Verb-Stranding Verb Phrase Ellipsis in Japanese," Journal of East Asian Linguistics. 25.2: 113–142.
Goldberg, Lotus. 2005a. Verb-stranding VP ellipsis: a cross-linguistic study. PhD diss., McGill University, Montréal.
Gribanova, Vera. 2013a. Verb-stranding verb phrase ellipsis and the structure of the Russian verbal complex. Natural Language and Linguistic Theory 31(1): 91–136.
Gribanova, Vera. 2013b A new argument for verb-stranding verb phrase ellipsis. Linguistic Inquiry 44(1): 145–157.
Hale, K. & S. J. Keyser. 1993. On argument structure and the lexical expression of syntactic relations. In K. Hale & S. J. Keyser (Eds.), *The View from Building 20: Essays in Linguistics in Honor of Sylvain Bromberger* (pp. 11–41). Cambridge, Mass: MIT Press.
Hale, K. and S. J. Keyser. 2000. Conflation. Cuadernos delingüística VII 2000, Documenos de trabajo. Lingüística Teórica, ed. by AnaBravo Martín, Carlos Luján Berenguel, and Isabel Pérez Jiménez, 39–76. Madrid: Instituto Universitario Ortega y Gasset
Hale, K. & S. J. Keyser. 2002. *Prolegomenon to a Theory of Argument Structure*. Cambridge: MA: MIT Press.

Halle, M. & Alec Marantz. 1993. Distributed Morphology and the pieces of inflection. In K. Hale & S. J. Keyser (Eds.), *The View from Building 20: Essays in Linguistics in Honor of Sylvain Bromberger* (pp. 111–176). Cambridge, Mass: MIT Press.
Hankamer, Jorge, and Ivan A. Sag. 1976. Deep and surface anaphora. *Linguistic Inquiry* 7: 391–426.
Hoekstra, E. 1993. Dialectal variation inside CP as parametric variation. Dialektsyntax, [Linguistische Berichte Sonderheft 5], Edited by W. Abraham and J. Bayer. 161–179.
Hoji, Hajime. 1998. Null objects and sloppy identity in Japanese. *Linguistic Inquiry* 28: 127–152.
Hook, Peter. E. 1974. *The Compound Verb in Hindi.* Ann Arbor: Center for South and Southeast Asian Studies, University of Michigan.
Hardt, Daniel. 1993. Verb Phrase Ellipsis: form, meaning and processing. PhD diss., University of Pennsylvania.
Jayaseelan, K. A. 1990. Incomplete VP deletion and gapping. *Linguistic Analysis* 20, 64–81.
Jespersen, Otto. 1965. A Modern English Grammar on Historical Principles, Part VI, Morphology. London: George Allen and Unwin Ltd.
Johnson, Kyle. 2001. What VP-ellipsis can do, and what it can't but not why. In *The handbook of contemporary syntactic theory*, edited by M. Baltin and C. Collins, 439–479. Oxford: Blackwell.
Karimi, Simin. 1999a. 'A Note on Parasitic Gaps and Specificity', *Linguistic Inquiry* 30: 704–713.
Karimi, Simin.1999b. 'Specificity Effect: Evidence from Persian', *Linguistic Review* 16: 125–141.
Kayne, Richard. 1990. Romance Clitics and PRO. *NELS* 20.
Kennedy, Chris. 2008. Argument contained ellipsis. In: Johnson (2008a), 95–131.
Kim, Soowon. 1999. Sloppy/strict identity, empty objects, and NP ellipsis. *Journal of East Asian Linguistics 8:* 255–284.
Koizumi, Masatoshi. 2000. String vacuous overt verb movement. Journal of East Asian Linguistics 9: 227–285.
Kumar, Rajesh. 2006. *Negation and Licensing of Negative Polarity Items in Hindi Syntax.* New York: Routledge.
Lacara, Nicholas. 2014. Why there is no verb-stranding in (Mainland) Scandinavian. 29th Comparative Germanic Syntax Workshop University of York, UK, 26 September 2014.
Lobeck, Anne. 1995. *Ellipsis: functional heads, licensing and identification.* New York: Oxford University Press.
Levin, Beth and Malka Rappaport Hovav. Unaccusativity: *At the Syntax-Lexical Semantics Interface.* Linguistic Inquiry Monograph Twenty-Six. Cambridge, Massachusetts. London, England: The MIT Press.
Mahajan, Anoop. 1990. The A/A-bar distinction and movement theory. PhD dissertation, MIT, Cambridge, Mass.
Mahajan, Anoop. 2012. Ergatives, Antipassives and the Overt Light v in Hindi. *Lingua 122.* 204–214.
Manetta, Emily. 2011. *Peripheries in Kashmiri and Hindi Urdu: The syntax of discourse-driven movement.* series: Language Faculty and Beyond, Amsterdam: John Benjamins.
Martins, Ana-Maria. 1994. Enclisis, VP-deletion and the nature of sigma. *Probus* 6: 173–205.
McCloskey, James. 1991. Clause structure, ellipsis and proper government in Irish. *Lingua* 85: 259–302.

Megerdoomian, Karine. 2012. The status of the nominal in Persian complex predicates. *Natural Language and Linguistic Theory* 30: 1.
Merchant, Jason. 2013. Voice and ellipsis. *Linguistic Inquiry* 44(1).
Mohanan, Tara. 1994. *Argument Structure in Hindi*. Stanford: CSLI Publications.
Oku, Satoshi. 1998. A theory of selection and reconstruction in the minimalist perspective. Doctoral dissertation, University of Connecticut.
Postal, Paul. 1993. Parasitic Gaps and Across-the-Board Phenomenon. *Linguistic Inquiry* 24: 735–754.
Otani, Kazuyo, and John Whitman. 1991. V-Raising and VP-ellipsis. *Linguistic Inquiry* 22: 345–358.
Payne, John R. 1985. Complex phrases and complex sentences. In *Language typology and syntactic description*. Vol. 2, Complex constructions, ed. by Tim Shopen, 3–41. Cambridge: Cambridge University Press.
Pollock, Jean-Yves. 1989. Verb movement, universal grammar, and the structure of IP. *Linguistic Inquiry* 20: 365–424.
Ramchand, Gillian. 2008. *Verb Meaning and the Lexicon: A First Phase Syntax*. Cambridge: Cambridge University Press.
Raza, G. 2011. Subcategorization Acquisition and Classes of Predication in Urdu. PhD thesis, University of Konstanz.
Rasekhi, Vahideh. 2014. Missing objects in Persian. Ms., Stony Brook University
Roberts, Ian & Anna Roussou. 2002. The Extended Projection Principle as a Condition on the Tense Dependency. In: Svenonius, P. (ed.). *Subjects, expletives, and the EPP*. Oxford: OUP, 125–156.
Ross, John Robert. 1969. Auxiliaries as main verbs. *Studies in Philosophical Linguistics* 1: 77–102.
Sag, Ivan and Jorge Hankamer, 1984. Towards a theory of anaphoric processing. *Linguistics and Philosophy*, 7: 325–345.
Sag, Ivan. 1979. *Deletion and logical form*. PhD diss., New York: Garland.
Sag, Ivan. 1981. Formal Semantics and Extralinguistic Context. In P. Cole (ed) *Syntax and Semantics*, Volume 9: Pragmantics. New York: Academic Press, 273–294.
Sailor, Craig. 2014. The variables of VP-ellipsis. PhD Dissertation, University of California, Los Angeles.
Saito, Mamoru. 1985. Some asymmetries in Japanese and their theoretical implications. PhD diss., MIT Press, Cambridge.
Simpson and Syed 2013 Simpson, Andrew, Arunima Choudhury and Mythili Menon. 2013. Argument Ellipsis and the licensing of covert nominals in Bangla, Hindi and Malayalam. *Lingua* 134: 123–138.
Sproat, Richard. 1985. On deriving the lexicon. PhD dissertation, Massachusetts Institute of Technology.
Sulger, Sebastian and Ashwini Vaidya. 2014. Towards Identifying Hindi/Urdu Noun Templates in Support of a Large-Scale LFG Grammar. 4th Workshop on South and Southeast Asian NLP. COLING 2014.
Takahashi, Daiko. 2006. Apparent parasitic gaps and null arguments in Japanese. Journal of East Asian Linguistics 15: 1–35.
Toosarvandani, Maziar. 2009. Ellipsis in Farsi complex predicates. *Syntax*, 2009, 12(1): 60–92.
Travis, Lisa. 1984. Parameters and Effects of Word Order Variation, PhD dissertation, MIT, Cambridge.

Williams, Edwin. 1977. Discourse and logical form. *Linguistic Inquiry* 8: 101–139.
Winter, Yoad. 1995. Syncategorematic conjunction and structured meanings. In *Proceedings of SALT 5*, ed. by Mandy Simons and Teresa Galloway. Available at http: //elanguage.net/journals /salt/issue/view/288.
Zwart, Jan-Wouter. 1993. Verb movement in Complementizer Agreement. *MIT Working Papers in Linguistics* 18: 297–340.

Anoop Mahajan

Case licensing in Hindi prenominal relative clauses

Abstract: This paper presents a range of data illustrating restrictions on Hindi prenominal relative clauses. While Hindi finite relative clauses, especially correlatives, have been well studied in existing formal linguistics literature in Hindi, the prenominal relative clauses have not received as much attention. Hindi prenominal relative clauses are non-finite and are built around perfective or imperfective participles or infinitival verb forms. I show that the choice of the verb form places restrictions on the grammatical function of the nominal head of the relative head noun. One of the aims of this paper is to propose an analysis of these restrictions by relating them to abstract case licensing and by suggesting that the movement of the relative head noun in these type of relative clauses is an abstract case seeking movement. In the second half of the paper, I present data that seems to indicate that while the syntax of Hindi prenominal relative clauses seems to involve movement of the head of the relative clause, there is also contradicting evidence that suggests that the head of the relative clause is base generated external to the relative clause. This sets up a paradox and I suggest that this paradox can be resolved in favor of a head movement analysis if we assume that this movement does not reconstruct for binding purposes. I suggest that this lack of reconstruction for binding may be related to the case seeking nature of this movement.[1]

Keywords: Prenominal relatives clause, Case licensing, determiner phrase

1 Introduction

This paper explores some asymmetries between prenominal and postnominal externally headed relative clauses in Hindi. While largely dwelling on the nature of

1 My thanks to the organizers and the audience at the International Conference on Hindi Studies 2016, INALCO, Paris. Thanks also to the participants at Formal Approaches to South Asian Languages (FASAL) 3, 2013, at USC where some of the material in this paper was presented.

Anoop Mahajan, Department of Linguistics, University of California, Los Angeles, USA. Email: amahajan@ucla.edu

https://doi.org/10.1515/9783110610796-004

prenominal relative clauses, I suggest that both externally headed relative clauses as illustrated by (1),[2] and internally headed relative clauses as illustrated by (2), involve externalization of the head by a movement process.[3]

Externally headed post-nominal:

(1) वो फूल [जो तुमने कल खरीदे थे] बहुत अच्छे हैं।
vo phūl [jo tum-ne kal kharīde
those flower.M.PL which you-ERG yesterday buy.PFV.M.PL
the] bahut aččhe hɛ̃.
AUX.PST.M.PL very nice.M.PL be.PRS.PL[4]
'The flowers that you bought yesterday are very nice.'

Externally headed pre-nominal:

(2) [तुम्हारे कल खरीदे हुए] वो फूल बहुत अच्छे हैं।
[tumhāre kal kharīde hue] vo phūl
your yesterday buy.PFV.M.PL be.PFV.M.PL those flower.M.PL
bahut aččhe hɛ̃.
very nice.M.PL be.PRS.PL
'The flowers that you bought yesterday are very nice.'

These two types of relative clauses differ in various ways. Some of these differences are very well known in the typological literature. For example, as Keenan (1985) pointed out, prenominal relative clauses are somewhat *reduced* compared to postnominal clauses in general. This holds true in Hindi as well, largely along the lines that Keenan noted. Thus, the prenominal relative clauses of the type in (2) cannot contain tense, nor can it contain a relative pronoun. Furthermore, the subject of the relative clause cannot have a nominative or ergative subject. Thus, the following variants of (2) are ungrammatical in Hindi:

---

2 There is fairly extensive work done on Hindi relative clauses as well as on relative clauses in related Indian languages. For a typological outline of the properties of Hindi and other South Asian languages, please see Subbarao (2012), Chapter 8. For restrictions on Hindi prenominal relative clauses, see also Hook and Koul, ms.

3 I will not discuss Hindi correlatives in this paper.

4 List of abbreviations used in this paper: AGT = agentive, AUX= auxiliary, DAT = dative, DO = direct object, DOM = differential object marking, ERG = ergative, F = feminine gender, GEN = genitive, IMP = imperative, IMPF = imperfective, M = masculine gender, NOM = nominative, OBL = oblique, PFV = perfective, PL = plural, PP = postposition phrase, PST = past, PROG = progressive , PRS = present, SG = singular, SUB = subject, and T =tense.

(3) *[तुम्हारे कल खरीदे थे] वो फूल बहुत अच्छे हैं।
*[*tumhāre kal kharīde the*] *vo phūl*
your yesterday buy.PFV.M.PL AUX.PST.M.PL those flower.M.PL
bahut ačče hɛ̃.
very nice.M.PL be.PRS.PL
'The flowers that you had bought yesterday are very nice.'

(4) *[जो फूल कल खरीदे हुए] वो बहुत अच्छे हैं।
*[*jo phūl kal kharīde hue*]
which flower.M.PL yesterday buy.PFV.M.PL be.PFV.M.PL
vo bahut ačče hɛ̃.
those very nice.M.PL be.PRS.PL
'The flowers which you bought yesterday are very nice.'

(5) *[तुमने/ तुम कल खरीदे हुए] वो फूल बहुत अच्छे हैं।
*[*tum-ne/ tum kal kharīde hue*]
you-ERG/you.NOM yesterday buy.PFV.M.PL be.PFV.M.PL
vo phūl bahut ačče hɛ̃.
those flower.M.PL very nice.M.PL be.PRS.PL
'The flowers that you bought yesterday are very nice.'

Another dimension of differences between the post-nominal and the pre-nominal relative clauses pertains to the *accessibility* of the types of nominal phrases that can be relativized. Thus, the post-nominal relative clauses in Hindi seem to be quite liberal in that they can modify various grammatical functions including the subject – as in (6), the direct object as in (7), and the indirect object as in (8). I leave out other positions since they will not be directly relevant for our subsequent discussion.

(6) वो फूल [जो मेज़ पर रखे थे] मुरझा गये।
vo phūl [*jo mez par rakhe the*]
those flower.M.PL which table on put.PFV.M.PL AUX.PST.M.PL
murjhā gaye.
wilt go.PFV.M.PL
'Those flowers which were put/lying on the table wilted.'

(7) वो फूल [जो तुमने मेज़ पर रखे थे] मुरझा गये।
vo phūl [*jo tum-ne mez par rakhe the*]
those flower.M.PL which you-ERG table on put.PFV.M.PL AUX.PST.M.PL
murjhā gaye.
wilt go.PFV.M.PL
'Those flowers which you had put on the table wilted.'

(8) वो लड़की [जिसको तुमने फूल दिये थे] आ रही है।
vo larkī [jis-ko tum-ne phūl diye the]
that girl who-DAT you-ERG flower.M.PL give.PFV.PL AUX.PST.M.PL
ā rahī hɛ.
come PROG.F.SG AUX.PRS.SG
'That girl to whom you gave flowers is coming.'

On the other hand, pre-nominal relatives are not as liberal. While the subject and the direct object are accessible for relativization in (9) and (10) respectively, (11) indicates that the indirect object cannot be relative using a pre-nominal relative clause.

(9) [मेज़ पर रखे हुए] वो फूल मुरझा गये।
[mez par rakhe hue] vo phūl murjhā gaye.
table on put.PFV.M.PL be.PFV.M.PL those flower.M.PL wilt go.PFV.M.PL
'Those flowers that are on the table wilted.'

(10) [तुम्हारे मेज़ पर रखे हुए] वो फूल मुरझा गये।
[tumhāre mez par rakhe hue] vo phūl
you-GEN.M.PL table on put.PFV.M.PL be.PFV.M.PL those flower.M.PL
murjhā gaye.
wilt go.PFV.M.PL
'Those flowers that you put on the table wilted.'

(11) *[तुम्हारी फूल दी हुई] वो लड़की आ रही है।
**[tumhārī phūl dī hui] vo larki*
you-GEN.F flower.M.PL give.PFV.F.SG be.PFV.F.SG that girl
ā rahī hɛ.
come PROG.F.SG AUX.PRS.SG
'That girl to whom you gave flowers is coming.'

In fact, pre-nominal relative clauses containing an imperfective verb are even less liberal in this *accessibility* respect. As illustrated by (13) and (14), even a direct object cannot be relativized if the pre-nominal relative clause has an imperfective as the main verb.

(12) [मुरझाते हुए] वो फूल बाहर फेंक दो।
[murjhāte hue] vo phūl bāhar phẽk do.
wilt.IMPFV.M.PL be.PFV.M.PL those flower.M.PL outside throw give.IMP
'Throw away those flowers that are wilting.'

(13) *[तुम्हारे खरीदते हुए] वो फूल मुरझा गये।
*[*tumhāre* *kharīdte* *hue*] *vo* *phūl* *murjhā* *gaye.*
you-GEN.M.PL buy.IMPFV be.PFV those flower.M.PL wilt go.PFV.M.PL
'Those flowers that you are buying wilted.'

(14) *[तुम्हारी फूल देती हुई] वो लड़की आ रही है।
*[*tumhārī* *phūl* *detī* *huī*] *vo* *laṛkī* *ā* *rahī* *hɛ.*
you-GEN.F flower give.IMPFV.F be.PFV.F that girl come PROG AUX.PRS.SG
'That girl to whom you are giving flowers is coming.'

Thus, while post-nominal externally headed relative clauses are clearly different in various ways from the pre-nominal externally headed relative clauses, even the prenominal relative clauses of the two types that we have seen, (namely, perfective participle and imperfective participle) are not identical. However, the *reduced* nature of the pre-nominal relative clauses is similar across the two types of pre-nominal relatives that we have seen – they cannot have tense, they cannot have a relative pronoun and they cannot have a nominative or ergative subject. In Mahajan (2017), an account is outlined of the restrictions on *accessibility* of argument nominals in Hindi prenominal relative clauses. This account ties the accessibility of arguments for relativization to structural case licensing restrictions that hold in pre-nominal relative clauses because of their *reduced* status. Given that the post-nominal relative clauses are not reduced, these restrictions are not applicable to those type of relative clauses. In section 2, I provide a sketch of Mahajan's (2017) account. In the section 3, I then provide evidence for externalization of the head both in pre-nominal and post-nominal relative clauses. This is followed by presenting some data that is somewhat puzzling for the externalization account of relative clauses followed by a proposal that may account for the relevant facts.

2 Basic Facts

The facts and analysis in this section follow Mahajan (2017). These facts are needed to later deal with the issues of externalization of the head in relative clauses. Hindi prenominal relative clauses come in various varieties. The verb form inside these relative clauses is always non-finite but can consist of perfective participle, imperfective participles and certain kind of infinitives.[5]

Of these, our main focus on this paper will be on perfective participle based prenominal relative clauses. Consider the data below. The brackets indicate the limits of the prenominal relative clause, the head of the relative clause is the NP that appears after the right bracket.

(15) [मोहन की लिखी हुई] किताब
[*Mohan-kī likhī huī*] *kitab*
Mohan-GEN.F write.PFV.F be.PFV.F book.F.SG
'a/the book written by Mohan'

(16) [बाजार से आयी हुई] ताज़ी सब्ज़ी
[*bāzār se āyī (huī)*] *tāzī sabzī*
market from come.PFV.F (be.PFV.F) fresh.F vegetable.F.SG
'fresh vegetables (which) arrived from the market'

(17) [मरी हुई] छिपकली
[*marī (huī)*] *čhipkalī*
die.PFV.F (be.PFV.F) lizard.F.SG
'a/the lizard that is dead'

(18) [मेज़ पर सोयी (हुई)] बिल्ली
[*mez par soyī (huī)*] *billī*
table on sleep.PFV.F (be.PFV.F) cat.F.SG
'a/the cat sleeping on the table'

(16)–(18) are cases of subject relativization. (15) is an instance of an object relativization. In (15), the subject of the relative clause is followed by the genitive postposition. The perfective participle verb, the participial aux *be* (which is optional) and the genitive postposition agree with the relativized head noun. The

5 A couple of examples of Hindi infinitival relative clauses are provided below. For some discussion of these, please see Mahajan (2013). *Vālī* and *vāle* in the glosses below are usually translated as an agentive markers and are therefore glossed here as AGT.

(i) [मेरी रोज़ पढ़ने वाली] किताबें
[*merī roz paṛhne vālī*] *kitābẽ*
I-GEN.F everyday read.INF.OBL AGT.F.PL book.F.PL
'Books which I read every day'

(ii) [किताब पढ़ने वाले] लोग
[*kitāb paṛhne vāle*] *log*
book read.INF.OBL AGT.M.PL people
'People who read book(s)'

subject can also be marked as a *by*-phrase instead with genitive (but can never be unmarked).

(19) [मोहन द्वारा लिखी (हुई)] किताब
[*Mohan-dvārā likhī (huī)] kitāb*
Mohan-by write.PFV.F (be.PFV.F) book.F.SG
'A/the book written by Mohan'

(15) is parallel to a non-relative perfective transitive ergative clause (20) below. Similarly, (16) is parallel to the normal non-relative intransitive perfective non-ergative (21) below.

(20) मोहन ने किताब लिखी (थी)।
Mohan-ne kitāb likhī (thī).
Mohan-ERG book.F.SG write.PFV.F.SG (AUX.PST.F.SG)
'Mohan had written the book.'

(21) बाज़ार से ताज़ी सब्ज़ी आयी (थी)।
bāzār-se tāzī sabzī āyī (thī).
market.from fresh vegetable.F.SG come.PFV.F.SG (AUX.PST.F.SG)
'The fresh vegetables had arrived from the market.'

Mahajan (2017) suggests that the perfective prenominal relatives in (15)–(19) are structurally parallel to normal non-relative clauses such as (20) and (21) with a crucial difference: they use the same perfective participle verbal forms and have similar agreement patterns, but while (15)–(19) lack a finite T, (20) and (21) have a finite T (though it can be phonetically null).

It should be noted that the prenominal relative clauses in Hindi cannot be finite. This is illustrated by the ungrammaticality of (22) below.

(22) *[मोहन की लिखी थी/ है] किताब
*[*Mohan-kī likhī thī/ hɛ] kitab*
Mohan-GEN.F write.PFV.F.SG AUX.PST.F.SG/ be.PRS.SG book.F.SG
'A/the book that was/is written by Mohan.'

Similarly, while a genitive subject is possible in (22), and a *by*-subject is possible in (19), an ergative subject is systematically impossible in prenominal relative clauses as shown by the examples below.

(23) *[मोहन ने लिखी (हुई)] किताब
*[*Mohan-ne* *likhī* (*huī*)] *kitāb*
Mohan-ERG write.PFV.F.SG be.PFV.F.SG book.F.SG
'A/the book written by Mohan'

(24) *[राधा ने मोहन को लिखी (हुई)] किताब
*[*Rādhā-ne* *Mohan-ko* *likhī* (*huī*)] *kitab*
Radha-ERG Mohan-DAT write.PFV.F be.PFV.F book.F.SG
'A/the book written to Mohan by Radha'

The reason for the ungrammaticality of (23) and (24) may be due to the non-finiteness of the prenominal relative clauses. It is also important to note that unmarked subjects are also systematically excluded from the prenominal relative clauses.

(25) *[मोहन पढ़ी (हुई)] किताब
*[*Mohan* *paṛhī* (*huī*)] *kitāb*
Mohan read.PFV.F (be.PFV.F) book.F.SG
'A/the book read by Mohan'

(26) *[राधा मोहन को लिखी (हुई)] किताब
*[*Rādhā* *Mohan-ko* *likhī* (*huī*)] *kitab*
Radha Mohan-DAT write.PFV.F be.PFV.F book.F.SG
'A/the book written to Mohan by Radha'

The ungrammaticality of (25) and (26) is perhaps not surprising since the prenominal relative clauses in Hindi are non-finite, and lack the finite T that could case license the subject. Thus, the subjects of the relative clauses *Mohan* and *Radha*, in (25) and (26) respectively, are not case licensed. In particular, they cannot receive a nominative case since a finite T is absent. Given that (23) and (24) are also ungrammatical, it may be possible to argue that ergative case licensing also requires finiteness. However, I do not develop that argument here.

The important generalization seems to be that subjects and objects can be relativized in prenominal perfective relatives in Hindi. Furthermore, when an object is relativized, the subject cannot be unmarked – it must either have a genitive case postposition or an agentive postposition. The crucial observation in Mahajan (2017) is that the direct object, if present because the verb is transitive, *must* be relativized. It cannot appear inside the perfective prenominal relative clause. (27)–(28) below involve attempted subject relativization with an overt direct object inside the relative clause. They are ungrammatical.

(27) *[किताब पढ़ा हुआ] लड़का
*[*kitāb* *paṛhā* *huā*] *laṛkā*
book.F write.PFV.M.SG (be.PVF.M.SG) boy.M.SG
'A/the boy who has read the book' (*even if agreement on V and AUX is F)

(28) *[अंग्रेज़ी अख़बार खरीदा हुआ] आदमी
*[*aṅgrejī* *axbār* *kharīdā* *huā*] *ādmī*
English newspaper buy.PFV.M.SG be.PFV.M.SG man.M.SG
'A/the man who had bought the English newspaper'

(27)–(28) show that an unmarked direct object cannot be present inside the relative clause while another nominal is relativized in Hindi perfective prenominal relative clauses. We have already seen that unmarked subjects are not possible inside prenominal relative clauses as in (25) and (26). It was suggested earlier that (25)–(26) are ungrammatical because there is no source of nominative case in the non-finite prenominal relative clause. The ungrammaticality of (27) and (28) can now similarly be attributed to the unavailability of any additional structural case inside the prenominal relative clause. In particular, the ungrammaticality of (27) to (28) tells us that perfective prenominal relative clauses are unable to license any non-PP arguments inside them. This would imply that a structural case licensing little v is absent in these clauses.[6]

The fact that a direct object, if present within a perfective prenominal relative clause, must be externalized (i.e., must be the head that appears outside the relative clause) indicates that the heads of prenominal relative clauses are externally case marked. Thus, the relativized DPs in (27)–(28) must appear in a structural case position in a clause as in (29) (in a subject position) and in (30) (as an object of a preposition). The oblique ending of the plural head in (30) is due to the postposition *-se*, supporting the idea that these heads are externally case marked.

(29) [मोहन की पढ़ी हुई] किताब खो गयी।
[*Mohan-kī* *paṛhī* *huī*] *kitāb* *kho* *gayī.*
Mohan-GEN.F read.PFV.F be.PVF.F book.F.SG lose go.PFV.F.SG
'A/the book written by Mohan was lost.'

6 I am assuming here, following Chomsky (1995) and Kratzer (1996), that the verb phrase structure includes an outer shell introduced by a little v, a head that is an accusative case assigner and it also introduces the external argument in its specifier position. See also, Mahajan (2012) for an argument for a particular implementation of this idea in the context of ergative case assignment in Hindi.

(30) राधा को [मोहन की लिखी हुई] किताबों से डर लगता है।
Rādhā-ko [*Mohan-kī likhī huī*] *kitābõ-se*
Radha-DAT Mohan-GEN.F write.PFV.F be.PVF.F books.OBL.F.PL-from
ḍar lagtā hɛ.
fear.M.SG feel.IMPFV.M.SG AUX.PRS.SG
'Radha is afraid of the books written by Mohan.'

Further support for the proposal that the heads of the prenominal relative clauses are externally case marked comes from the relativization possibilities of phrases like locatives, manner phrases and instrumental phrases (and other oblique phrases) which must be case licensed by their own postpositions. The prediction is that such nominals cannot be relativized using the perfective prenominal relative clause construction. This prediction is borne out as exemplified by the ungrammaticality of (31b), (32b) and (33b) below.[7]

(31a) मोहन कुएँ में डूब गया।
Mohan kuẽ mẽ ḍūb gayā.
Mohan well.M.OBL in drown go.PFV.M.SG
'Mohan drowned in the well.'

(31b) *[मोहन का डूबा हुआ] कुआँ/ कुएँ (में)
*[*Mohan-kā ḍūbā huā*] *kuā̃/ kuẽ* (*mɛ̃*)
Mohan-GEN drown.PFV.M.SG be.PFV.M.SG well/well.OBL.M.SG in
'=The well in which drowned.'

(32a) वो कार से गया।
vo kār-se gayā.
he car-with go.PFV.M.SG
'=He went with a car.' (He used a car to go.)

(32b) *[उसकी गयी हुई] कार
*[*uskī gayī huī*] *kār*
he-GEN.F go.PFV.F be.PFV.F car.F.SG
'=the car in which he went'

(33a) चोर ने लड़के को चाकू से मारा।
čor-ne laṛke-ko čākū-se mārā.
thief-ERG boy-DOM knife-with kill.PFV.M.SG
'The thief killed the boy with a knife.'

7 The morpheme *-ko* is glossed as DOM (Differential Object Marking) in (33). Whether the nominal that has this marking bears an accusative case or not is a debatable issue and is not directly relevant here. For some discussion, see Mahajan (2013).

(33b) *[चोर का लड़के को मारा हुआ] चाकू
*[*čor-kā* *laṛke-ko* *mārā* *huā*] *čākū*
thief-GEN boy-DOM kill.PFV.M.SG be.PFV.M.SG knife.M.SG
'The knife with which the thief killed the boy'

The proposal that the head in a Hindi prenominal relative clause must be externally case marked now helps us make sense of the restriction that in perfective prenominal relative clauses in Hindi, only subjects and direct objects can be relativized since they are the only type of arguments that can be structurally case licensed by clause internal spinal heads like T and v. The inability of a direct object to survive inside a perfective prenominal relative clause must therefore follow from the lack of a case licensing head inside these clauses. Given that a finite T is clearly absent in Hindi prenominal relative clauses, the only other plausible source for the structural case would have been an accusative assigning little v. On the basis of the evidence that we have seen so far, I suggest that this case assigning little v is absent in these perfective prenominal clauses. Furthermore, if the Hindi ergative case is inherently assigned by this same little v (as proposed in Mahajan, 2012), then the impossibility of licensing an ergative inside the perfective prenominal relatives in Hindi is also accounted for. This now provides us with an account for the ungrammaticality of (23), repeated below as (34). The perfective prenominal relative clause in (34) must not have the DO inside it because there is no ACC case licensing little v inside it, and at the same time the absence of this little v accounts for the absence of the inherent ergative case.

(34) *[मोहन ने लिखी हुई] किताब
*[*Mohan-ne* *likhī* *huī*] *kitāb*
Mohan-ERG write.PFV.F be.PFV.F book.F.SG
'A/the book written by Mohan'

To complete this line of argumentation, the big difference between a prenominal relative clause in (35) and a normal finite transitive clause like (36) is the absence/presence of finite T. The fact that the object is licensed in (36) and not in (35) must then be due to this finite T. Therefore, if the finite T licensed NOM, then the object in (36) must have NOM since we have already eliminated the possibility of the availability of an (ACC) licensing little v head.

(35) *[किताब पढ़ा हुआ] लड़का
*[*kitāb* *paṛhā* *huā*] *laṛkā*
book.F.SG read.PFV.M.SG be.PFV.M.SG boy.M.SG
'A/the boy who has read the book' (* even if agreement on V and AUX is F)

(36) लड़के ने किताब पढ़ी थी (*हुई)।
*laṛke-ne kitāb paṛhī thī/ (*huī)*
boy-ERG book.F.SG read.PFV.F AUX.PST.F.SG/ (be.PFV.F.SG)
'The boy had read the book.'

A by-product of this discussion is that it helps us make sense of why only certain kinds of grammatical function positions are accessible for relativization in the context of the typology of relativization as discussed in Keenan and Comrie (1977). Only subjects and (non-postpositional) direct objects are accessible for relativization in Hindi perfective prenominal relative clauses because firstly, only those two need structural case licensing, and secondly, structural case is not available in Hindi perfective prenominal relative clauses, and lastly, the relative clause head in Hindi perfective prenominal relatives is externally case marked. The fact that the indirect object and PPs in Hindi cannot be relativized in perfective prenominal relatives follows since they all receive a case from a postposition inside the relative clause.

Further evidence that prenominal relative clauses in Hindi involve case driven A-movement of the relative head comes from comparing perfective prenominal relative clauses with imperfective relative clauses. The latter differ from the former in interesting but completely predictable ways if the case licensing based A-movement analysis of Mahajan (2017) is right. For the purposes of the discussion that follows, our treatment of perfective prenominal relatives provides us with a good starting point.

3 The structure of the pre-nominal relative clauses

I start with an assumption about the structure of relative clauses as in Cinque (2010). Cinque's proposal is outlined in the tree below. The relative clause is a prenominal modifier in this structure and the external head dPext is pronounced while the internal head ~~dPint~~ is not pronounced.[8]

8 I am skirting the question of whether or not the internal head moves prior to deletion for now.

(37)

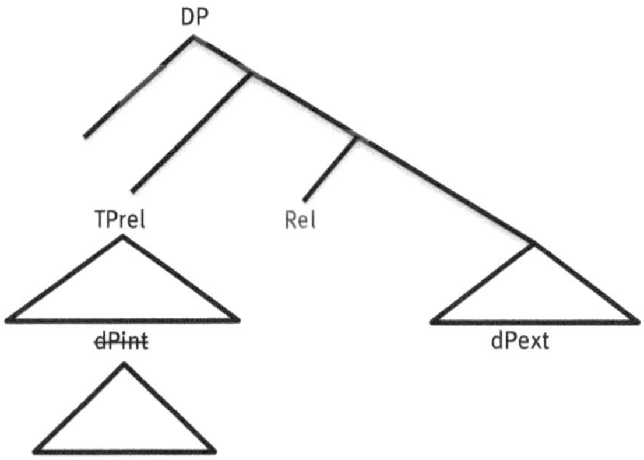

Fig. 1: Structure of pre-nominal relatives

An implementation of Cinque's proposal about matching analysis of externally headed (prenominal) relative clauses would be to delete the internal head in its base position. In fact, given that this internal head is not Case licensed in perfective prenominal relatives (as I suggested), it must delete. The external head is the head of the extended nominal projection, and this is the Case position (case being assigned by a head outside the relativized DP).

I now discuss data that is consistent with the proposal that the visible external head of the relative clause in (37) is base generated in its external position and thus Hindi perfective prenominal relative clauses must have a head 'matching' analysis as implemented in (37). The evidence comes from the lack of reconstruction effects.

3.1 Reciprocals do not reconstruct for binding

(38) and (39) below show that the reciprocals contained inside the external head cannot be bound by a relative clause internal DP. Thus, the subject DP fails to antecede the reciprocal in (38) and the indirect object DP fails to antecede the reciprocal in (39).

(38) *[उनकी पढ़ी हुई] एक दूसरे की किताबें खो गयी।
*[*unkī*$_i$ *paṛhī* *huī*] *ek* *dūsre-kī*$_i$ *kitābẽ kho gayī̃.*
they-GEN read.PFV.F be.PFV.F one other-GEN books lose go.PFV.F.PL
= 'Each other's books that they read were lost.'

(39) *[मोहन की उनको दिखायी हुई] एक दूसरे की किताबें खो गयीं।
*[*Mohan-kī*$_i$ *unko* *dikhāyī huī*] *ek* *dūsre-kī*$_i$ *kitābẽ*
Mohan-GEN they-DAT shown be.PFV.F one other-GEN book.F.PL
kho gayī̃.
lose go.PFV.F.PL
= 'Each other's books that Mohan gave them were lost.'

(40) and (41) below show that the genitive subjects and *-ko* indirect objects are otherwise legitimate binders for reciprocals inside direct objects in non-relative clauses.

(40) [उनका एक दूसरे का होमवर्क करना] ठीक नहीं है।
[*unkā*$_i$ *ek* *dūsre-kā*$_i$ *homwark* *karnā*] *ṭhīk* *nahī̃ hɛ.*
them-GEN one other-GEN.M.SG homework do.INF proper not be.PRS.SG
= 'Their doing each other's homework was not proper.'

(41) [मोहन का उनको एक दूसरे का होमवर्क दिखाना] ठीक नहीं है।
[*Mohan-kā un-ko*$_i$ *ek* *dūsre-kā*$_i$ *homwark* *dikhānā*] *ṭhīk*
Mohan-GEN they-DAT one other-GEN homework show.INF proper
nahī̃ hɛ.
not be.PRS.SG
= 'Mohan's showing them each other's homework was not proper.'

Furthermore, there is nothing inherently wrong with a reciprocal inside a relative head. Thus, as long as there is an external binder available, reciprocals inside relative heads are fine.

(42) उन्होंने [मोहन की पढ़ी हुई] एक दूसरे की किताबें फाड़ दीं।
unhõne$_i$ [*Mohan-kī* *paṛhī* *huī*] *ek dūsre* *kī*$_i$
they-ERG Mohan-GEN read.PFV.F be.PFV.F eachother GEN.F
kitābẽ *phāṛ dī̃.*
book.F.PL tear gave.PFV.F.PL
= 'They tore up each other's books that Mohan had read.'

(43) उन्होंने [मोहन की राधा को दिखायी हुई] एक दूसरे की किताबें फाड़ दीं।
unhõne$_i$ *[Mohan-kī Rādhā-ko dihkhāyī hui] ek dūsre-kī*$_i$
they-ERG Mohan-GEN Radha-DAT show.PFV.F be.PFV.F each other-GEN
kitābẽ phāṛ dī.
book.F.PL tear gave.PFV.F.PL
= 'They tore up each other's books that Mohan had shown to Radha.'

3.2 Reflexives do not reconstruct for binding

The facts here are parallel to those of reciprocals except for the fact that for many speakers of Hindi, reflexives can only be anteceded by subjects. In (44) and (45) below, the reflexive fails to be bound by the genitive subjects inside the relative clauses indicating that the head of the relative clause containing the reflexives could not have originated inside the relative clauses.

(44) *[उनकी पढ़ी हुई] अपनी किताबें खो गयी।
*[*unkī*$_i$ *paṛhī huī] apnī*$_i$ *kitābẽ kho gayī.*
them-GEN.F read.PFV.F be.PFV.F self's book.F.PL lose go.PFV.F.PL
= 'Self's books that they read were lost.'
(45) *[मोहन की उनको दिखायी हुई] अपनी किताबें खो गयीं।
*[*Mohan-kī*$_i$ *unko dikhāyī huī] apnī*$_i$ *kitābẽ kho gayī.*
Mohan-GEN they-DAT show.PFV.F be.PFV.F self's book.F.PL lose go.PFV.F.PL
= 'Self's books that Mohan showed to them were lost.'

Once again, the genitive subjects in Hindi can easily bind reflexives otherwise as shown in (46) and (47). Therefore it is not the genitive nature of the subjects in (44) and (45) that induces the ungrammaticality.

(46) [उनका अपना होमवर्क समय पर करना] अच्छी बात है।
[unkā$_i$ *apnā*$_i$ *homwark samay-par karnā] aččhī bāt hɛ.*
they-GEN self's homework time-on do.INF good thing AUX.PRS.SG
= 'Their doing self's homework on time is a good thing.'
(47) [मोहन का उनको अपनी तस्वीरें दिखाना] ठीक नहीं है।
[Mohan-kā$_i$ *unko apnī*$_i$ *tasvīrẽ dikhānā] ṭhīk nahī̃ hɛ.*
Mohan-GEN they-DAT self's picture.F.PL show.INF proper not AUX.PRS.SG
= 'Mohan's showing them self's pictures is not proper.'

Furthermore, there is nothing wrong with a reflexive inside a relative head, as long as there is a higher external binder available. Thus, in (48) and (49) below, the reflexive *apnī* is bound by the matrix subjects, and the resulting sentences are grammatical.

(48) सीता ने [मोहन की पढ़ी हुई] अपनी किताबें वापस ले लीं।
*Sītā-ne*ᵢ *[Mohan-kī paṛhī huī] apnī*ᵢ *kitābẽ*
Sītā-ERG Mohan-GEN read.PFV.F be.PFV.F self's book.F.PL
vāpas le lī̃.
back take take.PFV.F.PL
= 'Sita took back self's books that Mohan had read.'

(49) गीता ने [मोहन की सीता को दिखायी हुई] अपनी किताबें वापस ले लीं।
*Gītā-ne*ᵢ *[Mohan-kī Sītā-ko dikhāyī huī] apnī*ᵢ *kitābẽ*
Gītā-ERG Mohan-GEN Sita-DAT show.PFV.F be.PFV.F self's book.F.PL
vāpas le lī̃.
back take take.PFV.F.PL
= 'Gita took back self's books that Mohan had shown to Sita.'

3.3 Pronominal binding and reconstruction

The facts of pronominal binding parallel those we have observed in the previous two sub-sections. Thus, as shown in (50) below, a pronoun contained within the head of the relative clause cannot be bound by a quantifier contained inside the relative clause.

(50) *[मोहन की हरेक बच्चे को दिखायी हुई] उसकी किताब खो गयी।
*[*Mohan-kī harek bačče-ko*ᵢ *dilkhāyī huī] uskī*ᵢ
Mohan-GEN each one child-DAT show.PFV.F be.PFV.F he-GEN
kitābẽ kho gayī̃.
book.F.PL lose go.PFV.F.PL
= 'Hisᵢ books that Mohan gave to each childᵢ were lost.'

(50) is an example of a direct object relativization. The direct object relative head contains a pronoun that we are attempting to bind by a quantificational indirect object inside the relative clause. However, the sentence is ungrammatical in its intended meaning as provided in the translation. This suggests that the direct object could not have moved from within the relative clause from a position lower than that of the indirect object.

Whether or not the pronoun can co-refer with the genitive subject is not clear to me at this time. The relevant judgment would obviously be useful because of the subject obviation property of Hindi pronouns.[9]

That indirect object QPs in Hindi can bind a pronoun inside direct objects in other contexts is shown in (51):

(51) [मोहन का हरेक बच्चे को उसकी तस्वीर दिखाना] ठीक नहीं है।
[Mohan-kā harek bačče-ko$_i$ uskī$_i$ tasvīr dikhānā]
Mohan-GEN eachone child-DAT he-GEN.F picture.F show.INF
ṭhīk nahĩ hɛ.
proper not be.PRS.SG
= 'Mohan's showing each child$_i$ his$_i$ picture was not proper.'

Furthermore, as has been the case in the previous two sets of data concerning binding, there is nothing wrong with a bound pronoun inside a relative head, as long as there is an external binder available outside the relative clause.

(52) सीता ने हरेक बच्चे को [मोहन की साइन की हुई] उसकी किताबें लौटा दीं।
Sītā-ne harek bačče-ko$_i$ [Mohan-kī sāin kī huī]
Sita-ERG each child-DAT Mohan-GEN.F autograph do.PFV.F be.PFV.F
uskī$_i$ kitābẽ lɔṭā dĩ.
he-GEN.F book.F.PL return give.PFV.F.PL
'Sita returned to each child$_i$ his$_i$ books autographed by Mohan.'

---

9 A further argument against reconstruction of the external head can be developed to test whether or not the head reconstructs in examples such as (i).
(i) [मोहन की$_i$ बच्चों को दिखायी हुई] उसकी$_i$ किताबें खो गयीं।
[Mohan-kī$_i$ baččõ-ko dikhāyī huī] us-kī$_i$ kitābẽ kho gayĩ
Mohan.gen children.dat show.PFV aux.PFV.F he.GEN books lose go.PFV.F.PL
= 'His books that Mohan gave to the children were lost.'
Hindi pronouns display an anti-subject orientation. Thus the following is ungrammatical.
(ii) *[मोहन का उसकी तस्वीर फाड़ना] ठीक नहीं है।
**[Mohan-kā$_i$ us-kī$_i$ tasvīr phāṛnā] ṭhīk nahĩ hɛ*
*Mohan.GEN he-GEN picture tear.INF proper not be.PRS
= 'Mohan's tearing his picture was not proper.'
Unfortunately, the judgment in (i) is not clear and needs further testing. If (i) is substantially better than (ii), that would imply that the head of the relative clause is not base generated inside the relative clause and we would then have an additional test available to support the idea being put forward here.

To conclude this section, the anti-reconstruction evidence that we have seen in this section indicates that a matching analysis of Hindi perfective prenominal relative clauses is plausible.

4 Reconstruction of idiom chunks

In this section, I present data that conflicts with the anti-reconstruction data presented in the previous section, thus setting up a paradox. The evidence here concerns splitting idiom chunks. The following sentences from Schachter (1973) are often cited to support a head movement analysis of English relative clauses:

(53) The careful track that she's keeping of her expenses pleases me.
(54) I was offended by the lip service that was paid to civil liberties at the trial.

If the Hindi relative clauses that we have been discussing have a 'matching' derivation as opposed to a 'raising' derivation, we would expect that the matching derivation would exclude the possibility of splitting idioms with a part of the idiom inside the relative clause and another part inside the relative head. However, as (55)–(59) below show, idioms can indeed be split in prenominal relative clauses following a pattern more like we would expect in head raising relative clauses.

(55) [मेरे कंधों पर पड़ा हुआ] बोझ मुझे मार देगा।
mere kandhõ par paṛā huā bojh
I-GEN.OBL shoulder.OBL.M.PL on place.PFV.M.SG be.PFV.M.SG burden.M.SG
mujhe mār degā.
I-ACC kill give.FUT.M.SG
= 'The responsibilities placed on me will kill me.'

(56) [मोहन की फूटी हुई] किस्मत
[Mohan-kī phūṭī huī] kismat
Mohan-GEN break.PFV.F be.PFV.F fate/luck.F
= 'Mohan's misfortune/bad luck'

(57) [कटी हुई] नाक लेकर कहाँ जाओगे।
[kaṭī huī] nāk lekar kahā̃ jāoge.
cut.PFV.F be.PFV.F nose.F.SG take.ABS where go.FUT
= 'Where will you go with a bad reputation?'

(58) [मेरी राह में बिछाये हुए] काँटे तुम्हें भारी पड़ेंगे।
[merī rāh-mẽ bičhāe hue] kā̃ṭe tumhẽ bhārī paṛẽge.
I-GEN path-in spread.PFV.PL be.PFV thorn.M.PL you-DAT heavy fall.FUT.PL
= 'You will be sorry for making things difficult for me.'

(59) [कलेजे पर मारा हुआ] तीर
[kaleje-par mārā huā] tīr
liver-on hit.PFV be.PFV arrow.M
lit. the arrow shot through the liver; = the grievous hurt (that you caused me)

Given Schachter's idiom chunk argument, this Hindi data then suggests a raising analysis of the prenominal relative clauses.

5 Resolving the paradox

The anti-reconstruction data that we saw in section 3 supports a matching analysis for the perfective prenominal relative clauses while the idiom chunk data we saw in section 4 support a raising derivation for the same type of relatives. One possibility is that both types of derivations are in principle available for Hindi prenominal relative clauses. However, this way of thinking gives no ready answer for why an unbound anaphor does not trigger a raising derivation as well.

In section 2, I suggested that the syntax of prenominal relative clauses involves a crucial structural property – that of the unavailability of structural case inside the prenominal relative clause. I would now like to use that analysis and suggest that the apparent paradox presented by the data in section 3 and 4 can be solved by adopting an A-movement head movement analysis of prenominal relative clauses hinted at in section 2. This analysis can be implemented using Cinque's universal template for relative clauses with the following derivation in (60).[10]

The derivation in (60) involves movement of the relative clause internal head dP_{int} (dP indicates that the relative head itself is a phrasal projection) to a relative clause external position. I suggest that this position is the SPEC DP position as shown in the tree (60). Since I am employing Cinque's template here, the base generated external head must be silent and that is indicated by striking out the external head as ~~dP_{ext}~~ head. The head that is actually pronounced is the moved dPin that has moved from within the relative clause thus making this a raising

10 Other implementations of this idea are also possible, but I do not pursue them here.

derivation. The surface order in which the head follows the relative clause must then be achieved by leftward TP movement across the raised head (Kayne, 1994) that presumably adjoins the TP to the DP. This will place the head of the relative clause in the phase edge position of the DP where it can receive structural case from an external case assigning head.[11]

(60)

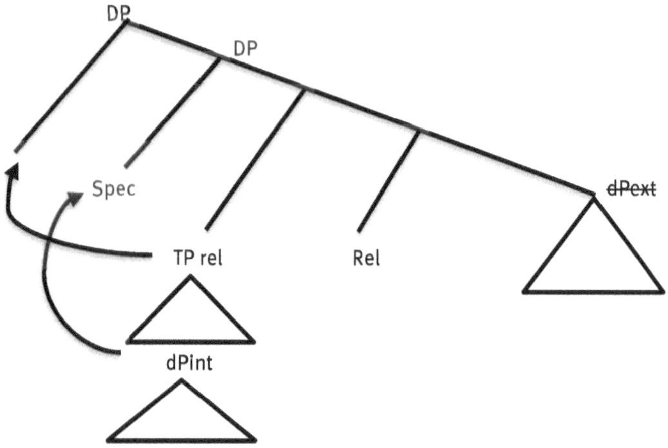

Fig. 2: Derivation of pre-nominal relative clauses

The movement of the head of the relative clause therefore ends up in a case position and therein lies our solution for the lack of the reconstruction effects of the sort that we observed in section 3. It is well known that certain kinds of A-movements do not reconstruct for binding (Mahajan, 1990; Tada, 1993; Wurmbrand, 2010). The following sentence illustrates this with the middle-field scrambling in German that arguably involves A-movement.

11 I am assuming here that a traditional view of phrase structure rather than a strict implementation of Kayne's (1994) view that specifiers are adjoined. Thus, (60) is a configuration where the DP projection has both a specifier and a TP adjoined to it. An alternative would be to treat both the moved relative head and the fronted TP be multiple Specs. That would also yield the result that we need. Neither of these options is available in Kayne (1994).

(61) *weil sie [ein Bild von $seinem_i$ Auftritt] [jedem $Kandidaten]_i$
since she a_{ACC} picture of his appearance every candidate
t_{ACC} zeigte
t_{ACC} showed
'Since she showed a picture of his appearance to every candidate' (Lechner, 1998)

(61) involves scrambling of the direct object above the indirect object in German, a movement that is arguably A-movement. The failure of pronominal binding indicates unavailability of reconstruction of the direct object, a fact that parallels the facts we observed in section 3. The Hindi relative clause data is perhaps more striking given that there is clearly a case motivation for relative clause head movement, and case driven movement is usually a good indicator of A-movement. The derivation suggested here, along with the case seeking nature of relative head movement in Hindi prenominal relatives, now provides us with a resolution to our paradox. Anti-reconstruction binding effects follow because the head does not reconstruct for binding purposes after A-movement and the idiom chunk data follows because idioms can standardly be split by A-movement, i.e., split idioms are diagnostics for movement and not for the type of movement.

6 Summary

In the data and the analysis that I have presented in this paper, I have suggested a framework that can account for restrictions on relativization in prenominal relative clauses in Hindi. That framework crucially relies on case licensing of argument nominals. If the analysis presented here is on the right track then it provides evidence for the concept of case licensing of argument nominals. I have furthermore presented data that presents a derivational paradox concerning the syntax of pre-nominal relative clauses in Hindi. I suggest that this paradox can be resolved if we assume that the externalization of the head in Hindi prenominal relative clauses is an A-movement process and that the head of the relative clause does not fully reconstruct to its base position. Thus while the "accessibility" restrictions (what grammatical functions can be relativized) can now be understood as a function of case properties of the reduced relative clauses, the non-reconstruction properties of the moved head of the relative clause can also be related to the case driven movement of the relative head.

References

Chomsky, N. 1995. *The minimalist program*. Cambridge, Mass.: MIT Press.
Hook, P. and O. Koul. ms. The noun phrase accessibility hierarchy and participial noun modifying constructions in Hindi-Urdu and Kashmiri.
Kayne, Richard S. 1994. *The Antisymmetry of Syntax. Linguistic Inquiry Monograph Twenty-Five.* Cambridge, Massachusetts: MIT Press.
Keenan, E. 1985. Relative Clause. In Timothy Shopen ed. *Language Typology and Syntactic Description, Vol. II: Complex Constructions*. Cambridge: Cambridge University Press, 141–170.
Keenan, E. and Comrie, B. 1977. Noun Phrase Accessibility and Universal Grammar. *Linguistic Inquiry* 8.1, 63–99.
Kratzer, A. 1996. Severing the external argument from its verb. In J. Rooryck and L. Zaring (ed.), *Phrase structure and the lexicon*. Dordrecht, The Netherlands: Kluwer Academic Publishers. 109–170.
Mahajan, A. 2012. Ergatives, antipassives and the overt light v in Hindi. *Lingua* 122, 204–214.
Mahajan, A. 2013. Argument Licensing and the Derivation of Prenominal Relative Clauses in Hindi. Paper presented at *FASAL III*, USC, March, 2013.
Mahajan, A. 2017. Accusative and Ergative in Hindi. In Coon, J., D. Massam, D. and L. Travis (Eds.), *The Oxford Handbook of Ergativity*. Oxford: Oxford University Press, pp. 86–108.
Schachter, P. 1973. 'Focus and Relativization', *Language 49* (1), 19–46.
Subbarao, K.V. 2012. *South Asian Languages, A Syntactic Typology*. Cambridge: Cambridge University Press.

Boris Zakharyin

Constraints on attributive functions of Hindi perfect participles manifesting the resultant state

Abstract: The paper deals with certain special cases of attributive usage of Hindi Perfect participles (PP hereafter). The research is provided mainly for contexts 'NP^1–PP–NP^2' wherein the participial relativizer syntactically modifies NP^2 serving as 'head' and shows agreement with the latter in gender, number and case. It is shown that, contrary to Hindi, participial relativizers in Telugu (representing Dravidian in general) imply no restrictions on attributive functions of the participles conditioned by transitivity, voice oppositions or agreement regularities. The analysis undertaken demonstrates that the explanation suggested for modifying potentialities of Hindi PPs is not to be based on syntax alone but sought in the spheres of semantics and pragmatics as resultant PPs must signify such changes in referents of NP^2 which are clearly noticeable by either the participants of the situation or by the performers of the speech-act.

Keywords: Hindi, derivation, participial relativizers, agreement

There is a number of participial formations in Hindi, and perfect participles (PPs) constitute one of the main types of them. Morphologically Hindi PPs are generated in the following way: 'root or stem (*V-*) + suffixes *-Ø-/-y-* + inflexions *-ā/e/ī*'. Thus produced the participle-proper may also imply a certain optional element *hu-Ø-ā/e/ī* (which formally is the PP produced from the stem of auxiliary *ho-* 'to be'). The morphemic structure of PPs -proper in Hindi is, thus, very much similar to that one of perfect participles which were in use in Ancient Indo-Aryan (AIA) and which were generated according to formula: 'V + suffix *-(i)ta-/-na-* + case/number inflections'. The process of derivation of PPs in AIA differed considerably from that implied by all other types of participles, as AIA PPs in *-(i)ta-/-na-* were produced straight from the roots while other participles were generated from the so called "tense-bound stems". The similarity existing between Hindi and AIA PPs concerns not only form alone but is also evident on a functional level as, like in Hindi, in Vedic (the most archaic variant of AIA) PPs might already be

Boris Zakharyin, Moscow State University, Moscow, Russia. Email: khokhl@iaas.msu.ru

https://doi.org/10.1515/9783110610796-005

used instead of finite verbal forms - either by themselves or in combinations with different auxiliaries, see, e.g., (1) and (2):

(1) ततं मे अपस तद् तायते पुनः।
ta-tá-ṃ *me* *ápas*
do-PP-N.NOM.SG 1.DAT/GEN.SG work-N.NOM.SG
tád *u* *tā-ya-te* *púnaḥ*
that PRVB weave-PASS-3.SG again
'My work [is] done (lit. 'woven'), it is to be woven again.' (RV I.110,1)

(2) धूमस् अभवद् दिवि श्रितः
dhūmá-s ... *a-bhava-d* *div-í* *śr-itá-ḥ*
smoke.M-NOM.SG PAST-AUX-3SG sky-LOC.SG raise-PP- M.NOM.SG

When in Middle Indo-Aryan (MIA) the finite tense-forms of Perfect, Imperfect and Aorist had actually ceased to exist, PPs with suffixes -(*i*)ta-/-*na*- came into use in their place. Later on, in New Indo-Aryan (NIA), perfect participles-proper started functioning as finite forms of the Preterit, and for adjectival and adverbial usage the new, secondary, PPs were elaborated – namely, those combining forms of the 'original' participles with the mentioned optional element *hu-Ø-ā*/e/*ī*. Both the components of secondary PPs in Modern Hindi usually demonstrate the identity of their final (agreement showing) affixes – e.g., *ā-y-ī* (*hu-Ø-ī*) *laṛk-ī* 'the girl who came' ↔ *ā-y-ā* (*hu-Ø-ā*) *laṛk-ā* 'the boy who came'. But there may also be instances of dissimilarity: the ending of the original participle-proper is then the 'fixed' -*e*, and the final inflections of the optional element vary in accordance with the grammatical characteristics of the 'head' NP - e.g., *skarṭ pahan-Ø-e hu-Ø-ā laṛk-ā* 'the boy who has put on skirt'.

Syntactically any PP – transitive or intransitive - may be used attributively. In such cases it functions as a relativizer that modifies the following NP, its 'head', and, correspondingly, through adjectival-like inflections agrees with the 'head' NP in gender, number and case. The intransitive perfect PPs imply orientation towards the agent, while their transitive counterparts are generally oriented towards the patient – see, e.g., examples (3) and (4):

(3) घर से निकली हुई औरत
ghar-ø *se* *nikal-ø-ī* *(hu-ø-ī)*
house.M.NOM.SG from go out-PP-F.NOM.SG be-PP- F.NOM.SG
ɔrat-ø
woman-F.NOM.SG
'The woman who has come out of the house'

(4) हनुमान को दी हुई ध्वजा
hanumān-ø ko d-ø-ī
Hanuman-M.NOM.SG to give-PP-F.NOM.SG
(hu-ø-ī) dhvaj-ā
be-PP-F.NOM.SG flag-F.NOM.SG
'The flag given to Hanuman'

The grammar of Hindi implies certain lexical restrictions on intransitive verbal stems that generate adjectively functioning PPs. In general we might agree with Subbarao's statement that perfective intransitive PPs in Hindi-Urdu *selectively* permit 'almost unlimited modifying usage'. Subbarao also mentions two "exceptions" represented by verbs *kūd-* 'jump' and *tɛr-* 'swim'; the PPs produced from these stems cannot be used as modifiers. Thus, e.g., Hindi sample (5) is ungrammatical while its Telugu equivalent (6) is acceptable:

(5) *दीवार कूदी हुई लड़की
dīwār-ø kūd-ø-ī (hu-ø-ī) laṛak-ī
wall-M.NOM.SG jump-PP.F.NOM.SG be-PP-F.NOM.SG girl-F.NOM.SG
'The girl who jumped the wall'

(6) *gōḍa-ø gent-ina pilla-ø*
wall-INAN.NOM.SG jump-PP girl-AN.F.NOM.SG
'The girl who jumped the wall'
(Subbarao 2012: 279, 289, 332).

In reality the group of "exceptions" is much greater than the one mentioned by Subbarao. It was Verma who already in 1971 described the stems *hãs-* 'laugh' and *dɔṛ-* 'run' as not allowing the corresponding PPs to function attributively and introduced for them the term 'statals' (Verma 1971: 160). A few years later Kachru extended the list having added to it 'statives' (that was the term she used) *učhal-* 'hop', *jhūl-* 'swing', *khel-* 'play', *phā̃d-* 'jump', *čal-* 'move' (Kachru 1980: 155). Still later Liperovskiy included some other 'statives' into the list – those were the verbs *mũd-* 'become turned down, fall down', *čaṛh-* 'rise, go up', *saj-* 'become dressed up', *mil-* 'be/become united' (Liperovskiy 1984: 69). Thus, utterances like **dɔṛ-θ-ā (hu-θ-ā) laṛk-ā* 'The boy who has run' or *'*hãs-θ-ī (hu-θ-ī) laṛk-ī* 'The girl who has laughed' and the like are not permitted by Hindi grammar. Even nowadays the list of *exceptions* still seems to be incomplete –a few other potential members may be found to add to it.

Subbarao's comment on the status of the "exceptional" participial modifiers described above has been limited to a single remark actually implying no reasonable explanation. According to him, usage of PPs of this type is "highly contextualized" (Subbarao 2012: 331). Meanwhile, the explanation still seems to exist, and it probably is to be looked for not in syntax alone but in the spheres of semantics and pragmatics. All the above listed "exceptional" stems are unaccusative verbs of motion, and the PPs generated on their basis function as resultatives, signifying such changes of position which are **clearly noticeable** by either the participants of the situation in question or by the performers of the speech-act.

Further on our attention will be concentrated on examining the relativizers' functioning in one of the most significant syntactic contexts – that of the type 'NP^1 – *PP* – NP^2'. When used here, intransitive PPs, syntactically modifying the 'head' (NP^2), show agreement in gender/number/case with the latter (and never with NP^1!) – see illustrative examples 7–11:

(7) किनारा टूटी प्याली पर।
kinār-ā *ṭūṭ-ø-ī* *pyāl-ī* *par*
brim-M.NOM.SG be broken-PP-F.NOM/OBL.SG cup-F.NOM/OBL.SG upon
'Upon the small cup with the broken brim.'

(8) काजल लगी आँखें।
kājal-ø *lag-ø-ī* *ā̃kh-ẽ*
eye-paint-M.NOM/OBL.SG/PL applied-PP-F.NOM/OBL.SG eye-F.NOM.PL
'Eyes with eye-paint applied [to them].'

(9) एक कोना मुड़े पन्ने पर।
ek *kon-ā* *muṛ-ø-e* *pann-e* *par*
one corner-M.NOM.SG be curved-PP-M.OBL.SG page-M.OBL.SG on
'On the page with the curved corner.'

(10) पानी पड़ी हुई राख।
pānī-ø *paṛ-ø-ī* *hu-ø-ī*
water-M.NOM.SG fall-PP-F.NOM.SG be-PP-F.NOM.SG
rākh-ø
ashes-F.NOM.SG/PL
'Ashes [upon which] water [has] fallen' - Liperovskiy's sample (Ibid.).

(11) कनौटी कतर डाला कुत्ता।
kanɔtī-ø *katar ḍāl-θ-ā* *kutt-ā*
ear-F.NOM.SG be bitten off-PP-M.NOM.SG dog-M.NOM.SG
'The dog whose ear got cut off.'

For some of the above given constructions the supposed explanation may be based on the 'part-whole' semantic relation existing between NP^1 and NP^2. For example, in samples (7), (11) and probably also in (9) the NPs in question are bound by the relation of inalienable possession. However, it is definitely not so in case of samples (8) and (10), and thus the potential explanation is non-universal, an *ad hoc* one. At the same time it is important that each one of the samples above implies as its underlying structure a sentence with a relative clause and a resultant PP in it that demonstrates agreement with NP^1 - see, e.g., (7a) or (11a):

(7a) ऐसी प्याली पर जिसका किनारा टूटा हुआ है।
[ɛs-ī] *pyāl-ī* *par* *jis* *k-ā*
such-F.OBL.SG cup-F.OBL.SG upon REL.OBL.SG PPS-M.NOM.SG
kinār-ā *ṭūṭ-ø-ā* *hu-θ-ā* *[hɛ]*
brim-M.NOM.SG break-PP-M.NOM.SG be-PP-M.NOM.SG AUX-PRS.3.SG
'Upon [such a] small cup the brim of which [is] broken.'

(11a) ऐसा कुत्ता जिसकी कनौटी कुतर डाली हुई है।
[ɛs-ā] *kutt-ā* *jis* *k-ī*
such-M.NOM.S dog-M.NOM.SG REL.OBL.SG PPS-F.NOM.SG
kanɔṭ-ī *kutar* *ḍāl-θ-ī* *hu-θ-ī* *[hɛ]*
ear-F.NOM.SG bite off-PP.F.NOM.SG be-PP-F.NOM.SG AUX-PRS.3 SG
'[Such a] dog whose ear has been bitten off.'

We may now turn to examining attributive functions of PPs produced from transitive stems which, being used in 'NP^1 – PP – NP^2 context, serve as modifiers of NP^2 (and thus, in traditional terms, have the so called 'passive meaning'). NP^1 in underlying (non-participial) structures may be characterized by different syntactic categories: it may imply the ergative subject – and the corresponding NP of the participial clause is then to be marked by genitive (see sample (12)); it may be associated with direct or indirect object – and in participial clause it is then marked by nominative (see samples (13) and (14)):

(12) राम की पढ़ी किताब
Rām-ø *k-ī* *paṛh-ø-ī* *kitāb-ø*
Ram-M.OBL.SG GEN-F read-PP.F book-F.N.SG
'The book thathas been read by Ram.'

(13) हिंदी सीखा नौकर
hindī-ø *sīkh-ø-ā* *nɔkar-ø*
Hindi-N.SG learn-PP-M.N.SG servant-M.N.SG
'The servant who learned Hindi'

(14) मेंहदी रचे हाथ
mẽhandī-ø *rač-ø-e* *hāth-ø*
henna dye-PP-M.N.PL hand-M.N.PL
'Hands on which the 'mehandi' paste has been put'[Subbarao2012: 331]
'Hands dyed with henna'

A common place in a number of Hindi grammars is that transitive PPs in this language always imply patient-bound orientation and thus cannot modify either ergative or dative subjects of underlying structures. Due to this, (12a) as a variant of (12) is ungrammatical; (12b), according to some language speakers, is permitted, but its meaning considerably differs from the basic (12):

(12a) *राम पढ़ी किताब
Rām-ø *paṛhṛ-ø-ī* *kitāb-ø*
Ram.M.N.SG read.PP.f book.f.N.SG
'Ram read the book.'
(12b) *राम को पढ़ी किताब
Rām-ø *ko* *paṛh-ø-ī* *kitāb-ø*
Ram.M.OBL.SG DAT read-PP.F book-F.N.SG
'[Someone] has read the book for/to Ram'

It seems useful to compare this usage of transitive participial modifiers in Hindi with seemingly analogical situation in Telugu (which may be looked at as representing Dravidian in general). The PP modifier in Telugu does not imply agreement with any NP and, being neither agent- nor patient-orientated, is neutral towards voice distinctions. Thus, exchange of positions between NP^1 and NP^2 does not affect the modifying transitive PP syntactically, though it changes radically the meaning of the corresponding clause:

(15) *Rāmuḍu-ø* *cadiv-ina* *kitābu-lu*
Ram-N.SG read-PP book-N.PL
'Books that Ram has read.'
(15a) *kitābu-lu* *cadiv-ina* *Rāmuḍu-ø*
book-N.PL read-PP Ram-N.SG
'Ram who has read books.'
(16) *Rāmuḍu-ø* *ćamp-ina* *Vasanta-ø*
Ram-N.SG kill-PP Vasanta-N.SG
'Vasanta killed [by] Ram.'

(16a) *Vasanta-ø* *ćamp-ina* *Rāmuḍu-ø*
Vasanta-N.SG kill-PP Ram-N.SG
'Ram killed [by] Vasanta.'

Subbarao's position concerning the oblique objects modification by PPs is rather contradictory: on page 286 of his work dedicated to participial modifiers in Hindi he bans participial modification of this type, but later on (on page 331) he still admits it by saying that "sometimes the modification is permitted" (and he supplies the illustrative sample (17)) and "sometimes not" (the illustrative sample (18) is given by him). He makes no attempt to further distinguish these occurrences or to provide any positive explanation for the phenomena:

(17) राम को लगी चोट
Rām-ø *ko* *lag-ø-ī* *čoṭ-ø*
Ram-M.OBL.SG DAT be attached-PP.F.N.SG injury-F.N.SG
'Injury that Ram got'

(18) *राम को लगी भूख
**Rām-ø* *ko* *lag-ø-ī* *bhūkh-ø*
Ram-M.OBL.SG DAT be attached-PP.F.N.SG hunger-F.N.SG
'Hunger that Ram got'

When describing the attributive functions of transitive PPs in Hindi Subbarao seems to fully agree with traditional grammarians in that PPs in question cannot modify the ergative transitive subjects of underlying clauses (Subbarao 2012: 279, 286). But statements of this kind contradict ordinary speech facts as Hindi (as well as Urdu) abounds in such pairs of sentences with PPs when in one case the modifying function is permitted, but in another it is banned – see, e.g., in addition to (17) ↔ (18) – other contrasting pairs, namely (19) ↔ (20) and (21) ↔ (22):

(19) *लस्सी पिया हुआ आदमी
**lassī-ø* *pi-y-ā* *(hu-ø-ā)* *ādmī-ø*
milkshake-F.N.SG drink-PP.M.N.SG AUX-PP.M.N.SG man-M.N.SG
'The man who drank milkshake'

(20) शराब पिया हुआ आदमी
śarāb-ø *pi-y-ā* *(hu-ø-ā)* *ādmī-ø*
wine-M.N.SG drink-PP.M.N.SG AUX-PP.M.N.SG man-M.N.SG
'The man who drank wine'

(21) *घड़ा रखी अलमारी
*ghaṛ-ā rakh-ø-ī almārī-ø
jug-M.NOM.SG keep-PP.F.NOM.SG cupboard-F.NOM.SG
'Jug kept cupboard'

(22) पाँव धोया पानी
pā̃v-ø dho-y-ā pānī-ø
leg-M.N.PL wash-PP-M.N.SG water-M.N.SG
'Water in which legs have been washed.'

The described usage of intransitive PPs and the above provided analysis of the contrasting pairs of sentences with transitive PPs (like (17 ↔ 18), (19 ↔ 20), etc.) lead us to the only possible explanation for modifying potentialities of Hindi PPs used in NP^1 – *PP* – NP^2 contexts: only in cases when as a result of accomplished action the state of the referent of NP^2 is changed and this change becomes evident either for the participants of the speech act, or for actual or virtual observers that take part in the situation presented, the attributive functioning of any Hindi *PP* (be it intransitive or transitive) is permitted and acquires the corresponding realization inside the sentence.

References

Kachru. Y. 1966. *Studies in a Transformational Grammar of Hindi*. Department of Linguistics, University of Illinois, Urbana, Illinois.

Liperovskiy, V. P. 1984. *Glagol v jazyke hindi* (= Verb in the Hindi language). Moscow: Nauka.

MacDonell, A. A. 1916. *A Vedic Grammar for Students*. [reprint 1993]. Delhi: Motilal Banarsidass.

Subbarao, K. V. 2012. *South Asian Languages. A Syntactic Typology*. New York: Cambridge University Press.

Verma, M. K. 1971. *The Structure of the Noun Phrase in English and Hindi*. Delhi-Patna-Varanasi: Motilal Banarsidass.

Annie Montaut

On the nature of the Hindi infinitive: History as an answer to its syntactic behavior?

Abstract: The Hindi infinitive has been traditionally considered a verbal noun but sometimes also, more recently, a gerund. Its unique feature within Indo-Aryan is due first to its form, since it is exclusively a *-n-* form as opposed to many other languages with several infinitival forms, then to the fact that this form behaves sometimes as a noun, inflecting for case, and sometimes as an adjective, inflecting for gender and number. The first of these peculiarities has been recently claimed by Southworth as a supplementary argument for revisiting the old Grierson hypothesis, according to which Hindi, with Urdu and Panjabi, as the central 'inner' languages, correspond to a first kernel of migrants, whereas Eastern and South Western languages, as 'outer' languages, correspond to a later wave of migration, sharing specific linguistic 'innovations'. One of these innovations is the use of the *-tavya* (> v/b) Sanskrit gerund as future, obligative or infinitive, shared by all Indo-Aryan languages except Hindi/Urdu/Panjabi. The paper is an attempt to counter this assumption and to relate the history of the Hindi infinitive to its agreement peculiarities, which display both nominal and adjectival behavior. The basic synchronic and diachronic facts will first be summarized, before an analysis of the alternate agreement patterns of transitive infinitives in their semantic content. The second half of the paper deals with similar alternations involving the subject of infinitives, with a final section devoted to some typological correlations and conclusions: how a categorial ambivalence (gerund or verbal noun) came to be used more and more for mapping semantic distinctions is a topic for further typological research on linguistic change.

Keywords: Hindi infinitive, gerund, verbal noun, diachrony, agreement

1 Introduction

The infinitive or verbal noun (क्रियावाचक संज्ञा) in standard Hindi is strikingly unique in Indo-Aryan. First, there is only one form (the *-n-* form) as opposed to many

Annie Montaut, SEDYL, Structure et Dynamique des Langues, CNRS/INALCO/IRD, 65 rue des Grands Moulins, Paris, France. Email: annie.montaut@inalco.fr

https://doi.org/10.1515/9783110610796-006

other languages with several infinitival forms (only Gujarati has a single form for the infinitive which is the *-v-* form). Second, this form behaves sometimes as a noun, inflecting for case, and sometimes as an adjective, inflecting for gender and number. These facts have been used by Southworth (2005) as a further evidence for revisiting the old Grierson hypothesis (1903) which was originally suggested by Hoernle (1880). According to that hypothesis, Hindi, along with Panjabi, is deemed to be the central 'inner' languages, corresponding to a first kernel of migrants, whereas Eastern and South Western languages, are 'outer' languages, corresponding to a later wave of migration. The evidence for this later migration consists in the linguistic "innovations" shared exclusively by the so-called outer languages. Among these distinctive innovations, the use of the *-tavya* Sanskrit gerund as future, obligative or infinitive, not taken into account by Hoernle or by Grierson, is considered crucial evidence in Southworth (2005). Gujarati has indeed a *-v-* infinitive, Marathi a *-v-* deontic form, Bengali a *b-* (< *v*) future, whereas Hindi/Urdu/Panjabi have no such forms in any of the above functions. Countering Southworth's assumption, the paper is an attempt to relate the history of the Hindi infinitive to its agreement peculiarities, all the more intriguing since they show a paradoxical behavior: sometimes a noun, sometimes an adjective, to which category does the Hindi infinitive really belong? The study starts with a summary of the basic synchronic and diachronic facts (section 1), and then analyzes the alternate agreement patterns of transitive infinitives in their semantic content (section 2). Section 3 deals with similar alternations when the subject of infinitives acts, or may act, as the controller. The last section presents some typological correlations and conclusions regarding the evolution in the use of the categorial ambivalence of the form (either a gerund or a verbal noun), which is now increasingly used for mapping semantic distinctions.

2 Nature and history of the 'infinitive'

2.1 Basic facts

The modern Hindi infinitive and verb entry in dictionaries is formed of the verbal root +*nā*, where *-ā* exhibits the standard masculine ending of nouns which inflect in the oblique case. As a direct argument, subject or object, it displays the *-nā* ending, and as an oblique the *-ne* ending, a reason why it is often referred to as a verbal noun, although it has no plural.

(1a) वहाँ जाना ज़रूरी होगा।
vahā̃ jānā zarūrī hogā.
there go.M.SG[1] necessary be.FUT.3F.SG
'It will be necessary to go there'

(1b) वह वहाँ जाना नहीं चाहता।
vah vahā̃ jānā nahī̃ čāhtā.
3SG there go.M.SG NEG want.IPFV.PTCP.M.SG
'He does not want to go there.'[2]

(1c) वहाँ जाने में कितना समय लगेगा।
vahā̃ jāne mẽ kitnā samay lagegā?
there go.OBL in how much time take.FUT.3.M.SG[3]
'How long will it take to go there?'

But in certain constructions, for instance in ability sentences or in the deontic mood, the ending varies in gender or number, more like a participle, similar in nature to adjectives. Example (2) shows a feminine agreement of the 'infinitive' with its complement which also controls the main verb agreement:

(2a) मुझे इस तरह की इंजिन चलानी नहीं आती।
mujhe is tarah kī injin čalānī
1SG.DAT this sort of motor.F.SG drive.INF.F.SG
nahī̃ ātī.
NEG come.PRS.F.SG
'I do not know how to make this motor work.'

---

1 The following abbreviations are used in this paper: 1 = first person, 2 = second person, 3 = third person, ABL = ablative, ACC = accusative, AG = agent, CVB = converb, DAT = dative, DEF = definite, DEM = demonstrative, ERG = ergative, F = feminine, FUT = future, GEN = genitive, GER = gerund, INF = infinitive, INS = instrumental, IPFV = imperfective, LOC = locative, M = masculine, N = neuter, NEG = negation, NOM = nominative, OBL = oblique, PFV = perfective, PL = plural, POT = potential, PPFT = pluperfect, PROG = progressive, PRS = present, PRSUMP = presumptive, PST = past, PTCP = participle, REL = relative, SG = singular

2 The auxiliary is often omitted in the present tense when the sentence is negative, and the predicate is a mere imperfective participle. I will further on gloss such forms as present for a more convivial reading.

3 The verb is difficult to gloss, being almost bleached in such expressions, and expressing bare contact, or a mere state, as an independent verb.

(2b) मुझे नए जूते ख़रीदने हैं।
mujhe *nae* *jūte* *kharīdne* *hɛ̃.*
1SG.DAT new shoe.M.PL buy.INF.M.PL be-PRS.PL
'I must buy new shoes.'

As a complement of transitive past verbs requiring the ergative constructions, like *jānnā*, *čāhnā*, the infinitive also agrees with its object as an adjective:

(3a) उसने मेरी जान लेनी चाही।
us.ne *merī* *jān* *lenī* *čāhī.*
3SG.ERG my.F.SG live.F.SG take-INF.F.SG want.PFV.F.SG
'He wanted to take my life (= to kill me).'

(3b) मैंने यह कहानी पढ़नी शुरू की थी।
mɛ̃.ne *yah* *kahānī* *paṛhnī* *śurū* *kī thī.*
1SG.ERG this story.F.SG read.INF.F.SG start do.PPFT.F.SG
'I had started reading this story.'

Significantly, the latter constructions crucially correlate with the marking of the subject, that is to say with non-nominative alignments. In ergative constructions, the non-finiteness of the main verb can be correlated with object agreement, with such paraphrases as 'by X Y done' which are easily traceable in the history of the language as nominal sentences with instrumental agent and patient-agreeing past passive participle. Similarly deontic modality used to be expressed by means of a passive participle, instrumental agent, and agreement with patient, but modern Hindi does not bear traces of this. Furthermore, the infinitive, also a non-finite form of the verb, is not immediately relatable to a passive participle, at least in 'central languages' with a nasal infinitive.

2.2 History of the infinitive in Hindi and related languages

Let us first roughly define the notion 'infinitive' and its various synonyms. A standard 'true' infinitive is usually invariable, like the Sanskrit infinitive ending in *-tu* (surviving only in one of the Marathi infinitives ending in *-u*), or the Latin infinitive ending in *-ere* or *-ire*, which is the origin of Romance infinitives. Such forms can syntactically behave as nouns (filling such positions as subject or object) but do not vary in case and have no gender as such although they can be nominalized (with a masculine article for instance in French or Spanish). Languages such as English make their infinitive with a preposition, which points to the nominal nature of the form. Hence the frequent designation of infinitives as *verbal nouns*,[4] until their current present-day designation as 'gerunds', following the ancient categorization of participle-like forms (Latin -*endus*, French -*ant*).

2.2.1 The nasal infinitive: a verbal adjective?

The -*n*- form is now present in Standard Hindi and in most of its dialects it is the only available form, something that Southworth interprets as a retention whereas all 'outer languages' display a *v/b* gerund which he considers as a shared innovation.

The -*nā* category's highly atypical behavior for an infinitive, since it can vary in gender and number like an adjective, has been the reason why it has long been assumed to derive from a gerundive in -*anya*, in the same way as the -*v*- Gujarati infinitive is derived from the -*tavya* gerund, and not from a nominal suffix.

The Gujarati infinitive in -*vũ* such as કરવું *karvũ* 'to do' indeed comes from the Sanskrit obligative verbal adjective (or gerund) *kartayam*, 'which has to be done' (Chatterji 1926, Cardona & Suthar 2003) and inflects like an adjective as did the Sanskrit form (cf. infra) when used in modal constructions: (4a) with a transitive infinitive it agrees with the feminine object, (4b) with an intransitive infinitive it remains in the neuter.[5]

(4a) *mar.e čɔpḍī vanč.v.i če, lekh*
1SG.AG book.F.SG read.V.F.SG be.PRS.3 article.M.SG
lakh.v.o če.
write.V.M.SG be-PRS.3SG
'I want to read a book, to write an article.'

(4b) *tam ne kyā ja.v.u če.*
2.DAT where go.V.N.SG be-PRS.3
'Where do you want to go?' (Cardona & Suthar 2003)

The classical assumption for modern nasal infinitives (Beames: 236, Hoernle: 153, followed by Haspelmath 1987) was that they were derived from an alternate form

4 Butt (1993) gives strong arguments to consider infinitival clauses as verbal nouns.

5 The deontic modality requires an enlarged form of the infinitive, suffixed with -an- and same agreement pattern:

mare caupdī vanc.van.ī che
'I had to read a book'
mare lekh lakh.vano che
'I had to write an article'.

of the Sanskrit obligative passive participle *-anya* until a convincing counter-derivation was proposed by Tagare (1948: 321), Bloch (1960: 280), Schwarzschild (1955), namely from the suffix *-ana* used to derive nouns of action. Apabhramsha indeed never used the *-any/aṇya* form for the infinitive (Bubenik 1998: 190).

Further evidence against the derivation from *-anya*: Where it survived, this -*anya/aṇya* form maintained its modal meaning as in Garhwali, it also maintains its syntax (agreement with patient and oblique agent in (5c)):

(5a) मैं नी करण्य।
mɛ̃ nī karṇya.
1SG NEG do-*ṇīya*
'I shall not do.' (Chatak 1980: 132)

(5b) करण्या काम।
karṇyā kām.
do-*ṇīya*.M.SG work.M.SG
'Work to be done.'

(5c) हमारी बात कैन जाणनी।
hamārī bāt kɛna jāṇnī.
our talk.F.SG who.OBL know-*ṇya*-F.SG
'Wo could know our talk.'[22] (Chatak 1980: 132)

Forms derived from the *-tavya* gerund are also (weakly) retained in Garhwali (*tavya > iya /ivaũ > iyũ >ayũ: karyũ* 'to be done', but rarely used as 'verbal nouns': the standard infinitive and verbal noun is *-no/ṇo*, from the nominal suffix *-ano*, formally similar in the feminine to the gerund but quite distinct in the masculine.

The only plausible explanation for the adjectival behavior of the nasal infinitive of Hindi is an analogy with the *-v-* forms inherited from the *-tavya* Sk gerund (or gerundive), which in turn can only be explained by a parallel retention of the -v/b gerund at least up to a certain time. These forms indeed proliferated everywhere in New Indo-Aryan and not only in 'outer' languages as claimed by Southworth, most of the time along with other forms for verbal nouns (*-n-,-t-, -l*).

In Bengali for instance, the *-b-*[6] form, derived from SK *-tavya*, is still used for verbal nouns in certain contexts such as *ja.b.ār somoy.i* [go.*b*.GEN time.LOC] "at the time of leaving", in Assamese *za.b.âr xâm.ât* leave.*b*.GEN time.LOC] 'at the time of leaving', both languages exhibiting other formations for infinitives in different contexts (*-t-*, *-l-*). Maithili allows both a *-l-* and a *-b-* form such as *dekh.lā me*

6 For the other (more consistent: with no alternation) grammaticalization as a future, see below example (15).

sunnar or *dekh.bā me sunnar* "beautiful to look at" (Jha 1958: 519). And the well-known single form of the Gujarati infinitive *bolvũ* "to speak" is for Southworth further evidence for presenting 'outer languages' as sharing distinctive innovations, in this case further grammaticalizations of the Sanskrit *-tavya* gerund.

But the fact is that *-b/v* infinitives are also present in 'central' or 'inner' languages. It is particularly well attested in the very language out of which MSH emerged, namely Braj, where *-v-* forms are used as verbal nouns and in alternation with the nasal form as final complement (7):[7]

(6a) सदा कहु सौं रहिवौ नाहि। [BRAJBHASHA]
sadā kahu sɔ̃ rah.iv.ɔ nāhi.
always somebody with stay.*iv*.M.SG NEG
'One does not remain always in the same company.'
(Lit. 'There is no staying always with anybody') from Kellogg 1876

(6b) मेरे पुत्रनि कौं पंडित करिवे जोग है। [BRAJBHASHA]
mere putrani kɔ̃ paṇḍit kar.iv.e jog hɛ.
my sons ACC paṇḍit do.*iv*.OBL worth be.PRS.3SG
'You are competent for making my sons wise men.' (Kellogg's translation)

(7a) मोकों पकरन कों आयौ। [BRAJBHASHA]
mokõ pakaran kõ āyɔ.
1.ACC seize.*an* DAT come.PST.3M.SG
'He came to catch me.'

(7b) मोकों स्पर्श करिवे कों आयौ। [BRAJBHASHA]
mokõ sparś karive kõ āyɔ.
1.ACC touch.*iv* DAT come.PST.M.SG
'He ran to touch me.' (Snell 1991)[8]

7 A common ambiguity when one speaks of Hindi is the recent origin of the association language/language name. Whereas the language has a definitely uninterrupted and well documented history and is in no way reducible to a recent lingua franca born out of the blue (Singh & Agnihotri 1997), the languages which contributed to its genesis are now labelled differently, most of them after the region, except for the Sant Bhasha, a mixed literary language of saint poets, which also contributed to the genesis of 'Hindi' between the Apabramsha stage and the modern stages. For Braj as the most direct ancestor of Hindi, cf. Drocco 2016 (oral presentation in Napoli SLE 16).

8 It seems however that the *-n-* form is preferred when complementing the inceptive auxiliary *lag* 'start':
rājā kah.ani lāgyau
king say.*an* start.PST.M.SG
'The king began to say'

In modern Bundeli, along with the *-n-* form the *-b-* form is found in similar contexts:

(8a) मोरो घर जानो। [MODERN BUNDELI]
moro ghar jāno.
my house go.*n*.M.SG
'My going home.'

(8b) तुमाओ दौरबो ऊके चलबे बराबर है । [MODERN BUNDELI]
tumao dɔr.b.o ūke čala.b.e barābar hɛ.
your run.M.SG 3.SG.GEN walk.OBL equal be.PRS.3SG
'Your running is equal to his walking.' (Jaiswal 1962: 133)

So the verbal noun inherited from the *-tavya* gerund is omnipresent today in the whole area, except MSH: it is in no way specific to 'outer' languages' but one may wonder how an obligative gerundive could grammaticize into an infinitive.

2.2.2 What is the *-tavya* form in reality?

The *-tavya* form is mainly documented as an obligative passive participle used as a predicate since classical Sanskrit, with a syntax similar to that of the past participle, except that it is more frequent than the past with intransitive verbs:[9]

(9a) मया तत कर्तव्यम्। [SANSKRIT]
mayā tat kartavyam.
1SG.INS DEM.NOM.N.SG do.GER.NOM.N.SG
'I have to/should do that.' (lit. 'by me this to-be-done')

Such a pattern prevailed up to the New Indo-Aryan everywhere for expressing obligation, with an instrumental agent and GN agreement with patient or default agreement if intransitive:

(10a) हिंसा न करवी। [OLD RAJASTHANI]
hinsā na kar.av.ī.
violence.F.SG NEG do-AV.F.SG
'Injury is not to be done.' (Tessitori 1915: 120)

9 *tribhir gantavyam* [three.INS.PL go.*tavyam*] 'the three should go' (lit. it must be gone by the three).

(10b) तैं न जैवु। [OLD RAJASTHANI]
tẽ na jāi.vu.
2.INS NEG go.V.M.SG
'You should not go.' (lit. 'It should not be gone by you')
(from Khokhlova 2013: 101)

This history is documented up to Jain Apabhramsha (*Paumacariu*):

(11a) अन्नु न नमेवउ। [APABHRAMSHA]
annu na nam.eva.u.
other.M.SG NEG respect.V.M.SG
'No other is to be respected.' (*Paumacariu* 26.3.2)

(11b) नवर एक्कु वौ मैं पालेव। [APABHRAMSHA]
navara ekku vau mẽ pāl.ev.au.
only one vow.M.SG 1SG.INS keep.ev.M.SG
'I shall/should observe only one vow.' (Bubenik 1998: 194)

It is still present in Marathi, both old (12a) and modern (12b) with the original non-nominative syntax and modal meaning.[10]

(12a) मझ्यानें धदा सिखवला। [OLD MARATHI]
majhyānẽ dhadā sikh.av.l.ā.
1SG.INS lesson.M.SG learn.POT.PST.M.SG
'I could/was able to learn the lesson.' (Bloch 1970: 265)

(12b) त्याने समइ उचलावी। [MARATHI]
tyānẽ samai učalā.v.ī.
3M.SG.INS/AG lamp.F.SG lift.*av*.F.SG
'He should lift the lamp.' (Wali 2004: 31)

It was similarly present in Eastern languages up until the 14th-15th century with the same non-nominative alignment and a meaning progressively shifting from obligation to future:

10 Also present with intransitive verbs:
tyānẽ gharī̃ yā.v.ẽ.
3M.SG.INS/AG home.LOC come.*av*.N.SG
'He should come home.' (in Bloch 1970).

(13) *toe* *sāma* *kariba* *maï* *sānga.* [OLD BENGALI]
2.OBL with do.*ba*(M.SG?) 1SG.OBL company-M.SG
'I shall have union (do company) with you.'
[from Chatterji 1926: 967]

The construction is inherited from the Ashokean Prakrit, as shown by the Sarnath rock edict quoted by Chatterji who interprets it as displaying "a vague mandatory sense, with an express future implication" (1926: 966):

(14) इयम् सासने विंनापयितव्ये।
iyam *sāsane* *vĩnāpayitavye.*
DEM NOM.M.SG principle.M.SG make.know-GER.NOM.M.SG
'This principle should/will be made known.' (made to be known)

It further shifted to a purely temporal meaning with nominative re-alignment similar to what happened for the past in Eastern languages (*tumi boi.ta par.l.e* 'you read the book').

(15) *tumi* *boi.ta* *por.b.e.*
2.NOM book.DEF read-*b*.2
'You will read the book.'

What logic can account for these diverging grammaticalization paths? From obligation to wish then future is a quite canonical pattern (Heine & Kuteva 2002). All Romance languages also display ex-obligative 'have' futures. But a shift from obligation to verbal noun, as suggested by Chatterji (1926) is an extremely weak probability. The fact is that both uses and meanings, modal meaning when used as a predicate and otherwise verbal noun, were already attested in Sanskrit:

(16) न अयम् वक्तव्यस्य कालः।
na *ayam* *vaktavya.sya* *kālaḥ.*
NEG this speak-*tavya*.GEN time
'It is not the time of speaking.' (*Panchatantra*, in Bloch 1970: 278)

One must conclude that right from the first stages, modality is not attached to the form but to the construction, and that the *-tavya* form is an undercategorized one, modal only when used as a predicate and agreeing like a participle, otherwise conveying the mere notion of the verb, exactly like its Latin counterpart the *-nd-* gerund: *Carthago dele.nd.a est*: 'Carthago is to be destroyed', 'we must destroy

Carthago', with feminine agreement *-a*, vs *ars loque.nd.i*, 'art of speaking', *ars ama.nd.i* 'art of love', with genitive case marking *-i*.

3 Embedded infinitives and the optional agreement with their object

3.1 Previous explanations

In two types of sentences, agreement is optional and the infinitive can either agree with its object or remain in the *-nā* form like an intransitive infinitive in the position of direct object or subject. The first type involves a transitive infinitive which is the direct complement of a main verb like *čāhnā* 'to want' or complex predicate like *śurū karnā* 'to begin' in a tense requiring the ergative construction. The second type involves a transitive infinitive theme of a dative-subject predicate like *ānā* 'to come > to know':

(17a) उसने चाय पीना चाहा।
us.ne čāy pīnā čāhā.
3SG.ERG tea.F.SG drink.M.SG want.PFV.M.SG
'S/He wanted to drink tea.'

(17b) उसने चाय पीनी चाही।
us.ne čāy pīnī čāhī.
3SG.ERG tea.F.SG drink.F.SG want.PFV.F.SG
'S/He wanted to drink tea.'

(18a) मैंने हिंदी सीखना शुरू किया।
mɛ̃.ne hindī sīkhnā śurū kiyā.
1SG.ERG Hindi.F.SG learn.M.SG start do.PFV.M.SG
'I started learning Hindi.'

(18b) मैंने हिंदी सीखनी शुरू की।
mɛ̃.ne hindī sīkhnī śurū kī.
1SG.ERG Hindi.F.SG learn.F.SG start do.PFV.F.SG
'I started learning Hindi.'

(19a) मुझे साइकिल चलाना आता है।
mujhe sāikil čalānā ātā hɛ.
1SG.DAT bike.F.SG ride.M.SG come.PRS.3M.SG
'I know how to ride a bike.'

(19b) मुझे साइकिल चलानी आती है।
mujhe sāikil čalānī ātī hɛ.
1SG.DAT bike.F.SG ride.F.SG come.PRS.3F.SG
'I know how to ride a bike.'[11]

Bhatt (2005) gives a new interpretation of the above alternation between local or long distance agreement (LDA), following previous analyses by Mahajan (1989), who argued that the infinitive may optionally assign a case, or as a phenomenon of incorporation when there is no LDA (Butt 1995; Mohanan 1995), or as a case of pseudo-incorporation (Dayal (2003). Bhatt's (2005) explanation relies on the notion of "restructuring verbs". According to this theory, inspired by Rizzi's analysis of clitic raising in Italian and Wurmland's analysis of long passives,[12] ordinary infinitives project a PRO (subject) which blocks long distance agreement, whereas restructuring infinitives (complement of restructuring verbs such as typically "want") have no such syntactic projection, hence only the object noun can discharge agreement features. Bhatt also notes that the semantic effects involved in this alternation have been little studied, apart from an intuitive reading of the LDA construction as "more specific", and he adds a relevant illustration of the noun scope, which is wider in the LDA construction:

(20a) नईम ने हर किताब पढ़ना चाहा।
Naīm ne har kitāb paṛhnā čāhā.
Naeem-ERG each book.F.SG read.M.SG want.PFV.M.SG
'Naeem wanted to read every book.'

(20b) नईम ने हर किताब पढ़नी चाही।
Naīm ne har kitāb paṛhnī čāhī.
Naeem-ERG each book.F.SG read.F.SG want.PFV.F.SG
'Naeem wanted to read every book.'

Whereas only (20b) allows the reading 'for every book, he wanted to read it' (every- > want: wide scope on matrix verb), (20a) and (20b) allow the reading of a paper-devouring Naim wishing to read every possible book (every > read).

11 Example discussed in Butt (1995), Mohanan (1995), Montaut (2012) among others. The gloss for present, formed by an imperfective participle agreeing in number and gender and the present auxiliary agreeing in person, is simplified as verb PRS, in two words, except for the 'short' present of the verb be as a copula (one word) in contrast to its 'long' present in example (21a).

12 Le ha voluto leggere (*Le ha deciso di leggere).

3.2 Agreement and the degree of individuation of the noun

I will concentrate on these semantic effects, before coming back to the hypothesis of restructuring verbs. Let us first have a look at the contexts favoring or requiring each construction. LDA (10b, 11b, 12b, 13), required when the object is specific or even only referential, is by far the most frequent construction. But in such expressions as ‘ride a bike/drive a car’, or ‘drink tea’ we find both.

The ‘incorporating’ construction is found in contexts where the topic is whether or not to drink tea. In (21a) after a warning against various habits (sugar, milk, quantity, etc.), all expressed with the LDA construction such as in (21b), the conclusion is the following (although the modal auxiliary is invariable in Hindi, the infinitive shows agreement):

(21a) उसका मतलब नहीं है कि चाय पीना नहीं चाहिए। पीना चाहिए। *सेहतमंद होती है।
uskā matlab nahī̃ hɛ ki čāy ***pīnā*** *nahī̃ čāhie.*
its meaning NEG is that tea-F.SG drink-M.SG NEG must
*pīnā čāhie. *sehatmand hotī hɛ.*
drink-M.SG must. healthy be PRS.F.SG
‘It does not mean that one should not drink tea. One should.
*It [tea] is good for health.’

(21a) shows that the noun cannot be anaphorized, only the process can be,[13] suggesting that the noun is not represented for its properties but only serves as a classifier for the verb (something drinkable). The object has a strictly classifying function (class of drinkable), and behaves as a mass noun which makes the process an activity, not an event, in the same way as standard incorporation in language which displays it (‘tea-drink’ like ‘baby-sit’) and the global process Object-Verb behaves as an intransitive verb.[14]

Conversely, when in the same article, a similar statement emphasizes the quantity of tea, the construction shifts to LDA (21b). Marked quantification correlates with a noun (and process) which is neither massive nor discrete (countable),

---

13 From (wiki-how.com, 26/5/16). Another acceptable prolongation could have been: *yah [cāy pīnā] bahut sahatmand hotā hɛ* ‘this [tea drink] is (M.SG) very healthy’.

14 Although not accepted in standard Hindi, such constructions occurred in speech and blogs, and the word *kāfī* “coffee”, a feminine as well as cāy, can also occur in similar constructions with a non-agreeing infinitive: *kāfī pīnā hī nahī̃, lagānā bhī cāhie* [coffee drink.M.SG just not apply.M.SG too must] ‘One must not only drink coffee but also apply it’ (on should make coffee massage and skin scrubs), in an advertisement from https://dusbus.com/hi/coffee-pina-nahi-lagana-chahiye/

what has been analyzed by Frankel & Paillard and then De Vogüé (1991) as 'dense', a form of intermediate individuation.[15]

(21b) कितनी चाय पीनी (*पीना) चाहिए। दो या तीन कप से ज़्यादा चाय पीनी नहीं चाहिए।
kitnī ***čāy*** *pīnī* **(pīnā)* *čāhie?*
how much-F.SG tea.F.SG drink.INF.F.SG drink.INF.F.SG must
do yā tīn kap se-zyādā ***čāy*** *pīnī* *nahī̃ čāhie.*
two or three cup more-than tea drink.INF.F.SG NEG must
'How much tea should one drink? One should not drink tea for more than two-three cups a day.'[16] (wiki-how.com)

And similarly, when the statement focuses on the variety of tea (black, green) the LDA construction is chosen (*pīnī čāhie*).

When the LDA construction occurs in general statements with a time/space limitation such as pregnancy or timing for drinking, the speakers who accept (21a) usually accept both constructions for (21b'), the LDA construction emphasizing the object as possibly contrasting with some other drink (or nothing):

(21b') खाने के तुरन्त बाद चाय नहीं पीनी (पीना) चाहिए।
khāne ke turant bād ***čāy*** *nahī̃ pīnī (pīnā) čāhie.*
meal of immediately after tea NEG drink-F.SG drink-M.SG must
'One should not drink tea right after a meal.'

Agreement is of course blocked with a markedly individuated (*ko*) object, for instance when a secondary process transforms the object into a requalified one, since Hindi displays default agreement with *ko*-marked objects.

(21c) चाय को बार बार गरम करके नहीं पीना चाहिए।
čāy ***ko*** *bār-bār garam karke nahī̃ pīnā čāhie.*
tea.F.SG **ACC** repeatedly hot do.CVB NEG drink-M.SG must
'One should not drink repeatedly boiled tea.'
(lit. 'Having boiled the tea several times drink')

15 Discrete occurrence: 'I had a hot a tea', 'one tea for each', etc.; mass occurrence: 'water is liquid', 'stone is hard'.
16 Although obligation is expressed by the invariable *cāhie*, the agreement pattern of the infinitive is the same as with a finite auxiliary as (2b).

This does not mean that (21c) is to be read as (21a): the embedded process does not refer to a routine activity like make tea (*čāy banākar*) but to a specific preparation emphasizing the transformation of the object. Both the noun and the embedded process can be anaphorized, which is not the case for (21a).[17]

3.2.1 Individuation, subject's imputed intention or discursive salience?

The notion *lakri kātnā* 'cut wood' may have as expected the two constructions each with a different reading. When it refers to an activity with the noun acting only as a classifier (classifying properties), absence of agreement is indeed current in contexts as *mẽne lakṛī kāṭnā sīkhā* 'I learnt how to cut wood/wood-cutting', or *lakṛī kāṭnā nahī̃ čāhie* 'one should not cut wood' (for ecological reasons: one should avoid deforestation).[18] The LDA with feminine agreement of infinitive and main verb is expected when a specific tree or a wooden board is at stake but both constructions occur in apparently very similar contexts:

(22a) अन्त में लकड़ी काटने लायक एक वृक्ष से उन्होंने लकड़ी काटना शुरू किया।
ant mẽ lakṛī kāṭne lāyak ek vr̥kś se unhõne ***lakṛī***
end in wood cut suitable a tree from 3PL-ERG wood.F.SG
kāṭnā śurū kiyā.
cut-M.SG start did-M.SG
'Finally he started cutting wood from a tree suitable for wood-cutting.'

(22b) जिसे बाबूलाल मीणा ने ख़ुद का बताते हुए उसकी लकड़ी काटनी शुरू कर दी। * काटना शुरू कर दिया।
jise Bābūlāl mīṇā ne khud kā batāte-hue uskī ***lakṛī***
REL.ACC Babulal Mina ERG self of telling its wood.F.SG
kāṭnī śurū kar dī. **kāṭnā śurū kar diyā.*
cut.F.SG start do gave.F.SG cut.M.SG start do gave.M.SG
'Claiming the tree to be his, Babulal Mina started cutting its wood.'
(lit. Which, claiming his own, Babulal Mina started cutting its wood.)

One could argue that (22b) is more definite, referring to the specific tree just felled in his yard, whereas (22a) just refers to a suitable tree (indefinite: *ek*). But the

17 ***usmẽ*** *esid kī mātrā zyādā hɛ*, (it-in acid of quantity more is) 'it contains more acid' or ***isse*** *cāy mẽ esid kī mātrā baṛh jātī hɛ* [this-by tea in acid of quantity increase goes] 'this increases the acidity rate in tea').

18 Again for those speakers who are not linguistically 'purist' and do not altogether reject non LDA constructions.

context in (22a) points to a specific tree, long searched for and perfectly identified by the wood cutter, who desperately wants fuel for his family and has travelled three days to find the suitable material. Simply the act is performed in view of getting wood for fire, hence the representation of the process as an activity (mass process) although it concerns an objectively identified occurrence of 'tree'. The process in (22b) on the contrary functions as a dense, or even discrete type of process.[19] Moreover, the salient entity in the discourse is the (litigious) tree, whereas in (22a) it is the need for fuel.

As for abstract nouns, highly favored as candidates for differential object marking in simple sentences in many languages (Company Company 2003), they are less likely to fit in pseudo-incorporation constructions with activity reading,[20] and more likely to retain the *ko* marking with default agreement with embedded infinitives.[21] Alternation is more frequently between the *ko* construction with default agreement and the LDA construction, the latter for the maintenance or discourse topicality (23a) after an initial occurrence of the *ko*-marked noun as the new relevant topic (23b):

(23a) गरीबी को मिटाना है,
garībī *ko* *miṭānā* *hɛ.*
poverty.F.SG ACC erase.M.SG be.PRS.3SG

(23b) तो पहले बड़े राज्यों से गरीबी हटानी होगी।
to *pahle* *baṛe* *rājyõ* *se* *garībī* *haṭānī* *hogī.*
then first big states from poverty.F.SG take.out be.FUT.F.SG
'If poverty is to be erased poverty (one) should first wipe poverty of from big States.'

(23c) ?गरीबी हटाना होगा।
?garībī *hatānā* *hogā.*
poverty.F.SG take.out.M.SG be.FUT.M.SG

19 In De Vogüé (1991: 57) discrete processes are characterized by aiming at a conformity with a standard realisation ("etalon de conformité"), paralleling Vendler's accomplishements, like 're-paired a given car' (so that the car is repaired), whereas dense processes only involve quantified objects and are not valuated for their conformity to a yardstick.

20 The classical incorporation tends to incorporate concrete objects (grass-gather, tree-chop, liquor-drink, etc., cf. Mithun 2009), hence the unavailability of pseudo-incorporation construction for verbo-nominal complex predicates never allow (*X kī madad kī* /**kiyā*), against Polinksky & Potsdam's (2001) proposal that CP never allows LDA.

21 Almost as frequently as concrete definite specific nouns: *usne vigyān ko jānnā cāhā* 'he wanted to know science', *prakriti ko vināś se bacānā hɛ* 'one has to save nature from destruction' (Jagaran 25/3/17). For Hindi DOM construction, see Montaut (forthcoming).

A striking fact is that similar semantic differences which correlate with LDA construction and pseudo-incorporation, accounted for by the relations between object and verb in both models (Bhatt's and Dayal's) are also observable in subject-verb relations, although (24a) is considerably less frequent than (24b) and not accepted by all:

(24a) बारिश आना शुरू हुआ।
bāriś ānā śurū huā.
rain.F.SG come.M.SG start was.M.SG
'It started raining.' (monsoon arrival)

(24b) बारिश आनी शुरू हुई।
bāriś ānī śurū huī.
rain.F.SG come.F.SG start was-F.SG
'Rain started falling/coming.'

Such facts could be made compatible with the hypothesis of restructuring verbs if we consider that *ānā* 'come' is unaccusative and has an object as main argument, not a subject ('rain': object, then same alternation of agreement pattern as in 11). But the verb *ānā* 'come' also allows the standard construction of subjects when nominalized, in the genitive, whether the noun is a mass type noun as 'rain' or a discrete/dense noun as 'imported coton': such genitive subjects are treated like animate subjects of non unaccusative verbs:[22]

(24c) बारिश का आना शुरू हुआ।
bāriś kā ānā śurū huā.
rain.F.SG GEN come.M.SG start was-M.SG
'It started raining.'

22 Like for instance:
माँ का मुझे इस तरह डाँटना।
mā̃ kā mujhe is tarah ḍā̃ṭnā...
mother GEN I-ACC this way scold
'The fact that Mother scolds me in this way...', where the word "mother" is in the genitive case.

(25) अमरीका के दक्षिणी भाग से आने वाली कपास का अन्तर्राष्ट्रीय बाज़ार में आना बंद हो गया।[23]
amrīkā ke dakṣiṇī bhāg se āne vālī kapās kā antarrāṣṭrīy
America of southern part from coming cotton GEN international
bāzār mẽ ānā band ho gayā.
market in come.M.SG stop became.M.SG
'The arrival in the international market of cotton coming from Southern America stopped.'

I will look at the constructions of nominalizations (true 'verbal noun') in the next section, after considering the alternation in potentially 'restructuring' contexts (main verb 'begin, or end'), assuming that what is at stake here is subject-verb relation.

4 Alternate constructions for subjects of non-finite verbs

4.1 Subject of embedded infinitive in a 'restructuring' context

The pseudo-incorporating construction of subjects such as (24c) is quite rare (apart from not being accepted by purists) and what in almost all cases occurs is the subject controlling the agreement of infinitive and main verb (LDA?), not only in the definite past/perfect/pluperfect as expected, but many times in the present or future.[24] Animate subjects are never to be incorporated even when collectivized in nouns such as *bhīṛ* 'crowd' and even inanimate are so only rarely (rain, snow).

23 Malik *Bhārtīya itihās ke pramukh pahlū* [Main Aspects of Indian History] Delhi: Sarasvati House, 2016, p. 366

24 The example *barf paṛna śurū hotā hɛ* [snow.F fall.M start is.PRS.M] 'Snow usually starts falling (in this high valley in October)' is no more frequent than *barf paṛnī śurū hogī / ho cukī hogī* [snow.F fall.F start will.F/ termiative FUT.F] 'Snow will start falling/ must have started falling. Thus, there is an extreme instability of the agreement pattern not only in blogs but also in the written press.

(26a) सुबह से ही जलाभिषेक के लिए श्रद्धालु आने शुरू हो गए थे।
subah se-hī jalābhiṣek ke-lie śraddhālu ***āne***
morning since lustration for devotee.M.PL come.M.PL
śurū ho gae the.
starting be go.PPFT.M.PL
'Since early morning pilgrims had started coming for the sacred bath.'

(26b) कल से श्रद्धालुओं की भीड़ आनी शुरू हुई *आना शुरू हुआ।
kal se śraddhāluõ kī bhīr ***ānī***
yesterday from devotees of crowd.F.SG come.F.SG
*śurū huī. *ānā śurū huā.*
starting be.PST.F.SG come.M.SG starting be.PST.M.SG
'Since yesterday the crowd of pilgrims started coming.'

In cases such as (26), the embedded infinitive is almost always 'restructuring', in other terms it always behaves as an inflectable gerund. The noun can be questioned, anaphorized, and relativized[25] and has a definite autonomy, including most often those nouns involved in meteorological expressions often represented by a single verb in many languages (to rain, to snow). The reason for the relative unavailability of non-restructuring constructions, semantically to the global process and not the action of a distinct entity, may lie in the availability of expressing the whole process by the noun alone (*bāriś śurū huī* rain started: it started raining). Rare contrasts are however observable. In (27a), the feminine noun *barf* 'ice/snow' does not control the agreement which is controlled by the infinitive (masculine verbal noun), whose subject does not surface as a genitive-marked subject but as a compound. The statement's context is an inquiry into (de)glaciation on earth where scientists may discover approximate datings by analyzing the chemical structure of glacier rocks.[26] (27b) in contrast makes *barf* 'snow' the salient entity in the context, with narration going on on the topic:

25 पूर्णिमा से स्नानार्थियों की जो भीड़ आनी शुरु हुई आना शुरु हुआ वह कम होने का नाम नहीं ले रही है।
pūrṇimā se snānārthiyõ kī jo bhīṛ anī śurū huī
full.moon from sacred.bath.seekers of REL crowd come.F.SG start was.F.SG
**ānā śurū huā vah kam hone kā nām nahī̃ le rahī hɛ*
come.M.SG start.was.M.SG3SG that less be of name NEG take PROG.PRS.3F.SG
'The crowd of bathers which has started coming since full moon does not seem to be decreasing.'

26 The interfering *kab* 'when' is not an argument against coalescence, since in verbo-nominal complex predicates also it is frequently found occurring between both elements like various particles and negation.

(27a) बरफ़ कब पिघलना शुरू हुआ होगा।
barf kab pighalnā śurū huā hogā.
snow.F.SG when melt.M.SG start was.M.SG PRSUMP.M.SG
'When snow melting may have started.'

(27b) वह फ़्लैट से बाहर निकला तो बरफ़ पड़नी बंद हो गई थी। लेकिन ठंडी शीत लहर चल पड़ी थी जिसका अर्थ था कि बर्फ अब जम जाएगी।
vah flɛṭ se bāhar niklā to **barf** **paṛnī**
3SG flat from out leave then snow.F.SG fall.F.SG
band ho gaī thī. lekin ṭhaṇḍī śīt lahar čal paṛī thī
finished be go.PFV.F.SG PST but cold frost wave go fall.PFV PST
jiskā arth thā ki yah barf *ab jam jāegī.*
whose meaning was that this snow now freeze go.FUT
'[When] He came out of the flat the snow had stopped falling. But an ice cold wave had arrived which meant that *snow* would now freeze.'

Yet the best standpoint to observe alternate constructions of subjects of non-finite verbs is the nominalized infinitive: no agreement is concerned, since only case marking varies, but the semantic alternation echoes the semantic difference between LDA and pseudo-incorporation constructions.

4.2 Subject of verbal noun

The genitive marking of the subject is required with nominalized infinitives, whether complementing restructuring verbs (28a) or not (28b).

(28a) श्रद्धालुओं का धरमदारी में आना शुरू हो गया था।
śraddhāluõ kā dharmadārī mẽ ānā śurū ho gayā thā.
devotees GEN Dharmadari in come.INF.M.SG start be go PPFT.M.SG
'The arrival of the pilgrims had started at Dharmadari.'

(28b) श्रद्धालुओं के आने से पहले।
śraddhāluõ ke āne se pahle.
devotee GEN come.INF.M.SG before
'Before the arrival of pilgrims.'

(28a), patterning like (25c), differs from the LDA construction in (26) in so far as the verbal noun is given a prominent syntactic and semantic status: noun and infinitive (verbal noun) are distinct, with an emphasis on the arrival and a reading of the noun as discrete entity. This construction is required for any infinitive subject when distinct from the main verb, inanimate as well as human.[27] But, as is the case for LDA in non-nominative alignments, there are cases of optionality. Besides, there are also systematic exceptions to the subject marking rule, with nouns like 'darkness', 'evening', 'night', 'morning'.[28]

(29a) अँधेरा आने पर सब भाग गए (*अँधेरे के आने पर)।
*ãdherā āne par sab bhāg gae. (*ãdhere ke āne par)*
darkness come at all run go.PFV.M.PL darkness GEN come at
'When it went dark all ran away.'

(28b) रात *(के) होने में कई घंटे बाकी हैं।
*rāt *(ke) hone mẽ kaī ghanṭe bākī hɛ̃.*
night (GEN) be in several hours remaining are
'There are still several hours more before it is night.'

(28c) पौ *(के) फटने (सुबह *(के) होने) से पहले घरवालों का खाना तैयार रहेगा।
*pɔ *(ke) phaṭne (=subah *(ke) hone) se-pahle gharvālõ kā*
dawn (GEN) burst morning GEN be before family of
khānā tɛyār rahegā.
meal ready stay.FUT
'Before dawn (= day-break) meal for the family will be ready.'

Statements such as *pɔ ke phaṭne se* or *andhere ke hone mẽ* are ruled out: the required coalescence between subject and verb corresponds to a global process in which the noun is not represented for any particular property, and which simply gives a temporal location to the main process. In case the statement concerns a particular night, marking of course is no longer ruled out.[29]

---

27 As is the case for participles: *mã̄ *(ke) āne par /mã̄ *(ke) āte hī sab cup ho gae* [mother GEN come.inf on /mother GEN coming just all silent became] 'When Mother came whole became silent'.

28 Since only genitive marking is the topic in this section, glosses will be further on limited to it, unless otherwise stated.

29 Even when represented for its general properties but in contrast with for instance 'day', night can also be marked as a distinct subject, and further pole of discursive continuity, as in this verse from Gulzar:
रात के आने से पहले ही कहीं ये दिन गिर के मर जाए
***rāt ke** āne se pahle hī kahī̃ ye din gir ke mar jāe ....*
'May this day not die *before night arrives* (Gulzar)
रात आएगी तो फिर से ज़ख़्म कुरेदेगी
(*rāt āegī to phir se zakhm kuredegī*
'when night comes my wound will open again')

Apart from these systematic 'exceptions', there are nouns which allow both constructions, particularly meteorological ones such as 'rain', 'monsoon', 'wind', 'snow', etc. They appear systematically unmarked in weather forecasts:

(30a) कमज़ोर मानसून आने की भविष्यवाणी।
kamzor mānsūn āne *kī bhaviśya-vāṇī.*
weak *monsoon come* of weather-forecast
'Forecast of weak monsoon (coming).'

(30b) कश्मीर में कुछ स्थानों पर बारिश होने या बर्फ़ गिरने की संभावना है जिससे घाटी में ठंड या शुष्क मौसम से परेशान लोगों को कुछ राहत मिलेगी।
kaśmīr mẽ kuč̌h sthānõ par bāriś hone yā barf girne kī
Kashmir in some places on *rain be* or *snow fall* of
sambhāvnā hɛ jisse ghāṭī mẽ ṭhaṇḍ yā śuṣk mɔsam se
possibility is by.which valley in cold or dry weather by
pareśān logõ ko kuč̌h rāhat milegī.
worried people to some relief will.get
'There is a possibility of *raining* or *snowing* at some places in Kashmir, which will relieve the people suffering from cold or dry weather.'

(30) both are predictions (non-specific events), and relativization bears as expected on the whole process (snow-fall) in (30b). This process may be qualified ('week' in (30a). It can even be added adverbial specifications can even be added such as 'late', 'early' in (31b) or the noun can have a coordinate such as 'storm or tempest' without opposing the coalescent construction (31a):

(31a) ज़ोर की आँधी या तूफ़ान आने पर वृक्ष गिर पड़ते हैं, छप्पर उड़ जाते हैं।
zor-kī ā̃dhī yā tūfān āne par vṛkṣ gir paṛte hẽ,
strong of *storm or tempest come* on, trees fall.PRS.M.PL
č̌happar uṛ jāte hẽ.
roofs fly go.PRS.M.PL
'On violent storm or tempest coming, trees fall down, roofs fly.'

Even a noun like *krānti* 'revolution' can be unmarked if used with 'come' for simply dating the main process and marked otherwise.

(31b) कभी बरसात देरी से शुरू होने से किसान बरबाद हुआ तो कभी मानसून जल्दी होने से।
kabhī barsāt derī-se śurū hone se kisān barbād huā to
once rain late start be by peasant destroy was then
kabhī mānsūn jaldī hone se.
once *monsoon early be* by
'Peasants were ruined either *by late rain-arrival* or by *early monsoon-arrival.*' (ETV Rajasthan, 9/7/15)[30]

What seems to be prevalent here is the non-specificity of the process. Like forecast as a modality for eventualities (30), the process in (31) does not refer to a definite event, as indicated by the tense of main verb (general assertion: habitual imperfect in (31a), or by the iteration 'once... once', in (31b). On the contrary, semelfactive events tend to display the genitive construction, which is required when the statement involves a specific tempest, particularly if named with a proper noun.[31] There is very little difference between (31a) and (32), both borrowed from the same article devoted to the disasters caused by the early monsoon in 2015.

(32a) मानसून का जल्दी आना बना वजह।
mānsūn kā jaldī ānā banā vajah.
monsoon GEN early come.M.SG become-PST cause
'The early arrival of the monsoon became the cause [of disaster in soya culture].'

(32b) मानसून के जल्दी आने से सोयाबीन की फ़सल पर ख़राब असर पड़ रहा है।
mānsūn ke jaldī āne se soyābīn kī fasal par kharāb
monsoon GEN early come by soya of crop on bad
asar paṛ rahā hɛ.
effect fall.PROG.SG.PRS
'The early arrival of the monsoon is having a bad impact on the soya crop.'

Actual present and preterit point to the specificity of the event in (32a) whereas (31b) was the conclusive sentence of the paper, presenting a generalization of this specific events of summer 2015 within a recurring frame. In addition, the term

---

30 For intervening elements between noun and verb, see note 26.

31 देश के पूर्वी तट पर समुद्री तूफान हुधुद के आने की आशंका
deś ke pūrvī taṭ par samudrī tūfān 'hudhud' ke āne kī āśaṅkā.
country of eastern coast on oceanic cyclon 'Hudhud' GEN come of fear
'Fear of tsunami Hudhud's arrival on the country's eastern coast'

itself 'monsoon' and its precocious arrival makes up for the whole dramatic scenario, and become the most salient event regarding soya bean cultivation.

Saliency is even more the discriminating feature in (33), without the specific/non-specific distinction. Genitive marking of the subject 'snow big flakes', 'heavy snow' is present in the first occurrence in the title, with an effect of sensational announcement, then the same subject occurs in the text without genitive marking, the process as a whole (coalescent) mentioned mainly as an explanation for the more salient fact, that the valley is now cold enough for winter sports (earlier than usual: end of August). The higher degree of coalescence is a compound noun (*himpāt* 'snow fall') in further occurrences:

(33a) रोहतंग दर्रे पर बर्फ़ के **फाहों का गिरना** जारी है।
rohtang darre par barf ke phāhõ kā girnā *jārī hɛ.*
Rohtang pass on snow of flakes GEN fall continue is
'Falling of heavy snow continues at Rohtang Pass.'
(Amarujala 21/08/2016)

(33b) रोहतंग दर्रे पर बर्फ़ के **फाहे गिरने** से पर्यटन नगरी में ठंड आग़ाज़ हो गया।
rohtang darre par barf ke phāhe girne *se paryaṭan nagarī*
Rohtang pass on snow of flakes fall by tourism city
mẽ ṭhaṇḍ āgāz ho gayā.
in cold arrival be went
'Because of heavy snow fall at Rohtang Pass, cold arrived in the touristic station.'

(33c) रात को हुए हिमपात के कारण ऊंची घाटी शीतलहर की चपेट में आ गई।
rat ko hue himpāt *ke kāraṇ ũ̃čī ghāṭī śītlahar kī*
night at been *snowfall* of reason high valley cold.wave of
čapeṭ mẽ ā gayī.
grip in come went
'Because of the night snowfall, the high valley came in the grip of in an ice-cold wave.'

The alternation between coalescent SV and genitive marked subject in nominalized infinitives is certainly not parallel to the alternation between LDA and pseudo-incorporated constructions. But similar factors are at play, namely the behavior of the noun as a mass noun vs a dense/count one, the specificity (of the main process) and the salience of the noun. Besides, since one might analyze the coalescent SV as an intransitive like verb, it comes close to the non LDA constructions of the object-infinitive in section 2.

5 Conclusion: Typological correlations and evolutions

Whatever the role played by the historical origin of infinitive in Hindi, namely through analogical remodeling of the *-an* ending after the *-tavya* gerund from Sanskrit and early New Indo-Aryan languages, it is clearly now behaving both as a gerund and as a noun (with typical genitive marking of its subject as a noun complement as seen above).

As a gerund used as a predicate, it is expected to agree in gender with its subject, particularly in non-nominative alignments such as (9) in Sanskrit, retained in pre-modern Hindi as well as in all other Indo-Aryan languages both Eastern and Western (10–14). This agreement pattern and non-nominative alignment share a similar history with the past participle used as a predicate in all Indo-Aryan languages up to the 14–16th century, when Eastern languages shifted both past and obligative statements to nominative alignments and changed the modal meaning of the gerund to a purely temporal meaning, whereas Western languages reinforced the non-nominative alignment of the past participle into a full-fledged ergative pattern.[32] The shared innovations then in no way distinguish 'outer' languages from central ('inner') ones, as opposed to Southworth's assumptions.

In modern standard Hindi, as well as other Indo-Aryan languages except Marathi (12b), the predicative use of the gerund (Sanskrit obligative passive participle) has not been retained, but the agreement pattern has extended to the non-predicative gerund (or adjectival infinitive), and is strictly limited to non-nominative alignments, with a nasal infinitive, as is the case with the -v- Gujarati infinitive. Regarding the rise of the infinitive's agreement, one can hypothesize that competing constructions for obligation, with and without copula in old Gujarati (14th c.) explain the modern behavior of the infinitive, the copula construction patterning exactly like the modern Gujarati gerund in (4) and triggering the reanalysis of the obligative verbal adjective as a gerund (infinitive):

(34a) *ṣisyiĩ* *te* *kārya* *tatkāla* *āčarivaũ.*
pupil.INS DEM.M.SG work.M.SG immediately do-*v*-M.SG
'The pupil should immediately do that work.' (Dave 1935: 94)

32 With altogether different futures, either inherited from the Sanskrit sigmatic future (Gujarati, Awadhi and Bhojpuri for certain persons), or periphrastic (+ *ga* 'go', + *la* 'touch').

(34b) *jīṇaĩ* *jīviĩ* *jīhā̃* *jāi.v.aũ* *čhɛ.*
REL.INS person.INS there go-*v*.M.SG be.3M.SG
'The person who is designated to go there' (= who should go) (Dave: 1935: 67)

More research should be done on the rise of the adjectival agreement of the nasal infinitive in Hindi, keeping in mind that the nominal behavior of the form is attested right from the beginning in Sanskrit (16) and even today Hindi has *tatsams* with both the obligative meaning (*kartavya* 'duty': what has to be done) and the purely notional meaning (*vaktavya* 'statement'). The -*v*- form was originally an uncategorized form, hence its availability for very divergent grammaticalizations, obligation leading to future, the meaning 'verbal notion' leading to infinitive.

An interesting parallel is offered by Romance languages derived from Latin. Latin also displayed a gerund (*dele-nd-us/um/a* 'to be destroyed) with obligative meaning when constructed with copula (optional dative agent) and a verbal noun otherwise, inflecting for case but not gender (*ars loque.nd.i,* 'art of speaking.GEN', *ars ama.nd.i* 'art of love.GEN'), the latter meaning, of simple verbal notion, probably the basic one (Ernoult & Thomas 1951, Touratier 1994). The obligative gerund behaved exactly as the past passive participle when used as a periphrastic perfect with copula, both with dative agents, in striking parallel with the evolution of Indo-Aryan till the 14–16th century. These non-nominative alignments prevailing in Late Latin further shifted to nominative alignments (Adams 2013), like Eastern Indo-Aryan languages, except that a new auxiliary 'have' was used for this shift (have something done/to be done), and modern languages now display 'have' perfects and futures.[33] This affinity between perfect and obligation in non-nominative alignments was explained for Latin at its daughter Romance languages and for Sanskrit/Old Persian as nominalizations involving views over action (as a result or as a goal aimed at) and not the direct expression of action (Benveniste 1966, Kurylowicz 1965). This is in conformity with the fact that only non-nominative alignments licence the special LDA agreement analyzed in section 2.

One should also mention that case marking in the non-nominative alignments for perfect and obligation was dative in Latin, instrumental in Old Indo-Aryan, and modern Gujarati (4) displays an alternation between ergative and dative. Once the passive reading of the participial forms is lost, what remains is an

33 *Mihi id factum est* [to.me this done is] 'I have done this' (// *maya tat kr̥tam*), and *mihi id faciendum est*, (to.me this to.be.done is) 'I must do this' (// *maya tat kartavyam*) where shifted to *ego id factum habeo* (I this done have] and *ego id fieri habeo* [I this be.done have].

oblique marking of the agent, and many languages close to Hindi still display such alternations, with no clear difference in meaning.[34]

(35a) तुमने जरूर रानो चाइए। [Modern Braj]
tum.ne jarūr rāno čāie.
1SG.ERG surely stay.INF must
'You must stay.'

(35b) छोकरी कु जरूर आराम करनो चाइए। [Modern Braj]
čhokrī ku jarūr arām karno čāie.
girl DAT surely rest do.INF must
'The girl must rest.'

(35c) तिननैं कल अउना है। [Modern Kangri, in Eaton 2008]
tin.nẽ kal auṇā hɛ.
3F.SG.ERG surely stay.INF is
'She is to come tomorrow.'

(35d) तिसाँ जो मदद करनी है। [Modern Kangri, in Eaton 2008]
tisā̃ jo madad karnī hɛ.
3F.SG DAT help.F.SG do.INF.F.SG is
'She should help.'

The origin of the *v-* infinitive as a gerund which could behave as a gerund in non-nominative alignments is clearly an important factor in the new agreement pattern of the Gujarati infinitive, and in the same way the analogical behavior of the nasal Hindi infinitive can explain its behavior as a gerund (in contrast with Romance infinitives, which all come from the Latin invariable infinitive in -re/ire and are consequently invariable). But the interesting fact is that this ambivalence (gerund or verbal noun) is now used by the language as a new possibility for marking semantic differences: gerund licensing LDA makes the noun more specific or salient, whereas the verbal noun may incorporate its objects (and coalesce with its subject?) and result in a reading of the process as an activity, in the same way as the subject marking alternation in nominalization allows for a reading of the noun as more or less independent, hence a reading of the process as activity or event. Haspelmath (1987)'s cognitive explanation, by the fact that agreement

34 For the origin of dative and ergative markers from similarly locative words (*ne* < *ṇai, kaṇṇai* < *karṇasmin* 'ear-locative', *ko* < *kakṣa* 'side') and the use of *ne/nai* as a dative marker in many Hindi dialects and Indo-Aryan languages, as well as both ergative and dative/accusative in Bangaru, see Montaut 2016.

of the Latin gerund echoes the higher salience of concrete nouns compared with verbs, matches the above analysis.[35]

Alternations of infinitive agreement with object are very limited in standard Hindi and not allowed with discrete nouns. However one finds today expressions where LDA is required in standard Hindi, rejected by purists but clearly used for imposing a reading of the process as an activity:

(36a) यूँ तो किताब पढ़ना हर किसी को नहीं भाता...।
yũ-to kitāb paṛhnā har kisī ko nahī̃ bhātā.
anyway book.F.SG read.M.SG everyone DAT NEG pleases
'Anyway everyone does not enjoy book-reading'

(36b) वैसे तो मुझे किताबें पढ़ना बहुत पसंद है।
vɛse to mujhe kitābẽ paṛhnā bahut pasand hɛ.
so then 1SG.DAT book.F.PL read.M.SG much taste is
'Anyway I don't like much reading books' (= book reading)

In subject position also, infinitives in sentences like Gujarati (36a), not allowed in standard Hindi (36b), seem to be allowed in what one might call 'advanced Hindi' like (36d) and (36e):

(36a) *ā čõpdī vāč.v.ī muśkel che.*
this book.F.SG read.INF.F.SG difficult is
'It is difficult to read this book' (from Khokhlova 2013: 97)

(36b) यह किताब पढ़ना (*पढ़नी) मुश्किल है/ ज़रूरी है।
*yah kitāb paṛh.n.ā (*paṛhnī) muśkil hɛ /zarūrī hɛ.*
this book.F.SG read.INF.M read.INF.F difficult is necessary is
'It is difficult to read this book' (my example)

35 *Cupidi bellorum gerendorum* (desirous war.GEN.M.MPL wage.ger.gen.m.pl) 'Desirous of waging wars' (lit. of wars to-be-waged), *ab urbe condita* (from city.ABL.F.SG found.ppp.abl.sg) 'from the foundation of the city' (lit. from the city founded). The paper also relates to the agreement of Hindi infinitive when complement of verb *čāhnā* 'want' and its conclusions hold valid although most examples are not (with main verb *čāhnā* in the present for instance).

(36c) किताब *मिलनी* बहुत ज़रूरी है [लेकिन नोटबंदी की वजह से] मुश्किल है *मिलनी*!
kitāb milnī *bahut zarūrī* *hɛ* [*lekin notbãdī*
book get.F much necessary is but demonetisation
kī vajah se] *muśkil* *hɛ* milnī.
because of difficult is get.F
'It is very much necessary to get the book [but because of the money change] how difficult they are to get [at shops].'
(Ankur Chauhan, *Notbandi*, Notion Press, 2017)

One may argue that *milnā* requires a non-nominative alignment in finite statements, yet the standard construction with nominalized infinitives in subject position blocks agreement (34c):

(36d) कक्षा एक से आठ तक [की] किताबें गर्मी की छुट्टियों से पहले *मिलना* मुश्किल है।
kakṣā ek se āṭh tak kī kitābẽ garmī kī čhuṭṭiyõ
class one from eight to of books summer GEN holidays
se pahle milnā muśkil hɛ.
before get.M difficult is
'Finding textbooks for class 1 to 8 before summer holidays is difficult'
(news.primarykamaster.com)

Such substandard alternations as (36c) and (36d) may well be rejected by lovers of standard grammar, they are none the less increasingly frequent and in most cases used purposely for conveying semantic differences. This suggests, with the progressive extension of the originally limited cases of optionality, that optionality in the infinitive agreement is increasingly used for conveying semantic distinctions, which are not marked in the purist standard grammar in these constructions but are in other constructions such as object marking. Significantly, the expression बात करनी चाहिए *bāt karnī čāhie*, [speech.F do.F must] 'one should speak' occurs with the 'wrong' masculine agreement in the best writers, whatever their regional origin, such as Phanisarnath Renu (Bihar) or Krishna Baldev Vaid (Panjab), when the intention is to give priority not to the exchange but to the simple fact of expressing oneself.[36]

36 And that, even when the noun is qualified: *himsā bāt nahĩ karnā čāhie* [violence.f speech.f do.m must] 'one should not speak violently' (Renu).

References

Adams, James Noel. 2013. *Social variations and the Latin language*. Cambridge: Cambridge University Press.

Benveniste, Emile. 1966. Les transformations des catégories grammaticales. *Problèmes de linguistique générale* (vol. 2), 127–136. Paris: Gallimard.

Bhatt, Rajesh. 2007. Unaccusativity and case licensing. handout (McGill University) *people.umass.edu/bhatt/papers/mcgill-may2007-handout1*

Bhatt, Rajesh. 2005. Long distance agreement in Hindi-Urdu. *Natural Language and Linguistic Theory* 23: 757–807.

Bloch, Jules. 1906. *La phrase nominale en sanscrit*. Paris: Champion.

Bloch, Jules. 1970. [1920]. *The formation of the Marathi language*. (English rendering of the French original *La Formation de la langue marathe*. Paris: Champion). Delhi: Motilal Banarsidass.

Bloch, Jules. 1970. *Indo-Aryan*: From the *vedas* to modern *times*. Paris: Adrien-Maisonneuve. (revised edition and translation of L'indo-aryen du Veda aux temps moderns. Paris: Adrien-Maisonneuve, 1965).

Bubenik, Vit. 1998. A historical syntax of late Indo-Aryan (Apabhraṃśa). Amsterdam: John Benjamins.

Butt, Miriam. 1993. Hindi/Urdu infinitives as NPs. *South asian language review* 3: 51–72.

Bybee, Joan, R. D. Perkins & W. Pagliuca (eds.). 1994. *The evolution of grammar, tense, aspect and modality in the Languages of the world*. Chicago: Chicago University Press.

Cardona, George. & B. Suthar. 2003. Gujarati. In *The Indo-Aryan languages*. In George Cardona & Dhanesh Jain (eds.), (658–97). London: Routledge.

Chatak, Govind. 1966. मध्यपहाड़ी का भाषाशास्त्रीय अध्ययन *Madhyapahāṛī kā bhāshāshāstrīya adhyayan*. Delhi: Radhakrishna Prakashan.

Chatterji, Suniti Kumar. 1986. [1926] *The Evolution of Bengali language*. Delhi: Rupa & Co.

Company Company, Concepcion. 2003. Grammaticalization and category weakness. In *New reflections on grammaticalization*, 201–6, Wischer Ilse & Diewald Gabrielle (eds.). Amsterdam: John Benjamins.

Dave, Trimbaklal, N. 1935. *A study of the Gujarāti language in the 16th century: with special reference to the* Bālāvabodha *to* Upadeśmālā (Suri). London: Royal Asiatic Society.

De Vogüé, Sarah. 1991. La transitivité comme question théorique. *LINX* 24: 37–65.

Dongde, Ramesh V. & Wali, Kashi. 2009. *Marathi*. Amsterdam: John Benjamins.

Eaton, Robert D. 2008. *Kangri in context: An areal perspective*. Michigan, Ann Arbor, University of Michigan PhD thesis.

Ernoult, Ernest & François Thomas. 1951. *Syntaxe latine*. Paris: Klincksieck.

Grierson, G.A. 1967. *Linguistic survey of India*, Delhi. Delhi: Motilal Banarsidass. [Originally published in 1903-1928]

Harris, Alice. 2003 Cross-linguistic perspective in syntactic change. In Joseph & Janda (eds.), *Handbook of historical linguistics*, 529–61. Delhi: Blackwell.

Haspelmath, Martin. 1987. Verbal noun or verbal adjective? The case of the Latin gerundive and gerund. (*Arbeitspapiere, N.F., Nr. 3*) Cologne: Institut für Sprachwissenschaft der Universität zu Köln.

Heine, Bernd & Tania Kuteva. 2005. *Language contact and grammatical change*. Cambridge: Cambridge University Press.

Hock, Hans Heinrich. 1992. *Studies in Sanskrit syntax*. Delhi: Motilal Banarsidass.
Hoernle, A. F. Rudolf. 1880. A comparative grammar of the Gaudian languages, with special reference to the eastern Hindi. London: Trübner & Co.
Jaiswal, Mahesh Prasad. 1962. *A linguistic study of Bundeli*. Leiden: Brill.
Jha, Subhadra. 1985. [1958] *The formation of the Maithili language*. Delhi: Munshiram Manoharlal.
Khokhlova, Liudmila. 2013. Obligational constructions in new Indo-Aryan languages of western India. *Lingua Posnianiensis* LV-2: 91–107.
Kuryłowicz, Jerzy. 1965. The evolution of grammatical categories. *Diogène* 51 (51–71).
Mahajan, Anoop K. 1989. Agreement and agreement phrases. In I. Laka & A. K. Mahajan (eds.), *Functional heads and clause structure*, 217–252, No. 10, MIT Working Papers in Linguistics, Cambridge, MA.
Malchukov, Andrej & Narrog, Heiko. 2009. Case polysemy. In Andrej Malchukov & Anrew Spencer (eds.), *The handbook of case*, 518–34. Oxford: Oxford University Press.
Mithun, Marianne. 1986. On the nature of noun incorporation. *Language*, *62* (1): 32–38.
Mohanan, Tara. 1995. Wordhood and lexicality: Noun incorporation in Hindi. *Natural Language & Linguistic Theory*. 13-1: 75–134
Montaut, Annie. 1997. Benveniste et Kuryłowicz: deux méthodes, deux trouvailles sur le système aspecto-temporel. *Linx* N° spécial 9 (*Emile Benveniste vingt ans après*. C. Normand ed.): 337–53. (available online: http://linx.revues.org/1080)
Montaut, Annie. 2012. Saillance et antisaillance en hindi. *La saillance, Faits de langue 39*: 83–100.
Montaut, Annie. 2013. The rise of non-canonical subjects and semantic alignments in Hindi. Ilja Serzant & Leonid Kulikov (eds.) *The diachronic typology of non-canonical subjects*, 92–117. Amsterdam: John Benjamins.
Montaut, Annie. 2016. Why ergative case marker in modal clauses? The historical evolution of aspect, modality, ergative and locative in Indo-Aryan. In Eystein Dahl & Kryzstof Stronski (eds.), *Ergativity in Indo-Aryan and beyond*, 135–165. Amsterdam: John Benjamins.
Montaut, Annie. 2017. Grammaticalization of participles and gerunds in Indo-Aryan; preterite, future, infinitive. In Andrej Malchukov & Bisang Walter (eds.), *Unity and diversity in grammaticalization scenario*, 95–134, Language Science Press (Studies in Diversity Linguistics 99).
Montaut, Annie. 2018. The rise of differential object marking in Hindi and related languages. In Ilja Serzant & Alena Witzlack Makarevich (eds.), *Diachrony of differential argument marking*. Language Science Press. Pp. 281-313. http://langsci-press.org/catalog/book/173
Pandharipande, Rasjeshari. 1997. *A grammar of the Marathi language*. London: Routledge.
Pandit, Prabodh Bechardas. 1976. *A Study of the Gujarati language in the 14th century with special reference to a critical edition of* Ṣaḍāvaśyakabālāvabodhavṛtti *of Taruṇaprabha*. Bombay: Bharatiya Vidya Bhavan.
Polinsky, Maria & Eric Potsdam. 2001. 'Long-distance agreement and topic in Tsez', *Natural Language and Linguistic Theory 19*, 583–646.
Saxena, Baburam. 1937. *Evolution of Awadhi*. Delhi [1971 reprint]. Delhi: Motilal Banarsidass.
Schwarzschild, L. A. 1955. Notes on the history of the infinitive in Middle Indo-Aryan. *Indian Linguistics* 16: 29–34
Singh, Rajendra & Ramakant Agnihotri. 1997. *Hindi morphology*: A word-based description. Delhi: Motilal Banarsidass.

Snell, Rupert. 1991. *The Hindi classical tradition: A Braj Bhasha reader*. London: School of Oriental and African Studies, University of London.
Southworth, Franklin. 2005. *Linguistic archeology of South Asia*. [the Grierson hypothesis revisited]. London: Routledge.
Stronski, Kryzstof. 2010. Variations of ergativity patterns in Indo-Aryan. *Poznan Studies in Contemporary Linguistics* 46(2): 237–253.
Stronski, Kryzstof. 2014. On the syntax and semantics of the past participle and gerundive in early NIA. Evidence from Pahari. *Folia Linguistica Historica 35*: 275–305.
Tagare, G.V. 1948. *Historical grammar of Apabhramsha*. Poona: Deccan College.
Tessitori, Luigi. 1914-16. Notes on the grammar of the Old Western Rajasthani, with special reference to Apabhramsha and to Gujarati and Marwari. *Indian Antiquary 42–44*.
Tiwari, Udayan N. 1970. [1961] *Hindi bhāṣā kā udgam aur vikās*. Ilahabad: Lok Bharati Prakashan.
Touratier, Christian. 1994. *Syntaxe latine*. Louvain: Peeters.
Wali, Kashi. 2004. *Marathi*. Munchen: Lincom Europa

Ekaterina Kostina

Main verb form in structures of ability/possibility in Hindi

Abstract: The paper aims to provide structural analysis of Hindi potential sequences with modals *saknā* and *pānā* 'to be able to'. Such sequences consist of the uninflected 'main' verb bearing the lexical meaning + an inflected modal auxiliary, expressing ability, possibility, or permission. While the semantics and morphological characteristics of the potential verbs themselves have been analyzed in detail in multiple works on Hindi grammar, specific features of the main verb form, usually referred to as the stem, have remained out of the researchers' scope of interest. However, defining the morphological status of this form might not only provide better understanding of Hindi grammatical patterns, but also help Hindi learners avoid some typical mistakes.

The paper begins with a brief description of potential structures existing in Hindi; this is aimed at drawing a general picture of the system and defining the place of modal auxiliaries *saknā* and *pānā* in it. The next section is dedicated to the analysis of the structure 'X + *x*' - its historical background and areal variations, the morphological features of the main verb, terms used for it in Hindi grammar books and articles, and the grammatical status of the whole sequence. The conclusion is made that the verb preceding *saknā*, although homonymous with the stem, actually takes the form of a non-finite verboid of adverbial nature, for which the term converb (CVB, hereinafter) seems the most preferable.

Sequences with *pānā*, analyzed in Section 4, appear to have a different history and nature, which leads to the possibility of using another verbal form, the oblique infinitive, before the auxiliary. Although interchangeable in some contexts, the converbial and the infinitival structures are used by some Hindi authors to serve different purposes, i.e. to describe one's (in)ability to do something (the converb) and acquisition of permission (the oblique infinitive). At the end of the paper, occasional infinitival and participial combinations with *saknā* are described.

Keywords: Ability & possibility in Hindi, modals, main verb, converb

---

Ekaterina Kostina, Faculty of Asian and African Studies, Saint-Petersburg State University Russia. Email: helkari@mail.ru

https://doi.org/10.1515/9783110610796-007

1 Introduction

Modality is one of the most 'fruitful' topics for a linguist, since the ways of its verbalization depict the linguistic world-image of a speech community in a vivid and distinct manner. Hindi is no exception to this rule, and the semantics and pragmatics of various modal structures to be found in the language has been described and analyzed in detail in a number of monographs and articles (Hook 1974, Daschenko 2002; Shlomper 2005; Bhatt et al. 2011; Poornima 2012).

The scope of this paper will be limited to the structures expressing ability, possibility and permission, particularly, those formed with the help of verbs *saknā* and *pānā,* translated into English as 'can', 'be able to', 'may' and their equivalents. The paper will concentrate not upon the differences in meaning between the modals, but upon the morphological features of the main verb, the bearer of the lexical semantics. This topic has almost escaped the researchers' attention; however it seems worth discussing since its ignorance may lead (and actually leads) to misunderstanding.

The most common mistakes are omitting the main verb (see for example (1a)) and putting the infinitive before the modal verb, as in (1b), both of which result from copying the patterns existing in other languages (like 'I can' in English or '*āmi karte pāri*' in Bengali). Such mistakes are usually not crucial: although examples (1a) and (1b) are found unacceptable by native speakers of Hindi, they still remain understandable and unambiguous. Nevertheless, since the semi-modal *pānā* can also be used in its initial meaning 'to obtain', putting the infinitive in the nominative before it may result in misunderstanding. In (1c) we see an acceptable sentence with the meaning 'Will he be able to sleep?' expressed by the canonical structure – the stem-like 'bare' lexical verb + *pānā*. However, if we mistakenly replace *so* with the infinitive *sonā* (1d), the sentence will be understood as 'Will he receive gold' (1e) due to the homonymy.

(1a) *मैं सकता हूँ।
**mẽ saktā hū̃*
I can.IPFV.M.SG AUX.PRS.SG
'I can.'

(1b) *मैं करना सकता हूँ।
**mẽ karnā saktā hū̃*
I do.INF can.IPFV.M.SG AUX.PRS.SG
'I can do.'

(1c) क्या वह सो पायेगा?
kyā vah so pāyegā
Q he sleep.CVB get.FUT.M.SG
'Will he be able to sleep?'

(1d) *क्या वह सोना पायेगा?
**kyā vah sonā pāyegā*
Q he sleep.INF get.FUT.M.SG
'Will he be able to sleep?'

(1e) क्या वह सोना पायेगा?
kyā vah sonā pāyegā
Q he gold get.FUT.M.SG
'Will he receive gold?'

Therefore, the main objectives of the paper are, first, to define the morphological status of the most frequently encountered form of the main verb in modal structures and, second, to search for and analyze its possible alternatives. Since the author of the paper is not a native speaker of Hindi, all examples have been borrowed from trustworthy literary sources with any exceptions separately justified.

2 Ways to express ability, possibility and permission in Hindi

Hindi has a wide range of patterns to express various aspects of ability and/or possibility and permission, thus providing the speaker with a powerful tool to convey all the subtleties of meaning. For the purpose of this paper, a brief observation of the most common of potential structures (without detailed discussion of the semantic nuances) seems to be sufficient.

2.1 Non-verbal means

The nominal potential structures are the most specified means of expressing modality: unlike the modal verbs, they are seldom (if ever) used to denote both ability and possibility. This leads to considerable diversity of adjectives and nouns of potential semantics. Here we will confine ourselves to those of them which usually form combinations with verbs and play the role of modal auxiliaries.

2.1.1 Ability

Verbal adjectives with the meaning 'able', 'capable of', derived from the Sanskrit root *śak* 'to be able to' (*śakt, śaktimān*) or derivations of *kṣam* 'to allow', 'to be able to' and *samarth* 'to be/make fit', 'to prepare' should be mentioned first. They are usually preceded by the oblique infinitive (ending in –*e*) with the locative case-marker (postposition) *mẽ*[1] 'in', as can be seen from the examples (2a) to (2d). In Urdu-styled Hindi, the word *qābil/kābil* of Arabic origin can be used with the the oblique infinitive of the main verb instead of the *tatsama* words listed above, see example (2e):

(2a) क्या जादू था उनकी लेखनी में जो... वातावरण को...सजीव और उत्फुल्ल करने में शक्त था।
kyā jādū thā un-kī lekhnī-mẽ jo
what magic.M AUX.PST.M.SG he.HON-GEN.F pen.F-LOC that...
vātāvaraṇ-ko sajīv ɔr utphull karne-mẽ
environment.M-ACC vivid and flowering do.INF.OBL-LOC
śakt thā
able AUX.PST.M.SG
'What magic was there in his pen, that was able to make the environment vivid and flowering.' (Brahmānand 1971: 201)

(2b) मनुष्य अपने को एकरस रखने में शक्तिमान है।
manuṣya apne-ko ekras rakhne-mẽ
man.M self's.OBL.ACC one.type keep.INF.OBL-LOC
śaktimān hɛ
able be.PRS.SG
'A man is able to keep him or herself unchanged.' (Premdās 1983: 89)

(2c) बच्चे... पाठ पढ़ने में सक्षम पाए गए।
bačče... pāṭh paṛhne-mẽ sakṣam pāe gae
child.M.PL lesson read.INF.OBL-LOC able find.PFV.M.PL go.PFV.M.PL
'Children... proved to be able to read the text.' (Mahrotrā and Śarmā 2015)

1 The question of the morphological status of the case-markers (or simple, underived postpositions) shall not be discussed here; these are glossed following Montaut (2004).

(2d) निविशेष शब्द... रचना को काव्यत्व की पदवी प्रदान करने में समर्थ नहीं होते।
niviśeṣ śabd... račnā-ko kāvyatv-kī padavī
ordinary word.M composition-ACC poetry-GEN.F status.F
pradān karne.mẽ samarth nahī̃ hote
provision do.INF.OBL-LOC able not be.IPFV.M.PL
'Ordinary words are not able to provide a composition with a status of poetry.' (Tripāṭhī 1973: 3)

(2e) अगर आप जाने क़ाबिल नहीं तो मत जाइये।
agar āp jāne qābil nahī̃ to mat jāiye
if you.HON go.INF.OBL able not then don't go.IMP.HON
'If you are not able to go, then do not go.' (Prasād 1998: 324)

Nouns of the same verbal origin (*śakti, kṣamtā, sāmarthya* etc.) can also express ability being accompanied by the infinitive in the Genitive form; see examples (3a) to (3c). These nouns can act as the grammatical subject of the sentence with the predicate represented by verbs *honā* 'to be', *rahnā* 'to stay' or *bāqī honā* 'be left' or as the direct object of the verb *rakhnā* 'to keep'. There are other words meaning 'power' in Hindi (such as *vaś/bas*), but they are less frequently used with verbs and do not usually denote ability *to do* something.

(3a) उसमें लिखने की शक्ति खूब बाक़ी है।
us-mẽ likhne-kī śakti khūb bāqī hɛ.
he.OBL-LOC write.INF.OBL-GEN.F power.F enough left be.PRS.SG
'There's enough ability to write left in him.' (Nāgar 2006: 331)

(3b) उसमें अपनी रक्षा करने की सामर्थ्य ही नहीं रही।
us-mẽ apnī rakṣā karne-kī sāmarthya
she.OBL-LOC self's.F protection.F do.INF.OBL-GEN.F power.F
hī nahī̃ rahī.
even not stay.PFV.F
'There was no more power to protect herself left in her.' (Premchand 2014)

(3c) इस शहर में कितने लोग ईश्वर की उपासना ... करने की क्षमता रखते हैं?
is śahar-mẽ kitne log īśvar-kī
this.OBL town-LOC how many people.M God-GEN.F
upāsanā karne-kī kṣamatā rakhte hɛ̃
worship.F do.INF.OBL-GEN.F ability.F keep.IPFV.M.PL AUX.PRS.PL
'How many people in this town posess the ability to worship God?' (Kohlī 2009: 404)

2.1.2 Possibility

The idea of *possibility* (and more often, impossibility) can be expressed by adjectives *sambhav* (or *mumkin*) and *asambhav* (or *nāmumkin*) meaning 'possible' and 'impossible', respectively, see examples (4a) and (4b). The example (4c) demonstrates an interesting combination of the two ideas: ability expressed by the modal auxiliary *saknā* and possibility expressed by an adjective. The noun *sambhāvnā* 'possibility' is also widely used with the infinitive of the lexical verb in the Genitive form, see Example (4d).

(4a) गली में लेटना मुमकिन नहीं था।
galī-mẽ *leṭnā* *mumkin* *nahī̃* *thā.*
street.F-LOC lie.INF possible not be.PST.M.SG
'It was not possible to lie down in the street.' (Kamaleśvar 2008: 170)

(4b) मेरे लिये वापस लौटना संभव नहीं।
mere *liye* *vāpas* *lɔṭnā* *sambhav* *nahī̃.*
1-GEN.OBL for back return.INF possible not
'It's not possible for me to come back.' (Kamaleśvar 2008: 422)

(4c) कश्मीर को भारत के... जबड़ों से निकाल सकना मुमकिन नहीं।
kaśmīr-ko *bhārat-ke...* *jabṛõ-se* *nikāl*
Kashmir.M.ACC India.M-GEN.M.OBL jaw.M.PL.OBL-ABL take out
saknā *mumkin* *nahī̃*
can.INF possible not
'It is not possible to take Kashmir out of India's... jaws.' (Kamaleśvar 2005: 102)

(4d) सफलता प्राप्त करने की संभावना काफ़ी अधिक है।
saphaltā *prāpt* *karne-kī* *sambhāvanā* *kāfī*
success.F obtained do.INF.OBL-GEN.F possibility.F quite
adhik *hɛ.*
more be.PRS.3.SG
'The possibility of getting success is quite great.' (Singh 2008: 99)

2.1.3 Permissive

As for the 'permissive' meaning, nouns *anumati* (*Skt.*) *and ijāzat* (*Ar.*), both preceded by the infinitive in the Genitive form, are the most common, see examples (5a) and (5b).

(5a) वे टकसाल देखने की भी अनुमति चाहती हैं।
ve *ṭaksāl* *dekhne-kī* *bhī* *anumati*
they mint.M see.INF.OBL-GEN.F also permission.F
čāhtī *hɛ̃.*
want.IPFV.F AUX.PRS.PL
'They also want a permission to see the mint.' (Bhaṇḍārī 2002: 146)

(5b) उसे... लिपस्टिक का इस्तेमाल करने की इजाज़त नहीं।
use... *lipsṭik-kā* *istemāl* *karne-kī*
she.OBJ lipstick.M-GEN.M.SG usage.M do.INF.OBL-GEN.F
ijāzat *nahĩ.*
permission.F not
'She is not allowed to... apply lipstick.' (Nāgar 2006: 54)

A brief observation of non-verbal means of expressing the idea of potential modality has shown that all of them are very specific and interchangibility between the semantic groups is impossible (one cannot use *śakti* instead of *sambhāvanā* or *anumati*). As for the form of the main verb, it is always the infinitive, playing the role of the indirect object or the modifier.

2.2 Non-modal verbs and potential moods

Besides nouns and adjectives, some verbs of non-modal nature can be used in potential structures. Putting the verb *ānā* 'to come' after the infinitive of the main verb, the speaker implies that a person (or a personified inanimate object) has a skill of doing something. The subject (the experiencer) here receives the Accusative-Dative *ko* case-marker or is put in the Objective case (personal pronoun), see Examples (6a) and (6b). The infinitive of the main verb usually acts as the grammatical subject and is in masculine singular; however, the infinitive of a transitive verb may sometimes follow the number and the gender of its direct object, causing the same changes in the form of *ānā* itself, as in example (6c). This phenomenon cannot but remind us of the more controversial structures of obligation with the auxiliaries *čāhie, honā* and *paṛnā* (6d):

(6a) पर स्वामी को खाना बनाना आता है क्या?
par svāmi-ko *khānā* *banana* *ātā*
but swami.M.DAT food.M prepare.INF.OBL come.IPFV.M.SG
hɛ *kyā?*
AUX.PRS.SG Q
'But is Swami really able to cook?' (Kohlī 2009: 321)

(6b) तुम्हें... टाइप करना आता है?
tumhẽ ... ṭāip karnā ātā hɛ.
you.DAT type do.INF.OBL come.IPFV.M.SG AUX.PRS.SG
'Can you type?' (Varmā 2009: 184)

(6c) मुझे आलोचना नहीं करनी आती।
mujhe āločanā nahī̃ karnī ātī.
I.DAT critics.F not do.INF.F come.IPFV.F.SG
'I can't write critics.' (Gopāl 2006: 235)

Compare:

(6d) बात उसे कहनी ही पड़ी।
bāt use kahnī hī paṛī.
story.F he.DAT tell.INF.F indeed fall.PFV.F
'He indeed had to tell (her) the story.' (Bhaṇḍārī 2002: 36)

Ability due to having a skill (particularly a learnt one) can also be expressed by the combination of the infinitive with the verb *jānnā, 'to know'*, see the examples (7a) to (7c). The subject here is in the Nominative; the infinitive usually retains the same masculine singular ending *-ā*, whether the verb is intransitive (7a) or transitive (7b). However, a transitive infinitive (but not the finite verb) may sometimes agree with the direct object, as in (7c).

(7a) नाविक... तैरना जानता है।
nāvik... tɛrnā jāntā hɛ.
boatman.M swim.INF know.IPFV.M.SG AUX.PRS.SG
'A boatman can swim.' (Mīcū and Tripāṭhī 2008: 73)

(7b) प्रजा... अपनी रक्षा करना जानती है।
prajā... apnī rakṣā karnā
people.F.SG self's.F protection.F do.INF.M
jāntī hɛ.
know.IPFV.F.SG AUX.PRS.SG
'People know how to protect themselves.' (Caudharī 2008: 316)

(7c) वह भी अपनी रक्षा करनी जानता था।
vah bhī apnī rakṣā karnī jāntā thā.
he also self's.F defense.F do.INF.F know.IPFV.M.SG AUX.PST.M.SG
'He also could protect himself.' (Śarmā 1973: 67)

In negative or quasi-negative structures, the combination of the perfective participle with the verb *jānā* 'to go', bears the meaning of 'impossibility due to some internal restrictions'. The subject is marked by the Instrumental *se*. The structure is usually referred to as the 'modal passive' (Montaut 2004: 208) or the 'passive of (dis)ability' (Van Olphen 1970). In works by Indian authors it may also be called the 'impersonal voice' (Kachru 2006: 94), Hin. *bhāv vāčya* (Pā̃ḍe 2012: 205–207). T. Oranskaya (Oranskaya 2006: 152–164) distinguishes between the 'structure of impossibility' (with an intransitive main verb, see example (8a)), and the 'modal passive' (with a transitive main verb, see example (8b)).

(8a) तारा से अधिक देर तक अपने घर में रहा नहीं गया।
tārā-se adhik der tak apne ghar-mẽ
Tara-INSTR much delay.F till self's.M.OBL house.M-LOC
rahā nahī̃ gayā.
stay.PFV.M.SG not go.PFV.M.SG
'Tara was unable to stay at her home for much time.' (Nāgar 2006: 224)

(8b) किसी का भी कष्ट मुझसे देखा नहीं जाता था।
kisī-kā bhī kaṣṭ mujh-se dekhā
anyone-GEN.M.SG even trouble .M I.OBL-INSTR look.PFV.M.SG
nahī̃ jātā thā.
not go.IPFV.M.SG AUX.PST.M.SG
'I could not look at anyone being in trouble.' (Jain 2012: 411)

The speaker's perception of possibility of any event can be expressed grammatically by putting the verb in the form of the *Conjunctive*, or the *Potential mood* (see example (9a)), or the *Presumptive* (see example (9b)).

(9a) तुम शायद सोच रही हो...
tum śāyad soč rahī ho...
you maybe think stay.PFV.F. AUX.CONJ.2.NEUT
'Maybe you think...' (Bhaṇḍārī 2002: 352)

(9b) ड्राइवर आ गया होगा तुम्हारा।
ḍrāivar ā gayā hogā tumhārā.
driver.M come go.PFV.M.SG AUX.FUT.M.SG you-GEN.M.SG
'Your driver must have come.' (Nāgar 2006: 33)

Permission can be expressed by the oblique infinitive + *denā* 'to give', both in affirmative (example (10a)) and negative (example (10b)) structures:

(10a) खुद कश्मीरियों ने उसे भारत में मिलने दिया था।
khud kaśmīriyõ-ne use bhārat-mẽ
self's Kashmiri.M.PL-ERG it.OBJ India.M-LOC
milne diyā thā.
meet.INF.OBL give.PFV.M.SG AUX.PST.M.SG
'The Kashmiris themselves let it merge in India.' (Kamaleśvar 2005: 102)

(10b) वह तो उसे कभी बाहर नहीं सोने देगा।
vah to use kabhī bāhar nahī̃ sone degā.
he EMPH she.OBJ ever outdoors not sleep.INF.OBL give.FUT.M.SG
'As for him, he will never allow her to sleep outdoors.' (Bhaṇḍārī 2002: 154)

The overview presented above should by no means be considered an attempt to cover all the ways of expressing the potential and permissive modality in Hindi. Its purpose was just to demonstrate how wide the variety of modal structures is. More surprisingly, almost all the aforementioned meanings can be covered (to some extent) by a pair of potential verbs: the modal *saknā* and the semi-modal *pānā*. G. Shlomper justifiably notices that 'the verb *sak-*... may turn out to be an important medium in all three subclasses.'[2] (Shlomper 2005: 158)

2.3 Saknā and pānā

It seems unnecessary to describe the semantics of the two potential verbs in detail here, as it has already been done in many works on Hindi grammar (see References). The most general idea can be formulated following H. Nespital: "... सकना meaning 'can, be able, mostly in the sense of having the intellectual, physical, artistic, or psychological ability, capacity of doing .... (s.th.); पाना meaning here also 'can, be able' [to] do... (s.th.) because internal or external conditions make it possible." (Nespital 2008: vi) The two modal verbs share some common features and also have a number of peculiarities.

The examples (11a) to (11f) will briefly illustrate the fact that both of the discussed verbs can express ability, possibility and permission.

2 G. Shlomper refers here to the three classes of modality, i.e. deontic, inherent, and epistemic.

2.3.1 Ability/inability

(11a) उसे कुछ काम है इसलिये वह... नहीं आ सकेगा।
use kuč̌h kām hɛ isliye vah...
he.OBJ some work.M be.PRS.SG therefore he
nahī̃ ā sakegā.
not come can.FUT.M.SG
'He's got some work to do; therefore, he will not be able to come.' (Rākeś 2008: 256)

(11b) मैं बात का सूत्र ... पकड़ नहीं पाया।
mɛ̃ bāt-kā sūtr... pakaṛ nahī̃ pāyā.
I word.F-GEN.M.SG thread.M catch not get.PFV.M.SG
'I was unable to catch the thread of the talk.' (Rākeś 2008: 70)

2.3.2 Possibility

(11c) पर अब क्या हो सकता था!
par ab kyā ho saktā thā.
but now what be can.IPFV.M.SG AUX.PST.M.SG
'But what could happen now!' (Bhaṇḍārī 2002: 270)

(11d) न्याय कैसे हो पाएगा?
nyāy kɛse ho pāegā.
justice.M how be get.FUT.3.M.SG
'How will justice be possible?' (Kohlī 2009: 2/67)

2.3.3 Permission

(11e) मैं तुम्हें रोकूँगा नहीं... तुम जा सकते हो।
mɛ̃ tumhẽ rokū̃gā nahī̃...
I you.OBJ stop.FUT.1.M.SG not
tum jā sakte ho.
you go can.IPFV.M.PL AUX.PRS.2.NEUT
'I won't stop you... You may go.' (Varmā 2009: 129)

(11f) नकाबपोशों की आज्ञानुसार वह उस कोठरी के अंदर नहीं जाने पाया था।
nakābpośõ-ki *āgyānusār…* *vah* *us*
masked.M.PL.OBL-GEN.F as per order he that.OBL
koṭhrī-ke *andar* *nahī̃* *jāne*
chamber.F-GEN.M.OBL inside not go.INF.OBL
pāyā *thā.*
get.PFV.M.SG AUX.PST.M.SG
'Due to the order of the masked people, he couldn't enter that chamber.' (Khatrī 2005: 30)

At the same time, it should be borne in mind that *pānā* is a semi-modal verb, widely used in its initial meaning 'to get', 'to find', 'to obtain' beyond the limits of potential modality (see examples (12a) and (12b)).

(12a) यह मंत्र मैं ने अपने गुरु से पाया था।
yah mantr *mẽ-ne* *apne* *guru-se*
this spell.M.SG I-ERG self's.M.OBL teacher.M.SG-ABL
pāyā *thā.*
get.PFV.M.SG AUX.PST.M.SG
'I was given this spell by my teacher.' (Kohlī 2008: 181)

(12b) उन्होंने तो कभी 'हर आदमी' और 'दुनिया' को अपने लिये ज़रूरी नहीं पाया।
unhõ-ne *to* *kabhī* *har* *ādmī* *ɔr*
he.HON.OBL-ERG certainly ever every man.M.SG and
duniyā-ko *apne-liye* *zarūrī* *nahī̃* *pāyā.*
world.F.SG.OBJ self's.M.OBL.for necessary not get.PFV.M.SG
'He never found 'every man' and 'the world' necessary for himself.' (Kamaleśvar 2013: 461)

However, this semi-modal goes much further along the way of grammaticalization then the verbs *ānā* and *jānnā*, occasionally used in modal structures (as it has been shown in Section 1.2). First, it is less specified and can be used in a wider range of contexts and in almost all tenses and moods (the restrictions will be discussed below). Moreover, when used as a modal verb, *pānā* changes its grammatical properties and does not require the ergative structure in the Perfective tenses (compare Examples (12a) (ergative) and (11b) (non-ergative)). Just like *saknā* and unlike *ānā* and *jānnā*, it cannot be used individually even in the case of anaphora (compare Examples (13a) and (13b) with (13d) and (13e)).

(13a) अच्छा साब, आप को गाना आता है? मेमसाब को तो Ø आता होगा।
aččhā sāb āp-ko gānā ātā hɛ?
ok Sir.M.SG you.HON.DAT sing.INF come.IPFV.M AUX.PRS.SG
memsāb-ko to Ø ātā hogā.
madam.F.SG-DAT EMPH Ø come.IPFV.M AUX.FUT.SG
'Ok Sir, can you sing? Madam certainly can.' (Kātyāyan 1994: 21)

(13b) तुम गीत गाना जानते हो? – चीनी ने कहा – Ø जानता हूँ, मगर तुम ... नहीं समझ सकोगे।
tum gīt gānā jānte ho? čīnī-ne
you song.M.SG sing.INF know.IPFV.M AUX.PRS.2.PL Chinese-ERG
kahā Ø jāntā hū̃, magar tum
say.PFV.M.SG Ø know.IPFV.M AUX.PRS.1.SG but you
nahī̃ samajh sakoge.
not understand.CVB can.FUT.2.M.PL
'Can you sing songs? – the Chinese said – Yes, I can. But you won't be able to understand.' (Rādhākr̥ṣṇa 1963)

(13c) तू मेरी बात तो सुन सकती है। हाँ, हाँ, सुन सकती हूँ।
tū merī bāt to sun saktī hɛ
you I-GEN.F word.F EMPH hear can.IPFV.F AUX.PRS.SG
- hā̃-hā̃, sun saktī hū̃.
- yes-yes hear can.IPFV.F. AUX.PRS.1.SG
'You can hear me, can't you? Yes, I can hear you.' (Singh 1999: 192)

(13d) सुन पायेगा जो मैं कहूँगा? ...सुन पाऊँगा, प्रशांत।
sun pāyegā jo mɛ̃ kahū̃gā?
hear get.FUT.M.SG what I say.FUT.1.M.SG
... sun pāū̃gā, Praśānt
... hear get.FUT.1.M.SG Prashant
'Will you be able to hear what I say? –... I'll be able to hear it, Prashant.' (Kamaleśvar 2008: 468)

Saknā and *pānā* have very similar usage restrictions. They are never used in the Imperative, are unable to form derived (causative) verbs, and cannot form compounds with light verbs (*kar sakiye, *kar sakānā, *kar sak lenā* or **kar pā lenā* are unacceptable).

The difference lies in the field of Progressive tenses: while *pānā* appears in such structures quite often (14a), *saknā* is not supposed to be used in the progressive (Montaut 2004, p. 128, Van Olphen 1970: 295). Rare examples of such usage can, however, be met in Hindi fiction, demonstrating an attempt to complete the defective paradigm of *saknā* (see example (14b)).

(14a) मगर मैं तय नहीं कर पा रही कि...
magar mẽ tay nahī̃ kar pā-rahī ki...
but I fixed not do get.PROG that
'But I cannot decide if...' (Rākeś 2008: 83)

(14b) लेकिन बात मन में इतने दिनों से घुमड़ रही थी कि वह रह नहीं सक रहा था।
lekin bāt man-mẽ itne dinõ-se
but matter.F mind.M-LOC so many day.M.OBL.PL-ABL
ghumaṛ-rahī thī ki vah rah nahī̃
cloud over.PROG AUX.PST.F.SG that he live not
sak-rahā thā.
can.PROG.M.SG AUX.PST.M.SG
'But the thing had been occupying his mind for so many days, that he was unable to live.' (Yādav 2007: 287)

Now, if we turn our attention to the topic of this paper, i.e. to the form of the main verb used with modals, we will see that both *saknā* and *pānā* usually require that the main verb be put in the special 'bare' form rather than the infinitive (examples (11a) to (11e)). In modern standard Hindi, this is always true for *saknā* (exceptions will be discussed in Section 5). *Pānā* allows the oblique infinitive in permissive contexts (11f).

One more considerable difference between these two verbs comes out when we speak about passive structures. The problem of the involvement of potential structures into passive transformations has been discussed in detail in Bhatt et al. 2011: 54–56. As an intransitive verb, *saknā* does not undergo passive transformation, but it allows the main verb to take the passive form, see Example (15a). On the contrary, *pānā* is not supposed to form structures with the main verb in passive. Unlike *āp kā kām nahī̃ kiyā jā sakā*, 'Your work couldn't have been done', **āp kā kām nahī̃ kiyā jā pāyā* is incorrect, see (Singh 1985: 113).[3] The passivisation of *pānā* in its modal meaning is also usually considered impossible; however, rare examples can still be found in newspapers and analytics, see examples (15b) and (15c).

3 Exceptions to this rule, however, can be found:
मुफ़लिसी और विलासिता का ऐसा संयोग इस दुनिया में बिरलों के पास देखा जा पाएगा।
mufalisī ɔr vilāsitā-kā ɛsā saṃyog is duniyā-mẽ
poverty.F and luxury.F-GEN.M.SG such.M.SG combination.M this.OBL world.F-LOC
biralõ-ke pās dekhā jā pāegā.
rare.m.pl.obl-gen.m.obl near see.pfv.m.sg go get.fut.m.sg
'Such a combination of poverty and luxury can be seen rather rarely in this world.' (Tripāṭhī 2014)

(15a) पैर नहीं रखा जा सकता था।
pɛr nahī̃ rakhā jā saktā thā.
foot.M.SG not put.PFV.M.SG go.CVB can.IPFV.M.SG AUX.PST.M.SG
'It was impossible to place one's foot.' (Kamaleśvar 2013: 275)

(15b) जनभाषा क्या होती है, यह भी आज तक नहीं समझ पाया गया।
janbhāṣā kyā hotī hɛ, yah bhī
mass-language.F.SG what be.IPFV.F AUX.PRS.SG this also
āj-tak nahī̃ samajh pāyā gayā.
today.until not understand.CVB get.PFV.M go.PFV.M
'But what the national language is, this proved impossible to be under stood until now.' (Nāth 2012)

(15c) ऐसा दु:साहस... विदेशी शासन के दौरान भी नहीं कर पाया गया...
ɛsā duḥsāhas... videśī śāsan-ke
such.M.SG audacity.M.SG foreign rule.M.SG-GEN.M.OBL
dɔrān bhī nahī̃ kar pāyā gayā...
during also not do.CVB get.PFV.M go.PFV.M
'Such recklessness couldn't have been done even during the ... foreign rule...' (Singh 2014: 82)

So, to sum up: Hindi applies various verbal and non-verbal tools to express potential modality; however, the verbs *saknā* and *pānā* stand apart for a number of reasons: firstly, they demonstrate a greater degree of universality, both semantic and grammatical; secondly, both are usually accompanied by the main verb not in the infinitive, but in a specific 'bare' form, lacking the affix *-nā*; thirdly, they are never used independently and lastly, *saknā* at least cannot undergo the passive transformation.

If we attempt to trace back Indo-Aryan potential patterns and compare the structures found in Hindi with those from ancient Indian literature, we will be surprised to see a totally different picture. The Sanskrit root *śak*, from which the modern *saknā* is derived, demonstrates combinations with the infinitive, it can be used in passive and can stand individually. In the following section a possible explanation of this difference will be provided.

3 *Saknā:* historical and areal overview

The Sanskrit root *śak* ('to be able') is quite often met in Epic, Classical and Medieval texts, with its forms and specific features of usage well described in Sanskrit grammars (e.g. Speijer 1993[1886]: 303–305). It was widely used in both finite and non-finite (p.p. *śakta*, p.fut.pass. *śakya* 'able') forms, and was usually complemented by the infinitive, see examples (16a) to (16c). However, the infinitive was not the only possible choice. In his monumental Dictionary, Sir Monier Monier-Williams notices that under some conditions *śak* can also be used 'with acc. dat. or loc., rarely acc. of a verbal noun .... e.g. with ग्रहणाय or ग्रहणे, 'to be able to seize'; वध-निर्णेकम् अ-शक्नुवन्, 'unable to atone for slaughter'' (Monier-Williams 2008: 1044), see example (16d).

(16a) यावद् अहं प्रचलितुं शक्नोमि...

yāvat	*aham*	*pračalitum*	*śaknomi.*
as soon as	I	walk away.INF	can.PRS.1.SG

'As soon as I can walk away...' (Kale 1986: 156)

(16b) परोक्षे खलीकर्तुं शक्यते...

parokṣe	*khalīkartuṁ*	*śakyate...*
invisibility.M.SG-LOC	beat.INF	can.PASS.PRS.3.SG

'(He) can be beaten when I don't see it.' (Tripāṭhī 2002: 150)

(16c) नित्यं प्रसारितकरो मित्रोऽपि न वीक्षितुं शक्यः।

nityam prasāritakaro	*mitro'pi*	*na*	*vīkṣitum*	*śakyaḥ.*
always extending.hands	sun even	not	see.INF	can.PFPASS.M.SG

'The sun always keeps extending his hands (rays) and is unbearable to look at.' (Kale 1986: 111)

(16d) भवान् ... मम न ग्रहणे शक्तः ...

bhavān...	*mama*	*na*	*grahaṇe*	*śaktaḥ...*
Sir.M.SG.NOM	I.GEN	not	seizure.N.SG.LOC	can.PPASS.M.SG

'You, unable to seize me...' (Mahābhāratam 12:136:106)

The possibility of employing nouns with *śak* indicates the specific relation between the potential verb and the lexeme denoting the action. This can be illustrated by a quotation from the explanation by Dr. Rāmśaṅkar Tripāṭhī of a verse from the classical drama *Mr̥č̌čhakaṭikam* (example (17a)).

(17a) अयं पट: प्रावरितुं न शक्यते।

ayaṁ	*paṭaḥ*	*prāvarituṁ*	*na*	*śakyate.*
this.M.SG.NOM	cloth .M.SG.N	cover.INF	not	can.PASS.PRS.3.SG

'This cloth cannot be worn to cover (the body).'

Dr. Tripāṭhī explains: 'अयम् - यह, पट: - वस्त्र, प्रावरितुम् - (शरीर) ढकने के लिए अर्थात् ढकने में, न - नहीं, शक्यते - समर्थ है... अर्थ - ... यह वस्त्र शरीर ढकने लायक नहीं है' (Tripāṭhī 2002: 143). His treatment of the infinitive *prāvarituṁ* as '*for* covering, i.e. *in* covering' demonstrates that the infinitive or the verbal noun used with *śak* played the role of an indirect object, something to which the potential is applied, and the verb *śak* was not an auxiliary, but a contentive verb, capable of being used independently, see example (17b).

(17b) यदि शक्नोषि काकुत्स्थ द्वन्द्वं दास्यामि ते ततः।
yadi śaknoṣi kākutstha dvandvaṁ
if can.PRS.2.SG descendant of Kakutstha.VOC duel.M.ACC.SG
dāsyāmi te tataḥ.
give.FUT.1SG you.SG.ACC then
'O the descendant of Kakutstha! If you can <fix an arrow>, I will engage you in a duel.' (Vālmīki Rāmāyanam 1:75:28)

The same observations remain true for the Pali verb *sak-*, consider example (18).

(18) न हि सक्खिन्ति धेनुपापि छेत्तुम्...
na hi sakkhinti dhenupāpi čhettum.
not for can.FUT.3.PL calve even break.INF
'For even calves shall not be able to break...' (Johansson 2012: 157)

However, in the course of phonetic and grammatical changes, the infinitive gradually began to blend with another quasi-nominal verbal form, usually referred to as the *conjunctival participle, the absolutive, the gerund or the converb* (this term seems the most appropriate for a number of reasons which will be presented in Section 3). The main function of this form is to denote the action completed or begun prior to the action expressed by the finite form of a verb. The abundant usage of such forms for a sequence of actions has been one of the characteristic features of Indo-Aryan languages since ancient time, see example (19).

(19) एवं विचिन्त्य तं दर्भैः सञ्छाद्य धनुषि समारोप्य स्कन्धे कृत्वा गृहं प्रति प्रस्थितः।
evam vičintya tam darbhaiḥ sañčhādya dhanuṣi samāropya
so think.CVB it.ACC grass-INSTR.PL cover.CVB bow-LOC.SG put upon.CVB
skandhe kṛtvā gṛham-prati prasthitaḥ.
shoulder-LOC.SG do.CVB house.ACC.SG.towards leave.PPP.NOM.SG
'Having thought so, (he) covered it (the turtle) with the grass-ropes, fastened the rope to his bow.tip, put it on his shoulder and started home.' (Kale 1986: 131).

In his Pali grammar, Thomas Oberlies observes that the absolutival (i.e. converbial) suffix *-tūna* 'seems to be based on **tŭ̄*, which resulted from a blending of (absol.) *-tvā* and (inf.) *-tum*' (Oberlies 2001: 269). Although at the Old Indo-Aryan stage the infinitive and the converb were never used interchangeably, in Prakrits other than Pali, according to R. Pischel, absolutives may well be used in infinitival meaning and *vice versa* (Pischel and Jha 1999: 461, 467).

In Apabhraṃśa languages, the trend becomes even more evident. Interchangeability of the infinitive and the converb (now often formed by the new suffix *-i*) has been recorded for the structures of purpose with the verbs of motion (Bubenik 1998: 207), with *lag(g)-* 'be attached' (Bubenik 1998: 218), with *jā-* 'go' to denote completion or result (Bubenik 1998: 113). As for the modal structures, we find only the converb and no longer the infinitive with the potential *sakkai:* 'The main verb complementing the modal verb *sakkai* 'can' (or the adjective *samathu* 'capable') is expressed by the gerund in Apabhraṃśa' (Bubenik 1998: 206), see example (20).

(20) *ko sakkai rāya gaṇevi tāiṃ.*
who can.PRS.3.SG king count.GER those
'King, who can count them?' (Paumacariu 37.5.8, cited in Bubenik 1998: 206)

Old Hindi also employs converbs with *sak-* (Strnad 2013: 446), as in the well-known Kabir's saying, see example (21a). Here it is the same form that is used to denote actions preceding or accompanying the predicate verb, and it usually takes the ending *–I*, with two exceptions: *de-* 'to give' and *le-* 'to take', which have the zero-ending. According to J. Strnad, 'the reason for the loss of the final *-i* may be found in the weakening of unstressed short vowel following immediately after a stressed long one' (Strnad 2013: 447). Converbial forms in *–i* can be found in combination with the potential auxiliary in early samples of modern Hindi (21b) along with the zero-ending form (21c). However, in standard Hindi the 'bare' form appears to have always been considered more preferable (see Greaves 1921: 253).

(21a) न कछु किया न करि सका।
nā kačhu kiyā na kari sakā.
not anything do.PFV.M.SG not do.CVB can
'I haven't done anything and cannot do anything.' (Kabir)

(21b) अथवा तू अपने भाई को क्यों कर कहि सकता है ...।

athavā	*tū*	*apne*	*bhāī-ko*	*kyõkar*	*kahi*
otherwise	you	self's.OBL	brother.M.ACC	why	say.CVB
saktā	*hɛ.*				
can.IPFV.M.SG	AUX.PRS.SG				

'Otherwise how can you say to your brother...' (New Testament 1849: 16)

(21c) और कोई... उसे एक बात न कह सका।

ɔr	*koī...*	*use*	*ek*	*bāt*	*na*	*kah*	*sakā.*
and	anyone	he.OBJ	one	word.F	not	say.CVB	can.PFV.M.SG

'And no one was able to say a single word to him?' (New Testament 1849: 9)

A brief history of Indo-Aryan potential structures has demonstrated that in combinations with the potential modal verb originating from the Sanskrit root *śak* the converb gradually replaced the infinitive, 'which was lost or confused with the former in later Middle Indo-Aryan...' (Tikkanen 1987: 263). In Medieval Hindi literature converbs are quite easily distinguishable from both the infinitive and the stem, and researchers never hesitate in postulating the nature of the lexical verb form complementing *sak-* (the difference between the concepts concerns only the terminology). Modern standard Hindi has lost the converb in *-i* in favor of the bare one, homonymous with the stem, and this fact resulted in the appearance of the two-way interpretation of this form.

The possibility of one more shift, this time from the converb to the stem (similar to the shift from the infinitive to the converb), needs extra examination. In this paper, we will restrict ourselves to a discussion of the formal compliance of the lexical verb form complementing *saknā* with the requirements for a language unit to be referred to as the root, the stem or a verboid (Section 3).

Some evidence to support the converbial nature of the form in question can be collected from other modern languages of the area. They also have the converb in potential structures with the verbs originating from *śak-* (Zograf 1976: 256), and this converb is different from the stem. Gujarati presents a classical illustration of the phenomenon (Nespital 2008: v), although G. Cardona considers the form before the potential verb the infinitive, homonymous with the converb (Cardona 2004: 1728). Marathi is supposed to have the infinitive, but this form (ending in nasalized *-ũ*) has more in common with the adverbial participle (in *-ūn*) than with other quasi-nominals (Kuznetsov 1978: 110–111, Zograf 1976: 257). In Hindi dialects the so-called 'reduced'/'shortened' form of the converb, ending in *–i(y)* or equal to the verbal root (depending on the root type), may also combine with *sak*, see examples (22a) and (22b) from modern Awadhi and (22c) from modern Braj.

(22a) कोऊ हमारे मुकाबिले ठहरि न सकी।
koū hamare mukābile ṭhahari na sakī.
anyone I-GEN.OBL confrontation.M.OBL stand.CVB not can.FUT.3.SG
'No one will be able to confront me.' (Liperovskiy 1997: 142)

(22b) *tum dui jane kā kām kar sakat ho?*
you two man.M.PL what work.M do.CVB can.IPFV.M AUX.PRS.2.NEUT
'What work can the two of you do?' (Liperovskiy 1997: 142)

(22c) अब तू बेखटके जाय सकइ ऐ।
ab tū bekhaṭke jāy sakai ai.
now you without fear go.CVB can.CONJ.2.SG AUX.PRS.2.SG
'Now you can go without fear.' (Liperovskiy 1988: 108)

Whether the converb has turned into the stem or not, the initial replacement of the infinitive with the converb changed the roles of the components of the potential structure. In Hindi the lexical verb no longer takes the substantival form of a verbal noun or a noun-like verboid (the infinitive); therefore, it cannot be perceived as an indirect object – the area in which the potential manifests itself. In Hindi the lexical verb has truly become the main one, the center of the verbal phrase. This resulted in the impossibility of using *saknā* in the Passive form, since it is the lexical verb and not the modal that has the ability to take the direct object now. Moreover, it became impossible to separate the modal *saknā*, now acting as an auxiliary, from the lexical verb (see deletion restrictions in Masica 1991: 375). The impossibility of dropping the lexical verb (even in answers) is a characteristic property of all verbal combinations on the basis of the converb, see examples (23a) and (23b).

(23a) प्रमोद खा चुका? ... हाँ, खा चुका।
pramod khā čukā?... hā̃, khā čukā.
Pramod.M.SG eat.CVB finish.PFV.M.SG yes eat.CVB finish.PFV.M.SG
'Has Pramod eaten yet?... Yes, he has.' (Amarkānt 2007: 100)

(23b) तू पंडित... से मिल आया क्या?... हाँ, माँ! मिल आया।
tū paṇḍit... -se mil āyā kyā?...
you pandit.M.SG- with meet.CVB come.PFV.M.SG Q
hā̃, mā̃! mil āyā.
yes mom meet.CVB come.PFV.M.SG
'Have you met Pandit?... Yes, mom. I have met him.' (Kohlī 2009: 59)

At the same time, the similarity between the potential sequence and 'Main Verb + Light/Vector /Intensive verb' combinations is only superficial. A more precise examination demonstrates that there are more differences than similarities between them (see Hook 1974, Poornima 2012 etc.). G. Cardona considers the criterion of more/less restricted distribution to be the most crucial one (Cardona 1965: 122, 124). Taking into account the history of the main verb form, we can add that the 'Vv' combinations were formed on the basis of the converb or the participle from the very beginning, hence the more evident converbial nature of the lexical verb in them. The main verb of the potential structure has lost its substantival properties, but still it has not acquired the truly converbial meaning. Unlike Western scholars, native speakers of Hindi seldom describe the form of the main verb used before *saknā* as an adverbial verboid (e.g. *pūrvakālik kr̥dant*), as they do not usually perceive it as a converb.

It may be supposed that in the course of linguistic changes on both the phonetic and morphological level, some modern Indo-Aryan languages (including Hindi) have developed a specific structure to denote the potential modality, formed on the basis of the converb, an adverbial form of secondary representation. This structure is different from 'sequences of verbs which are the result of embedding (*learn* to V, *forget* to V, *enjoy* V-ing, etc.) on the one hand, and from 'Vv' or Main Verb + Specifier (Explicator) ... on the other' (Masica 1991: 374). The question is how this peculiar combination should be treated: can it be perceived as a compound verb (a new lexical unit), an analytical verbal form or a syntactic structure? The answer to this question will help us solve one more problem. So far, the term 'the converb' was used for the form of the lexical verb combined with *saknā*. However, this term has many competitors in books and articles on Hindi grammar. In the next section, the advantages and disadvantages of the most popular terms employed for the main verb form will also be observed.

4 Grammatical status of the potential sequence and terms used for the main verb form

The main verb may be referred to as the *root* (Schmidt 2007: 333, Kachru 2006: 83), the *stem* (Montaut 2004: 128, Shapiro 1989: 104, McGregor 2008: 97); *the bare verb* (Bhatt et al. 2011: 49), the *base* (Cardona 2004: 1728), the *base infinitive* (Poornima 2012: 37), or the *absolutive* (Nespital 2008 etc.). Russian authors of Hindi grammars propose the term 'deyeprichastiye' (Zograf 1976: 256) meaning roughly 'a participle used to describe properties of an action' and usually translated as the *adverbial participle*.

All these terms can be easily divided into two groups, representing the form of the lexical verb in potential structures either as a morpheme or as a whole word. It may seem unnecessary to discuss the terms of the first group in light of the conclusions made in the previous section. However, since they appear in many works on Hindi grammar, I will attempt to explain why they seem to be unsatisfactory even if we do not take into consideration the history of the form.

At first glance, the term *root* is quite adequate: the form in question definitely bears the lexical meaning of the verbal complex and denotes the 'pure' action without any temporal, modal or aspectual connotation. Since prefixes play no part in verbal derivation processes in Hindi, this form seems to be not further analyzable. E. Greaves considers the verb preceding *saknā* as 'remaining unchanged throughout' (Greaves 1921: 327). However, if we widen the scope of examined structures, we will easily find analyzable causative forms in sequence with *saknā*, see example (24a). Another type of derivative forms before *saknā* is represented by compound verbs, see example (24b).[4]

(24a) वह मंदिर नहीं बनवा सका।
vah mandir nahī̃ banvā sakā.
he temple.M.SG not build.CAUS.CVB can.PFV.M.SG
'He was unable to build the temple.' (Kohli 2009: 5/244)

(24b) कुछ भी कह दे सकता है।
kuč̌h bhī kah de saktā hɛ.
anything also say.CVB give.CVB can.IPFV.M.SG AUX.PRS.SG
'He can say anything at all.' (Caudharī 2001: 257)

Furthermore, the main verb of the potential structure can be involved in passive transformation, and the result of a transformation cannot be considered a root. Example (25a) demonstrates the most frequently met impersonal passive structure with *saknā*; (25b) illustrates the personal structure.

(25a) समुद्रतल को खुली आँखों से देखा जा सकता है।
samudratal-ko khulī ā̃khõ-se dekhā
seafloor.M-ACC open.F eye.F.OBL.PL-INSTR see.PFV.M.SG
jā saktā hɛ.
go can.IPFV.M.SG AUX.PRS.SG
'The seafloor can be seen by the open eye.' (Kamaleśvar 2005: 66)

4 Such usages, though not infrequent, are restricted to a definite range of light verbs, see (Kachru 1966: 57, 89–91).

(25b) यह आशा नहीं की जा सकती है कि ...
yah āśā nahī̃ kī jā saktī hɛ ki...
this hope.F not do.PFV.F go.CVB can.IPFV.F.SG AUX.PRS.SG that
'One cannot hope that...' (Yaśpāl 2007: 207)

The aforementioned statement causes us to conclude that the form in question does not fulfill the requirements for a morpheme to be a root (see Matthews 2007: 350): it may be analyzable, derivative or present the result of a grammatical transformation. The solution to the question of whether the terms 'stem' or 'base' would suit it better partially depends on the general perception of the potential modal structure. A language unit can be treated as a base or a stem only if it is involved in a *morphological* process, either inflectional or derivational one. It means that the whole sequence should be perceived as an analytical form of the main verb or as a complex, compound verb derived from it.

Treatment of combinations like *kar saknā* 'to be able to do' as a single lexical unit, i.e. a compound verb (H. *sañyukt kriyā*) can be found in works like (Katenina 1960), (Guru 1962) or (Pā̃ḍe 2012). The main reason for this interpretation is that *saknā* cannot be used individually, and therefore its role is similar to that of a morpheme. However, although *saknā* is definitely non-autonomous (see example (13c)), it is still autosemantic, unlike formative verbs in sequences like *mar jānā*, both parts of which jointly have one meaning: 'to die' (see Nespital 2008: v).

Interpreting the potential structures as one lexeme also contradicts the possibility of incorporating particles and interrogative pronouns between their parts; see example (26a). Moreover, in the language of poetry, the modal and the main verb may even exchange their places, although such word order cannot be considered canonical; see example (26b).

(26a) इसका दूसरा साधन हो भी क्या सकता है?
is-kā dusrā sādhan ho bhī kyā saktā hɛ?
it-GEN.M.SG other.M means.M be even what can.IPFV.M.SG AUX.PRS.SG
'What indeed can its means be?' (Yaśpāl 2007: 7)

(26b) सकेगा कर क्या दीन सहाय?
sakegā kar kyā dīn sahāy?
can.FUT.3.M.SG do what poor help
'What the helper of the poor will be able to do?' (Baccan 2009: 52)

Some Hindi grammarians describe the modal structure discussed here as a 'secondary analytic form' (Zograf 1976: 256), i.e. a morphological unit. The structure with *saknā*, indeed, demonstrates high regularity and 'the top level of grammaticalization of a free syntactic combination of words' (Ultsiferov 2005: 590). However, proclaiming something a grammeme requires that it be involved in opposition with at least one another form. Finding such a form in the modern Hindi language seems to be impossible.[5]

It appears more appropriate to treat the potential modal sequence with *saknā* as a semi-syntactic unit, a complex predicate (Poornima 2012) or a morpho-syntactic structure, bound at the syntagmatic level (Liperovskiy 1997). The term 'analytic construction', proposed by O.G. Ultsiferov (Ultsiferov 2005: 590) also seems satisfactory.

Treating the potential sequence as a syntactic unit forces us to avoid the terms 'stem' or 'base', as the structure no longer remains on the morphological level. The form employed with *saknā* is definitely equal to the stem, but it cannot be called *the stem proper*; it is a word, not a part of a word.[6] Then we need to analyze the terms 'bare verb', 'gerund', 'adverbial / conjunctival participle', 'absolutive', '(base) infinitive' and 'converb', proposed for it in grammars.

The term *bare verb* may well suit the purposes of a brief Hindi grammar for beginners or a semantic study: the lexical verb in a potential structure is indeed bare, lacking not only the infinitival affix *-nā*, but also any other morphological marker. However, this term does not reflect the form's nature and is not suitable for a work on morphology.

The term '(base) infinitive' seems unsatisfactory as its usage may lead to confusion or the substitution of the correct form with the infinitive proper (ending in *-nā* or *-ne*) – a typical mistake for Hindi learners (see Section 5).

The other terms, as becomes evident from the explanations of scholars who use them, denote one and the same indeclinable non-finite verbal form of adverbial nature. Since there is no such form in the English language, there has been much controversy surrounding its definition (see Tikkanen 1987: 36–37). Following the tradition of Sanskrit grammars of the 19th century based on the works by Franz Bopp (e.g. Whitney 2004[1889]: 989–995, Spejer 1993[1886]: 296–300 etc.), some scholars use the term 'gerund' (Tikkanen 1987, Bubenik 1998). However, according to the Concise Dictionary of Linguistics, a gerund is 'A nominal form of verbs in Latin <...>.' Hence a term available for verb forms with a noun-like role in other languages: e.g. English *fighting* is traditionally a gerund in *Fighting used*

5 The contrast between the potential sequence and the Progressive (durative) participle e.g. *kar rahā*, also originating from the combination of a converb with an auxiliary (see Strnad 2013: 445–446), is particularly noticible in this context.

6 M. Shapiro, however, lists the *stem* among other non-aspectual verbal forms, along with the infinitive, the subjunctive and the future (Shapiro 2007: 267–268).

to be fun, as opposed to the participle, also ending in *-ing* but with a different syntactic role, as in *people fighting*' (Matthews 2007: 158). Using this term for an adverbial verboid (not only when it complements the potential auxiliary, but also when it describes the preceding action), though justified by the tradition of Sanskrit studies, seems inappropriate.

Other scholars adopt terms that employ the word 'participle': *the* (*conjunctival*) *participle* (Greaves 1921: 253, Schmidt 2007: 328, Montaut 2004: 93[7]), the *adverbial participle* (Dymshits 1986: 248), the 'adverbial participle-stem' (Ultsiferov 2005: 593). The problem with these terms is that participles are supposed to be adjectival (Matthews 2007: 288), and there are other (proper, adjectival in nature) participles in Hindi, which may also be used adverbially to denote conjunction of actions. This is demonstrated by example (27a), where the perfective participle in its adverbial form *kiye*, 'having done' and *ūbkar*, 'having got bored' (the adverbial verboid) are used as homogeneous parts of the sentence. Although adverbial perfective participles may participate in the formation of compound verbs (see McGregor 2008: 190–191 and example (27b)), they are inacceptable with *saknā*, and therefore, in order to avoid confusion, it seems better not to use 'participial' terms for the form preceding this modal auxiliary.

(27a) नेता भइया ऊपर मुँह किये ऊबकर झुँझला रहे थे।
netā *bhaiyā* *ūpar* *mũh* *kiye*
leader.M.SG brother.M.SG upwards face.M.SG do.PFV.M.OBL
ūbkar *jhũjhlā-rahe* *the.*
be bored.CVB get irritated-PROG.M.PL AUX.PST.M.PL
'Leader Brother turned his face upwords; he was bored and was getting angry.' (Yādav 2007: 327)

(27b) इतनी महत्त्वपूर्ण चीज़ आप मुझे क्यों दिये दे रहे हैं?
itnī *mahattvapūrṇ* *čīz* *āp* *mujhe* *kyõ*
such.F.SG important thing.F.SG you.HON I.OBJ why
diye *de-rahe* *hɛ̃.*
give.PFV.M.OBL give-DUR.M.PL AUX.PRS.PL
'Why are you giving me such an important thing?' (Yādav 2007: 292)

The term *absolutive* (Nespital 2008: v; Strnad 2013: 445) is also quite popular. It originated in the middle of the 19th century and is supposed to indicate the indeclinable character of this form. The term has been 'widely used especially by

7 This term is used by A. Montaut only for the forms expressing adverbial subordination, not for those used with *saknā*.

Neogrammarians for corresponding categories in other Indo-European languages as well' (Tikkanen 1987: 37). However, to some extent it is semantically void, resembling the term 'bare verb', and also not altogether unambiguous: it is often used for the case of the direct object of transitive verbs and of the subject of intransitive verbs in ergative languages (see Matthews 2007: 3). Since Hindi adopts the ergative pattern in perfective tenses, the term 'absolutive' is likely to appear in works on Hindi grammar with this meaning, and it seems more preferable to avoid it when speaking either of the adverbial verboid or the form in sequences with *saknā*.

The only unambiguous term in the list is 'the converb'. It stands only for an adverbial non-finite verbal form (see Matthews 2007: 80) and has already been adopted by some Hindi scholars for the verbals in *-kar* (e.g. Montaut 2013: 91–120). Since it has been demonstrated in Section 2 that from the historical point of view the form of the lexical verb in potential sequences is an adverbial verboid, I suggest that the term be extrapolated to the form of the main verb in *saknā* structures.

5 Converbial and infinitival sequences with *pānā*

The verb *pānā* originates from the Sanskrit root *āp-* 'to obtain' modified by the prefix *prā-*. *Hindī Śabdsāgar* dictionary derives the verb from *prāpaṇā* (Sanskrit) and *pāvaṇa* (Prakrit) (Śyāmsundardās 1969: 2948). Unlike *saknā*, the verb *pānā* is not purely modal; its basic lexical meaning is 'to get', 'to obtain' (mostly abstract, non-material objects, such as personality characteristics or an opportunity, see examples (28a) and (28b)). The initial meaning can transform into 'to find (out)' (especially when the verb is preceded by a participial clause, see example (28c)).

(28a) बचपन से ही ऐसी प्रकृति पायी थी।
bačpan-se *hī* *ɛsī* *prakr̥tī*
childhood.M-ABL EMPH such.F nature.F
payī *thī.*
obtain.PFV.F.SG AUX.PST.F.SG
'From the very childhood obtained such nature.' (Jain 2012: 411)

(28b) सुभागी ने मौका पाया तो भागी।
subhāgī-ne *mɔkā* *pāyā* *to* *bhāgī.*
Subhagi.F-ERG chance.M get.PFV.M.SG then run away.PFV.F.SG
'When Subhagi got a chance, she ran away.' (Premchand 2002: 106)

(28c) अपने को एक सजे हुए कमरे में पाया।
apne-ko *ek* *saje* *hue*
self's.OBL-ACC one decorated.PFV.M.OBL be.PFV.M.OBL
kamre-mẽ *pāyā.*
room.M.OBL.SG-LOC find.PFV.M.SG
'Found himself in a decorated room.' (Premchand 2002: 33)

Being used as a modal, the verb *pānā* turns into an auxiliary verb and changes some of its grammatical properties (see Montaut 2004: 128). As can be concluded from examples (28a) and (28b) above, the initial verb is morphologically and syntactically transitive: it may have a direct object and requires that the sentence be built according to the ergative pattern in perfective tenses and moods. Examples of its modal usage in the same tenses demonstrate that it becomes intransitive and always follows the gender and the number not of the direct object, but of the Nominative-marked subject, see examples (29a) and (29b).

(29a) गोबिन्दी इस अचानक सवाल का... जवाब न दे पायी।
gobindī *is* *ačānak* *savāl-kā*
Gobindi.F this.OBL sudden question.M-GEN.M.SG
javāb *na* *de* *pāyī.*
answer.M not give get.PFV.F.SG
'Gobindi was unable to answer this sudden question.' (Singh 1999: 23)

(29b) नाज़ी सिपाही... बियर का पहला गिलास समाप्त नहीं कर पाये थे।
nāzī *sipāhī...* *biyar-kā* *pahlā* *gilās...*
Nazi soldier.M beer-GEN.M.SG first.M.SG glass.M.SG
samāpt *nahĩ* *kar* *pāye* *the.*
finished not do get.M.PL AUX.PST.M.PL
'Nazi soldiers were unable to finish the first glass of beer.' (Yaśpāl 2007: 281)

Unlike *saknā*, modal *pānā* has no prototype in Old or Middle Indo-Aryan languages. However, the usage of a lexeme with the meaning 'to obtain' to denote *conditional ability* or more precisely *incapability*, was not totally unknown: Duroiselle suggests using the indeclinable *labbha* (Skt. *labh* 'to obtain') in modal infinitival structures in Pali: *daŋ na labbhhā evaŋ kartuŋ* 'It is not possible to do it in this way' (Duroiselle 2014: 120).

The semi-modal with the root *pā-* can be encountered in a number of New Indo-Aryan languages (Punjabi and Assamese, among others), but 'it is not clear without further investigation whether they are equivalent' (Masica 1991: 377). In

Baṅglā, *pāoẏā* appears alongside the basic potential modal verb *pārā* in restricted environments, see example (30). Baṅglā potential modals *pārā* and *pāoẏā* are preceded by the infinitive.

(30) কিন্তু আপনার মত আনাড়ীর ওপরে মোড়লি করতে পাই ত আমি আর সমস্ত ছেড়ে দিতে পারি।

kintu	*āpnār*	*mata*	*ānāṛīr*	*opare*	*moṛali*	*karte*	*pāi*
but	you.HON-GEN	alike	stranger	above	power	do.INF	get.PRS.1

ta	*āmi*	*ār*	*samasta*	*čheṛe*	*dite*	*pāri.*
then	I	else	all	leave.CVB	give.INF	can.PRS.1

'But if I manage to tame a strange like you, I will be able to leave everything else.' (Caṭṭopādhyāẏ 2014: 235)

As for Old Hindi, J. Strnad notices that the 'verbal substantive can be followed by the verb *pā-* 'to be able to', 'to get the chance' (*mil.na [...] pā̃u* in 253.3), and the collocation with the verb *de-* (as in *na dei čaraṇā̃* in the verse 390.2) probably connones permission 'to allow', 'to let'' (Strnad 2013: 449). There is no trace of the converb used with *pā-* at this stage, while it is prevalent in the case of *sak-*.

It is most likely that the first modal sequences featuring *pānā* in modern Hindi also contained not the bare converb, but the infinitive (apparently in the oblique form) and appeared together with the active permissive structure 'the oblique infinitive + *denā* 'to give'' as its opposition. It is worthwhile to consider what E. Greaves proposes:

> These two sets of compounds, though in one sense contrasted, have much in common, and may conveniently be considered together. They are used with the inflected infinitive. This may be regarded as the Dative Case, with the को or के लिए unexpressed. Thus उसने उसको जाने दिया, might be more fully written, उसने उसको जाने के लिए... दिया *He gave (permission) to him to go*, and so वह जाने पाया, might, similarly, be more fully written, उसने जाने को (or जाने के लिए)... पाया, *He obtained (permission) to go.'* (Greaves 1921: 329)

There are almost no traces of such 'reconstructed' postpositional sequences, at least not with the permissive meaning; however, the theory itself appears quite attractive and was supported by other grammarians (see McGregor 2008: 147). Under the influence of the *saknā* structure, *pānā* gradually began to be used with the converb. However, the infinitival structure did not become extinct, and now it is even possible to find both options in the same text, see examples (31a) and (31b).

(31a) कभी उसे देख पाती तो उसका मुँह चूम लेती।
kabhī use dekh pātī to us-kā
when she.OBJ see.CVB get.IPFV.F.SG then she-GEN.M.SG
mũh čūm letī.
face.M.SG kiss.CVB take.IPFV.F.SG
'If I ever saw her, I would kiss her face' (Prasād 2014:120)

(31b) मेरी सहृदयता घूँघट उलटने नहीं पाती।
merī sahṛdaytā ghũghaṭ ulaṭne
I-GEN.F.SG tenderness.F.SG veil.F.SG unroll.INF.OBL
nahī̃ pātī.
not get.IPFV.F.SG
'My tenderness never has a chance to take off the veil.' (Prasād 2014:120)

Although ignored by some researchers (Katenina 1960, Zograf 1976), this phenomenon has not remained entirely unnoticed, and multiple explanations of the difference between the converbial and the infinitival structures can be found in works on Hindi grammar.

Hindī Śabdsāgar explains the existing duality of the main verb form from the aspectual point of view. In the entry 'पाना' we read that both structures denote ability (Hin. *śakyatā*), but the converbial one also implies completeness (Hin. *samāpti*), see examples (32a) for *śakyatā* and (32b) for *śakyatā* +*samāpti* (both examples have been taken from *Hindī Śabdsāgar* dictionary, see (Śyāmsundardās 1969: 2949)).

(32a) तुम वहाँ जाने नहीं पाओगे।
tum vahā̃ jāne nahī̃ pāoge.
you there go.INF.OBL not get.FUT.2.M.PL
'You will not be able to go there.'

(32b) मैं अभी वह चिट्ठी नहीं लिख पाया।
mɛ̃ abhī vah čiṭṭhī nahī̃ likh pāyā.
I yet that letter.F not write.CVB get.PFV.M.SG
'I haven't been able to write that letter yet.'

Examples from the dictionary cannot illustrate the phenomenon well enough, as they contain different aspectual forms of *pānā* itself. On the basis of these examples it may be concluded that only the converbial, not the infinitival structure, should be used in perfective tenses, which is clearly incorrect. However, this theory is not altogether incorrect: in a way, it supports the suggestion that the converbial form preceding *pānā* is somehow related to the idea of completeness (remember the initial meaning of the converb!)

The majority of modern works on Hindi grammar distinguish between the two structures on the basis of the modality type. According to them (Montaut 2004, Nespital 2008 etc.) the converbial structure denotes conditional *capacity* (in negative or quasi-negative environments, inability despite effort (Kachru 1980: 50, Masica 1991: 377)), while the combination of *pānā* with the oblique infinitive (also in negative sentences) bears the permissive or permissive passive[8] meaning, indicating that the subject is (was or will be) prevented from doing something by an outer obstacle.

This observation can be supported by examples (33a) and (33b). Both sentences describe the impossibility of an idea coming to someone's mind; but in the first example this is due to the thinker's incapability, where in the second example the thinker does not allow the thought to appear in his mind.

(33a) लाख कोशिश करने पर भी मेरे मन में कोई भी विचार नहीं आ पाएगा।
lakh *kośiś* *karne* *par-bhī* *mere*
100 thousand attempt.F do.INF.OBL despite I-GEN.M.OBL
man-mẽ *koī* *bhī* *vičar* *nahī̃* *ā* *pāegā.*
mind.M-LOC any also thought not come.CVB get.FUT.3.SG
'Despite making thousands of attempts, not a single thought will be able to enter my mind.' (Dvivedī 2005: 54)

(33b) वह अमरता प्राप्त कर लेगा – इसका विचार ही उसके मन में नहीं आने पाया था।
vah *amartā* *prāpt* *kar* *legā –* *is-kā*
he immortality obtained do.CVB take.FUT.M.SG this-GEN.M.SG
vičar *hī* *us-ke* *man-mẽ* *nahī̃*
thought.M even he-GEN.M.OBL mind.M-LOC not
āne *pāyā* *thā.*
come.INF.OBL succeed.PFV.M.SG AUX.PST.M.SG
'...That he will obtain immortality – this thought could not enter his mind.' (Varmā 2009:121)

Unfortunately, it is not always easy to define whether a sentence implies the permissive (acquisitive) sense or not. For example, it remains unclear whether the subject of the sentence (34a) speaks of his capability to come after having completed his work, or informs the hearers of the fact that he was given permission

8 The term 'passive' here implies that it is the patient, not the agent under the scope of the modal in the infinitival structure (see Montaut 2004: 129–130).

to leave only after the work had been completed. The difficulty of modality type interpretation can also be illustrated by observing the difference between the translations made by two Russian linguists of one Hindi sentence, see example (34b).

(34a) नम्बर ठट्ठी को निकालकर तब आने पाया हूँ।
nambar *ṭhaṭṭhī-ko* *nikālkar* *tab* *āne*
number thirty-ACC take out.CVB then come.INF.OBL
pāyā *hū̃.*
get.PFV.M.SG AUX.PRS.1.SG
'Having taken out number thirty, I was able to come.' (Premchand 2009: 294)

(34b) वहाँ नौ बजे के बाद कोई पढ़ने नहीं पाता।
vahā̃ *nɔ* *baje-ke* *bād* *koī*
there nine ring.PFV.M.OBL-GEN.M.OBL after anyone
paṛhne *nahī̃* *pātā.*
study.INF.OBL not get.IPFV.M.SG

Z. M. Dymshits translates this sentence in the permissive clue:

No one is allowed to study there after nine o'clock' (Dymshits 1986: 142). At the same time, O. G. Ultsiferov, trying to include in his translation the Russian verb *poluchat'sia* 'to come out', a cognate of *poluchat* 'to obtain', strips the sentence of the permissive meaning: 'No one has the option of studying there after nine o'clock' (Ultsiferov 2005: 277).In other cases, permissive interpretation of the infinitival structure becomes nearly impossible. The subject of the situation, described in example (35a) is the Sun, and it seems unlikely that the Sun should ask for anybody's permission to rise. Z. M. Dymshits notices that the infinitival construction can also point towards the subject's (in)ability to do something in time before something else happens (see Dymshits 1986: 151); a similar observation has been made by R. L. Schmidt for Urdu in (Schmidt 2007: 333). This observation explains the usage of this structure in (35a) and may also be illustrated by (35b). However, (35c) demonstrates that the converbial structure may also be used in such an environment.

(35a) शरद ऋतु का सूर्य... ऊँचा नहीं होने पाया था कि... एक नौजवान... आ धमका।
śarad *ritu-kā* *sūrya...* *ū̃čā* *nahī̃* *hone*
autumn.M season.F-GEN.M.SG sun.M high.M.SG not be.INF.OBL
pāyā *thā* *ki...* *ek* *nɔjavān...* *ā*
get.PFV.M.SG AUX.PST.M.SG that one soldier.M come.CVB
dhamkā.
descend.PFV.M.SG
'The Sun hadn't risen high yet as a soldier stumbled in.' (Singh 1999: 98)

(35b) अभी एक घाव नहीं भरने पाया था कि दूसरा चरका लगा।
abhī ek ghāv nahĩ bharne pāyā thā
now one wound.M not fill.INF.OBL get.PFV.M.SG AUX.PST.M.SG
ki dūsrā čarkā lagā.
that second.M.SG bruise.M. apply.PFV.M.SG
'Hardly had one wound filled when another bruise appeared.' (Premchand 2002: 166)

(35c) उसका वाक्य पूरा भी न हो पाया था कि बाहर से आवाज़ आयी...
us-kā vākya pūrā bhī na ho pāyā
he-GEN.M.SG speech.M complete.M.SG also not be.CVB get.M.SG
thā ki bāhar-se āvāz āyī...
AUX.PST.M.SG that outside-ABL voice.F come.PFV.F
'Hardly had his speech been finished when there was a sound.' (Singh 1999: 177)

Some linguists treat both the sequences we have discussed as stylistic variants of the same structure. It will be interesting to notice that while D. Phillot describes the converbial structure as a spoken, non-literary variant of the infinitival one (Phillot 1909: 33), contemporary researchers are inclined to consider the infinitival variant a rather marginal and rarely met alternative of the converbial sequence (Hook 1974: 90). Indeed, most examples of the infinitival structure will be met in stories and novels by Premchand and his contemporaries, although occasional occurrences can be found in works of later periods as well. Some of these usages can be explained by one or another syntactic or semantic reason, but counter-examples are quite easy to find in literary works, which means most theories are not universal. It may be supposed that the initially prevailing infinitival structure[9] has gradually become substituted by the converbial one. While some Hindi authors continue to use it in standard environments (permission, 'hardly had... when...'), in other cases its usage merely provides additional linguistic characteristics to the text.

The last observation is true for comparatively few instances of infinitival structures with *saknā*. They are incorrect from a grammatical point of view, but are sometimes still met in Hindi literature. The most interesting of these occasions will be described in Section 6.

9 E. Greaves even does not mention the converbial sequence with *pānā* in the list of 'compound verbs', see (Greaves 1921: 326).

6 Non-converbial main verb in combination with *saknā*

In early Hindi grammars one can find traces of the infinitive before *saknā*. W. Yates notices that potentials 'are formed by adding sakná *to be able* to a verbal root, or to the infinitive mood of the verb; as, *khá sakná* or *kháne sakná* '*to be able to eat*' (Yates 1855).

The language of that time provides us with examples of such usages, along with the standard, converbial ones, see examples (36a) and (36b) from the New Testament translation.

(36a) मनुष्य जो है सो मुझ पर क्या करने सकता है?
manuṣya jo hɛ so mujh-par kya
man.M what be.PRS.SG that I.OBL-on what
karne saktā hɛ?
do.INF.OBL can.IPFV.M.SG AUX.PRS.SG
'What is man able to do to me?' (New Testament 1948: 559)

(36b) और वह वहाँ कोई आश्चर्य कर्म न कर सकता था।
ɔr vah vahā̃ koī āśčarya karm na kar saktā
and he there any miracle deed not do.CVB can.IPFV.M.SG
thā.
AUX.PST.M.SG
'And he was unable to do any work of power there.'
(New Testament 1948: 97)

However, during the process of Hindi standardization, this structure began to be considered unacceptable and disappeared from grammar books. E. Greaves characterizes it as an archaic, 'antiquated' one (Greaves 1921: 327); however, as we have already seen, the infinitive in *–nā* was not used in Old Hindi or its dialects in sequences with *sak-*. The phenomenon seems more likely to be explained by the influence of other languages, e.g. Bengali: the New Testament translation in (36a) and (36b) was prepared and published in Calcutta, and Bengali has infinitives in potential structures (see example (30)). Another translation of the same period (The New Testament, 1949) was made in Agra, and it contains no traces of the infinitive in combination with *saknā*. Nowadays, Hindi writers use the structure 'infinitive + *saknā*' along with other grammatical and spelling mistakes to imitate the Bengali accent, see examples (37a) and (37b). Further examples demonstrate that English (37c) and other foreign (e.g. Nepali, (37d)) accents are also sometimes imitated this way.

(37a) बात ये लोग अपना फीर बी करने सकता है।
bāt ye log apnā phīr bī karne
word.F this.PL people.M. self's.M.SG later too do.INF.OBL
sakta hɛ.
can.IPFV.M.SG. AUX.PRS.SG
'These people can continue their talk later on.' (Yaśpāl 2009, 134)

(37b) हम ईहां कुछ बी करने शकता, शमझा?
ham īhā̃ kuč̌h bī karne śaktā
we here anything too do.INF.OBL can.IPFV.M.SG
śamjhā.
understand.PFV.M.SG
'I can do everything here, understand?' (Kamaleśvar 2009: 160)

(37c) हाम भी नहीं जाने सकता साहेब जी।
hām bhī nahī̃ jāne saktā sāheb jī.
we too not go.INF.OBL can.IPFV.M.SG Sir HON
'I can't go there either, Sir.' (Śivmūrti 2007: 56)

(37d) कल तो हम रूकने नहीं सकेंगे।
kal to ham rūkne nahī̃ sakẽge.
tomorrow EMPH we stop.INF.OBL not can.FUT.M.PL
'I won't be able to stay for tomorrow.' (Mitr 2008: 26)

If one continues to check for other possible verbal forms used in combination with *saknā* either in standard or in spoken Hindi, he or she will encounter the combination of a perfective participle with the modal verb, see examples (38a) and (38b).

(38a) प्रयोग सिर्फ़ किताबों तक सीमित रखकर अमल में कैसे देखा सकता है?
prayog sirf kitābõ-tak sīmit rakhkar
experience.M only book.F.PL.OBL.up to limited keep.CVB
amal-mẽ kɛse dekhā saktā hɛ?
practice-LOC how see.PFV.M.SG can.IPFV.M.SG AUX.PRS.SG
'How can the result be seen in reality if the experience is limited to the books?' (Nandan 1988: 82)

(38b) समय की गति को पीछे नहीं ले जाया सकता।

samay-kī	*gatī-ko*	*pīče*	*nahī̃*	*le*
time.M-GEN.F	progress.F.ACC	backwards	not	take.CVB
jāyā	*saktā.*			
go.PFV.M.SG	can.IPFV.M.SG			

'It is impossible to turn time back' (Upādhyāy 2014: 79)

These structures appear to be the result of the omission process; the 'complete' verb of (38a) will be '*dekhā jā saktā hɛ*' and in (38b) it should be '*le jāyā jā saktā*'. The reasons leading to omissions like these and the degree of acceptability of this structure cannot be postulated without proper investigation. However, their existence supports our general conception that potentials in Hindi are not complemented by a verbal root or a stem.

7 Conclusion

In summary, the following conclusions can be made:

(i) There are multiple structures to denote potential modality (ability, possibility and permission) in Hindi; some of them are restricted to specific usages (modal nouns and adjectives), while others cover a wide range of meanings. The most universal ones are verbs *saknā* and *pānā*.

(ii) Unlike European and some other Indian languages, Hindi potentials are normally complemented not by the infinitive, but by a form that is homonymous with the verbal stem. An analysis of the morphological features of this form, supported by historical and areal observation, has demonstrated that it is not the verbal root or the stem proper; it is a non-finite verbal form of adverbial nature, for which the term 'converb' appears to be the most adequate. The whole sequence in its turn is not a compound verb, but a complex predicate with the modal (or semi-modal) auxiliary.

(iii) At the same time, the semi-modal *pānā* can be preceded by the infinitive in its oblique form. Numerous attempts have been made to distinguish between the converbial and the infinitival sequences with *pānā*. Correct to some extent, all the existing explanations of the phenomenon seem to be not universal, and a gradual substitution of the infinitival structure by the converbial one appears to be the general trend, although some writers still employ the infinitive in permissive contexts and in order to denote narrow escape.

(iv) Similar infinitival structures with *saknā* can also be found in Hindi literature; however, in modern standard Hindi they are absolutely non-conventional,

appearing in the speech of those who are not native speakers of Hindi. Combinations like these are often used by writers to imitate foreign accents.
(v) In scientific and periodical publications, though not frequently in fictional writing, one can encounter the structure 'Perfective Participle + potential modal'. This structure appears to be the result of omitting the passive auxiliary *jānā*, and its existence proves once again that the verb in sequence with *saknā* and *pānā* should not be referred to as the root or the stem.

References

Amarkānt. 2007. *Pratinidhi Kahāniyā̃*. Dillī: Rājkamal Prakāśan.
Baccan, Harivañśrāy. 2009. *Khɛyām kī Madhuśālā*. Dillī: Rājpāl & Sons.
Bhaṇḍārī, Mannū. 2002. *Nāyak, Khalnāyak, Viduṣak*. Dillī: Rājkamal Prakāśan.
Bhatt, Rajesh, Tina Bögel, Miriam Butt, Annette Hautli and Sebastian Sulger. 2011. *Urdu/Hindi Modals* in *Proceedings of the LFG11 Conference*. CSLI Publications, pp. 47–67
Brahmānand. 1971. *Rāhul Sāṅkr̥tyāyan*. Dillī: Hariyāṇā Prakāśan.
Bubenik, Vit. 1998. *A Historical Syntax of Late Middle Indo-Aryan (Apabhraṃśa)*. Amsterdam, Philadelphia: John Benjamins Publishing.
Cardona, George. 1965. *A Gujarati reference grammar*. Philadelphia: University of Pennsylvania Press.
Cardona, George. 2004. From Vedic to Modern Indic Languages. In Booij, Geert E., Lehmann, Christian Christian, Mugdan, Joachi, and Skopeteas, Stavros (eds.). *Morphologie / Morphology. 2. Halbband*. Berlin:Walter de Gruyter GmbH & Co.
Caṭṭopādhy āẏ, Śaratcandra. 2014. *Pather Dābi*. e-book: editionNEXT.com
Caudharī, Raghuvīr. 2008. *Gokul, Mathurā, Dvārikā*. Dillī: Rādhākr̥ṣṇa Paperbacks.
Caudharī, Rājkamal. 2001. *Agnisnān evaṃ Anya Upanyās*. Dillī: Rājkamal Paperbacks.
Daschenko, Galina Mikhɛlovna. 2002. Modasnost' Vozmozhnosti v Yazike Urdu [Potential Modality in the Urdu Language]. Moscow: MGU Publishing House.
Duroiselle, Charles. 2014. [1906] *Duroiselle's Pali Grammar: A New Edition of 'A Practical Grammar of the Pali Language'*. Electronic text by Eisel Mazard.
Dvivedī, Bhojrāj. 2005. *Hipnotizm (Sammohan Vigyān)*. Dillī: Dimond Pocket Books.
Dymshits, Zalman Movshevich. 1986. *Grammatika Yazyka Xindi [Grammar of the Hindi language]*. Part 1. Moskva: Nauka.
Gopāl, Madan. 2006. *Kalam kā Mazdūr: Premchand*. Dillī: Rājkamal Prakāśan.
Greaves, Edwin. 1921. *Hindi Grammar*. Allahabad: The Indian Press, LTD.
Guru, Kamtāprasād. 1962. [1921]. *Hindī Vyākaraṇ*. Banāras: Nāgari-Pracāriṇī Sabhā.
Hook, Peter Edwin. 1974. *The Compound Verb in Hindi*. Michigan: The University of Michigan, Center for South and Southeast Asia Studies.
Jain, Vīrendrakumār. 2012. *Anuttar Yogī*. Dillī: Rājkamal Paperbacks.
Johansson, Rune E. A. 2012. *Pali Buddhist Texts: An Introductory Reader and Grammar*. London and New York: Routledge.
Kachru, Yamuna. 1966. *An Introduction to Hindi Syntax*. Urbana, Illinois: Department of Linguistics, University of Illinois.

Kachru, Yamuna. 1980. *Aspects of Hindi Grammar*. New Delhi: Manohar.
Kachru, Yamuna. 2006. *Hindi*. Amsterdam, Philadelphia: John Benjamins Publishing Co.
Kale, M. R. (ed.). 1986. *Pañcatantra of Viṣṇuśarman*. Delhi: Motilal Banarasidass.
Kamaleśvar. 2005. *Ā̃khõ Dekhī Pākistān*. Dillī. Rājpāl & Sons.
Kamaleśvar. 2008. *Samagr Upanyās*. Dillī: Rājpāl & Sons.
Kamaleśvar. 2009. *Jhūṭhī dīvārẽ* in *Pratinidhi bāl kahāniyā̃*. Dillī: Ātmārām & Sons.
Katenina, Tatiana Yevgenievna. 1960. *Yazyk Xindi [Hindi Language]*. Moskva: Izdatelstvo Vostochnoy Literatury.
Kātyāyan, Hemkānt. 1994. *Lāl kiraṇõ kā sūraj*. Dillī, Lakhnaū: Ātmārām & Sons.
Khatrī, Devakīnandan. 2005. *Candrakanta santati-3*. Dillī: Rājkamal Prakāśan.
Kohlī, Narendra. 2009. *Toṛo Kārā Toṛo*. Dillī: Rājkamal Prakāśan.
Kumār, Mahendra and Śarmā, Omprakāś (ed.). 1985. *Sāhitya-manīshā: Ḍô. Omprakāś Śāstrī smṛti granth*. Naī Dillī: Ārya Book Depot.
Kuznetsov, Boris Ivanovich. 1978. *Glagolniye imena yazyka Marathi* [Nominal Verbs in the Marathi Language]. Moskva: Nauka.
Liperovskiy, Vladimir Petrovich. 1988. *Ocherk Grammatiki Sovremennogo Bredzha* [An Outline of Modern Braj Grammar]. Moskva: Nauka.
Liperovskiy, Vladimir Petrovich. 1997. *Ocherk Grammatiki Sovremennogo Avadhi* [An Outline of Modern Awadhi Grammar]. Moskva: Vostochnaya Literatura.
Mahrotrā, Mamtā, Śarmā, Maheś. 2015. *Śikṣā kā adhikār*. Dillī: Prabhāt Prakāśan.
Masica, Colin P. 1991. *The Indo-Aryan Languages*. Cambridge: Cambridge University Press.
Matthews, Peter Hugoe. 2007. *The Concise Oxford Dictionary of Linguistics*. Oxford: Oxford University Press.
McGregor, Ronald Stuart. 2008. *Outline of Hindi Grammar*. Third Edition. New Delhi: Oxford University Press.
Mīcū, Rohit and Tripāṭhī, Kṛṣṇa Candra. 2008. *Cāy, Śarāb ɔr Zahar*. Dillī: Rādhākṛṣṇa Prakāśan.
Mitr, Paṅkaj. 2008. *Huḍuklullu*. Dillī: Rājkamal Prakāśan.
Monier-Williams, Monier. 2008. [1899]. *A Sanskrit-English Dictionary Etymologically and Philologically Arranged*. Oxford: Oxford University Press.
Montaut, Annie. 2004. *A Grammar of Hindi*. Munich: LINCOM Europa.
Montaut, Annie. 2013. The rise of non-canonical subjects and semantic alignments in Hindi. In *The Diachronic Typology of Non-Canonical Subjects* (ed. Ilja A. Serzant, Leonid Kulikov). Amsterdam/Philadelphia: John Benjamins Publishing.
Nandan, Kanhɛyālāl. 1988. *Ghāṭ Ghāṭ kā Pānī*. Dillī: Subodh Pocket Books.
Nāgar, Amṛtlāl. 2006. *Bū̃d ɔr Samudr*. Dillī: Rājkamal Prakāśan.
Nāth, Amarendr. 2012. Gujarāt Hāī Korṭ kā Nirṇay...//Bargād. 06.01.2012. URL: https://bargad.org/2012/01/06/hindi-amrendra/
Nespital, Helmut. 2008. Hindī Kriyā-Koś. Dictionary of Hindi Verbs: Containing all Simple and Compound Verbs, their Lexical Equivalents in English and Illustrations of their Usage. Allahabad: Lokbharati Prakashan.
New Testament. 1948. The New Testament of our Lord and Savior Jesus Christ, in the Hindi Language. Calcutta: Baptist Mission Press.
New Testament. 1849. *The New Testament of our Lord and Savior Jesus Christ*, Translated from the Original Greek. Agra: Secundra Orphan Press

Oberlies, Thomas. 2001. *Pali: A Grammar of the Language of the Theravada Tipitaka. With a Concordance to Pischel's Grammatik der Prakrit-Sprachen*. Berlin: Walter de Gruyter GmbH & Co.

Oranskaya, Tatiana Iosifovna. 2006. Pochemu jā- 'ukhodit', idti' ispolzuyetsia kak vspomogatel'niy glagol v passive hindi? [Why is jā- 'to leave', 'to go' used as an auxiliary verb in Hindi passive]. In *Indoitanskoye yazykoznnie i tipologiya yazykovykh situatsiy*. SPb: Nauka

Pā̃ḍe, Hemcandra. 2012. *Samasāmayik hindī vyākaraṇ*. [Contemporary Hindi Grammar] Dillī: Granthalok.

Phillot, Duglas C. 1909. *Hindustani Stumbling-blocs*. London: Crosby and Son.

Pischel, Richard and Jha, Subhadra. 1999. *A Grammar of the Prakrit Languages*. Delhi: Motilal Banarasidass.

Poornima, Shakthi. 2012. *Hindi Complex Predicates at the Syntax-Semantics Interface*. PhD thesis submitted to State University of New York, Buffalo.

Prasād, Dvārak. 1998. *Pahiye*. Dillī: Subodh Pocket Books.

Prasād, Jayśaṅkar. 2014. *Merī Kahāniyā̃. Bhāg 1*. Bhāratīya Sāhitya Inc.

Premchand. 2002. *Raṅgbhūmi*. Nayī Dillī: Star Publications.

Premchand. 2009. *Raṅgbhūmi. Bhāg 2*. Dillī: Ātmārām & Sons.

Premchand. 2012. *Maṅgalsutr//Pratigyā*. Bhāratīya Sāhitya.

Premdās, Viśāl. 1983. *Muktidvār. Śri Kabīr Mandir Dalasarāy*. Dillī: Rājkamal Prakāśan.

Rādhākṛṣṇa. 1963. *Sapne bikāū hẽ*. Vārāṇasī: Hindī Pracāraka Pustakālaya.

Rākeś, Mohan. 2008. *Ādhere Band Kamre*. Dillī: Rājkamal Paperbacks.

Śarmā, Śrīrām. 1973. *Adṛśya Rekhāẽ*. Dillī, Āśā Prakāśan.

Schmidt, Ruth Laila. 2007. Urdu. In Jain, Danesh and Cardona, George (eds.) *The Indo-Aryan Languages*. London and New York: Routledge.

Shapiro, Michael C. 1989. *A primer of modern standard Hindi*. Delhi: Motilal Banarasidass.

Shapiro, Michael C. 2007. Hindi. In Cardona, George and Danesh Jain (eds.) *The Indo-Aryan Languages*. London and New York: Routledge.

Shlomper, Genady. 2005. *Modality in Hindi*. Munich: Lincom Europa.

Singh, Aruṇ Kumār. 2008. *Samāj manovigyān kī rūprekhā*. Dillī: Motilāl Banārasīdās.

Singh, Balvant. 1999. *Kāle Kos*. Dillī: Rājkamal Prakāśan.

Singh, Rājnāth. 2014. *Bhāratīya Rājnīti ɔr Hamārī Soc*. Dillī: Prabhāt Prakāśan.

Singh, Sūraj Bhān. 1985. *Hindī kā vākyātmak vyākaraṇ*. Dillī: Sāhitya Sahakār.

Śivmūrti. 2007. *Keśar-Kastūrī*. Dillī: Rādhākṛṣṇa Paperbacks.

Spejer, Jacob Samuel. 1993. [1886]. *Sanskrit Syntax*. Delhi: Motilal Banarasidass.

Strnad, Jaroslav. 2013. *Morphology and Syntax of Old Hindī: Edition and Analysis of One Hundred Kabīr vānī Poems from Rājasthān*. Leiden: Brill.

Śyāmsundardās (chief editor). 1969. *Hindī Śabdsāgar*. Sampūrṇ 10 khaṇḍõ mẽ. Khaṇḍ 6. Banāras: Kāśī Nāgarī Pracāriṇī Sabhā.

Tikkanen, Bertil. 1987. *The Sanskrit Gerund: A Synchronic, Diachronic and Typological Analysis*. Helsinki: Finnish Oriental Society.

Tripāṭhī, Anurāg. 2014. Dalit Āndolan ke 'Painthar' kā Ant //*Navbhārat Times*. 16.01.2014

Tripāṭhī, Ramāśaṅkar. 2002. *Mahākaviśūdrakapraṇītaṁ Mṛcchakaṭikam*. Dillī: Motilāl Banārasīdās.

Tripāṭhī, Rāmsāgar. 1973. *Mammaṭācāryakṛt Kāvyaprakāśaḥ. Bhāg 2*. Dillī: Motilāl Banārasīdās.

Ultsiferov, Oleg Georgievich. 2005. *Prakticheskaya Grammatika Sovremennogo Literaturnogo Yazyka Xindi* [A Practical Grammar of the Modern Standard Hindi Language]. Moskva: AST: Vostok-Zapad.
Upādhyāy, Dīndayāl. 2014. *Ekātm Mānavvād*. Dillī: Prabhāt Prakāśan.
Van Olphen, Herman Hendrick. 1970. *The Structure of the Hindi verb Phrase*. Dissertation. Austin, Texas: University of Texas.
Varmā, Bhagavatīcaran. 2009. *Cāṇakya*. Dillī: Rājkamal Prakāśan.
Varmā, Bhagavatīcaran. 2009. *Rekhā*. Dillī: Rājkamal Prakāśan.
Varmā, Bhagavatīcaran. 2009. *Ṭeṛhe-Meṛhe Rāste*. Dillī: Rājkamal Prakāśan.
Whitney, William Dwight. 2004. [1889]. *Sanskrit Grammar. Including both the Classical Language, and the older Dialects of Veda and Brahmana*. New Delhi: Munshiram Manoharlal Publishers Pvt. Ltd.
Yādav, Rājendr. 2007. *Ukhṛe hue log*. Dillī: Rādhākṛṣṇa Prakāśan.
Yaśpāl. 2007. *Yaśpāl kī racnāvalī: khaṇḍ 13*. Allāhābād: Lokbhāratī Prakāśan.
Yaśpāl. 2009. *Dādā kāmreḍ*. Illāhābād: Lokbhāratī Paperbacks.
Yates, William. 1855. [1836]. *Introduction to the Hindustání Language. : In Three Parts, Viz., Grammar, Vocabulary, and Reading Lessons*. Calcutta: Printed and sold at the Baptist Mission Press.
Zograf, Georgiy Aleksandrovich. 1976. *Morfologicheskiy stroy novykh indoariyskikh yazykov* [The Morphological Structure of New Indo-Aryan Languages]. Moskva: Nauka.

Pradeep Kumar Das

Agreement in conjunct verb construction: let's solve the problem

Abstract: The present paper re-examines the puzzling agreement patterns of the phenomenon known as conjunct verb construction in Hindi-Urdu. Conjunct verbs consisted of a noun and a light verb have been the most challenging for their agreement patterns and remained a puzzle ever since it was first discussed by Bahl (1974: 24). The present study draws some ideas from Chomsky (1981 and 1993), mainly the distribution of structural cases and combines it with the intrinsic properties of the verbal and nominal elements and comes up with the solution that there must be some mechanism to account for the dispersal of structural-cases which may be available canonically with the verbal elements (Comrie 1981). In doing so, the nominal host of the light verb sometimes behaves as an integral part of the verb when it does not show any agreement with the light verb. However, in other instances, this nominal host acts as one of the arguments and shows the agreement with the light verb. The present research paper is an attempt to analyze the puzzling agreement patterns of conjunction verb construction and presents a tangible solution to the unsolved problem of agreement patterns in conjunct verb construction in Hindi-Urdu.

Keywords: Conjunct verbs, Structural case, Intrinsic agreement-pattern

1 The problem of agreement in conjunct verb

Bahl (1974: 24) has observed that there is a problem in providing an account for the patterns of agreement in 'conjunct verb construction' in Hindi-Urdu. Let us see the two examples that he presents in favor of his claim:

(1a) उसने मोहन को याद किया।

us-ne	*Mohan-ko*	*yād*	*kiyā.*
3M/F.SG-ERG	Mohan.M.SG-ACC	memory.F.SG	do.PFV.M.SG

'S/he remembered Mohan'.

Pradeep Kumar Das, Department of linguistics, Jawaharlal Nehru University, New Delhi, India.
Email: pradeep11@hotmail.com

https://doi.org/10.1515/9783110610796-008

(1b) उसको मोहन की याद आई।
us-ko *Mohan-kī* *yād* *āyī.*
3M/F.SG-DAT Mohan.M.SG-GEN.F.SG memory.F.SG come.PFV.F.SG
'S/he remembered Mohan'.

The sentences (1a) and (1b) pose a problem for the analysis of the agreement facts in Hindi-Urdu. The agreement pattern that is shown in these two sentences, i.e. the verb does not agree with 'left most unmarked nominal element' in (1a), while in (1b) we see that the verb shows agreement with the same nominal, remains a problem for almost all the accounts of agreement that have been given in the literature. What appears to be the case is that, the agreement facts that have been given in the literature are mostly based on the structure of simple predicate in Hindi-Urdu. It is for this reason that the rules that are given for the agreement facts for simple predicate do not account for the patterns of agreement for conjunct verb construction in Hindi-Urdu. But, before we go into the details of agreement facts of complex predicate, it is important for us to have an outline of rules of agreement for simple predicate in Hindi-Urdu.

2 Agreement in Hindi-Urdu in simple predicate

In order to understand the agreement pattern in Hindi-Urdu with regard to the simple predicate, we need to examine the following sentences and discuss the rules of agreement in Hindi-Urdu. The agreement patterns and their rules that explain the structure of simple predicates will help us later to understand the problem of agreement patterns in conjunct verb construction in the next section.

Let us examine the structure of the following sentences in order to understand the agreement facts of simple clauses in Hindi-Urdu:

(2a) लड़का रोटी खाता है।
laṛkā *roṭī* *khātā* *hɛ.*
boy.M.SG.NOM bread.F eat.IPFV.3M.SG AUX.PRS
'The boy eats bread.'

(2b) लड़के ने रोटी खायी है।
laṛke-ne *roṭī* *khāyī* *hɛ.*
boy.M.SG-ERG bread.F eat.PFV.F.SG AUX.PRS
'The boy has eaten bread.'

(3a) लड़की भात खाती है।
laṛkī bhāt khātī hɛ.
girl.F.SG.NOM rice.M eat.IPFV.F.SG AUX.PRS
'The girl eats rice.'

(3b) लड़की ने भात खाया है।
laṛkī-ne bhāt khāyā hɛ.
girl.ERG rice.M.SG eat.PFV.M.SG AUX.PRS
'The girl has eaten rice.'

(4) लड़की/लड़के ने जली हुई रोटी को खाया है।
laṛkī/laṛke-ne jalī huī roṭi-ko khāyā hɛ.
girl/boy-ERG burn.PFV.F be.PFV.F bread.F-ACC eat.PFV.M.SG AUX.PRS
'The girl/boy has eaten the burnt bread.'

The examples (2)–(4) summarize the agreement facts of simple predicate in a nutshell in Hindi-Urdu. This agreement pattern has long been understood and established by various kinds of research works that the verb of a simple predicate in Hindi-Urdu agrees with its leftmost unmarked[1] noun phrase in the sentence. Saksena (1985) has diligently captured the agreement facts in Hindi-Urdu and has hypothesized about the agreement pattern of simple predicate in just one simple sentence. She notes:

> Rule A: "The verb agrees with the leftmost phonologically null instance of case-marking" (Saksena 1985: 468)

If we examine the agreement facts given in the sentences (2)–(4), we would agree with Saksena's hypothesis, as it seems to work pretty well with regard to the agreement patterns of these sentences in Hindi-Urdu. In each of these sentences (2)–(4), the agreement pattern changes from 'subject-verb agreement' i.e. (2) and (3) to 'object-verb agreement' e.g. (2a) and (3a) and finally to what is known as 'default agreement'[2] in (4), and in doing so, the agreement pattern follows the abovementioned rule.

However, if we consider the agreement patterns shown in examples (1a)–(1b), we realize that Saksena's proposed rule in Hindi-Urdu does not account for

1 The nouns that don't bear any overt case marker is called 'unmarked noun phrase' in the literature.
2 We know that in Hindi-Urdu when there is no unmarked noun phrase (noun phrases with overt case marker), the verb exhibits a form of marker which is third person singular masculine and this marker with the verb in such cases has been termed as the 'default agreement' in the literature.

agreement facts displayed by the sentences. Meaning, as per the rule of agreement proposed by Saksena, the leftmost phonologically null instance of case-marked NP in (1a) is *yād* , 'memory' (a feminine noun) but the verb in the sentence in marked with 'masculine' inflection, while in (1b), the same nominal host qualifies the null instance of case-marked NP and shows agreement with the light verb. Therefore, it is important for us to examine the formation and function of complex predicates in Hindi-Urdu and account for the agreement pattern that they display.

3 Conjunct verb construction as one of the complex predicates

Like many languages, 'conjunct verb construction' is a part of complex predicate in Hindi-Urdu. It is formed by conjoining either a noun or an adjective with some verbs that are often called light verb.[3] The complex predicate is an important area of research today and there are many researchers who have worked on various aspects of complex predicate. Thus, it is pertinent to discuss as to how complex predicate is formed, used and differentiated from 'simple predicate' in the literature.

In general, a predicate is the part of a sentence that contains the verb (main verb) and the meaning of the sentence finds its 'predication' on it. This is how the simple predicate is defined but we must address the question as to how does the verb manifest in a complex predicate. Given the fact that a simple predicate must contain a verb of its own in the sentence, in case of a complex predicate, it must contain more than one verbal element in the verb phrase and thus the form, function and even the nature of the predicate is complex. The second co-existent element in the verb phrase could be a verb (e.g. in case of a compound verb), noun (e.g. in case of a conjunct verb), adjective (e.g. also in case of conjunct verb) or any other grammatical construct[4] which not only co-exists with the verb in the predicate position but also helps to explicate the meaning of the sentence.

3 The verb is called light verb because it goes through a process of 'grammaticalization'. There are lots of works that have been done for the explanation of the 'light verb'. For a more detailed description of 'light verb' see Butt (2003).

4 In case of Persian language, a complex predicate can have a postposition/preposition and even an adverb as the second element in the predicate position with main verb to form the complex predicate.

The present paper examines the conjunct verb construction as one of the 'complex predicates' that is formed out of a noun (abstract) and a verb (light verb). By definition, such a *complex predicate* is a grammatical category which is formed with the help of the mutual sharing of semantic features and a co-occurrence of two lexical items i.e. a *host noun* and a *light verb*. It is interesting to note that this co-occurrence has a very special function with regard to the agreement pattern in the case of a conjunct verb construction.

The main thrust of the paper is to examine this unique agreement pattern of the *host noun* and the light verb in such a construction. We will see shortly that this host-noun has two functions. In certain linguistic environments, it functions as an integral part of the verb phrase, and in some other contexts, the similar host-noun acts as one of the arguments of the light verb and controls the agreement properties of the light verb despite the fact that host-noun co-occurs with it for the purpose of predication as it contributes to the meaning of the predicate in Hindi-Urdu.

The conjunct verb construction has always been an area of interest for the scholars working on South Asian languages. Scholars such as Kellogg (1875), Guru (1922), Sharma (1958), Kachru (1966), Verma (1971), Hook (1974), Masica (1976), Butt (1995), Mohanan (1994), and Das (2009) have dealt with such conjunct verb construction of one or the other types. Despite abundant research in this area, one of the complex predicates known as conjunct verb construction remains descriptively and theoretically puzzling. Researchers have attempted to establish the reasons for such puzzling behavior of the nominal host in such complex predicate. However, beyond pointing out the mere structural descriptions[5] or the order of organization of the post-positions in the sentence, not much has been said about the theoretical ground. Thus, it is important to find out an explanation and solution to the everlasting puzzle of the agreement patterns of conjunct verb construction. The present research work is an earnest attempt to solve the puzzle and to provide an agreeable solution to the problem of agreement facts of conjunct verb construction in Hindi-Urdu.

5 Mohanan (1994) 'The Argument Structure in Hindi' has tried to analyze the structural dependencies of the complex predicates and she has at least been able to say something about the order of the postpositions in the sentences and she thinks this order itself is the reason for such quizzical behavior of the complex predicate. This has been at least a good start in terms of giving a path to find out the theoretical reason for this unique behavior of the construction.

4 The formation of the conjunct verbs

It is an interesting point to notice that any combination of a noun and a verb does not automatically qualify as a 'conjunct verb construction'. In other words, there are instances where the co-occurrence of a noun and a verb in a sequence of N+V cannot be called a 'conjunct verb construction'. Let us consider the following examples:

(5a) मानस ने अपना होमवर्क किया।
Mānas-ne *apanā* *homwark* *kiyā.*
Manas.M-ERG self's homework.M.SG do.PFV.M.SG
'Manas did his homework.'

(5b) नीतू ने महेश को एक किताब दी।
Nītu-ne *Mahesh-ko* *ek* *kitāb* *dī.*
Neetu-F Mahesh.M-DAT one book.F give.PFV.F.SG
'Neetu gave a book to Mahesh.'

The examples (5a)–(5b) may also be mistaken as 'complex predicates' because they are also formed with a sequence of N+V. However, we do not consider these examples as a 'conjunct verb construction' because the predicate contains just a simple verb and the NPs such as 'homework' and *kitāb* 'book' are the direct object of the verbs that have been used in the sentence. So, the thematic role and the valency of the argument-structure of the verbs, such as *karnā*, 'to do' and *denā*, 'to give', are well-satisfied and all the semantic and syntactic requirements of these verbs are in place. Therefore, there is no semantic or syntactic reason that could motivate us to consider the examples given in (5a)–(5b) as the complex predicates.

Nevertheless, there are expressions such as *pyār karnā*, 'to love', *yād karnā*, 'to remember', *bharosā karnā*, 'to rely', *ghriṇā karnā*, 'to hate', *tarakkī* (or *pragati*) *karnā*, 'to progress', *āwāz denā*, 'to call someone', *apmān karnā*, 'to insult', *tārīf* (or *praśaṃsā*) *karnā*, 'to praise', and *kṣamā* (or *māf*) *karnā*, 'to forgive' etc. that cannot be verbalized in many South Asian languages by using just one verb. In fact, it is almost impossible to verbalize such expressions by using a verb in many Indian languages and even in some other South-East-Asian languages outside the subcontinent, such as Korean, Japanese, and Bahasa Indonesia. If we see the linguistic traits in these languages, it seems that in order to fulfill the pattern-gap,[6] the speakers of these languages adopt a unique, uniform and interesting strategy. The strategy seems to select **abstract nouns** and verbs which go through a process of 'semantic change' or what is known as **'semantic bleaching'**[7] and then incorporate these nouns into VP in order to create the verbal equivalents so that they can meet the requirement of the structural pattern-gap for such expressions in these South Asian languages. This is how a 'complex predicate' is formed by conjoining an abstract noun/adjective with a light verb (a semantically bleached verb) and it brings forth a complex structure of a 'conjunct verb construction', where the meaning is primarily derived from the abstract noun/adjective and the light verb helps to explicate the meaning of non-verbal elements into a complex predicate.

Let us examine such instances of complex verb forms and compare the linguistic attributes of such constructions with that of non-complex verb forms that were given above in (5a)–(5b):

(6a) संगीता ने कमल पर भरोसा किया।
Sangītā-ne *kamal-par* *bharosā* *kiyā.*
Sangeeta.F-ERG Kamal.M-LOC faith.M do.PFV.M.SG
'Sangeeta placed faith in Kamal.'

(6b) धीरज ने बच्चों पर ध्यान दिया।
Dhīraj-ne *baččõ-par* *dhyān* *diyā.*
Dhiraj.3M.SG-ERG child.M.PL.OBL-LOC attention.M.SG give.PFV.M.SG
'Dhiraj paid attention to children.'

Let us now compare the examples (5a)–(5b) and (6a)–(6b) in order to prove that the 'nominal host' in (6a)–(6b) is an integral part of the predicate, while the same is not true for the examples given in (5a)–(5b).

In example (5a), we have an agent Mānas and 'an accomplished action' *apnā homework* 'his(own) homework'. These two arguments have been licensed in the

6 Pattern-gap refers to a situation of not being able to verbalize these expression purely in terms of employing a verbal element.

7 The best example of the process of grammaticalization that I can think of is the process of putting two verbs together where one of the verbs has to be grammaticalized, or semantically bleached in order to co-exist together. The examples of 'Compound verb' can be something like *mar jānā*, 'to die', *khā jānā*, 'to eat', *bol uṭhnā*, 'to speak' etc. However, even in the normal case when we make use of a verb to express any aspectual marker in the sentence, the verb seems to go through the same process of grammaticalization. For example, *jā rahā hɛ*, 'is going', *khā rahā hɛ*, 'is eating'. In these examples, the V2 in case of compound verb and auxiliary verb in normal verbal expression are said to have gone through the process of grammaticalization.

clause by the transitive verb *karnā* 'to do'. If we examine the example given in (6a), we would say that there is an agent, namely Sangeeta and the accomplished action is *bharosā* 'reliance'. This much is fine; however, we also have another argument in example (6a) namely Kamal. The verb in the sentence *karnā* 'to do', is a transitive one and cannot accommodate the third argument Kamal in the sentence as per the argument structure or sub-categorization principle of a transitive verb. Thus, the question that has to be answered is: where does this third argument come from, and how is this being accommodated/licensed in the sentence in terms of thematic roles, case-markings and counting of arguments/valences?

If we follow Mohanan's (1994) proposal, we could argue that the third argument in this transitive sentence has been licensed/ accommodated by the complex predicate i.e. the 'conjunct verb' – *bharosā karnā* 'an act of reliance' – as a single linguistic unit and not by examining the light verb '*karnā*', 'to do' in the sentence. If we accept this, we would realize that the 'conjunct verb', *bharosā karnā* would need a benefactor and thus, the third argument has been accommodated in the clause by the semantic value of the complex predicate.

Mohanan (1994) has also discussed the case-markers and their associations with different arguments in the complex predicate and it is useful to discuss them here. Moreover, before we discuss the case markers and their association with different arguments, it is important to map (count) the number of arguments first. In (6b), we have an agent Dhīraj i.e. the giver, a receiver *bačče* 'children' and a thing that is being given *dhyān* 'attention' (in personified form). Now, this is quite similar to what we have in example (5b), Neetu (agent), Mahesh (the receiver) and *a book* (the thing that is given). In both the examples, we have two internal arguments and one external argument, as the verb of these clauses is a ditransitive one (i.e. a three-place predicate).

However, there is something very interesting and important to discuss with regard to the distribution of the case-markers in (6b) and (5b). We know that the receiver/benefactor (i.e. the goal of the giving) normally takes the *dative case* as it is shown in the example (5b), *Mahesh-ko* 'to Mahesh'. But, the receiver/benefactor in example (6b) *bačče* has a locative case marker. Mohanan (1994) has shown, following Gruber's (1965) 'Semantic field',[8] that the locative case marker *par* 'on' is not a part of the semantic structure of the verb *denā* 'to give'. Therefore, *denā* 'to give' cannot give/license a locative case to its actant/argument. However, if we consider *dhyān denā* 'to pay attention' as a single unit (i.e. a complex predicate), we can definitely say that it assigns the locative case *par* 'on' to one of its arguments i.e. *bačče* 'children'. The aforementioned explanation proves

8 For a detailed analysis of Gruber's proposal of 'Semantic field', see Mohanan (1994).

that the 'nominal host' is an integral part of complex predicates on the basis of the intrinsic linguistic properties that have been discussed here. This is why this nominal host plays a crucial role in deciding the number of linguistic attributes such as valency, theta role, and case-association with actants/arguments in the sentences. These linguistic factors prove that there is a semantic bonding between the host noun and the light verb in a conjunct verb construction.

The above discussion of mismatch of the number of arguments and the 'distribution of case-markers' beyond the semantic capacity of their respective 'light verb' also makes the structure of conjunct verb construction very puzzling. Though puzzling, the abovementioned linguistic function is in fact an interesting topic for further research in linguistics. This is so because it requires a careful analysis of the problem before we could propose a solution for the agreement facts in a conjunct verb construction.

5 Conjunct verb and noun incorporation

Some researchers Mohanan (1994), Hock (2017), Dayal (2011), Verbeke (2013), Klaiman, (1990) etc. have used to term 'noun incorporation' while explaining the puzzling functions of a conjunct verb construction in different contexts i.e. the host-noun remains dormant inside the VP and does not show agreement with the light verb in some cases and yet in some other cases, the host-noun behaves as an argument of the light verb and also controls the agreement. Mohanan (1994) and Dayal (2011) have mainly used the term 'noun incorporation' in order to explain the agreement pattern in complex predicate where the general rule of agreement proposed by Saksena (1985; 468) does not seem to apply.

Chakrabarti (2014) Bhattacharyya et. al (2007) and Dayal (2011) have mentioned that '... Mohanan (1995) was the first to explicitly claim that Hindi has incorporation'. There are various kinds of incorporations, especially the incorporation of a nominal element into the VP that has light verb. There are several interesting accounts and findings given in Dayal (2011). The accounts and arguments that she gives in order to explain the syntactic and semantic structures of VPs which are borne out due to the noun incorporation in Hindi are thought provoking and convincing. However, Dayal (2011) does not directly deal with the agreement phenomenon in a conjunct verb construction in Hindi.

Chakrabarti (2014; 06) mentions that while addressing noun incorporation in Hindi Mohanan (1995) argues that the incorporated noun is an argument of the verb. Mohanan (ibid) has used the term *host* and *Light Verb* and shown that in this type of combination, the number of arguments, meaning, and case of the arguments are jointly determined by the noun and the verb. A large number of conjunct verbs are N+V combinations. The main question to answer with this type of 'verb construction' concerns the status of the noun, i.e., whether the noun is incorporated into the verb complex or if the noun is an overt argument of the verb.

Chakrabarti (2014; 06) provides these two types of examples which can be presented as:

Type-A: *čāy lenā* 'to have tea' *homwark karnā,*'to do the homework', and *kitāb denā,*'to give a book' etc.
Type-2: *jamhāī lenā* 'to yawn', *bharosā karnā,* 'to rely', *dhyān denā* 'to pay attention', *yād karnā,* 'to remember' and *yād ānā,* 'to remember', etc.

Mohanan (1994; 1995) opines that in the former cases, *cāy,* 'tea' *homwark* 'homework' and *kitāb* 'book' are overt objects of the verb whereas in the latter *jamhāī* 'yawn' *bharosā* 'reliance', *dhyān* 'attention', and *yād* 'remembrance' etc. are the instances of noun incorporation into the VP. It is for this reason that Mohanan (1994; 1995) has used the term 'noun incorporation' to explain the instances of 'conjunct verbs' in which the host nominals do not show the agreement with the light verb. The proposal has some impact especially when applying the general rule of agreement that has been proposed by Saksena (1985: 468). The noun incorporation strategy has helped Mohanan to explain why the left most unmarked feminine noun, namely *yād,* 'memory' in Bahl's sentence given in example (1a) cannot show agreement with the verb form *kiyā* 'did', which shows the masculine inflection. Bahl's sentences are presented in (7a) and (7b):

(7a) उसने मोहन को याद किया।
us-ne *Mohan-ko* *yād* *kiyā.*
3M/F.SG-ERG Mohan.M.SG-ACC memory.F do.PFV.M.SG.M
'S/he remembered Mohan'.

(7b) उसको मोहन की याद आई।
us-ko *Mohan-kī* *yād* *āyī.*
3M/F.SG-DAT Mohan.M.SG-GEN.F.SG memory.F.SG come.PFV.F.SG
'S/he remembered Mohan'.

As discussed above, these two sets of conjunct verb constructions and their agreement patterns pose problems of any theory/analysis in linguistics. One set allows the 'host noun' to be dormant and thus does not show agreement with the light verb; however, in the other set, the same 'host noun' for some good linguistic reason steps out of the bonding of the conjunct verb and almost functions as one of the arguments of the light verb and shows agreement with it.

There is no explanation for this puzzling behavior of the 'host noun' in a conjunct verb construction in Hindi-Urdu. Mohanan (1994 and 1995) is the only work prior to this research work which has attempted to explain the puzzle; however, having failed to offer any concrete explanation, she evokes the issue of 'noun incorporation' in her research work to overcome the shortcomings of her research. It is only after her work that many researchers, whom I have mentioned above, have either referred, quoted or mentioned about the terms such as 'incorporation' 'quasi incorporation' or 'pseudo incorporation' of the nominal with the light verb to form a 'conjunct verb construction'.

The present paper has taken the suggested recommendations of Mohanan (1994 and 1995) and analyzed the agreement patterns of two different behaviors of conjunct verbs comprehensively and theorized the patterns of agreement facts of conjunct verb construction in Hindi. Mohanan (1994; 230) couldn't solve this agreement puzzle and left the issue at the observational level that has been mentioned as '... if an argument, which precedes the nominal host, bears a *genitive* or a *locative* or an *instrumental* case, the light verb will show agreement with the nominal host, however, if the argument, which precedes the host, has an *accusative* or a *nominative* case marker, the light verb does not agree with the nominal host.'

Despite the fact that Mohanan (1994) has evoked the notion of 'noun incorporation' to account for the agreement pattern of conjunct verb construction, her observation did not bring any solution to the two sets of conjunct verb constructions and their puzzling behavior of the agreement facts that was noticed by Bahl's sentences as shown in example (7a) and (7b) above.

The present paper, however, does not need any support from the term called 'noun incorporation' as it has not only solved the puzzle of agreement patterns in the two sets of the conjunct verb constructions but has also provided the theoretical ground for such puzzling behavior of the 'host noun' in triggering and not triggering the agreement with the light in a conjunct verb construction.

The present paper suggests the following functional requirements for the dispersal of the case(s) that is/are structurally available with different types of verbs based on their +/- transitivity:

(i) If the light verb is an intransitive verb, it has only one case associated with it i.e. the nominative case, and unless this case is dispersed to an NP in the sentence, the light verb cannot form VP with the host nominal. However, if there is no scope to disperse this structural case in the sentence, the host nominal can receive the case and thus shows agreement with the verb.

(8) राम को मोहन से घृणा हुई।
Rām ko *Mohan se* *ghr̥ṇā* *huī.*
Ram.M.SG-DAT Mohan.M.SG-INSTR hatred.F be.PFV.F.SG
'Ram hated Mohan.'

(9) श्याम से मोहन की लड़ाई हुई।
Śyāmse *Mohan kī* *laṛāī* *huī.*
Shyam-INSTR Mohan.M.SG-GEN fight.F be.PFV.F.SG
'Shyam fought with Mohan.'

(10) मोहन की श्याम से लड़ाई हुई।
Mohan-kī *Śyām-se* *laṛāī* *huī.*
Mohan.M.SG-GEN Shyam.M.SG-INSTR fight.F be.PFV.F.SG
'Mohan fought with Shyam.'
[A fight took place between Mohan and Shyam.]

We see that the nominal host of the conjunct verb bears the structural case in each of these examples and shows the agreement with the light verb.

(ii) If the light verb is a transitive verb, it has two core (structural) cases associated with the verb i.e. Nominative (ergative) and Accusative and unless these cases are dispersed to NPs in the sentence, the light verb can't form VP with the host nominal. Let's consider some examples:

(11) राम ने मोहन को याद किया।
Rām-ne *Mohan-ko* *yād* *kiyā.*
Ram.M.SG-ERG Mohan.M.SG-ACC remembrance-F do.PFV.M.SG
'Ram remembered Mohan.'

(12) समीरा ने महेश को पसंद किया।
Samīrā-ne *Maheś-ko* *pasand* *kiyā.*
Sameera-ERG Mahesh.M.SG-ACC liking.F do.PFV.M.SG
'Sameera liked Mahesh.'

(13) निहारिका ने चन्दन को क्षमा किया।
Nihārikā-ne *Čandan-ko* *kśamā* *kiyā.*
Niharika-ERG Chandan.M.SG-ACC forgiveness-F to.PFV.F.SG
'Niharika forgave Chandan.'

In the above examples, both the cases i.e. Ergative and Accusative that are with the transitive light verb have been dispersed/given to the NPs in the sentence and thus the 'host nominal' in all these conjunct verb constructions remains dormant/incorporated in the VP as there is no contextual need for the nominal host to take the structural case from the light verb and show the agreement with it. However, let us consider the following examples:

(14) राम ने अपनी लड़ाई शुरू की / कर दी। (NB: कर दी is the compound verb of करना)
Rām-ne apnī laṛāī śurū kī/
Ram-ERG self's fight.F.SG-ACC start.ADJ do.PFV.F.S
kar dī.
do.V_1 + give.V_2.PFV.F.SG
'Ram started his (own) fight.'

The above example is very interesting but can be very well explained for its agreement pattern by the schema suggested by Das (2018). The explanation of the agreement pattern for the above sentence is similar. Since Hindi does not mark the inanimate and indefinite nouns with the overt accusative marker, the NP '*laṛāī* acts as the grammatical subject of the sentence and thus it shows the regular agreement pattern which can be compared with sentences like (15) and (16):

(15) राम ने अपना भात खाया।
Rām-ne apnā bhāt khāyā.
Ram-ERG self's rice.M eat.PFV.M.SG
'Ram ate his (own) rice.'

(16) राम ने अपनी रोटी खायी।
Rām-ne apnī roṭī khāyī.
Ram-ERG self's bread.F eat.PFV.F.SG
'Ram ate his (own) bread.'

(iii) If the light verb is a ditransitive one, it has three core (structural) cases associated with it, namely, Nominative (Ergative), Accusative and Dative, and unless these cases are dispersed to NPs in the sentence, the light verb cannot form VP with the host nominal. Let us consider some examples:

(17) राम ने मोहन को आवाज़ दी/ लगाई।
Rām-ne Mohan-ko āwāj dī/ lagāī.
Ram-ERG Mohan.M.SG-DAT calling sound.F give.PFV.F.S/ put.PFV.F.SG
'Ram called (for) Mohan.'

(18) राजा ने मंत्री को इनाम दिया।
Rājā-ne mantrī-ko inām diyā.
Raja-ERG minister.M.SG-DAT reward.M give.PFV.M.SG
'The king rewarded the minister.'

(19) शिक्षक ने छात्र को शाबासी दी।
śikṣak-ne čhātr-ko badhāī dī.
Shikshak-ERG student.M.SG-DAT congratulation.F give-PFV.F.SG
'The teacher congratulated the student.'

(20) मेरे दोस्त ने मुझे गाली दी।
mere dost-ne mujhe gālī dī.
my friend.M.SG-ERG I.M.SG-DAT abuse.F give.PFV.F.SG
'My friend abused me.'

In all these examples, the NPs have the Ergative, Dative as the overt cases and the light verb has not yet given away/ dispersed the Accusative case as a ditransitive verb. So, contextually, the nominal host accepts the covert accusative case and it functions as the grammatical subject of the ditransitive light verb and shows agreement with it. This kind of mediation of agreement is something which is very common in Hindi-Urdu. For example,

(21) राम ने मोहन को मिठाई दी।
Rām-ne Mohan-ko miṭhāī dī.
Ram-ERG Mohan.M.SG-DAT sweet.F give.PFV.F.SG
'Ram gave sweet to me.'

(22) सीता ने राम को अमरूद दिया।
Sītā-ne Rām-ko amrūd diyā.
Sita-ERG Ram.M.SG-DAT guava-M give.PFV.M.SG.
'Sita gave guava to Ram.'

(23) शर्मा जी ने मुझे हिन्दी पढ़ाई।
Śarmā-jī-ne mujhe Hindī paṛhāī.
Sharma-HON-ERG I.M.SG-DAT Hindi.F teach.PFV.F.SG
'Sharma ji taught me Hindi.'

Thus, on the basis of the above discussion, we can conclude the section that the present research work has proposed a solution for the patterns of agreement and the proposal is simple, yet exceptionless, and it only after the careful analysis of different types of verbs and their cooccurrences with different nominal hosts for the purpose of 'conjunct verb construction', I have come to the conclusion that there is no need to refer to the notion of 'noun incorporation' that has been evoked in Mohanan (1994) in order to explain the two different functions of agreement patterns of the 'host nominal' in a conjunct verb construction in Hindi.

6 Two different functions of Conjunct Verbs in Hindi-Urdu

At the beginning of this paper, it was discussed that the function of the nominal host in the 'conjunct verb construction' with regard to its agreement pattern with the light verb in the sentences (1a) and (1b) is descriptively and theoretically puzzling. There seems to be two distinct functions of the given nominal host in a conjunct verb construction. In the first case, the nominal host remains completely dormant in the verb phrase and does not act as one of the arguments of the VP, even when other arguments are overtly case marked and the nominal host is the only unmarked NP. Therefore, it seems that the host NP does not come out of its semantic bonding with the light verb and since other arguments have already been overtly case marked, the verb is marked with default agreement marking, namely, 3MS.

Nevertheless, in the second environment, the same nominal host does not remain dormant inside the verb phrase and for some reason does not seem to be an integral part of the VP as it breaks through the bonding with its light verb and seems to acquire some nominal properties due to the linguistic requirement of the context. The hypothesis gets strengthened when this nominal host – which was paired with a light verb in the conjunct verb construction for the purpose of semanticity of the verbalization – behaves as one of the arguments of the light verb in the sentence and controls the verb agreement of the construction when other nominal elements are overtly case marked. It somewhat functions like the grammatical subject in the conjunct verb construction. Let us examine these two sets of conjunct verb constructions:

Tab. 1: Agreement in Set A of conjunct verbs

Set A

No agreement (Host ↔ Light)

Subject	**Object**	**Host**	**Light**
Sangītā-ne +	*Kamal-ko* +	*yād* +	*kiyā*
Sangītā-ERG	Kamal-ACC	memory-F.SG	do.PFV.M.SG

(24) समीरा ने महेश को पसंद किया।

Samīra-ne	*Mahesh-ko*	*pasand*	*kiyā.*
Sarmeela.F-ERG	Mahesh.M-ACC	liking.F.SG	do.PFV.M.SG

'Sarmeela liked Mahesh.'

(25) दिनेश ने मधु को याद किया।

Dinesh-ne	*Madhu-ko*	*yād*	*kiyā.*
Dinesh.M-ERG	Madhu.F-ACC	memory.F.SG	do.PFV.M.SG

'Dinesh remembered Madhu.'

(26) निहारिका ने चन्दन को क्षमा किया।

Nihārikā-ne	*Čandan-ko*	*kṣamā*	*kiyā.*
Niharika.F-ERG	Chandan.M-ACC	forgiveness.F	do.PFV.M.SG

'Niharika forgave Chandan.'

The examples (24)–(26) support our generalization of one of the sets of conjunct verbs in Hindi-Urdu. The host noun in all these examples is a feminine singular noun, and it is the only unmarked nominal element in all the sentences. Therefore, this noun phrase is the most eligible and suitable candidate that can function as the controller of the agreement according to the rule that has been proposed by Saksena (1985). However, if we examine the agreement morphology of the verb phrase of these sentences (24)–(26), we find that the verb exhibits the default agreement i.e., 3MS. So, it is clear that the verb does not show any agreement with the nominal host in this set of examples.

There has been no explanation available for such mismatch of agreement patterns of conjunct verbs in Hindi-Urdu. To the best of our knowledge, Mohanan (1994: 230) has attempted to give some structural description to the problem of this mismatch. If we summarize Mohanan's hypothesis, it would read as '... if an argument, which precedes the nominal host, bears a *genitive* or a *locative* or an *instrumental* case, the light verb will show agreement with the nominal host, however, if the argument, which precedes the host, has an *accusative* or a *nominative* case marker, the light verb does not agree with the nominal host.' This observation is quite convincing and somewhat summarizes the structural distributions of case-markings and the agreement facts of conjunct verbs in Hindi-Urdu. However, we cannot consider this observation a solution to the problem since it is not difficult to find exceptions to the above-mentioned observations. Consider, for example, (27):

(27) संगीता ने मोहन को आवाज़ दी।
Sangītā-ne *Mohan-ko* *awāz* *dī.*
Sangeeta.F.ERG Mohan.M-DAT callinig sound.F give.PFV.3F.SG
'Sangeeta called for Mohan.'

The above example refutes the observation made in Mohanan (1994) because the argument that precedes the host nominal in the above sentence does bear an accusative/dative case marker and yet the light verb shows agreement with the nominal host in the sentence. Thus, this cannot be the solution to the problem of conjunct verb and agreement pattern in Hindi-Urdu. We will discuss the solution but let us first see the other type of examples (Set-B) of conjunct verb construction.

Tab. 2: Agreement in Set B of conjunct verb

Set B — **Agreement** (→ Host, → Verb(1v))

Subject	Object	Host	Verb(1v)
Nurīn-ne +	*Salīm-par* +	*kripā* +	*kī*
Nurīn-ERG	Salīm-LOC	favour-F.SG	do.PFV.F.SG

(28) समीर ने नगमा का अपमान किया।
Samīr-ne *Nagamā-kā* *apmān* *kiyā.*
Sameer.3M.SG-ERG Nagma.3F.SG-GEN insult.N.M do.PFV.M.SG
'Sameer insulted Nagma.'

(29) सुरेश को बच्चों का ध्यान आया।
Suresh-ko *baččõ-kā* *dhyān* *āyā.*
Suresh.3M.SG-DAT child.3M.PL-GEN remembrance.M.SG come.PFV.M.SG
'Suresh remembered the child.'

(30) नूरीन ने सलीम को आवाज़ दी।
Nurīn-ne *Salīm-ko* *āwāz* *dī.*
Nureen.3F.SG-ERG Saleem.3M.SG-DAT sound.N.F give.PFV.F.SG
'Nureen called for Saleem.'

(31) नसीर ने सबनम की तारीफ़ की।
Nasīr-ne *Sabnam-ki* *tārīf* *kī.*
Naseer.3M.SG-ERG Sabnam.3F.SG-GEN praise.N.F do.PFV.F.SG
'Naseer praised Sabnam.'

(32) सुजाता को दिनेश से नफ़रत हुई।
Sujātā-ko Dinesh-se nafrat huī.
Sujata.3F.SG-DAT Dinesh.3M.SG-INSTR hatred.N.F happen.PFV.F.SG
'Sujata hated Dinesh.'

(33) भारत में इस वर्ष काफी प्रगति हुई।
bhārat-mẽ is varsh kāfī pragati huī.
India.M.SG-LOC this year lots of development.F.SG happen.PFV.F.SG
'Lots of development happened in India this year.'

The above-cited examples (28)–(33), in which the 'light verb shows agreement with its nominal 'host', help us to hypothesize that the nominal host in all the examples in 'Set-B' is one of the arguments of the clause. Unlike 'Set-A', the placement of the 'host nominal' is in a separate box in 'Set-B' and this depicts the fact that even though the 'host noun' forms a 'complex predicate' by a mutual semantic sharing/bonding and co-occurrence with a 'light verb', it does not give up all its nominal characteristics in Set-B. The nominal characteristics can be checked through different processes of linguistic description available in the literature and let us bring some of such descriptions to prove our point.

7 Subjecthood in a sentence

Dixon (2001), Onishi (2001), Kachru (1990) and Comrie (1981) have discussed the importance of canonical and non-canonical arguments in order to establish the notion of subjecthood in linguistic literature. The notion can be shown in the following table:

Tab. 3: Markings in Hindi

Canonical vs Non-canonical markings	
More A/S properties	Less A/S properties
Nominative >	Objective > Genitive/Locative > Instrumental
← Canonical →	← Non-canonical →

In trying to highlight the implications of this canonical and non-canonical marking of the arguments, Comrie (1989: 93) suggests "... there is a glaring priority of subject over object in the structure of a sentence and it has a functional explanation. Presumably, a deeper cognitive organization of linguistic information that underlies the pattern in which the subject and object(s) (both DO & IO) occur". This hypothesis is better understood when we have the structural shift of a grammatical and logical subject for the purpose of mediating the agreement in Hindi-Urdu. To make the point clear, reconsider the examples (2) and (2a) in (34) and (35):

(34) लड़का रोटी खाता है।
laṛkā *roṭī* *khātā* *hɛ.*
boy.3M.SG.NOM bread.F eat.IPFV.3M.SG AUX.PRS
'The boy eats bread.'

In this example (34), the noun '*laṛkā*', 'boy' is both the logical as well as the grammatical subject in the sentence and gets the priority over the object that Comrie mentions for the purpose of selecting the controller of the agreement by the verb phrase. Let us see the shift of the role of the grammatical and logical subject in the following sentence:

(35) लड़के ने रोटी खायी है।
laṛke-ne *roṭī* *khāyī* *hɛ.*
boy.3M.SG-ERG bread.F eat.PFV.3F.SG AUX.PRS
'The boy has eaten bread.'

The agreement pattern of the sentence given in (35) is different from that of the (34) in Hindi-Urdu. The verb does not agree with the subject (i.e. *laṛkā*, 'boy'), rather it agrees with the direct object (e.g. *roṭī*, 'bread') in sentence (35). The agreement pattern of (34) is called 'Subject-verb agreement, however, the pattern of agreement in sentence (35) is known as 'Object-verb agreement'. The nomenclature of these agreement patterns may be different, but the linguistic process of mediating the agreement between the subject (logical/grammatical) and the verb phrase is the same at the deeper level of linguistic analysis that Comrie (ibid) articulates in his hypothesis. In other words, the logical subject in (35) is overtly case marked and thus it loses the candidacy of being the controller of the agreement by the rule proposed by Saksena (1985). Moreover, the direct object is not overtly case marked in sentence (35) and thus, it qualifies the linguistic prerequisite requirements of being the eligible controller for the agreement with the verb. The canonical marking of the arguments empowers the direct object of (35) to be the grammatical subject and shows the agreement with the verb in the sentence. Such explanation of agreement pattern and the priority of subject (both the logical and grammatical) over object in mediating the agreement with the verb justifies that there is a deeper cognitive organization of linguistic information, which allows this system of prioritizing the supremacy of subject over object to take place. Comrie's hypothesis claims the above fact in terms of marking the canonical arguments in linguistic expression will help us prove our point and provide a tangible solution to standing problem of agreement patterns in conjunct verb construction.

8 Finiteness of the verb in a sentence

The finiteness of the verb is a process of putting the phi-features[9] and the TAM[10] on the verbal element. The way a verb becomes finite in its usage in a sentence is the process that establishes the verb's relationship with the subject/object and identifies the case-markers (e.g. nominative, accusative or dative). It further links these markers with their respective thematic relations of the noun phrases in a sentence. Different theories of grammar capture and classify this procedure by applying different methods and mechanisms. The tree-diagram given below (figure-1) outlines the basic principles of canonical case assignment and the configuration of head(s) and modifier(s) that works as the backbone of the generative school of thought in linguistics (Chomsky 1965; 1981; 1986; 1993).

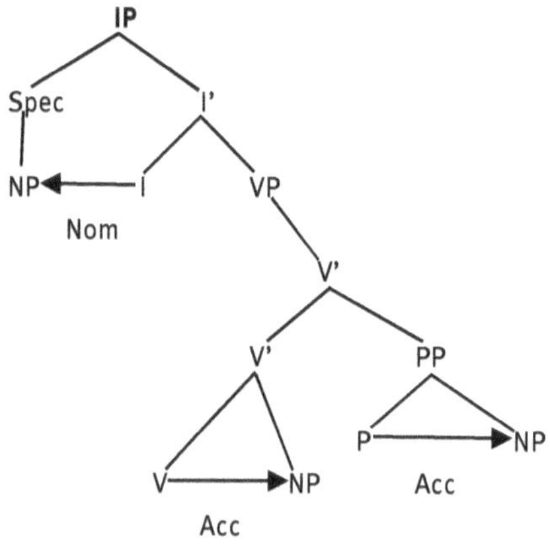

Fig. 1: Canonical case alignment in Hindi

9 The phi-features in the literature is known as the person, number and gender marking of the noun phrase on the verb.

10 TAM is the tense, aspect and the mood markings of the particular sentence in the context.

The tree-diagram also points out that the INFL/Tense of IP/TP is a case assigner and it assigns the nominative/subjective case to the NP in Spec position. The verb or V assigns an accusative case to the NP i.e., the direct object in the sentence. It is interesting to notice that the head P (e.g. preposition) is also a case assigner and it assigns an accusative case to the NP[11] i.e. the prepositional object in the sentence. The principles of generative grammar that explain the notion of canonical case-markings and the cognitive ability to understand the places/positions of the subject and object NPs may help us to establish a link between theorization of generative grammar and the structural description of agreement patterns in conjunct verb construction in Hindi-Urdu. We want to establish a link between the principles of generative grammar that help to understand the structural/canonical case marking of different NPs in a sentence and the principles of typological classification of canonical and non-canonical marking of the arguments in a sentence. By doing this, we will be able to achieve the explanatory adequacy of our hypothesis that we are going to purpose. After all, it is one and same thing whether we say that every NP must have a case in order to be the part of a sentence (Case theory in Chomsky 1980) or we say that the verb has to disperse its structural cases with the help of functional heads i.e. nominative case which is given to the subject NP by INFL/T (Tense) and the objective case (accusative case) to the object NP with the help of the verb i.e. the lexical head of a transitive sentence.

9 Canonical cases of the verb phrase and their displacement

The hypothesis that we want to propose here draws inferences from Comrie (1981) and Chomsky (1981) and amalgamates the best arguments given in these two theories and tops it up with the core argument of case-theory (or the *kāraka* theory) of Pāṇini. The hypothesis will help us solve the problems/puzzles of agreement patterns of conjunct verb constructions. The Pāṇinian hypothesis is as follows:

> Every verb, whether it is intransitive, transitive or ditransitive, has to give away or disperse semantically canonical cases. This entails:
> (a) An intransitive verb: has a nominative case as its canonical case
> (b) A transitive verb: has a nominative and an accusative case as its canonical cases

11 This place i.e. prepositional object may also be the place of an indirect object but this place is generated by a very complex mechanism in generative framework.

(c) A ditransitive verb: has a nominative, an accusative and a dative case as its canonical cases

Let us discuss as to how this hypothesis works. It is basically a blend or amalgamation of all three different approaches in linguistics i.e. the generative school of thought, the typological studies to languages and the Pāṇinian model of language analysis. The Pāṇinian model of linguistics analysis has always believed that it is compulsory to treat the centrality of verbal elements as the most fundamental principle in order to explain the structural dependencies in languages. There is a sutra in the Pāṇinian tradition which reads as follows:

क्रियान्वित्वं कारकत्वम् = क्रिया जिसको अन्वित करती है वह कारक होता है।
The verb assigns its noun(s) its/their grammatical role(s) with the help of case(s).

The Pāṇinian approach to the language analysis that establishes the centrality of the verbal element has helped not only the researchers in Sanskrit to explain the complex structural dependencies related to the morphosyntactic and semantic properties of the language but also computer-scientists who have been able to solve different structural issues in computer programming by applying the Pāṇinian model. We want to inbuilt the centrality of the verbal element in our hypothesis and use it as the key-factor to explain as to how our hypothesis works better in explaining the problem/puzzle of the conjunct verb construction in Hindi-Urdu.

10 Application of our hypothesis

The functional requirement of our hypothesis in order to account for the agreement patterns of the conjunct verb construction demands the followings:

(i) The canonical/structural case(s) that is/are available with the verb i.e. nominative of intransitive, nominative/ergative and accusative cases of the transitive verb and the nominative/ergative, accusative and dative case of the ditransitive verb must be dispersed/given away to the noun phrase(s) in the sentence before the verb becomes finite by taking the phi-features and the TAM in the sentence.

(ii) If the canonical/structural case(s) is/are dispersed/ given away to the NP(s) in the sentence, the nominal host remains dormant inside the verb phrase and the light verb inflects for the default agreement. However, if any of the canonical/structural case has not been dispersed to the NP(s) in the sentence, the nominal host acts as an argument (grammatical subject) and exhibits agreement with the light verb in the conjunct verb construction.

The application of our hypothesis proposed here, in principle, has all the core linguistic and cognitive features of three approaches mentioned above for solving the puzzle of the agreement patterns of the conjunct verb construction in Hindi-Urdu. Let us take some of the examples given in the present paper and explain how the puzzle of agreement patterns of the conjunct verb is actually solvable by our proposed hypothesis. Let us discuss Bahl's (1974: 24) classic examples first:

(34) उसने मोहन को याद किया।
us-ne *Mohan-ko* *yād* *kiyā.*
S/he.3S-ERG Mohan.3M.SG-ACC remembrance.N.F do.PFV.3M.SG
'S/he remembered Mohan.'

The verb in the above sentence (34) is a transitive one, and thus it has two canonical/structural cases as per our hypothesis e.g. the nominative/ergative case for the subject and accusative case for the direct object. We observe that both of these core/canonical/structural cases have been dispersed in the above sentence, and therefore, the nominal host remains dormant/idle inside the verb phrase and thus the light verb bears the default agreement. Let us explain the other example:

(35) उसको मोहन की याद आयी।
us-ko *Mohan-kī* *yād* *āyī.*
s/he.3M/SG-DAT Mohan.3M.SG-GEN memory.N.F come.PFV.F.SG
'S/he remembered Mohan.'

The light verb in the above example (35) is an intransitive verb, and according to its semantic value, it has only one canonical/structural case i.e. nominative that has to be given away before the verb becomes finite by taking the phi-features and TAM properties of sentential conjugation. If we observe more carefully, we notice that we don't find any nominative case being dispersed with any noun phrase in the sentence (*-ko* and *-kī* are dative and genitive case markers, respectively). It is in this context that the nominal host has to get out of its bonding with the light verb and receive the nominative case from the light verb and act as a grammatical subject and exhibit agreement with the verb. This may not be difficult for any theory to accommodate as this is a pretty common pattern of agreement where 'object-verb agreement' is facilitated through the process of 'grammatical subject' as one of the eligible candidates for the agreement of verb when the 'logical subject' is not available due to some linguistic constraints or discrepancies. All the above-mentioned examples and any other possible examples which have a conjunct verb and mark their agreement in Hindi-Urdu can easily be explained using our hypothesis. Let us explain the agreement pattern of the following sentences before we conclude the paper:

(36) मोहन संगीता को याद करता है।

Mohan	*Sangītā-ko*	*yād*	*kartā*	*hɛ.*
Mohan.M.SG.NOM	Sangeeta.F.SG-ACC	memory-F	do.IMPFV.3M.SG	AUX.PRS

'Mohan remembers Sangeeta.'

The sentence in (36) has a transitive verb and thus it has two canonical cases i.e. nominative and accusative cases. We see that the direct object in the sentence 'Sangeeta' has an overt accusative case '*-ko*' and the subject of the sentence, 'Mohan' has a nominative case that is covert (the canonically marked zero form of the structural case). The agreement morpheme on the verb matches the phi-features of the subject noun for two reasons: firstly, it is the left-most unmarked noun in the sentence and thus shows agreement with the verb, secondly, the nominal host remains dormant/idle inside the verb phrase as the dispersal of canonical/structural cases has already taken place, therefore, the nominal host does not acquire any nominal characteristics and maintains the bonding of conjunction with the light verb in the sentence.

(37) मोहन ने संगीता को याद किया।

Mohan-ne	*Sangītā-ko*	*yād*	*kiyā.*
Mohan.3M.SG-ERG	Sangeeta.3F.SG-ACC	remembrance.F.SG	do.PFV.3M.SG

'Mohan remembered Sangeeta.'

The agreement morphology of the verb in example (37) remains same i.e. 3MS despite the fact that the case association of sentence (36) and (37) are different. The subject NP has an overt ergative case marker in (37). We could wonder as to why the nominal host i.e. '*yād*', 'remembrance-N.F' – which is an unmarked NP – does not mediate the verb agreement in example (37). Saksena's (1985) proposed rule for agreement in Hindi-Urdu would make the nominal host as the left-most unmarked NP and thus it should act as the controller of agreement in (37). However, our hypothesis would not support this suggestion. If we check the dispersal of the canonical/structural cases with the verb, we realize that both ergative (a type of subjective case) and accusative cases have been assigned to their respective recipients and thus the nominal host remains dormant with the verb phrase and the verb is marked with default agreement morpheme.

(38) संगीता को मोहन याद आया।

Sangītā-ko	*Mohan*	*yād*	*āyā.*
Sangeeta.3F.SG-DAT	Mohan.3M.SG	remembrance.F.SG	come.PFV.3M.SG

'Sangeeta remembered Mohan.'

The sentence in (38) provides an interesting piece of evidence of agreement pattern in Hindi-Urdu. Such instances are called 'Dative subject[12] construction or 'Non-nominative Subjects[13] construction' and the subject NP is case marked with the dative subject in the sentence and that is what we have in (38). The direct object like NP[14] 'Mohan', however, is unmarked in example (38) and this becomes the grammatical subject in the sentence and thus marks its phi-features on the verb for the purpose of agreement in Hindi-Urdu. The nominal host remains dormant inside the VP because the only canonical/structural case i.e. 'Nominative case' of the intransitive verb *ānā*, ' to come' has already been dispersed in (38).

(39) संगीता को मोहन की याद आयी।

Sangītā-ko	*Mohan-ki*	*yād*	*āyī.*
Sangeeta.3F.SG-DAT	Mohan.3M.SG-GEN	remembrance.F.SG	come.PFV.3F.SG

'Sangeeta remembered Mohan.'

The sentence given in (39) adds up a genitive case to the object like-NP of the earlier example (38), and the effect is interesting. The nominal host that was dormant/idle in (38) becomes active and it acquires the nominal features by breaking the semantic/linguistic bond with the light verb as the canonical/structural case of the intransitive verb i.e. nominative case has not been dispersed in (39). Thus, by getting the nominative case from the light verb, the nominal host functions as the 'grammatical subject' in the sentence and mediates agreement with the light verb. This is what our hypothesis of agreement pattern in conjunct

---

12 See Verma, M. K., and K.P. Mohanan (eds.) (1990) for further details of 'Dative/Experiencer subject in Hindi.

13 See Bhaskarorao, P. & K.V. Subbarao (eds) (2004) for more detailed account on Non-nominative subjects in Hindi.

14 It noun 'Mohan' in example (23) is a direct object like NP only if we consider '*yād ānā*', 'to come to remembrance' as a conjunct verb and single unit.

verb construction predicts and it is able to explain the puzzle of agreement patterns of two sets of conjunct verb construction. Let us consider one last example before we conclude the paper (we have discussed in example (27)):

(27a) संगीता ने मोहन को आवाज़ दी।
Sangītā-ne *Mohan-ko* *awāz* *dī.*
Sangeeta.3F.SG-ERG Mohan.3M.SG-DAT sound.F.SG give.PFV.3F.SG
'Sangeeta called for Mohan.'

In example (27a), we have a ditransitive verb i.e. *denā*, 'to give'. According to the 'semantic valency rule' (i.e. the rule to count the total number of arguments with the verb), the ditransitive verbs have three canonical/structural cases e.g. nominative/ergative, accusative and dative cases. Therefore, according to our hypothesis that has been proposed here, these canonical cases must be distributed to the eligible candidates in the sentence before the verb gets changed into a finite verb by conjoining the TAM and phi-features of nominal and verbal elements of the sentence. We observe that the subject is marked with overt ergative case and the object noun, 'Mohan' bears '-*ko*' which is a dative case morpheme because of the verb that is ditransitive. The nominal host, '*āwāz*-N(f)', 'sound' has to come out from the semantic bonding of conjunct verb because one of the canonical/structural cases i.e. accusative case has not yet been dispersed. So, the nominal host comes out from the semantic bonding and receives the nominal attributes from the verb and acts as the grammatical subject of the verb *denā* 'to give' in (27) and (27a) and thus mediates the agreement with the light verb in the above sentence.

11 Conclusion

The present paper has taken up a serious issue of agreement pattern in Hindi-Urdu and has shown how this issue has remained a puzzle despite so much of research work being carried out in order to account for agreement facts of the conjunct verb construction. The present research paper has discussed various compatible proposals from three major schools of thought e.g. the Generative School of thought, the Functional School of thought and the Pāṇinian School of thought in order to propose an eclectic hypothesis that can solve the problems of agreement patterns shown by two distinct types of conjunct verbs in Hindi-Urdu. The paper, in the end, has explained with examples how the proposed hypothesis works across various kinds of data of conjunct verbs that have been drawn from Hindi-Urdu.

References

Aikhenvald, Alexandra Y., Robert M. W. Dixon & Masayuki Onishi (eds.). 2001. *Non-canonical marking of subjects and objects*. Amsterdam/Philadelphia: John Benjamins.

Anderson J. 1971. *The Grammar of case: towards a localistic theory*. Cambridge: Cambridge University Press.

Bahl, K.C. 1967. *A reference grammar of Hindi*. Chicago: South Asian Centre, University of Chicago.

Bahl, K.C. 1974. Studies in the Semantic Structure of Hindi: synonymous nouns and adjectives with 'karnā', Volume 1. Delhi: Motilal Banarasidass.

Balachandran, L. 1988. *A case grammar of Hindi*. Agra: Central Institute of Hindi.

Barlow, M & C. A. Ferguson (eds.). 1988. *Agreement in Natural Languages: Approaches, Theories, Descriptions*. Stanford: CSLI Publication.

Barlow, M. 1988. A situated theory of agreement. PhD Dissertation. Stanford University, Stanford.

Bhaskararao, Peri & Karumuri V. Subbarao (eds.). 2004. *Non-nominative subjects*, Vols. 1–2. Amsterdam/Philadelphia: John Benjamins.

Bhattacharyya, P., D. Chakrabarti, and V. Sarma. 2007. Complex Predicates in Indian languages and Wordnets. *Language Resources and Evaluation*, 40(3-4): 331–355.

Bickel, B. & Y. P. Yadav. 2000. A fresh look at grammatical relations in Indo-Aryan. *Lingua* 110: 343–373.

Blake, B. J. 1994. *Case*. Cambridge, Cambridge University Press.

Borik, O. and B. Gehrke. 2105. *The Syntax and Semantics of Pseudo-Incorporation*, Syntax and Semantics. Leiden: Brill Publishers.

Butt, M. 1993a. Object specificity and agreement in Hindi/Urdu. In Katharine Beals (ed.), *Papers from the 29th Regional Meeting of the Chicago Linguistic* Society 1: 89–103.

Butt, M. 1993b. Hindi-Urdu Infinitives as NPs. In Y. Kachru (ed.), *South Asian Language Review: Special Issue on Studies in Hindi-Urdu* III(1): 51–72.

Butt, M. 1995. *The Structure of Complex Predicate in Urdu*. Stanford: CSLI Publications.

Butt, M. 2003. The Light Verb Jungle. In G. Aygen, C. Bowern, and C. Quinn (eds.) *Harvard Working Papers in Linguistics*, 9: Papers from the GSAS/Dudley House Workshop on Light Verbs, 1–49.

Chomsky, Noam. 1965. *Aspects of the Theory of Syntax*. Cambridge: The MIT Press.

Chomsky, Noam. 1981. *Lectures on Government and Binding: The Pisa Lectures*. Holland: Foris Publications.

Chomsky, Noam. 1986. *Knowledge of Language: Its nature, origin and use*. New York: Praeger publishers.

Chomsky, Noam. 1993. *A minimalist program for linguistic theory*. In K. Hale & S. Keyser (eds.) *The View from Building 20*. Cambridge, Mass.: The MIT Press.

Chomsky, Noam. 1995. *The Minimalist Program*, Cambridge, Mass.: The MIT Press.

Comrie, B. 1973. The ergative: variations on a theme. In *Lingua* 32: 239–253.

Comrie, B. 1981. *Language Universals and Linguistic Typology*. Chicago: The University of Chicago Press.
Comrie, B. 1984. Reflections on Verb agreement in Hindi and related languages. *Linguistics* 22: 857–64.
Corbett, G. G. 1979. The Agreement Hierarchy. *Journal of Linguistics* 15: 203–24.
Corbett, G. G. 2003. Agreement: Terms and boundaries. In: William Griffin (ed.) *The Role of Agreement in Natural Language*: TLS 5 Proceedings (Texas Linguistic Forum 53); 109–122. [Available at: http://uts.cc.utexas.edu/~tls/2001tls/2001proceeds.html.]
Das, P.K. 1997. Agreement in Hindi-Urdu. An unpublished MPhil dissertation submitted to Centre for Linguistics and English, JNU, New Delhi.
Das, P.K. 2006. *Grammatical Agreement in Hindi-Urdu and its Major Varieties*. München: Lincom Europa.
Das, P.K. 2009. The form and function of Conjunct verb construction in Hindi. *Journal of South Asian Studies*, July 2009, HUFS, Vol.5 , No.1, 191–208.
Das, P.K. 2012. Agreement in Kinnauri. *Indian Linguistics*, 73(1-4), 19–33.
Das, P.K. 2013. Ergativity in Khortha: an enigmatic phenomenon. *Journal of South Asian Studies*, HUFS, South Korea, Vol 18, No. 3, 1–21.
Das, P.K. 2015. The linguistic prerequisites and grammaticalization of 'compound verb' in Hindi. *Journal of South Asian Studies*, HUFS, South Korea. Vol 21, No.2, 51–76.
Das, P.K. 2017. Case and Agreement in Khortha. In *Aligarh Journal of Linguistics*, Vol. 7, Number 1, 1–2.
Das, P.K. & J. C. Choi. 2017. Causativization in Hindi: an alternative view. In the *Journal of South Asian Studies*, HUFS, South Korea, Vol. 23, No.3, 147–178.
Davison, A. 1985. Case and control in Hindi-Urdu. *Studies in linguistics Science* 15 (2): 9–23.
Davison. A. 2002. Agreement features and projections of TENSE and ASPECT. In Rajendra Singh (ed.) *Yearbook of South Asian Languages and Linguistics*. Delhi: Sage Publications, 27–87.
Dayal, Veneeta. 2011. "Hindi pseudo-incorporation." *Natural Language & Linguistic Theory* 29, no. 1, 123–167.
Dayal, Veneeta. 2015. Incorporation: Morpho-Syntactic vs. Semantic Considerations. In O. Borik and B. Gehrke (eds.) *The Syntax and Semantics of Pseudo-Incorporation, Syntax and Semantics*, 47–87.
Dixon, R.M.W. 1994. *Ergativity*. Cambridge: Cambridge University Press.
Fillmore, C.J. 1968. The Case for Case. In E. Bach and R.T. Harms (eds.) *Universals in Linguistic Theory*. New York: Holt Rinehart and Winston.
Foster J.F. & L.F. Hofling. 1987. Word Order, Case and Agreement. In *Lingua* 25: 87–133.
Gair J. W. and K. Wali. 1989. Hindi Agreement as Anaphora. *Linguistics* 27: 45–70.
Grimshaw, J. 1990. *Argument Structure*. Cambridge, Mass.: The MIT Press.
Haegeman, L. 1994. *Introduction to Government and Binding Theory*. London: Basil Blackwell.
Hock, H. H. & Elena Bashir (eds.). 2017. *The Languages and Linguistics of South Asia*. Berlin: De Gruyter Mouton.
Hook, P. E. 1974. *The Compound Verb in Hindi*. Ann Arbor, Michigan: Center for South and Southeast Asian Studies.
Jackendoff, Ray. 1990. *Semantic Structure*. Cambridge, Mass.: The MIT Press.
Kachru, Y. 1966. *An Introduction to Hindi Syntax*. Urbana, Department of Linguistics, University of Illinois.

Kachru, Yamuna. 1990. Experiencer and other oblique subjects in Hindi. In Verma and Mohanan 1990. Pp. 59–75.
Kellogg, S. H. 1972. *A Grammar of the Hindi Language*. (Indian reprint) New Delhi: Oriental Books Corp.
Klaiman, Miriam H. 1990. The prehistory of noun-incorporation in Hindi. *Lingua* 81(4). 327–350.
Lapointe, S. 1985. *A Theory of Grammatical Agreement*. New York: Garland Publications.
Lehmann, C. 1988. On the Function of Agreement. In M. Barlow & C. A. Ferguson (eds.) *Agreement in Natural Languages: Approaches, Theories & Descriptions*. Stanford: CSLI Publications.
Masica, C. P. 1976. *Defining a linguistic area: South Asia*. Chicago: The University of Chicago Press.
Masica, C. P. 1991. *The Indo-Aryan Languages*. Cambridge: Cambridge University Press.
Mohanan, T. 1994. *Argument Structure in Hindi*. Stanford: The Stanford University Press.
Mohanan, T. 1995. Wordhood and lexicality. *Natural Language & Linguistic Theory* 13: 75–134.
Moravcsik, E. A. 1978. "Agreement.". In J. H. Greenberg, C. A. Ferguson and E. A. Moravcsik (eds.), *Universals of Human Language: IV: Syntax*, 331–374. Stanford: Stanford University Press.
Saksena A. 1981. Verb Agreement in Hindi. *Linguistics* 14: 467–474.
Saksena A. 1985. Verb Agreement in Hindi Part-II: a Critique of Comrie's Analysis. *Linguistics* 23: 137–142.
Sharma, A. 1958. *A Basic Grammar of Modern Hindi*. Delhi: Government of India, Central Hindi Directorate.
Singh, J. 1993. Case and Agreement in Hindi: A GB Theory. PhD dissertation, Department of Linguistics, York University, UK.
Singh, U.N. 1979. Agreement rule, Language Universal and Maithili. *South Asian Language Analysis* 1: 107–114.
Vajpeyi, Kishoridas. 1967. *Hindi Shabdanushasan*. Varanasi: Kashi Nagari Pracharini Sabha.
Verbeke, Saartje. 2013. *Alignment and Ergativity in New Indo-Aryan Languages*. Berlin: De Gruyter Mouton.
Verma, M.K. 1971. *The Structure of Noun Phrase in English and Hindi*. Delhi: Motilal Banarasidass.
Verma, Manindra K. (ed.). 1993. *Complex Predicates in South Asian Languages*. New Delhi: Manohar Publications.
Verma, Manindra K. and K. P. Mohanan (eds.). 1990. *Experiencer Subjects in South Asian Languages*. Stanford, CA: CSLI, Stanford University.

Shamim Fatma

Conjunct verbs in Hindi

Abstract: Hindi is extremely rich in complex verbs which are formed by the combinations of noun/adjective and a verb. They are also called conjunct verbs. These combinations are very systematic and intertwined. The paper intends to analyze the process leading to such orderliness. Conjunct verbs are of two types: transitive and intransitive. The transitive verbs are obtained by combining nouns/adjectives with verbs such as *karnā* 'to do', *lenā* 'to take' *denā* 'to give' *jītnā* 'to win' etc. The intransitive verbs are formed with the help of verbs such as *honā* 'to be/become', *lagnā* 'to feel', *ānā* 'to come' etc. The paper examines semantic patterns/ontological features of several such combinations to arrive at plausible conclusion about the productivity of conjunct verbs and their collocational restrictions.

Keywords: Hindi conjunct verbs, Ontology, complex predicate

1 Introduction

Like many South Asian Languages, Hindi is rich in complex verbs (Complex predicates). They are either the combination of noun/adjective+verb or verb+verb where noun, adjective or first verb contributes the semantic content and the verb or second verb accounts for the syntactic information of the construction. Noun/adjective and verb combinations are termed conjunct verbs, as in (1) and (2) whereas the combinations of two verbs are called compound verbs, as in (3).

(1) शीला ने काम किया।
Śīlā-ne *kām* *kiyā.*
sheela.F.SG-ERG work.M.SG do.PFV.M.SG
'Sheela did the work.'

(2) शीला ने कमरा साफ़ किया।
Śīlā -ne *kamrā* *sāf* *kiyā.*
Sheela.F.SG-ERG room-M.SG clean do-PFV.M.SG
'Sheela cleaned the room.'

Shamim Fatma, Mahatma Gandhi International Hindi University, Wardha, India. Email: sh_fatma2002@yahoo.com

https://doi.org/10.1515/9783110610796-009

(3) शीला ने सच बोल दिया।
Śīlā-ne *sač* *bol* *diyā.*
Sheela.F.SG-ERG truth.M.SG tell give.PFV.M.SG
'Sheela told the truth.'

In (1)–(3), we find three types of Hindi verbal constructions which can be grouped into two categories of complex verbs in Hindi, namely, conjunct verbs and compound verbs. (1) and (2) are examples of conjunct verbs since in (1) we find a noun *kām* 'work' and a perfective form of the verb *karnā*, 'do' whereas in (2) the verbal predicate exhibits a complex construction made of two elements, namely an adjective *sāf* 'clean' plus a verb *karnā*, 'do'. The example in (3), on the other hand, is considered be a compound verb as its predicate exhibits two verbal elements, namely *bol* 'tell' and *denā* 'give'. According to Mohanan (1990), "the large number of verbs in Hindi serves an auxiliary or modal function in which some of them combine productively with other verbs, adjectives and nouns to form complex predicates. In doing so, the verb may lose to varying degrees the syntactic and semantic that is associated with its main verb counterpart. Such a verb has been called a "light verb", and the entity it combines with is its "host"." Hook (1974) places the light verb in an aspectual complex on a par with the other auxiliaries in the language.

Hence, the Conjunct verbs are also termed as Light Verb Constructions. This type of verbal construction is common in South Asian languages such as Hindi (Burton-Page 1957). In Hindi, they are highly productive. As reported by Butt (2003) "Light Verbs are generally readily identifiable as a separate syntactic class. They have distinct distributional properties which coincide with a distinct (though hard to characterize) semantic contribution." In line with Butt, Bhattacharyya et. al (2007) sustain the idea that there are unique Indian language phenomena that bear upon the lexicalization vs. syntactically derived choice. One such example is the occurrence of conjunct and compound verbs (called Complex Predicates) which are found in all Indian languages. Automatic identification of Conjunct Verbs, and making distinction between Conjunct Verbs and ordinary combinations of verbs and their arguments, are important tasks of NLP (Natural Language Processing) applications such as parsing (Begum et al, 2011), Detection of MultiWord Expression (Singh, Dhirendra et al, 2015) and Machine Translation (Pal et al 2011). Lexical, Semantic, syntactic and pragmatic information is needed here for the task. Wei-Te Chen et. al. (2015) used the classifier, categorized into three different types: Basic Features, OntoNotes Word Sense Features, and WordNet Features for the identification of English light verb construction using lexical database. Begum et. al (2011) have discussed seven features of conjunct verbs classified into three areas, i.e., Lexical features, Binary Features and Collocation-based features. The Lexical category consists of Word based features having f1 (Verb), f2 (Object-Noun/Adjective) and f3 (Semantic category of Object, e.g. artifact, abstraction, state etc.). The Binary feature consists of f4 (Post-position Indicator) and f5 (Demonstrative Indicator). The Collocation-based feature has f6 (Frequency of verbs corresponding to particular object) and f7 (Verb Argument Indicator). Begum et. al (ibid.) used these feature sets for binary classification of conjunct verbs and non-conjunct verbs. Every feature discussed here has its role in increasing accuracy of identification of conjunct verbs.

This paper deals with the f3 features, i.e. the semantic categories of objects (Noun/Adjective) and the semantic compatibility of these features with particular light verbs. Hindi WordNet is a good source of semantic features of Nouns, Adjectives and verbs but the mapping of Noun and Adjective with Light Verbs for the formation of conjunct verbs is not available there. Such mapping of the semantic features of nouns and adjectives with those of the Light Verbs will make it more specific. This may aid Intelligent Text Processing and Interlingua-based Machine Translation such as UNL (Universal Networking language). UNL is an electronic language for computers to express and exchange all levels of information i.e. meaning, sentence by sentence (Uchida, 1999). Classifying verbs and categorizing them in a structure according to their selectional preferences and their semantic properties are essential tasks in most forms of text-information processing (Levin, 1993) like machine translation, information extraction etc.

The Predicate is a grammatical category which is formed by the mutual sharing of semantic features and co-occurrence of two lexical items i.e. a host and a light verb. According to Das (2006) "the lexical meaning of the term 'conjunct' ensures 'a semantic bound in close association with X'. The 'conjunct verb' is formed in Hindi-Urdu by replacing this X either with a noun or an adjective and therefore satisfying the semantic requirement by ensuring a close association with either of these categories of the word". More clearly, the semantic features of the host (noun/adjective/verb) must accord with the light verbs for the formation of complex predicates. Any sequence of noun/adjective/verb and verb (light verb) cannot be termed as conjunct/compound verb. For example:

(4a) लड़की इम्तिहान में अच्छा कर रही है।
laṛkī imtihān-mẽ aččhā kar rahī hɛ.
girl.F.SG exam.M-LOC well do PROG.F.SG AUX.PRS.SG
'The girl is doing well in exam.'

(4b) *लड़की इम्तिहान में अच्छा ले रही है।
*laṛkī imtihān-mẽ aččhā le rahī hɛ.
girl.F.SG exam.M-LOC good take PROG.F.SG AUX.PRS.SG
*'The girl is taking good in exam.'

(5a) लड़की ने मुझ पर भरोसा किया।
laṛkī-ne mujh-par bharosā kiyā.
girl.F.SG-ERG me-on trust do.PFV.M.SG
'The girl trusted me.'

(5b) *लड़की ने मेरा भरोसा लिया।
*laṛkī-ne merā bharosā liyā.
girl.F.SG-ERG my trust.M.SG take.PFV.M.SG
*'The girl took my trust.'

(6a) वो सो गया।
wo so gayā.
he sleep go.PFV.M.SG
'He slept.'

(6b) *वो सो पड़ा/बैठा।
*wo so paṛa/ bɛṭhā.
he sleep lie.PFV.M.SG/ sit.PFV.M.SG
*'He slept lying.'

In (4a) and (4b) we may see that the adjectival element *aččhā* good' is attached to the verb *karnā* 'to do' only. It cannot generate a conjunct verb by combining with the verb such as *lenā*. In (5a) and (5b) the nominal element *bharosā* 'faith' is attached to the verb *karnā* 'to do' rather than *lenā* 'to take' to produce the conjunct verb. In (6a) and (6b), the verb *sonā* is attached to the verb *jānā* and it is a correct compound verb while the combination of *sonā* with *bɛṭhnā* and *paṛnā* leads to the wrong constructions. This means that these elements are not combined in a haphazard manner, but are very much synchronized, ordered or interwoven. The hypothesis of the paper is that noun/adjective+ verb combinations have patterns of adjoining; they are not randomly attached to each other. The paper intends to analyze the processes leading to such synchronization or orderliness by examining several such combinations taking into account their ontological or semantic features and presenting those semantic patterns which lead to the formation of conjunct verbs. Only conjunct verbs which have the verbalizers *honā* 'to become', *karnā* 'to do', *lenā* 'to take' and *denā* 'to give' are discussed in this paper.

2 The nature of some conjunct verbs in Hindi

Conjunct verbs in Hindi are combinations of Noun/Adjective and verbs. Verbs in these combinations are assumed to be light verbs which carry functional features such as tense and agreement. There is a limited number of verbs in Hindi which act as light verbs, such as *karnā*, *honā*, *lenā*, *denā*, *jītnā*, *lagnā*, *uṭhnā*, etc. These light verbs are called 'verbalizers'. These verbalizers combine with noun/adjective and form conjunct verbs.

As shown in Figure 1, verbalizers are of two types: transitive and intransitive. Transitive conjunct verbs are formed by combining nouns/adjectives with transitive verbalizers such as *karnā* 'to do' (*silāī karnā* 'to stitch'), *lenā* 'to take'(*qasam lenā* 'to take oath), *denā* 'to give' (*hukm denā* 'to order'), *jītnā* 'to win' (*bharosā jītnā* to win faith') etc. Intransitive conjunct verbs are generated by combining nouns/adjectives with intransitive verbalizers such as *honā* 'to become' (*āsān honā* 'to be easy'), *lagnā* 'to feel' (*bhūkh lagnā* 'to be hungry'), *ānā* 'to come' (*čakkar ānā* 'to feel dizzy'), etc.

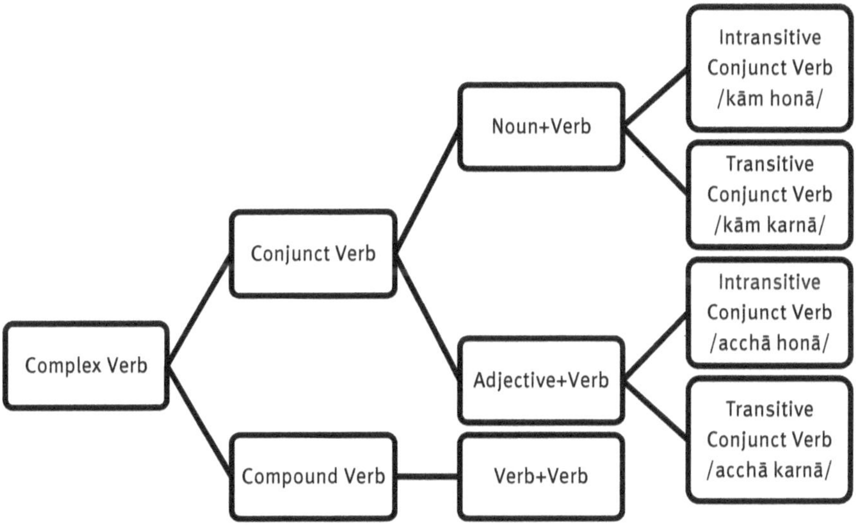

Fig. 1: Taxonomy of Complex Verbs in Hindi

The aim of the paper is to analyze ontological and semantic features of some conjunct verbs. Everything which exists in the universe, whether concrete or abstract, has some shared relations and internal features which make them related to or distinct from one another. For example, humans and animals are different creatures, but they both have life. Hence, they come under the category of living beings. Two things alike in nature or sharing some features somehow may show compatibility in some respect and may be combined, if necessary. In short, the 'combination' of things or concepts has some reasons for attachment; they are not attached randomly.

3 Ontology

Ontology is a knowledge source for semantic analysis and interpretation of natural language. It is a set of concepts consisting of Object, Events and Properties and the relations between them. The concept of Ontology has been borrowed from Engineering. In NLP and Machine Translation, we use this concept in defining the attributes and semantic features of the Lexicon. I have used the set of ontological features for Nouns and Adjectives in Hindi WordNet to represent the mapping between Nouns/Adjectives and Light Verbs. Following is the List for the Noun and Adjective Ontology. Here I have listed only the semantic attributes of Noun and Adjective by using what I have discussed as light verb constructions or conjunct verbs in this paper.

3.1 Noun ontology

The ontology of Hindi nouns is as follows:

- SEMANTIC Attributes
    - ANIMT [Animate]
    - INANI [Inanimate]
        - OBJCT [Object]
            - IMGN [Imaginary]
            - PHSCL [Physical]
                - ARTFCT [Artifact]
                    - MEDICINE [Medicine]
                - CHML [Chemical]
                - DRNKBL [Drinkable]
                - EDBL [Edible]
                - NAT [Natural Object]
                    - ANTM [Anatomical Object]
                    - MYTHO [Mythological Object]
        - PLACE [place]
            - IMGY [Imaginary Place]

    - MYTHO [Mythological Place]
    - PHSCL [Physical Place]
- EVENT [Event]
    - FTL [Fatal Event]
    - FTFL [Fateful Event]
    - HIST [Historical Event]
    - NAT [Natural Event]
    - PLND [Planned Event]
    - SCL [Social Event]
- ABS [abstract]
    - ACT [Action]
        - ANTISCL [Anti-social]
        - COMM [Communication]
        - OCP [Occupation]
        - SCL [Social]
        - PHSCLACT [Physical Action]
    - ART [Art]
    - COGN [Cognition]
    - COLOR [Color]
    - CONCEPT [Concept]
    - INFRM [Information]
        - COMM [Communication]
            - SYMBL [Symbol]
    - MSRMNT [Measurement]
    - OBJCT [Object]
    - PRCP [Perception]
    - POSS [Possession]
    - PSYFTR [Psychological Feature]
    - QUAL [Quality]
    - QUAN [Quantity]
    - STYL [Style]
    - TIME [Time]
        - PRD [Period]
        - SSN [Season]
    - TITL [Title]
        - GRP [Group]
    - SCTY [Society]
    - ORGZN [Organization]
        - POF [Part of]
        - STE [State]
    - MNTL [Mental State]
        - FEEL [Feeling]
            - EMOT [Emotion]
    - NAT [Natural State]
        - SSN [Season]
        - WTHR [Weather]
    - PHSCL [Physical State]

- PHSSLGCL [Physiological State]
  - DIS [Disease]
  - BIO [Biological State]
- SCL [Social State]
  - PRCS [Process]
- MNTL [Mental Process]
- NAT [Natural Process]
- PHSCL [Physical Process]
- SLD [Solid]

3.2 Adjective ontology

We can represent the adjective ontology as follows:

- SEMANTIC ATTRIBUTES
  - DESCRIPTIVE
    - ACT [Action]
    - APPR [appearance]
    - CLR [color]
    - DPTH [depth]
    - DIRCTN [directional]
    - EMOT [emotion]
    - EXST [existence]
    - MSRMNT [measurement]
    - NUM [numeral]
    - PLACE [place]
    - QUAL [qualitative]
    - QUAN [quantitative]
    - RESP [respective]
    - SHP [shape]
    - SIZE [size]
    - SND [sound]
    - SPD [speed]
    - STE [stative]
    - STRNGTH [strength]
    - TSTE [taste]
    - TEMP [temperature]
    - TIME [time]
    - TCH [touch]
    - WT [weight]
    - DMON [demonstrative]
    - INTRO [interrogative]
    - REL [relational]

4 Diagnosis of the conjunct verbs

Three things are represented by the verbs: Action, Event and State. The intransitive verbalizer *honā* is stative when it represents a STATE and inchoative when it represents an EVENT. The transitive verbalizers 'to do', *lenā* 'to take' and *denā* 'to give' represent ACTION, as in (7), (8), (9) and (10). Sometimes the entailment of ACTION is EVENT too, as in (11).

(7) काम ख़त्म हुआ। *(State)*
kām ***xatam huā.***
work.M.SG finish become.PFV.M.SG
'The work *got finished.*'

(8) काम ख़त्म हो रहा है। *(Event)*
kām ***xatam*** ***ho*** *rahā hɛ.*
work.M.SG finish be PROG.M.SG AUX.PRS.SG
'The work is getting over/ through.'

(9) बच्चों ने काम किया। *(Action)*
baččõ -ne ***kām*** ***kiyā.***
children-ERG work.M.SG do.PFV.M.SG.
'The children finished the job/assignment.'

(10) बच्चों ने मुझसे मुक़ाबला किया। *(Action)*
baččõ -ne mujh-se ***muqāblā*** ***kiyā.***
children-ERG me-ABL competition.M.SG do.PFV.M.SG
'The child competed with me.'

(11) लड़की ने मुझे दावत दी। *(Action)*
laṛkī-ne mujhe ***dāwat*** *dī.*
girl-ERG me-DAT party.F.SG give.PFV.F.SG
'The girl gave me party.'

In (11), the action verbs *dāwat denā* 'to give party' entails '*dāwat honā* 'to get the party held'. Conjunct verbs with *honā* do not always have their transitive counterpart with *karnā* but most transitive verbs have an event/ state as their intransitive counterpart. The conjunct verbs involving *honā* may not have their transitive counterpart with *karnā*. For example:

(12a) अभी दिन हो रहा है।
abhī ***din*** ***ho*** *rahā hɛ*
just now day.M.SG be PROG.M.SG AUX.PRS.SG
'The day is breaking right now.'

(12b) *अभी कोई दिन कर रहा है।
*abhī koī din kar rahā hɛ.
just now someone.SG day.M.SG do PROG.M.SG AUX.PRS.SG
*'Someone is doing day right now.'

The arrangements of relations between Action, Event and State are as follows:

(A) Action → Event → State
(B) Event → State
(C) Action → State

It is clear from 'A' that an action may lead to an event which may lead to a state, as in *phāṛnā* 'to tear', *phaṭnā* 'to get torn', *phaṭā honā* 'to be torn' respectively. In other words every conjunct verb with a transitive light verb has an intransitive counterpart with *honā* but not vice versa. Since *honā* means both 'to be' and 'to become', some intransitive verbs with *honā* may indicate an 'event' rather than a 'state'.

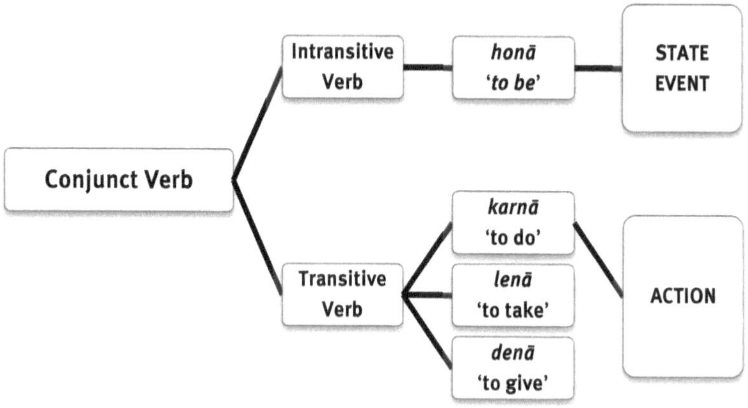

Fig. 2: Taxonomy of Conjunct verbs in Hindi

Only inanimate nouns have been found so far to be attached to the light verbs to form conjunct verb constructions. Both types of inanimate nouns, concrete and abstract, are attached to the verbs in this process. In cases of adjective and verb combination, only adjectives of quality or descriptive adjectives are attached to the verbs for the formation of conjunct verbs. Inanimate nouns which are concrete or abstract and contain adjectives of quality cannot be attached to any of the verbalizers; but there are nouns which are attached only to *honā* 'to become' and *karnā* 'to do', a few to *honā* 'to become', *karnā* 'to do' and *lenā* 'to take', a few attached only to *honā* 'to become', *lenā* 'to take', *denā* 'to give' and so on and so forth, and there are a few adjectives which are only attached to *honā* 'to become'; some can be attached to both *honā* 'to become' *and karnā* 'to do'. These nouns and adjectives have further sub-semantic or ontological features such as object, physical action, feeling, etc., and experience, appearance, etc., respectively which distinguish them from each other. The ontology of nouns and adjectives discussed in section 3 decides their combinations with the verbalizers.

4.1 Conjunct verbs having only *honā* 'to become' or 'to be'

Nouns which represent natural events have only *honā* but not *karna* 'to do', *lena* 'to take' or *dena* 'to give'[1] for the formation of conjunct verbs. Let us examine (13) and (14).

(13a) बारिश हो रही है। (*Natural Event*)
bāriś *ho rahī hɛ.*
rain.F.SG be PROG.F.SG AUX.PRS.SG
'It is raining.'

(13b) *बारिश कर रही है।
* **bāriś** *kar rahī hɛ.*
rain.F.SG do PROG.F.SG AUX.PRS.SG
*'It is doing rain.'

(14a) दिन हो रहा है।
din *ho rahā hɛ.*
day.M.SG be PROG.M.SG AUX.PRS.SG
'The day is breaking.'

(14b) *दिन कर रहा है।
* **din** *kar rahā hɛ.*
day.M.SG do PROG.M.SG AUX.PRS.SG
*'It is doing day.'

1 However such events may be indicated by some other *intransitive* verbs such as *ā̃dhī calnā* 'blowing of dust storm', *hawā calnā* 'blowing of winds', *barf girnā* 'snowing', *ole paṛnā* 'hailing' etc. having verbalizers *calnā* 'to blow', *girnā* 'to fell' and *paṛnā* 'to fell'. The paper is restricted only to the types of noun which take the verbalizers *honā* 'to become', *karnā* 'to do', *lenā* 'to take' and *denā* 'to give' only. So we will not discuss other verbalizers in this paper.

As is clear from (13a), (13b) and (14a), (14b), *bāriś honā* 'raining' and *din honā* 'day breaking' are correct collocations while **bariś karnā* *'doing raining' and *din* **karnā* 'doing day' are not. Natural phenomena cannot be controlled or done by anyone. They happen on their own. Such nouns cannot take the verbalizers *karnā* 'to do', *lenā* 'to take' or *denā* 'to give' for the formation of conjunct verbs because these verbs are the properties of human beings and animate objects. The semantic patterns of these noun-verb combinations are shown in table 1:

Tab. 1: Semantic patterns of the nouns of natural event and the verbalizer *honā* 'to be'.

NOUN
↓
INANIMATE
↓
EVENT
↓
NATURAL
↓
honā

Some of the possible combinations of these nouns and verbalizer *honā* 'to be' are as follows:

(15) Natural Event
  a. *rāt honā* 'to be night'
  b. *barsāt honā* 'to be rainy'
  c. *garmī honā* 'to be hot'
  d. *ṭhanḍ honā* 'to be cold'
  e. *āndhī/tūfān honā* 'to be blowing'

The adjectives which represent the internal quality of human beings/things combine with *honā* (in the sense of *be*) to generate conjunct verbs which indicate the internal quality of someone or something. For example:

(16a) इंसान को चालाक होना चाहिए। (*Internal Quality*)
insān ko ***čālāk honā*** *čāhiye.*
person.M-DAT clever become should.MD
'A person should be clever.'

(16b) *इंसान को चालाक करना चाहिए।
*insān- ko **čālāk karnā** čāhiye.
person.M-DAT clever do should.MD
*'A person should do the clever.'

(16c) इंसान को चालाकी करनी चाहिए।
insān-ko **čālākī** karnī čāhiye.
person.M-DAT cleverness.F.SG do.F should.MD
'A person should do the cleverness.'

We can see in (16a) that *čālāk honā* 'to be clever' is a possible combination whereas **čālāk karnā* 'to do the clever' in (16b) is not. (16c) shows that when an abstract noun derived from an adjective is used, the combination converges (*čālākī karnā*). We may note that *karnā* 'to do' converges with the abstract noun counterpart of these adjectives of light verb *honā* 'to be'. These natural or cognitive qualities are internal. They cannot be done or transferred to each other so these adjectives cannot be attached to the verbalizers *karnā* 'to do', *lenā* 'to take' or *denā* 'to give'. These verbalizers have the sense of doing, taking and giving something respectively which is incompatible with the semantics of the adjectives concerned here. The adjectives of this type can attach to the verbalizer *honā* 'to be' only. The semantic pattern of the adjectives of this category for the formation of conjunct verbs with the verbalizer *honā* is shown in Table 2.

Tab. 2: Semantic pattern of the Adjectives of internal quality and the verbalizer *honā* 'to be'.

ADJECTIVE
↓
QAULITY
↓
INTERNAL
↓
NATURAL-COGNITIVE
↓
honā

Some of the possible combinations of these adjectives with light verb *honā* are as follows:

(17) Internal Quality — Noun counterpart with *karnā*

a. *aqalmand honā* 'to be clever' — *aqalmandī karnā* 'to act cleverly'
b. *jośīlā honā* 'to be enthusiastic — *joś karnā* 'to enthuse'
c. *bewaqūf honā* 'to be foolish' — *bewaqūfī karnā* 'to show foolishness'
d. *śakkī honā* 'to be suspicious' — *śak karnā* 'to doubt/suspense'
e. *beīmān honā* 'to be dishonest' — *beīmānī karnā* 'to act dishonestly'
f. *ābhārī honā* 'to be obliged' — *ābhār karnā* 'to oblige'

4.2 Conjunct verbs having *honā* 'to become' and *karnā* 'to do' only

The nouns for physical action, psychological features representing mental perception, and communication are attached to the light verbs *honā* 'to be/become' and *karnā* 'to do'. In other words, the combinations of these nouns with the light verb *honā* 'to become' have their transitive counterpart with the light verb *karnā* 'to do', as we can see in sentences (17), (18) and (19).

(18a) कमरे की सफ़ाई हो रही है। (Physical Action)
kamre-kī safāī ho rahī hɛ.
room.M-gen cleaning.F be PROG.F AUX.PRS.SG
'The room is getting clean.'

(18b) मैं कमरे की सफ़ाई कर रहा हूँ।
mɛ̃ kamre-kī ***safāī*** *kar rahā hū̃.*
I room.M-GEN.F cleanliness.F do PROG.M.SG AUX.PRS.SG
'I am cleaning the room.'

(19a) उसे भरोसा होना चाहिए। (Mental Perception)
use ***bharosā honā*** *čāhiye.*
he/she.DAT trust.M be should.MD
'He/She should believe.'

(19b) वो मुझ पर भरोसा करता है।
wo mujh-par ***bharosā*** *kartā hɛ.*
he me-LOC trust.M do.IPFV.M.SG AUX.PRS.SG
'He believes me.'

(20a) आज इस बात का इज़हार हुआ। (*Communicative*)
āj is bāt-kā ***izhār*** *huā.*
today this matter-GEN expression.M be-PFV.M.SG
'Today this matter was expressed.'

(20b) शीला ने आज इस बात का इज़हार किया।
śīlā-ne āj is bāt-kā ***izhār***
Sheela-ERG today this matter.F-GEN.M expression-M.SG
kiyā.
do-PFV.M.SG
'Today Sheela has expressed this matter.'

The ontological or semantic patterns of nouns which combine with verbalizers *honā* and *karnā* only to form conjunct verbs are presented in Table 3:

Tab. 3: Semantic patterns of nouns in combinations with both *honā* 'to be' and *karnā* 'to do'.

Pattern 1	**Pattern 2**	**Pattern 3**
Noun	Noun	Noun
↓	↓	↓
Inanimate	Inanimate	Inanimate
↓	↓	↓
Abstract	Abstract	Abstract
↓	↓	↓
Action	Psychological feature	Action
↓	↓	↓
Physical	Mental Perception	Communication
↓	↓	↓
honā & karnā	*honā & karnā*	*honā & karnā*

Physical actions and communication are done by someone, the result of which is Event (something happened or is done. Nouns representing physical action can be attached to the verbalizers *honā* and *karnā* bearing these semantic features of *to happen* or *to do* (*something*) respectively. Similarly, nouns bearing psychological features representing mental perception are also attached to the verbalizers *honā* and *karnā*. Here the verbalizer *honā* stands for *verb indicating occurrence* or *Event* and the verbalizer *karnā* has sense of *bodily action*, *mental action* and *communication* respectively.

Some of the conjunct verbs combining these nouns with *honā* 'to become' and *karnā* 'to do' are as follows:

(21) Physical action
- *khel honā/karnā* ‘to be playing/to play’
- *paṛhāī honā/karnā* ‘to be studied/ to study’
- *rangāī honā/karnā* ‘to be dyeing/to dye’
- *pitāī honā/karnā* ‘to get beaten/to beat’
- *dhulāī honā/karnā* ‘to get washing, to wash’
- *marammat honā/karnā* ‘to get mend/to mend’
- *intezām honā/karnā* ‘to get manage/to manage’

Mental perception
- *bharosā honā/karnā* ‘to be trusted/to trust’
- *dillagī honā/karnā* ‘to be joked/to joke’
- *ehsās honā/karnā* ‘to be realized/to realize’
- *yaqīn honā/karnā* ‘to be believed/to believe’
- *afsos honā/karnā* ‘to be regretted/to regret’
- *bardāśt honā/karnā* ‘to get tolerated/to tolerate’

Communication
- *inkār honā/karnā* ‘to be refused/to refuse’
- *iqrār honā/karnā* ‘to be confessed/to confess’
- *bāt honā/karnā* ‘to be talking/to talk’
- *bahānā honā/karna* ‘to pretend’

The adjectives which represent the experience of the action and event and the condition of something can be classified as *adjectives of experience* and the adjectives which represent the appearance of an entity can be grouped as *appearance adjectives*. These adjectives are attached to *honā* and its transitive counterpart *karnā*. Senses of experience, condition and appearance make the adjectives eligible to combine with the light verbs *honā* ‘to become’ and *karnā* ‘to do’ as in (22a)–(22b) and (23a)–(23b) and restrict them to combine with other verbalizers i.e. *lenā* ‘to take’ and *denā* ‘to give’.

(22a) सारा सामान बर्बाद हुआ है। (*Condition*)
sārā sāmān **barbād** *huā.*
all stuff-M.PL spoiled be-PFV.M.SG
‘All stuff got spoiled.’

(22b) उसने सारा सामान बर्बाद किया है। (*Condition*)
us-ne sārā sāmān **barbād** *kiyā hɛ.*
s/he-ERG all stuff-M.PL spoiled do-PFV.M.SG AUX.PRS.SG
‘He/she has spoiled everything.’

(23a) कमरा साफ़ हो रहा है। (*Appearance*)
kamrā ***sāf*** *ho rahā* *hɛ.*
room-M.SG clean be-PRS.PROG.M.SG AUX.PRS.SG
'The room is getting clean.'

(23b) शीला कमरा साफ़ कर रही है। (*Appearance*)
śīlā *kamrā* ***sāf*** *kar rahī* *hɛ.*
sheela-F.SG room-M.SG clean do-PRS.PROG.F.SG AUX.PRS.SG
'Sheela is cleaning the room.'

The Adjectives which account for shape and size of anything also take *honā* 'to become' and *karnā* 'to do', as in (24).

(24a) इसका आकार धीरे धीरे छोटा हो रहा है। (*Shape*)
is-kā *ākār* *dhīre dhīre* ***čhoṭā*** *ho rahā* *hɛ.*
it-GEN shape.M.SG gradually short be-PROG.M.SG AUX.PRS.SG
'Its shape is reducing gradually.'

(24b) शीला ने इसका आकार छोटा किया है। (*Shape*)
śīlā-ne *is-kā* *ākār* ***čhoṭā*** *kiyā* *hɛ.*
Sheela-ERG it.SG-GEN shape.M.SG short.M.SG do.PFV.M.SG AUX.PRS.SG
'Sheela has reduced its shape.'

(24c) * शीला ने इसका आकार छोटा लिया। (*Shape*)
* *śīlā-ne* *iskā* *ākār* ***čhoṭā*** *liyā.*
Sheela-ERG it-GEN shape.M.SG small.M.SG take.PFV.M.SG
? 'Sheela took its shape small.'

(24d) * शीला ने इसका आकार छोटा दिया। (*Shape*)
* *Śīlā-ne* *iskā* *ākār* ***čhoṭā*** *diyā.*
Sheela-ERG it-GEN shape.M.SG small.M.SG give.PFV.M.SG
* 'Sheela gave its shape small.'

Adjectives having the sense of shape and size cannot be compatible with transfer verbs i.e. *lenā* 'to take' and *denā* 'to give' as is clear from (24c, d). The semantic patterns of these adjective and light verb *honā* 'to become' and *karnā* 'to do' combinations are shown in Table 4:

Tab. 4: Semantic patterns of some of the adjectives in combination with light verbs *honā* 'to be' and *karnā* 'to do'.

a. Adjective → Result of action or event → State/ Condition → *honā* 'to become' and *karnā* 'to do'
b. Adjective → Shape/Size → *honā* 'to become' and *karnā* 'to do'
c. Adjective → Appearance → *honā* 'to become' and *karnā* 'to do'

The conjunct verbs combining these adjectives with *honā* 'to be/become' and *karnā* 'to do' are as follows:

(25) a. Experience/Condition
- *zalīl honā/karnā* 'to get humiliated/to humiliate'
- *ruswā honā/karnā* 'to get disgraced/to disgrace'
- *badnām honā/karnā* 'to become infamous/to make infamous'
- *ājiz honā/karnā* 'to get irritate /to irritate
- *tãṅg honā/karnā* 'to get hack off/to hack off
- *beqarār honā/karnā* 'to be impatient/to make impatient'
- *bedam honā/karnā* 'to become breathless/to make breathless'*etc.*

b. Apppearance
- *gandā honā/karnā* 'to get dirty/to make dirty'
- *xūbsūrat honā/karnā* 'to become beautiful/to make beautiful'
- *badsūrat honā/karnā* 'to be ugly/to make ugly'
- *sastā honā/karnā* 'to become cheap/to cheap'
- *mãhṅgā honā/karnā* 'to become costly/to make costly'

c. Shape/Size
- *baṛā honā/karnā* 'to get big/to make big'
- *lambā honā/karnā* 'to become long/to make long'
- *patlā honā/karnā* 'to become thin/to make thin'
- *moṭā honā/karnā* 'to become fat/to make fat'
- *dublā honā/karnā* 'to become thin/to make

4.3 Conjunct verbs having *lenā* 'to take' and *denā* 'to give'

There are nouns of the *give* and *take* type having senses of transfer from giver to receiver implied in them. They take the verbalizers *lenā* 'to take' when the giver is the receiver and *denā* 'to give' when the receiver is someone else only. In some sense they are deictic verbs. They do not form conjunct verbs with *honā* 'to be/become' and *karnā* 'to do'. For example:

(26a) शीला ने सीता से पैसे उधार लिए हैं। (*Sense of giving and receiving*)
śīlā-ne *sītā-se* *pɛse* ***udhār***
Sheela.F.SG-ERG Sita.F.SG-ABL money.M.PL loan
liye *hɛ̃.*
take.PFV.M.PL AUX.PRS.PL
'Sheela has borrowed money from Sita.'

(26b) शीला ने सीता को पैसे उधार दिए हैं। (*Sense of giving and receiving*)
śīlā-ne *sītā-ko* *pɛse* ***udhār***
Sheela.F.SG-ERG Sita.F.SG-DAT money.M.PL loan
diye *hɛ̃.*
give.PFV.M.PL AUX.PRS.PL
'Sheela has lent money to Sita as borrowing.'

Some of the conjunct verbs of this combination are as follows:

(27) Sense of 'give' and 'take'
a. *qarz lenā/denā* 'to take/give loan
b. *ārśīvād lenā/denā* 'to accept/give blessing'
c. *vačan lenā/denā* 'to accept/give oath'
d. *badlā lenā/denā* 'to take/give revenge'
e. *firɔtī lenā/denā* 'to accept/give ransom money'

In (27) we see that the nouns which combine with the verbalizers *lenā/denā* can be categorized further on the basis of their attributes. The ontological/semantic patterns of such types of nouns in Table 5 show this clearly.

Tab. 5: Semantic patterns of nouns bearing the attribute of transfer to com-bine with *lenā* 'to take/ accept' and *denā* 'to give' both.

a. Noun → Inanimate → Object → Artifact → Transfer → *lenā* 'to take/ accept' and *denā* 'to give'
b. Noun → Abstract → Action → Communication/ Physical Action → Transfer → *lenā* 'to take/ accept' and *denā* 'to give'

We do not have conjunct verbs which have the combination of Adjective+ *lenā* 'to take/accept' and *denā* 'to give' i.e., *lenā* 'to take/accept' and *denā* 'to give' do not occur as verbalizers when we have adjectives as the first elements.

4.4 Conjunct Verbs having *honā* 'to become', *karnā* 'to do', *lenā* 'to take' and *denā* 'to give'

Some abstract nouns of *psychological features representing mental perception and state bearing feelings and emotions* combine with all four verbalizers i.e. *honā* 'to become', *karnā* 'to do', *lenā* 'to take' and *denā* 'to give'. They imply physical sensation too. For example:

(28a) शीला को अमर से मोहब्बत हो रही है। (*mental perception and state*)
śīlā-ko *amar-se* ***mohabbat*** *ho*
Sheela.F.SG-DAT Amar.M.SG-ABL love.F.SG be
rahī *hɛ.*
PROG.PRS.F.SG AUX.PRS.SG
'Sheela is falling in love with Amar.'

(28b) वो ग़रीबों से मोहब्बत करती है।
wo *ġaribõ-se* ***mohabbat*** *kartī* *hɛ.*
she poor.M.PL-ABL loves.F.SG do.IPFV.F.SG AUX.PRS.SG
'She loves the poor.'

(28c) वो दूसरों से मोहब्बत लेता है।
wo *dūsrõ-se* ***mohabbat*** *letā* *hɛ.*
he others.M.PL-ABL love-F.SG take.IPFV.M.SG AUX.PRS.SG
'He receives love from others.'

(28d) वो बच्चों को मोहब्बत देता है।
wo *baččõ-ko* ***mohabbat*** *detā* *hɛ.*
he children.M.PL-DAT love.F.SG give-M.SG AUX.PRS.SG
'He gives love to children.'

We can see in (28a)–(28d), the noun *mohabbat* 'love' is attached to the verbs *honā* 'to become', *karnā* 'to do', *lenā* 'to take' and *denā* 'to give' and the resulting conjunct verb has meaning derived from its combination with all these verbalizers. The semantic patterns of the nouns of this type which combine with all four verbalizers *honā* 'to become', *karnā* 'to do', *lenā* 'to take' and *denā* 'to give' are shown in Table 6:

Tab. 6: Semantic patterns of the nouns of mental feeling and emotion which take all four verbalizers *honā* 'to become', *karnā* 'to do', *lenā* 'to take' and *denā* 'to give' to form conjunct verbs

Noun →	Inanimate →	State/Perception →	Mental →	Feeling →	Emotion
honā 'to become', *karnā* 'to do', *lenā* 'to take/accept' and *denā* 'to give'					

Some of the conjunct verbs of these combinations are as follows:

(29) Mental perception and state
a. *dard honā/karnā/lenā/denā* 'to get/to take/to give pain
b. *ġam honā/karnā/lenā/denā* 'to have/to take/to give sorrow
c. *dukh honā/karnā/lenā/denā* 'to have/to take/to give sorrow'
d. *pyār honā/karnā/lenā/denā* 'to fall in/to take/to give love'

Nouns that suggest social status may also be found to be attached to these verbalizers.

(30a) मोहन की इन दिनों बहुत इज़्ज़त हो रही है। (*Social State*)

mohan-ki	*in*	*dinõ*	*bahut*	***izzat***
Mohan.M.SG-GEN	these	days	lot	honour.F.SG

ho	*rahī*	*hɛ.*
be	PROG.F.SG	AUX.PRS.SG

'Mohan is receiving lot of honour these days.

(30b) लोग मोहन की इज़्ज़त करते हैं।

log	*mohan-kī*	***izzat***	*karte*	*hɛ̃.*
people	Mohan.M.SG-GEN.F	respect.F.SG	do.IPFV.M.PL	AUX.PRS.PL

'People respect Mohan.'

(30c) इज़्ज़त लो और इज़्ज़त दो।

izzat	*lo*	***izzat***	*do.*
respect.F.SG	take.IMP.2PL	respect.F.SG	give-IMP.2PL

'Be respected and respect other.'

(30d) वो बड़ों को इज़्ज़त देता है।

wo	*baṛõ-ko*	***izzat***	*detā*	*hɛ.*
he-M.SG	elders-M.SG-ACC	respects-F	give-IPFV.M.SG	AUX.PRS.SG

'He respects elders.'

Tab. 7: Semantic patterns of nouns of social state with the verbalizers *honā* 'to become', *karnā* 'to do', *lenā* 'to take' and *denā* 'to give'

Noun → Inanimate → State → Social State →
honā 'to become', *karnā* 'to do', *lenā* 'to take' and *denā* 'to give'

Some of the conjunct verbs of this combination are as follows:

(31) Social State
a. *badnāmī honā/karnā/lenā/denā* 'getting notoriety/to dishonor/to slander/to give notoriety'
b. *ruswāī honā/karnā/lenā/denā* 'getting notoriety/to dishonor/to slander/to give notoriety'
c. *madad honā/karnā/lenā/denā* 'to get/to/to take/to give help'

Nouns bearing the sense of 'recommendation-cum-communication' in itself are also found to be attached to the verbalizer *honā* 'to become', *karnā* 'to do', *lenā* 'to take' and *denā* 'to give'. These conjunct verbs are employed in sayings rather than in ordinary sentences. For example:

(32a) वहाँ उसके लिए दुआ हो रही है। (*Recommendation-cum-communication*)
wahã̄ uske liye ***duā*** *ho rahī hɛ.*
there her for prayer.F.SG become PROG.F.SG AUX.PRS.SG
'Prayers are offered for him/her over there.'

(32b) वो दुआ कर रहा है।
wo ***duā*** *kar rahā hɛ.*
he.M.SG prayer do PROG.M.SG AUX.PRS.SG
'He is praying.'

(32c) बड़ों की दुआ लो।
baṛõ-ki ***duā*** *lo.*
elders.M.PL-GEN.F blessing.F.SG take.IMP.2PL
'Take blessing of elders.'

(32d) उसने मुझे दुआ दी।
usne mujhe ***duā*** *dī.*
he/she-ERG me.DAT blessing.F.SG give.PFV.F.SG
'He gave me blessing.'

Semantic mapping of the combination of these types of nouns and the light verbs is shown in Table 8:

Tab. 8: Semantic mapping of the combination of Nouns of Recommendation-cum-communication and the light verbs *honā* 'to become', *karnā* 'to do', *lenā* 'to take' and *denā* 'to give'

Noun → Inanimate → Abstract → Action → Recommendation-cum-communication →
honā 'to become', *karnā* 'to do', *lenā* 'to take' and *denā* 'to give'

Here is the list of some conjunct verbs of this type:

(33) Recommendation-cum-Information
a. *salāh honā/karnā/lenā/denā* 'be consulted/to consult/to take suggestion/to give suggestion'
b. *maśwarāh honā/karnā/lenā/denā* 'be consulted/to consult/to take suggestion/to give suggestion'
c. *badduā honā/karnā/lenā/denā* 'to have adverse wishes'
d. *śubhkāmnā honā/karnā/lenā/denā* 'to receive/give good wishes' etc.

We do not find such adjectives which take all these four verbalizers i.e. *honā* 'to become', *karnā* 'to do', *lenā* 'to take' and *denā* 'to give'.

Although a conjunct verbs may have synonyms, but it is not necessary that they behave alike. For example, synonyms of Hindi Noun/Adjective, borrowed either from Sanskrit may behave differently in accepting verbalizers from those which are from Persian source. For instance, if we take the word *xabar* 'news, information', which is borrowed from Persian, we get the following conjunct verbs.

(34) – *xabar honā* 'to be informed'
मुझे इस बात की ख़बर है।
mujhe is bāt-ki ***xabar hɛ.***
I- DAT this matter.F.SG-GEN.F information.F AUX.PRS.SG
'I have information about this matter.'

(35) – *xabar karnā* 'to inform'
उसने मुझे ख़बर की।
usne mujhe ***xabar kī.***
he/she-ERG I-DAT information.F do.PFV.F.SG
'He informed me.'

(36) – *xabar lenā* ‘to take information’
उसने लोगों से ख़बर ली।
usne logõ-se ***xabar lī.***
he/she-ERG people.M.PL-ABL information.F take.PFV.F.SG
‘He/she took information from people.’

(37) – *xabar denā* ‘to give information’
लोगों ने उसे ख़बर दी।
logõ-ne use ***xabar dī.***
people.M.PL-ERG 3-DAT information.F give.PFV.F.SG
‘People have given information to him/her.’

However, if we take the synonym of *xabar* ‘news, information’, namely, *sūčnā* ‘information’ we will have the following combinations.

(38) – *sūčnā honā* ‘to be informed’
शीला को इस बात की सूचना है।
śīlā-ko is bāt-ki ***sūčnā hɛ.***
Sheela-DAT this matter.F.SG-GEN.F information.F.SG AUX.PRS.SG
‘Sheela has information about this matter.’

(39) –**sūčnā karnā* ‘to inform’
*शीला ने पुलिस को इसके बारे में सूचना की।
śīlā-ne pulis-ko iske bare mẽ* ***sūčnā kī.*
Sheela-ERG police-DAT about this information.F.SG do.PFV.F.SG
‘Sheela informed police about it.’

(40) – *sūčnā lenā* ‘to take information’
शीला ने मुझसे सारी सूचना ली।
śīlā-ne mujh-se sārī ***sūčnā lī.***
Sheela-ERG I-ABL all information.F.SG take.PFV.F.SG
‘Sheela took all information from me.’

(41) – *sūčnā denā* ‘to give information’
शीला ने मुझे सारी सूचना दी है।
śīlā-ne mujhe sārī ***sūčnā dī*** *hɛ.*
Sheela-ERG I-DAT all information.F.SG give.PFV.F.SG AUX.PRS.SG
‘Sheela has given all information to me.’

(39) is not possible in standard Hindi[2] as the noun *sūčnā* 'information' cannot be attached to the verb *karnā* 'to do'. However, its adjectival form i.e., *sūčit* 'informed' can take the verb *karnā* 'to do' to form a conjunct verb *sūčit karnā* 'to inform'.

Nevertheless, we cannot generalize that the Persian source is more productive than the Sanskrit one. For instance, there are nouns/adjectives borrowed from Sanskrit in Hindi which also take all these four verbalizers to form conjunct verbs whereas their synonyms borrowed from Persian do not take all these four verbalizers for the formation of conjunct verbs. To understand the phenomenon, let us consider the noun *āgyā* 'permission', borrowed from Sanskrit, which forms the following conjunct verbs (42)–(45):

(42) – *āgyā honā* 'to be permitted'
रमन को यह काम करने की आज्ञा है।
raman-ko yah kām karne kī ***āgyā*** ***hɛ.***
Raman.M.SG-DAT this work do-GEN.F permission.F AUX.PRS.SG
'Raman is permitted to do this work.'

(43) – *āgyā karnā* 'to order'
आप सिर्फ़ आज्ञा करें, मैं यह काम कर दूँगा।
āp sirf ***āgyā karẽ*** *mɛ̃ yah kām kar dū̃gā.*
you .HON only order do.SBJV.PL I this work do give.FUT.M.SG
'You only order me I will do this work.'

(44) – *āgyā lenā* 'to take permission'
सीता ने इस काम को करने की आज्ञा ली है।
sītā-ne is kām-ko karne-kī ***āgyā***
Sita.F-ERG this work.M.SG-ACC do-GEN.F permission.F.SG
lī ***hɛ.***
take.PFV.F.SG AUX.PRS.SG
'Sita has taken permission to do this work.'

(45) – *āgyā denā* 'to give permission'
आप मुझे इस काम को करने की आज्ञा दें।
āp mujhe is kām-ko karne-kī ***āgyā*** ***dẽ.***
you.HON I.DAT this work-ACC do-GEN.F permission.F.SG give.SBJV.PL
'You give me permission to do this work.'

2 In some areas of Hindi-Urdu, it is possible to encounter constructions such as '*sūcnā karnā*' 'to inform'. However, such constructions are not considered standard by Hindi grammarians.

However its synonym from Persian i.e., *ijāzat* 'permission' do not form all these four conjunct verbs mentioned in (42)–(45), as it is clear from (46)–(49).

(46) – *ijāzat honā* 'to be permitted'
मुझे इस काम को करने की इजाज़त है।
mujhe is kām-ko karne-kī ***ijāzat*** ***hɛ.***
I-DAT this work-ACC do-GEN.F permission.F.SG AUX.PRS.SG
'I have permission to do this work.'

(47) – **ijāzat karnā* 'to permit'
* आप सिर्फ़ इजाज़त करें, मैं यह काम कर दूँगा।
* *āp sirf* ***ijāzat*** ***karẽ*** *mɛ̃ yah*
2.HON only permission-F.SG do-SBJV.PL 1.M.SG this
kām kar dū̃gā.
work do give.FUT.1M.SG
'You only give permission; I will do this work.'

(48) – *ijāzat lenā* 'to take permission'
मैंने इस काम को करने की इजाज़त ली है।
mɛ̃ne is kām-ko karne-kī ***ijāzat***
I-ERG this work-DAT do-GEN.F permission.F.SG
lī *hɛ.*
take.PFV.M.SG AUX.PRS.SG
'I have permission to do this work.'

(49) – *ijāzat denā* 'to give permission'
आप मुझे इस काम को करने की इजाज़त दें।
āp mujhe is kām-ko karne-kī
2.HON I-DAT this work-ACC do-GEN.F
ijāzat ***dẽ.***
permission.F.SG give.SBJV.PL
'You give me permission to do this work.'

5 Conclusion

There is a need for a detailed study and analysis of the nature of nouns and adjectives which forms conjunct verbs which is not possible in a short paper. I have presented a brief study of the some semantic patterns and features of noun/adjective which enable them to combine with certain verbalizers for the formation of conjunct verbs. I have grouped the nouns and adjectives according to their semantic properties and tried to find out their patterns. The point is that the convergence is not arbitrary; they follow certain patterns. I have discussed ontological patterns and semantic features of conjunct verbs having the verbalizers-*honā* 'to become', *karnā* 'to do', *lenā* 'to take' and *denā* 'to give' in this paper. Ontological features which have also been discussed in this paper are important tool to provide better semantic interpretation. Incorporation of this analysis may be useful for knowledge base resource development and the Interlingua based study and research.

References

Bhattacharyya, Pushpak, Debasri Chakrabarti, and Vaijayanthi Sarma. 2007. Complex Predicates in Indian languages and Wordnets. *Language Resources and Evaluation*, 40(3–4): 331–355.

Burton-Page, J. 1957. Compound and conjunct verbs in Hindi. In *Bulletin of school of oriental and African study*, University of London, VOL 19. 469–78.

Butt, Miriam. 2003. 'The Light Verb Jungle.' In G. Aygen, C. Bowern, and C. Quinn (eds.). 2003. Harvard Working Papers in *Linguistics, 9*: Papers from the GSAS/Dudley House Workshop on Light Verbs, 1–49.

Das, P. K. 2006. Grammatical Agreement in Hindi-Urdu and its major varieties, Munchen: Lincom Europa.

Hook, P. E. 1974. 'The Hindi compound verb: What it is and what it does?' In K. S. Singh (ed.) *Readings in Hindi-Urdu linguistics*. Delhi: National Publishing House.

http://www.cfilt.iitb.ac.in/~gaja/tree/tree/adjtree.html

http://www.cfilt.iitb.ac.in/~gaja/tree/tree/ntree.html

Levin, B. 1993. English Verb Classes and Alternations - A Preliminary Investigation. Chicago: University of Chicago Press.

Mohanan, T. 1990. *Arguments in Hindi*. Stanford: Department of Linguistics, Stanford University.

Rafiya, Begum, Karan Jindal, Ashish Jain, Samar Husain, and Dipti Misra Sharma. 2011. Identification of Conjunct Verbs in Hindi and their effect on Parsing Accuracy. In *Proceedings of the 12th CICLing*, Tokyo, Japan.

Singh, Dhirendra, Sudha Bhingardive, Kevin Patel, and Pushpak Bhattacharyya. 2015. Detection of Multiword Expressions for Hindi Language using Word Embeddings and WordNet-based Features. In *Proceedings of ICON*-2015.

Uchida, H., Zhu, M. et al. 1999. *Universal Networking Language: A gift for a millennium.* The United Nations University, Tokyo, Japan.

Wei-Te Chen, Claire Bonial, and Martha Palmer. 2015. English Light Verb Construction Identification Using Lexical Knowledge. In *Proceedings of the AAAI-15*, Austin, TX, USA.

Peter Edwin Hook, Omkar N. Koul

Impersonal expressions in Hindi-Urdu and phantom valents in Kashmiri

Abstract: The word acephaly denotes the absence of a head ['headlessness']. We* use it here in our discussion of two sets of idiomatic construction in Hindi-Urdu in which an expected syntactic agent is absent. We compare this 'headless' construction to a Kashmiri counterpart in which the missing 'head' is indicated by a non-referential ergative pronominal suffix affixed to the finite verb and conclude that the absence of pronominal suffixes in Hindi-Urdu may be at the root of what appears anomalous. This paper is not only an exploration of an unstudied area of Hindi grammar (that is, the absence of ने-marking [i.e., ergative marking] with some सकर्मक [i.e., transitive] verbs in the preterite or perfect tenses) but is also intended to be a step toward a more scientific way of gathering data.[1]

Keywords: Impersonal expression, phantom valents, Hindi-Urdu

1 Set I. V-ne kā man and V-ne kā dil karnā

In Hindi-Urdu [and in many other split ergative languages belonging to Indo-Aryan] use of a transitive verb like *kar-* 'do' in the preterite tense requires a syntactic agent[2] in the ergative:

* It is with deep sorrow that we must record the death of the co-author, Professor Omkar Koul, who was not able to see this chapter through to its final figuration in print. After a lifetime full of efforts and accomplishments, Dr. Koul passed away on the third of May 2018.

1 An earlier version of this paper was presented in Moscow at ICOSAL-10 (Tenth International Conference of South Asian Languages) in July 2012. It has benefited from comments and suggestions made at that meeting, before it and afterwards by Rajesh Bhatt, Ghanshyam Sharma, Prashant Pardeshi, Alice Davison, Bertil Tikkanen, Lakhan Gusain, Kusum Jain, and Elena Bashir. The authors have not always followed their suggestions and are the ones to be held to account for any damages done to the field of South Asian linguistics.

2 The term "syntactic agent" may require some explanation and illustration. A syntactic agent is to be distinguished from the participant or thematic role "Agent" as elaborated by Dowty and others with the consequence that unlike definitions of the latter there are no necessary semantic conditions (such as volitionality or causality) for designating a noun or noun phrase as a syntac-

Peter Edwin Hook, University of Virginia, USA. Email: peter.e.hook@gmail.com
Omkar N. Koul, Indian Institute of Language Studies, New Delhi, India.

https://doi.org/10.1515/9783110610796-010

(1) उन्होंने कार ख़रीदने का फैसला किया। [nayaindia][3]
unhõ-ne *kār xarīd-ne-kā fɛslā kiyā.*
them-ERG[4] car buy-INF-GEN decision.NOM did
'They decided to buy a car.'

(2) हमने कार खरीदने का मन बनाया। [blogspot]
ham-ne *kār xarīd-ne-kā man banāyā.*
we-ERG car buy-INF-GEN mind.NOM made
'We decided to buy a car.'

In (1) and (2) it is clear that the pronouns *unhõ-* and *ham-* are syntactic agents, since they are marked with the ergative postposition *ne* that is expected in a clause headed by the transitive verb *karnā* 'to do' or *banānā* 'to make' when it is in the preterite tense.

But what to make of (3) and (4)? In each of them the preterite form *kiyā* of *karnā* 'to do' governs the rection of the clause but the ergative case marker *ne* is not seen:

---

tic agent. The only requirement is that it be either the subject of an intransitive clause or the subject of a transitive clause that is not in the passive voice or be the object of *by* in the corresponding passive clause. Thus in (a) the noun phrase [what *is pleasurable*] is the syntactic agent of the clause even though it meets none of the conditions needed in order to merit the designation of Agent [participant role]: (a) *If* [what *is pleasurable*] *exceeds* [what *is painful*]... In the corresponding passive the syntactic agent of (a) corresponds to the object [what *is pleasurable*] of the preposition *by* in the passive: (b) *If* [*what is painful*] is exceeded by [what *is pleasurable*] ... See Hook, Pardeshi and Liang (2012: fn 16). Designations like "syntactic agent", "syntactic object" and "syntactic recipient" have no semantic content other than to keep track of functional identities across clause types. Compare the notion of *kāraka* in Panini (Cardona 1976).

3 Including URLs [that are not dead links] is a way for the reader to check on the meaning and validity of the examples. This [we maintain] is a corrective to the traditional reliance on the "intuitions" of "native speakers" who can be confused by the unnatural speech act of elicitation, who may be limited in imagination, and whose knowledge of the mother tongue is necessarily partial. Do any native speakers know the full extent of a language spoken by millions, even tens or hundreds of millions of other fellow speakers?

4 Abbreviations used in this paper include: 1 = first person; 3 = third person; ABL = ablative; ACC = accusative; DAT = dative; EMPH = emphatic; ERG = ergative; F = feminine; GEN = genitive; GER = gerund; HAB = habitual; INF = infinitive; INS = instrumental; LOC = locative; M = masculine; N = neuter; NOM = nominative; OBL = oblique; P = participle; PST = past; PL = plural; PRF = perfect; PRS = present; SBJV = subjunctive; SG = singular

(3) मुझे फिर वहाँ जाने का मन किया। [Prabhat Ranjan; *www.jankipul.com*]
mujhe phir vahā̃ jā-ne-kā ***man kiyā.***
me.DAT again there go-INF-GEN mind.NOM did
'I felt like going there again.'

(4) उनको कुछ फूल खरीदने का मन किया। [*facebook*]
un-ko kuch phūl xarīd-ne-kā ***man kiyā.***
him-DAT some flowers buy-INF-GEN mind.NOM did
'He (Nehru) felt like buying some flowers.'

In the future tense, the finite form *karegā* agrees in gender and number with the noun *man* 'mind':

(5) कभी आपको अकेले रहने का मन करेगा। [*onlymyhealth*]
kabhī āp-ko akele rah-ne-kā ***man kar-egā.***
sometimes you-DAT alone stay-INF-GEN mind.M.SG do-FUT.3M.SG
'At times you'll feel like being alone.'

Is *man* then the syntactic agent? In (6) the preterite form *kiyā* of *karnā* does not allow what we might otherwise consider its syntactic agent [namely, *man* 'mind'] to occur in the ergative:

(6) *कभी आपको अकेले रहने के मन ने किया। [Compare example (5)]
kabhī āp-ko akele rah-ne-ke* ***man-ne kiyā.*
sometimes you-DAT alone stay-INF-GEN mind-ERG did
'At times you felt like being alone.'

Therefore, we must conclude that *man* is not the syntactic agent of *karnā* in examples (3) and (4).

Perhaps the one who feels like doing something is to be taken as an experiencer-subject. In (7) we find a dative subject [*mujhe*] of *man kiyā* controling a gerund (aka, conjunctive participle or absolutive) *paṛh-kar*:[5]

5 For many speakers the dative of (7) alternates with a genitive. See the genitive *merā* in (a):
(a) *ɛsī sundar jagah-par* ***merā*** *kavitā likh-ne-kā man kiyā.*
such beautiful place-at my poem write-INF-GEN mind.NOM did
'In such a beautiful spot I felt like writing a poem.'
(manmohan-uniyal.blogspot.com)
We have no explanation to offer for this alternation, other than to suggest that it may be a precursor to the marking of all experiencers with the genitive case that is found in Bangla and other eastern varieties of Indo-Aryan.

(7) इसे पढ़कर मुझे कविता लिखने का मन किया। [blogvani.com]
*ise **paṛh-kar** mujhe kavitā likh-ne-kā man kiyā.*
it read-GER me.DAT poem write-INF-GEN mind.NOM did
'Reading it I felt like writing a poem.'

But *karnā* 'to do' is transitive, while other verbs or complex predicates taking experiencer dative subjects are *in*transitive.

In Hindi-Urdu most pairs of complex predicates in which there is an alternation of *kar-* 'do' with *ho-* 'become' [or 'be done'] show a uniform difference in valency. In (8) there are two valents (*ham-ne* and *jīn-kī khoj*) whereas in (9) there is only one (*jīn-kī khoj*):

(8) हमने काफ़ी जल्दी इस जीन की खोज की। [*www.patrika.com*]
***ham-ne** kāfī jaldī is jīn-kī **khoj** **kī**.* [two valents]
we-ERG quite quickly this gene-GEN discovery did
'We made the discovery of this gene quite soon.'

(9) तभी एक नई जीन की खोज हुई। [*blogspot*]
*tab-hī ek naī jīn-kī **khoj** **huī**.* [one valent]
then-only one new gene-GEN discovery became
'Only then was a new gene discovered.'

However, there is no diathetic or valency difference between *man kar-* and *man ho-*. In (10) we find the same number of valents [*use* and *jāne-kā man*] as in (3) [*mujhe* and *jāne-kā man*]:

(10) उसे घर से कहीं बाहर जाने का मन हुआ। [jagran]
***use** ghar-se kahī̃ bāhar jā-ne-kā*
him.DAT house-from somewhere outside go-INF-GEN
***man** **huā**.* [two valents]
mind.NOM became
'He felt like going somewhere out of the house.'

In (11) we find the same number of valents [*mujhe* and *kuch likhne-kā man*] as in (12):

(11) मुझे कुछ लिखने का मन हुआ। [karanmisra]
***mujhe** kuch likh-ne-kā **man** **huā**.* [two valents]
me.DAT something write-INF-GEN mind.NOM became
'I felt like writing something.'

(12) मुझे कविता लिखने का मन किया। [blogvani]
mujhe *kavitā* *likh-ne-kā* ***man*** ***kiyā.*** [two valents]
me.DAT poem write-INF-GEN mind.NOM did
'I felt like writing a poem.'

In our analysis of them, we would like to draw attention to a construction in Kashmiri which indicates a possible explanation for the absence of the ergative case in examples (3), (4), (7) and (12). Compare Hindi-Urdu (4) with Kashmiri (13) in which a parallel complex predicate V-*nu-k man karun* 'to feel like [V-ing]' is present:

(13) ***tyiman*** *koru-n*[6] *pōš* *hye-nu-k* *man.* [Kashmiri][7]
them.DAT did.3SG-ERG flowers buy-INF-GEN mind.NOM
'He (= Nehru) felt like buying some flowers.'[8]

Notice that in example (13) **three** valents are present: the dative form of the experiencer [*tyiman*], the nominative form of the syntactic direct object [*pōš hy-enu-k man*], and a third valent, a non-referential one, represented by the third person singular ergative affix –*n* on the finite verb.[9] In contemporary Kashmiri, therefore, we must regard the verb in (13) as a trivalent or ditransitive. The literal meaning of (13) is something like 'To him (i.e., to Nehru) Z (= dummy syntactic-agent) made a mind to buy flowers.' The construction in (13) is one of Kashmiri's many impersonal constructions.[10]

---

6 Notice that in Kashmiri matrix clauses, the finite element of the verb appears in verb-second position while in relative clauses the finite element is clause-final. This word-order rule, first observed by Jules Bloch nearly one hundred years ago (Bloch 1920:270-1; 1970:283), is nearly the same as in German and Dutch.

7 The values of two vowel symbols in transcriptions of Kashmiri differ from those of Hindi-Urdu. In Kashmiri an /*i*/ is a high unrounded central or back vowel – unless fronted by an immediately preceding or following /*y*/ or /*š*/ or /*c*/. Similarly the symbol /*e*/ represents a mid-central schwa-like vowel – unless fronted by a palatal (/*y*/ or /*š*/ or /*c*/).

8 Omkar Koul is responsible for Hindi to Kashmiri and Kashmiri to English rendering of all Kashmiri examples cited in this paper.

9 Whether the -*n* suffix is a fossil representing a notional or an anciently worshipped spiritual agent or is simply a dummy element required in order to satisfy the predicate argument structure of *karun* 'to do' as in (26) is a question whose answer may depend on input from cultural historians.

10 Kashmiri has at least four types of constructions featuring non-referential -*n*: Inceptives in *hye*- "take" when governing intransitive infinitives; weather and health expressions; and natural

On the basis of the construction in (13) we propose a solution for the anomalous absence of the ergative case in (3) and (4) and in a synonymous construction: V-*ne kā dil kar-* 'decide to V / feel like V-ing' which, like *man karnā*, has only two core valents, a preverbial noun in the nominative and an experiencer in the dative:

(14) मुझे उनसे ... ये पूछने का दिल किया कि ... [*blogspot*]
mujhe *un-se ...* *ye* ***pūch-ne-kā*** ***dil*** *kiyā* *ki ...*
me.DAT them-ABL this ask-INF-GEN heart.NOM did that
'I felt like asking them this, that...'

(15) **mye** *koru-n* ***dyil*** *tyiman* *yi* ***pritsh-nu-k*** *zyi ...*[11]
me.DAT did-3SG.ERG heart.NOM them.DAT this ask-INF-GEN that
'I felt like asking them this, that ...'

The hypothesis we are putting forward is that the trivalent construction that still exists [in fossilized form] in Kashmiri was at one time more generally distributed in Indo-Aryan. The *man kar-* and *dil kar-* constructions are remnants of it in Hindi-Urdu. Seen from that perspective the correct analysis of (3), (4) and (14) is:[12]

(16) [Z] Y-*ko* *man / dil* *kar-*
[dummy syntactic-agent] experiencer-DAT [direct object] do

---

processes such as melting, rusting, ageing, etc., and the idioms like those in (13) and (15) that are the topic of this chapter.

11 Notice that in ex (15) *dyil*'s complement *yi pritshnuk* is separated from it and displaced to the right even though semantically they function as a single unit.

12 This analysis comports with what is reported by Malchukov and Ogawa (2011: 45) as being Mel'čuk's 1979 analysis of Russian impersonals like those in (a) and (b):

(a) *dorog-u* *zanes-lo* $Ø_A$ *sneg-om.*
road-ACC cover-PST-N.SG (dummy) snow-INS
'The road got covered with snow.' [Lit: 'Z covered the road with snow.']
[Malchukov and Ogawa (2011: 45)]

(b) *kamchatk-u* *nakry-l-o* $Ø_A$ *pepl-om.*
Kamchatka-ACC blanket-PST-N.SG (dummy) ash-INS
'Kamchatka blanketed with ash.'
[Lit: 'Z blanketed Kamchatka with (volcanic) ash.'] (*www.wday.ru*)

Compare (a) and (b) with the Kashmiri construction in (c):

(c) *asmān* *boru-n* *oburi-sīty.*
sky.NOM filled-3SG.ERG cloud-with
'The sky clouded over.'
[Lit: 'Z filled the sky with cloud.'] [Hook and Koul (MS)]

Since in Hindi-Urdu there are no pronominal suffixes to represent the place of the non-referential 'dummy' syntactic agent [registered by the ergative suffix *-n* in Kashmiri], it's no longer possible to detect the trivalent nature of V-*ne kā man / dil karnā*. They are now orphaned lexical constructions.

2 Set II. Afflictional expressions

Hindi-Urdu has other constructions showing a similar [but not identical] anomaly in predicate-argument structure, namely *laqvā mārnā* 'to be paralyzed; have a stroke' (17) and (18), *lū mār-* 'suffer sunstroke' (19), *ṭhaṇḍ / pālā mār-* 'be chilled; be ruined by cold' (20) and (21):[13]

(17) ज़ू के दो बब्बर शेरों को लकवा मारा। [navbharattimes]
zū-ke do babbar śērõ-kō ***laqvā mārā.***
zoo-GEN two lions-DAT paralysis.NOM hit
'Two of the zoo's lions were paralyzed.'

(18) मुझे छह माह पूर्व लकवा मारा है। [jagran]
mujhe čhah māh pūrv ***lakvā mārā*** *hɛ.*
me.DAT six months before stroke.NOM hit is
'I had a stroke six months ago.'

(19) पार्क मार्केट के पास एक व्यक्ति को लू मार दिया और वहीं पर वो गिर गया। [*prabhatkhabar*]
pārk mārkeṭ-ke.pās ek vyakti-ko ***lū mār diyā*** *ɔr*
Park Market-near one person-DAT sunstroke hit GAVE and
vahī̃-par vo gir gayā.
there-LOC he fall WENT
'Someone got sunstroke near Park Market and fell down right there.'

(20) घर से निकलते ही उसे ठंड मारा तथा बेहोश हो गया। [*jagran*]
ghar-se nikal-te.hī use ***ṭhaṇḍ mārā***
house-from emerge-on him.DAT cold hit
tathā be.hoś ho.gayā.
and unconscious became
'As soon as he stepped out of his house he got a chill and passed out.'

---

13 As pointed out to us by Ghanshyam Sharma and Rajesh Bhatt the evidence for two of these (*lu mār-* and *ṭhaṇḍ mār-*) is limited to online reports from Bihar and Jharkhand. As local languages in Jharkhand and Bihar lack gender agreement this might explain the absence of gender agreement in examples (19)–(20).

(21) हरी सब्जियों को पाला मार दिया है। किसानों की हालत काफी खराब हो गयी है। [jagran]
harī sabziyõ-ko ***pālā mār diyā*** *hɛ.*
green veggies-DAT frost hit GIVEN is
kisānõ-kī hālat kāfī xarāb ho gayī hɛ.
farmers-GEN situation quite bad become WENT is
'Frost has hit green vegetable [crops]. Farmers are in dire straits.'

Differences include the following: The experiencer or entertainer of a desire or urge in V-*ne kā man / dil kar*-constructions may take either the dative or the genitive case[14] whereas the afflictee in *laqvā mār-* and *pālā mār-* always gets the dative case, never the genitive. The verb *mār-* in afflictives can be vectored with either *jā-* GO (37) or *de-* GIVE (21) whereas the verb *kar-* in V-*ne kā man / dil kar*-constructions, when compound, is vectored with *jā-* (41), never with *de-*.

As in the previous instances [(4) & (13) and (14) & (15)] Kashmiri has equivalent constructions featuring a dummy pronominal suffix *-n* on finite verb forms indicating a third non-referential 'phantom' valent:

(22) *zū-kyen dwan sĩhan* ***keri-n*** *phālij.*[15] [cf (17)]
zoo-GEN.DAT two.DAT lions.DAT did.F.SG-3SG.ERG paralysis.F.SG
'Two of the zoo's lions were paralyzed.'
[Lit: 'Z did paralysis to two of the zoo's lions.']

(23) *mye* ***keri-n*** *phālij śe ryeth brõh.* [cf (18)]
me.DAT did.F.SG-3SG.ERG stroke.F.SG six months ago
'I had a stroke six months back.'
[Lit: 'Z did a stroke to me 6 months ago.']

(24) *temyis* ***khēri-n*** *suban gari.*
him.DAT raised.F.SG-3SG.ERG morning.ABL home.ABL
cakras-pyeṭh nyīr-yith tīr. [cf (20)]
walk.DAT-at emerge-GER cold.F.SG
'He got a chill while going on a walk in the morning.'
[Lit: 'Z raised cold to him .']

---

14 See example (a) in footnote 5 above.

15 The words *laqvā* and *fālij* [Kashmiri *phālij*] are borrowings from Persian which in turn borrowed them from Arabic. In Hindi-Urdu the noun *fālij* usually occurs with the operator *gir-* 'fall'; *laqvā*, with *mār-*. They appear to be freely interchangeable [semantically if not syntactically] and depending on context mean either 'stroke' or 'paralysis'.

(25) *ezici tīryi sīty* ***che-n*** *nyīji sabzyiyi*
today's cold.OBL with are.F.PL-ERG.3SG green vegetables .F.PL
šiṭh-irāv-yi-matsi. [cf (21)]
freeze-CAUS-PST.F.PL-PSTPART.F.PL
'With today's cold the greens have [been] frozen.'
[Lit: 'Z has frozen the greens.']

Examples (22)–(25) are among a large number of impersonal constructions in Kashmiri that involve health or [more commonly] its absence.[16] Example (26) is from a paper on the grammar of expressions of weather and health in Kashmiri:[17]

(26) *temyis* ***keryi-n*** *pyēch.*
him.DAT did.M.PL-3SG.ERG cramps.NOM.M.PL
'He got cramps.'
[Lit: 'Z did cramps to him.']

The ostensibly trivalent construction in (26) alternates with the bivalent (27):

(27) *temyis* ***āyi*** *pyēch.*
him.DAT came.M.PL cramps.M.PL
'He got cramps.'

In similar fashion trivalent *phālij kar-*, *tīr khār-*, and *šiṭhirāv-* alternate with bivalent counterparts:

(28) *mye* ***geyi*** *phālij še ryeth brõh.* [Cf. (23)]
me.DAT went.F.SG stroke.F.SG six months ago
'I had a stroke six months back.'

16 In her recent monograph on Kashmiri Verbeke appears to cast doubt on the existence of the non-referential 3rd person ergative pronominal suffix *-n*. (2018: 59-61). However, instances of it can be found in published material:
(a) *šurah agasT 1973 pyeṭha-y lōgu-**n** tshadi rusituy rūd.*
sixteen August 1973 from-EMP applied-3SG.ERG halt without rain
'From the 16th of August it rained without a break.' (Pompur 1986: 69)
Published attestations include textbooks written for elementary school pupils:
... *yelyi sani 1489 tas manz ath hyotu-**n** naar.*
when year 1489 it in it.DAT took-3sE fire.NOM
'... when in 1489 it (= Jamia Masjid) caught fire.' (Kashmiri Reader 4, p. 23)
17 See Hook (1986) for discussion of examples provided by Omkar Koul.

(29) *temyis* ***khets*** *suban* *gari* *cakras-pyeṭh*
he.DAT rose.F.SG morning.ABL home.ABL walk.DAT-at
nyīr-yith *tīr.* [Cf. (24)]
emerge-GER cold.F.SG
'He caught a chill while leaving home for a walk in the morning.'

(30) *ezi.ci* *tīryi* *sīty* ***che*** *nyīji* *sabzyiyi*
today's cold-OBL with are.F.PL green vegetables.F.PL
šiṭh-ye-matsi. [Cf (25)]
freeze-PST.F.PL-PST.PART.FPL
'With today's cold the greens have [been] frozen.'

The Hindi-Urdu expressions also alternate with bivalent intransitives:

(31) दो साल पहले भी उनको लकवा हुआ था। [*dainiktribuneonline*]
do *sāl* *pahle* *bhī* *un-ko* *lakvā* ***huā*** *thā.* [Cf (18)]
two years ago also him-DAT stroke become was
'He had had a stroke two years ago, too.'

(32) लगातार गिर रहे तापमान से फसलों को पाला लग सकता है। [*bhaskar*]
lagātār *gir-rahe* *tāpmān-se* *fasalõ-ko* *pālā*
constantly fall-ing temperture-from crops-DAT frost
lag *saktā.hɛ.* [Cf (21)]
attach can
'Constantly falling temperatures can cause frost-damage to crops.'

The fact that (23)–(25) alternate with the corresponding bivalent intransitive clauses in (28)–(30) with no easily definable difference in meaning [at least no difference in the number of real-world participants – compare the contrasting pair (8) and (9)][18] indicates that the ergative pronominal suffixes in (23)–(25) are non-referential. They are present only to satisfy the formal requirement for a syntactic agent that comes with the use of the verbs *karun* 'to do', *khārun* 'to raise', and *šiṭhirāvun* 'to freeze' in Kashmiri. The fact that the preterite forms of *karun* and *khārun* and the present perfect form of *šiṭhirāvun* show agreement in gender and number with *phālij* and *tīr* (feminine singular) and *sabzyiyi* (feminine plural)

18 Of course the number of participants *in the real world* is the same in (9) as it is in (8); namely, two: the discoverer and the thing discovered. But (9) explicitly refers to only one of them - the thing discovered.

indicates that these nouns are direct objects.[19] The victims of strokes, chills, and frost in (23)–(25) then are syntactic recipients (even though they may have some properties of syntactic agents, such as the ability to antecede the reflexive possessive *panun* 'self's' and govern gerundial phrases).[20]

Seen in this light, Hindi-Urdu's *laqvā mār-* 'suffer paralysis' and *pālā mār-* 'be damaged by frost' are best analyzed as impersonal or acephalous predicates. Exceptions that help to prove the validity of our analysis are the following overtly trivalent 'cephalous' examples:

(33) तुम्हारे शरीर को तुम्हारे प्राणों ने लकवा मारा होता है। [*pustak.org/home.php?bookid=2462*]
tumhāre śarīr-ko ***tumhāre prāṇõ-ne*** *lakvā*
your body-DAT your spirits-ERG paralysis
mārā ho-tā hɛ.
struck.PST.PART be-HAB is
'Your soul has paralyzed your body.'

(34) उलटे राजधानी ने तमाम डाइट की रचनात्मकता को पाला मार दिया। [*humsamvet*]
ulṭe ***rāj.dhānī-ne*** *tamām 'ḍāīṭ'-kī račnātmak.tā-ko*
reverse capital-ERG entire D.I.E.T-GEN creativity-DAT
pālā mār diyā.
frost hit GAVE
'On the contrary the Centre has frozen all D.I.E.T[21] creativity.'

As we can see from (33) and (34) when speakers use *laqvā mār-* and *pālā mār-* metaphorically they supply the missing agent valent correctly and instinctively.[22]

---

19 As in Hindi-Urdu, Gujarati, Marathi, and most other split ergative western and northern Indo-Aryan languages, the rection of a preterite or perfect tensed clause in Kashmiri requires the agreement of the finite verb with a bare direct object in gender and number. See Masica (1991: 341–346) and Verbeke (2012).

20 In (a) *temyis* [the victim of the stroke] controls the gerundial phrase *panun vatan vētyith* 'returning to his country' and is the antecedent of the possessive reflexive *panun*:
(a) *panun vatan vēt-yith keri-n temyis phālij*
self's country arrive-GER did-3SG.ERG him.DAT stroke
'On returning to his country he suffered a stroke.' [O.N. Koul]

21 The acronym 'DIET' stands for 'District Institute of Education and Training', a renaming of India's BT colleges.

22 In similar fashion speakers of Kashmiri when making figurative use of an impersonal expression are free to fill the phantom agent slot with an explicit valent [or syntactic argument. See Tesnière (1969) for our use of "valent"].

Their ability to do so indicates their unconscious understanding of *mār-* as a trivalent predicate - even though for *laqvā mār-* and *pālā mār-* in their normal senses only two of the three valency slots are filled.

There is yet another class of afflictional expressions that may be used impersonally:[23]

(35) उसे करंट मार दिया जिससे वो ज़मीन पर गिर गया। [*jagran*]
use ***karanṭ mār diyā*** *jis-se vo*
him.DAT current hit GAVE which-from he
zamīn-par gir gayā.
ground-on fall WENT
'He got an electric shock and fell to the ground.

(36) नवदीप का हाथ कूलर पर लग गया और उसे करंट मार दिया। [livehindustan]
navdīp.kā hāth kūlar-par lag-gayā ɔr use ***karaṇṭ mār diyā.***
Navdip's hand cooler-on hit-WENT and him.DAT current hit GAVE
'Navdip's hand touched the cooler and he was electrocuted.'

While *karanṭ mār-* 'get a shock' may occur with nouns like *bijlī* 'electricity' (or 'lightning') as its syntactic agent as in (37) there are instances of *karanṭ mār-*'s use in which neither electricity or lightning is a participant (38) and (39):

(37) ट्यूबवेल स्टार्ट करते समय बिजली ने उसे करंट मार दिया। [*amarujala*]
ṭyūbvel sṭārṭ kar.te-samay ***bijlī-ne*** *use*
tubewell start doing-time electricity-ERG him.DAT
karanṭ mār diyā.
current hit GAVE
'While starting up the tubewell, he was electrocuted.'

(38) यह सुनकर मुझे मानो करंट मार दिया।
yah sun-kar mujhē mānō ***karanṭ mār diyā.***
this hear-GER me.DAT as.if current hit GAVE
'I was like shocked to hear this.'
[from Ravindra Bharti's *jan-vāsā*, 'The meeting place', p. 44]

(a) *emyi khyāl-an khēr temyis tīr*
this idea-ERG raised him.DAT cold
'This idea frightened him.' [cf. (24)]

23 Thanks to Lakhan Gusain for drawing our attention to this class of impersonal expressions.

(39) *yi* *buuzy-ith-iy* *zan* *mooru-n* *mye* *karanṭ.*
this hear-GER-EMPH as.if struck-3SG.ERG me.DAT current
'I was as if shocked to hear this.'

In the meaning 'lightning' *bijlī* itself may occur as the preverbial noun in an impersonal clause:[24]

(40) मूर्तियाँ जो मिलती हैं उन्हें देखकर लगता है कि जैसे अभी-अभी बिजली मारी है।
mūrtiyā̃ *jo* *mil.tī.hɛ̃* *unhẽ* *dekh-kar* *lag-tā.hɛ* *ki*
images that meet-PRS them see-GER seem-PRS that
jɛse *abhī-abhī* ***bijlī*** ***mārī*** *hɛ.*
like now-now lightning struck is
'Looking at the images there it seems like lightning has just now hit (them).'

Speakers seem to be aware of a mismatch between the predicate argument structure of *laqvā/pālā/karanṭ mār-* (as well as *man/dil kar-*) and the real world situations that they typically represent. One means of recognizing and to some extent relieving this tension may be the frequent use of the intransitive vector *jā-* 'go':

(41) शाम को मुझे अचानक उबले हुए अंडे खाने का मन कर गया।
śām-ko *mujhe* *ačānak* *uble.hue* *aṇḍe* *khā-ne-kā*
evening-LOC me.DAT suddenly boiled eggs eat-INF-GEN
man ***kar*** ***gayā.***
mind do WENT
'In the evening I suddenly felt like eating boiled eggs.'
[*mail.sarai.net/pipermail/deewan/*]

(42) क्या देश को लकवा मार गया है। [*samaylive.com*]
kyā *deš-ko* ***lakvā*** ***mār*** ***gayā*** ***hɛ.***
QM nation-DAT paralysis hit GONE is
'Has the country been paralysed?'

(43) फसल को भले पाला मार जाए या उसमें आग लग जाए ... [*hindi.webdunia*]
phasal-ko *bhale* ***pālā*** ***mār*** ***jā-e*** *yā* *us-mẽ*
crop-DAT even.if frost hit GO-SBJV or it-LOC
āg *lag* *jā-e ...*
fire stick GO-SBJV
'Let the crop freeze or catch fire ...'

24 The example is one of a kind but has impressive credentials: It occurs in the 2008 republication of Sūrykānt Tripāthi "Nirālā"'s *sampūrṇ kahāniyā̃* [*Complete stories*], p. 483.

(44) यह दृश्य देख हमें मानो करंट मार गया।
yah dr̥šy dekh hamẽ māno ***karaṇṭ mār gayā.***
this scene seeing us.DAT as if current hit WENT
'Seeing this scene we were like shocked.'
[Mahua Maji's *Maĩ, borišailla*, p. 206]

When *mār-* and *kar-* are vectored with *jā-* GO the syntactic status of the preverbial nouns *man, dil, laqvā,* and *pālā* is masked by default agreement. With *lū* and *ṭhaṇḍ* as preverbials agreement is optional, a stage perhaps on the path to eventual incorporation into the class of *yād kar-* expressions.[25]

3 Acephaly in the neighborhood

Other South Asian languages that have impersonal constructions include Marathi (45), Kalasha (46), Shina of Gilgit (47), Burushaski of Gilgit (48), and West Tibetan Balti (49):[26]

(45) *tyā-ts divaśi ti-lā* ***lakvā mār-lā.***
that-EMPH day her-DAT stroke.M.SG hit-PST
bol.ṇa hal.ṇa sāra band dzhāla [see (17-18)]
speaking moving all.NSG closed became.NSG
'That very day she had a stroke. Speech, walking, everything shut down.'
[*www.orkut.com*]

(46) *mɛ* ***žu-alyak ne kar-iu-dɛ.*** [Kalasha: compare (3-4)]
me.OBL eat-feeling not do-NON-PST-3SG
'I don't feel like eating.' [from Bashir 1990: 307]

(47) *ro* ***ṣey-ar-eégi-n*** ⇔ *ro ṣey-iílo.*
he.NOM blind-CAUS-PFV.P3SG.F-PRS.3SG[27] he.NOM blind-PST.3SG.M
'He has gone blind.' [lit: 'Z has blinded him.'] 'He went blind.'
[Hook & Zia 2005: 167]

25 Metaphorical uses of *lū mār jā-* and *ṭhaṇḍ mār jā-* seem more likely to show feminine gender agreement than literal uses do but relevant data is sparse.

26 For studies of impersonal constructions in non-South Asian languages see Malchukov and Siewierska (2011).

27 The verb's morphology indicates that the phantom valent is (or was) a grammatically feminine entity. See Hook and Zia (2005: 175–177) for discussion.

(48) *je* *qhus* ***á-a-t-i.m-i.*** [involuntary action][28]
I.NOM cough 1SG-CAUS-do-PST-3SG[29]
'I coughed. / I felt the urge to cough'
[lit: 'Z made me cough.' – quoted from Berger 1998:182, §16.14]

(49) *charpha mala **taŋma**-med.*
rain never release-NEG
'It never rains ....'
[lit: 'Z never releases rain.'] [Read 1934: 81]

Other than Shina and Kashmiri to our knowledge the only Indo-Aryan language that features a phantom valent is the closely related Poguli:

(50) *rod **lāg-tu-in*** ⇔ ***rod læg go.***
rain apply-PST.3SG-ERG rain attach.GER WENT
'It has begun to rain.' [lit: 'Z applied rain.'] ('Manzoor' Katoch, p.c.)

4 Alternative analyses

One possible objection to our analysis is that the examples we present are ungrammatical and merely reflect marginal forms of Hindi-Urdu current among provincial speakers. It is true that some examples come from reporters (local stringers?) in Bihar and Jharkhand, i.e. from speakers whose Hindi-Urdu does not observe standard rules governing the use of the ergative *ne* nor recognize gender. Example (51) for instance is from near Ranchi:

(51) मटर टमाटर और आलू सब को पाला मार दिया है।
[http://www.im4change.org/hindi]
*maṭar ṭamātar ɔr ālū sab-ko **pālā mār diyā** hɛ.*
peas tomatoes and potatoes all-DAT frost hit GIVEN is
'Peas, tomatoes, and potatoes. Frost has hit them all.'

28 These data were provided by Sherbaz Khan Bercha [Gilgit Public Library]. Similar impersonal constructions in Burushaski are noted by Lorimer (1938: 245) and Berger (1998: 359) and are reported by Yoshioka (2012) as well.

29 According to Bertil Tikkanen (p.c.), the *aá-* prefix on the verb in (48) indicates that the first person is the causee in a grammatically causative clause. According to Elena Bashir it also indicates a first person singular beneficiary.

According to some Hindi-Urdu speakers (51) should be corrected to (52):

(52) मटर टमाटर और आलू सब को पाले ने मार दिया है।
maṭar ṭamātar ɔr ālū sab-ko ***pāle-ne mār diyā*** *hɛ.*
peas tomatoes and potatoes all-ACC frost-ERG hit GIVEN is
'Peas, tomatoes, and potatoes. Frost has hit them all.'

However, "correcting" (51) to (52) is problematic. Available online examples of *pāle-ne mār diyā* and *pāle-ne mārā* are from reports out of rural parts of Rajasthan:

(53) अनेक लोगों ने बताया कि सब्जी की पैदावार को पाले ने मार दिया। [*bhaskar*]
anek logõ-ne batāyā ki sabzī-kī pɛdāvār-ko
many people-ERG said that green-GEN crop-ACC
pāle-ne mār diyā.
frost-ERG hit GAVE
'According to many people, frost hit vegetable crops.'

While some online examples of *pālā mār diyā* and *pālā mārā* come from Bihar and Jharkhand others come from the central Hindi provinces Haryana and UP:

(54) किसान-मजूर का जीना दूभर हो गया है। फसलों को पाला मार दिया है। [*jagran*]
kisān-majūr-kā jīnā dūbhar ho.gayā hɛ.
farmer-laborer-GEN living unbearable become is
fasalõ-ko ***pālā mār diyā*** *hɛ.*
crops-DAT frost hit GIVEN has
'Life for the farm laborer has become hard to bear. Frost has hit the crops.'
[as reported from Nangal Choudhary, Mahendragarh, Haryana]

More to the point, the "correction" in (52) cannot be extended to *laqvā mār- / mār de-*. The ergative forms *laqve ne* [or *lakve ne*] simply do not occur as agent-subjects of *mārā* or *mār diyā*. Thus, even if we drop all the others [*pālā mār-, ṭhaṇḍ mār-, lū mār-*] as being grammatical errors or dialectal aberrations, we must still accept the existence of at least one set of impersonal expressions in Hindi-Urdu: *laqvā mār- / mār de-*.

There is, however, another scenario that may allow us to exclude impersonals altogether from the grammar of Hindi-Urdu. By defining certain verb stems as being 'labile', one may reclassify the impersonal use of a transitive verb as the personal use of a formally identical intransitive verb. Thus, Molesworth (1857) has given the Marathi transitive *dhar-* 'hold, retain; apply, keep [something] at [a place]' a separate entry as an intransitive 'stick to, adhere; be borne, produced; bear fruit, etc.'[30]

(55) *jun-čyā prārambh-i* ***pāus dhar-l.ā*** *tar*
June-GEN beginning-LOC rain apply-PST then
pāṇi-ṭantsāi kami ho-il. [*dainikekmat*]
water-shortage less be-3SG.FUT
'If the rains set in at the start of June the water shortage will be less.'

Accordingly if we allow *mār-* and *mār de-* [when occurring with *laqvā*] and *kar-* [when occurring with V-*ne kā man* or *dil*] to be classified as intransitives, we may purge Hindi-Urdu grammar of a rare form of predication.

30 Molesworth's decision to set up a separate entry for intransitive *dhar-* accords with Marathi's agreement patterns. While the nominative plural *phaḷa* in (a) could possibly be either the direct object of an impersonal transitive or the syntactic agent of an intransitive [since the neuter plural agreement suffix *-i* on the finite verb form *dharli* would be required in either case], the number agreement with *phaḷa* in (a')'s plural form *dhartil* precludes the first possibility:

(a) *dzhāḍa bahar-li* ***phaḷa*** ***dhar-li*** *ki pakṣi ā-le-ts.* (*www.loksatta.com*)
trees blossom-PST fruits.NOM hold-PST that birds come-PST-EMPH
'Once trees blossom and fruit is borne, there will be no lack of birds!'

(a') *čār varṣān-ni* ***phaḷa*** ***dhar-til.*** (*maharashtratimes.indiatimes.com*)
four years-in fruits.NOM hold-3PL.FUT
'In four years fruit will be borne / will appear.'

In one type of impersonal construction in Kashmiri analysis of the agreement pattern leads to the opposite conclusion:

(b) ***tārakh*** ***keḍ-yi-n-as*** *neny.*
stars.NOM drew-M.PL-3SG.ERG-3SG-DAT bright.M.PL
'The stars came out bright.' [lit: 'Z drew the stars out bright. ']

(b') ***tārakh*** ***kaḍ-y-as*** (not: ***kaḍ-an-as***) *neny.*
stars.NOM draw-FUT3SG-3SG.DAT draw-FUT3PL-3SG.DAT bright.M.PL
'The stars will come out bright.' [lit: 'Z will draw the stars out bright.']

Although Marathi in the past – like Hindi-Urdu and Kashmiri in the present – may have harboured acephalous constructions, the lability of *dhar-* in the present language cannot be considered to be anything more than possibly a fossil remnant of impersonal constructions. Similarly the use in English of normally transitive predicates like *hold, lift,* and *set in* for weather phenomena is suggestive but cannot be considered as proving the earlier existence of phantom valents:

(c) *If warmer weather* ***holds,*** *the fog* ***will lift.*** *If not, by next week the rainy season* ***will have set in.***

5 Summary

In this paper we have examined two sets of idiomatic construction in Hindi-Urdu in which an expected syntactic agent is absent and have compared these 'headless' construction to Kashmiri in which the missing 'head' in parallel constructions is indicated by a non-referential ergative pronominal suffix affixed to the finite verb. We conjecture that the absence in Hindi-Urdu of pronominal suffixes similar to those found in Kashmiri masks the true nature of what otherwise seem to be syntactic anomalies.[31]

---

31 About acephaly in Hindi-Urdu there is undoubtedly more to be discovered and described, especially from the diachronic point of view. We leave that to others but not without noting the intriguing conjecture (made informally by Elena Bashir) that an analysis as frozen causative constructions may account for the unusual morphology of expressions like *X-ko dikhāī denā* 'to be visible to X' and *X-ko sunāī denā* 'to be audible to X':

(a) तभी उसे एक भारी भरकम मगरमच्छ दिखाई दिया।

tabhī	*use*	*ek*	*bhārī.bharkam*	*magarmacch*	***dikh-ā-ī***	***diyā*.**
then.EMPH	him.DAT	one	massive	crocodile	see-CAUS-GER	GAVE

'Just then he saw an enormous crocodile.' (*panchjanya.com*)

(b) उन्हें एक कड़क स्वर सुनाई दिया – ठहर जाओ!

unhẽ	*ek*	*kaṛak*	*svar*	***sun-ā-ī***	***diyā*:**	*ṭhahar*	*jā* !
him.DAT	one	loud	voice	hear-CAUS-GER	GAVE	halt	GO

'He (the Buddha) heard a loud voice: "Stop!"' (*bhaskar.com*)

Taking these expressions to be fossils of an impersonal construction one could analyze (a) and (b) as (a') and (b'):

(a') '[Z] showed him [made him see] an enormous crocodile.'

(b') '[Z] made him hear a loud voice.'

Under an analysis as causatives the long final /ī/ in *dikhāī* and *sunāī* would be a survival of the gerundial suffix of Old Hindi, a suffix that is still found in dialects. See the –*y* of *batā-y* in (c) [the fourth *dohā* of Kabir]:

(c) गुरु गोविन्द दोऊ खड़े काके लागूँ पाय। बलिहारी गुरु आपनो गोविन्द दियो बताय॥

guru	*govind*	*doū*	*khaṛe*	*kā.ke*	*lāgū̃*	*pāy?*
guru	Govind	both	stand	whose	touch.SBJV.1SG	feet

balihārī	*guru*	*āpno*	*govind*	*diyo*	***batā-y*.**
sacrifice	guru	our	Govind	GAVE	show-GER

'God and Guru both before me, whose feet shall I first touch?
Since it was Guru who showed me God, I owe him that much!'

References

Bashir, Elena. 1990. Involuntary experience in Kalasha. In Manindra K. Verma & K. P. Mohanan (eds.), *Experiencer subjects in South Asian languages*, 297–318. Stanford: CSLI Stanford University Press.
Berger, Hermann. 1998. *Die Burushaski-Sprache von Hunza und Nager*. Wiesbaden: Otto Harrassowitz.
Bloch, Jules. 1914-20. *La formation de la langue Marathe*. Paris: E. Champion. Translated into English by Dr. Dev Raj Chanana and published by Motilal Banarsidass in 1970.
Butt, Miriam. 2004. The role of pronominal suffixes in Punjabi. *stujay.com/wp-content/uploads/public/*particles%20in%20panjabi.pdf
Cardona, George. 1976. *Panini: A survey of research*. The Hague: Mouton
Davison, Alice. MS. Reversible and non-reversible dative subjects: A structural account.
Dowty, David R. 1991. Thematic proto-roles and argument selection. *Language* 67: 547–619.
Hook, Peter Edwin. 1986. Null valents in the expression of impersonal action in Russian and Kashmiri. *Papers from the Twenty-second Regional Meeting*. Chicago Linguistics Society. 179–194.
Hook, Peter Edwin, and Muhammad Amin 'Zia'. 2005. Searching for the Goddess: A study of sensory and other impersonal causative expressions in the Shina of Gilgit. In Rajendra Singh and Tanmoy Bhattacharya (eds.), *The Yearbook of South Asian Languages and Linguistics: 2005*, 165–188. Berlin & New York: Mouton de Gruyter.
Hook, Peter E., Prashant Pardeshi and Hsin-hsin Liang. 2012. Semantic neutrality in complex predicates in East and South Asian languages. *Linguistics* 50: 605–632.
Lorimer, D. L. R. 1938. *The Burushaski Language*. Oslo: Instituttet for Sammenlignende Kulturforskning.
Malchukov, Andrej, and Akio Ogawa. 2011. Towards a typology of impersonal constructions. In Andrej Malchukov and Anna Siewierska (eds.), *Impersonal constructions: A cross-linguistic perspective*, 19–56. Amsterdam: John Benjamins.
Masica, Colin P. 1991. *The indo-Aryan languages*. Cambridge: Cambridge University Press.
Mel'čuk, Igor. 1979. Syntactic or lexical zero in natural language. In *Proceedings of the Berkeley Linguistics Society*. 224–260.
Molesworth, James Thomas. 1857. *A dictionary, Marathi and English*. 2d ed., revised and enlarged. Bombay: Printed at the Bombay Education Society's press. [online version at *http://dsal. uchicago. edu*]
Pompur, Syed R. 1986. *Yath aadim vanas manz* (*In this human jungle*). Bijbehara: Sangar Publishing House.
Read, A. F. C. 1934. *Balti grammar*. London: Royal Asiatic Society.
Tesnière, Lucien. 1969. *Éléménts de syntaxe structurale*. 2nd edition. Paris: Klincksieck.
Verbeke, Saartje. 2012. *Alignment and ergativity in New Indo-Aryan languages*. Berlin-New York: Mouton de Gruyter.
Verbeke, Saartje. 2018. *Argument structure in Kashmiri*. Leiden and Boston: Brill.
Yoshioka, Noboru. 2012. *A reference grammar of eastern Burushaski*. University of Tokyo. Available online at http://repository.tufs.ac.jp/handle/10108/72148.

Andrea Drocco

An attempt to understand the encoding of reduced transitivity in Hindi: the case of compound verbs with *jānā*

Abstract: Since the 1960s, significant attention has been paid to the categorization and development of the so-called New Indo-Aryan 'compound verbs', albeit to different degrees in different languages. Thanks to the work of several scholars, we possess numerous investigations into the phenomenon, especially in respect to Hindi. Many analyses have been devoted to the semantic contrast between simple and compound verbal constructions. However, it is surprising that no significant investigations into the semantic contrast between the use of different vector verbs with the same polar verb have been published. This is especially true of those polar transitive verbs which can be compounded with both transitive and intransitive vectors; for example, *khā lenā* and *khā jānā*. The primary aim of the paper is to discuss the factors involved in this choice and, more particularly, whether these factors are semantic or pragmatic. The analysis is synchronic and grounded in a corpus-based examples taken from modern Hindi sources. It focuses on the polar transitive verbs *khānā* and *pīnā* compounded with the intransitive vector *jānā*.[1]

Keywords: Reduced transitivity, Hindi compound verbs

1 My thanks first and foremost to Giuliano Bernini, Pinuccia Caracchi, Peter Hook, Rajesh Bhatt and Ghanshyam Sharma for their very helpful comments on earlier drafts of this paper. Thanks also to the audience in a) New Haven (Connecticut, USA) at Yale University on the occasion of the workshop 'South Asian Languages: Theory, Typology, and Diachrony', 28-30 September 2012 and b) Lisbon (Portugal) on the occasion of the 32nd South Asian Languages Analysis Round Table (SALA-32), where I have presented earlier versions of this work. I would like also to thank my Hindi mother-tongue informants: Neha Tiwari, Chandra Bhushan, and Mohd Raza Ali. All errors and inadequacies are my own.

Andrea Drocco, Ca' Foscari University, Venice, Department of Asian and North African Studies, Ca' Cappello, San Polo 2035, Venice, Italy. Email: andrea.drocco@yahoo.it

https://doi.org/10.1515/9783110610796-011

1 Introduction

One of the salient innovations in the New Indo-Aryan languages is the use of so-called 'compound verbs' (Masica 1991: 326). Several works, with a focus on Hindi, have been devoted to the semantic and syntactic contrast between the compound and simple verb (see, among others, Hacker 1961, Hook 1974, 1991, Butt 1995, 2001, Butt & Geuder 2001, Butt & Ramchand 2005). However, few studies have addressed the semantic contrast between different vector verbs used with the same polar verb, particularly in respect to those polar transitive verbs which are compounded with an intransitive vector. After some preliminary remarks, this paper will aim to determine the semantic and/or pragmatic factors involved in the choice of *jānā* 'to go' as an intransitive vector compounded with a transitive polar verb. First, I will try to demonstrate that in Hindi the use of an intransitive vector verb with a transitive polar verb must be considered the formal encoding of intransitivity (§ 2). I will then summarize the hypothesis of the few scholars who have devoted attention to the topic of the present paper. According to them, the lack of volitionality of the agent is the primary factor involved in the choice of *jānā* as an intransitive vector verb compounded with a transitive polar verb (§ 3). In an attempt to verify the truth of this claim, I will use the well-known parameters of transitivity presented by Hopper & Thomson (1980). Based on these parameters, I will argue that a lack of agent volitionality is not a factor governing the choice of the type of compound verbs considered here (§ 4). Dismissing volitionality as a factor, I will present and discuss synchronic data in order to understand which other factor(s) are relevant. I will argue that these factor(s) are primarily pragmatic (§ 5). The conclusions of the study are presented in the last section (§ 6).

2 The relationship between compound verbs and transitivity in Hindi

First, let me illustrate what is meant by a 'compound verb' in Hindi. According to Hook (2001: 101), "[...] a compound verb (is) a sequence of two verbs AB ('polar A' plus 'vector B') that alternates with A (the 'polar') with little or no difference in meaning, that is a difference not easily translatable into languages which do not have compound verbs ". The principal vector verbs in the modern Indo-Aryan languages are those that, as full lexical verbs, mean 'give', 'take', 'go', 'come', 'fall', 'rise', 'sit', etc. Let us consider the following examples in Hindi, where the non-compound verb *lɔṭā* (cf. 1) alternates with the compound verb *lɔṭ gayā* (cf. 2):

(1) वह दुकान पर लौटा।
vah dukān par lɔṭā.
3SG shop LOC go back.PFV.M.SG[2]
'He went back to the shop.'
(adapted from McGregor 1977: 31)

(2) वह दुकान पर लौट गया।
vah dukān par lɔṭ gayā.
3SG shop LOC go back go.PFV.M.SG
'He went back to the shop.'
(adapted from McGregor 1977: 50)

As mentioned above, the semantic contrast between the compound and simple verb has received significant attention. According to the majority of scholars, constructions like (2) express a perfective aspect in contrast to constructions like (1) (see, among others, Hook 1974, 1991). However, it is rather surprising that no significant research has been conducted to investigate possible combinations of polar and vector verbs. This is especially true in regards to the principle(s) determining which vector verbs may or may not occur with which main verbs and, moreover, the semantic contrast between the use of different vector verbs with the same polar verb. Some exceptions are the studies of Hook (1978), Pandharipande (1981) and Nespital (1997). There are also general remarks found in Hindi grammars; for example, that the vector verbs *lenā* 'to take' (cf. example 3) and *denā* 'to give' (cf. example 4) express a flow of benefit toward or away from the doer, respectively.

(3) कविता पढ़ लो।
kavitā paṛh lo.
poem read take.IMP
'Read the poem to yourself.'
(adapted from Snell 2010: 156)

2 The following abbreviations are used in this article: ACC = accusative; AUX = auxiliary; CP = conjunctive participle; DAT = dative; DIR = direct; EMPH = emphatic; ERG = ergative; F = feminine; GEN = genitive; IMP = imperative; IMPF = imperfective; INSTR = instrumental; LOC = locative; M = masculine; NEG = negation; OBL = oblique; OIA = Old Indo-Aryan; PART = participle; PST = past; PFV = perfective; PRS = present; PROG = progressive; SG = singular.

(4) कविता पढ़ दो।
kavitā paṛh do.
poem read give.IMP
'Read the poem out.'
(adapted from Snell 2010: 156)

Even if infrequent, the most interesting and in some sense atypical constructions (cf. Hook 1976 and Montaut 1991, 2004) are realized with a combination of a transitive polar verb and an intransitive vector. These constructions are very important for many reasons. First, because they change the syntactical status of the transitive construction to an intransitive one. According to some scholars (see, among others, Pandharipande 1981, Kachru 1981 and Mahajan 2012) this is illustrated by the fact that using an intransitive vector verb with a transitive polar one:

(i) changes the canonical perfective case-marking of an original ergative construction; that is, one with an agent-like argument followed by the postposition *ne* and the verb in agreement with the object-like argument (if not followed by the accusative postposition *ko*), to a non-ergative one;
(ii) precludes passivization.

Regarding the first point, the relationship between the presence of the Hindi ergative case-marker *ne* and a compound verb is illustrated by the contrast between different vector verbs with + *ne* polar verbs. In particular, Hindi perfective sentences with compound verbs occur with the agent-like argument + *ne*, only if both the polar verb and the vector verb are themselves used independently with the agent-like argument + *ne* (cf. McGregor 1977: 104), exactly as in (5):

(5) राम ने युद्ध में रावण को मार डाला।
Rām-ne yuddh-mẽ Rāvaṇ-ko mār ḍālā.
Rām.M-ERG battle.M.SG.OBL-LOC Rāvaṇ.M-ACC kill pour.PFV.M.SG
'Rām killed Rāvaṇ in the battle.'
(adapted from Kachru 2006: 89-90)

Thus in (5):

The polar verb *mārnā* 'to kill' [+ *ne*] + vector verb *ḍālnā* 'to pour' [+ *ne*] = agent-like argument + *ne*

In all other instances the Hindi ergative case-marker *ne* is absent, exactly as in (6), with related synthetic explanations:

(6) वह गुस्से में बहुत कुछ कह गया।
vah guss-e mẽ bahut kuč̌h kah gayā.
3SG anger.M.OBL LOC much a lot say go.PFV.M.SG
'He said many things in anger.'
(adapted from Kachru 2006: 87)

Thus in (6):

The polar verb *kahnā* 'to say' [+ *ne*] + vector verb *jānā* 'to go' [+ zero] = agent-like argument + zero

As a consequence, the presence of an intransitive ZERO-argument polar or vector verb is a satisfactory condition for the intransitive status of the whole polar vector verb construction. Therefore:

polar+ ERG + vector+ ERG = agent-like argument + *ne* (Example n. 5)
polar+ ZERO + vector+ ZERO = agent-like argument + ZERO
polar+ ERG + vector+ ZERO = agent-like argument + ZERO (Example n. 6)
polar+ ZERO + vector+ ERG = agent-like argument + ZERO

Regarding the inability to passivize constructions where an intransitive vector verb is compounded with a transitive polar one (cf. example 7) (the second point above), Pandharipande (1981: 165) clearly maintains:[3] "Similarly, verbs such as *kar bɛṭhnā* 'to do by mistake' and *kah jānā* 'to say (something) unintentionally' fail to undergo passive and fail to qualify as transitive verbs."

In addition, the author (1981: 165) quotes the following ungrammatical sentence and states that it "[...] show[s] that the verb *kar bɛṭhnā* fails to undergo passivization":

3 The same seems to hold true according to the most authoritative Hindi grammars as, for example, McGregor (1977), Caracchi (2002), Montaut (1991, 2004) and Kachru (2006).

(7) *उससे सारा काम कर बैठा गया।
*us se sārā kām kar bɛṭhā gayā.
3SG.OBL INSTR whole work.M do sit.PFV.M.SG go.PFV.M.SG
'The whole work was done (by mistake) by him.'
(adapted from Pandharipande 1981: 166)

Based on these remarks, it is correct to assert that (9) is the intransitive version of (8):

(8) उसने काम किया। (*वह)
us-ne kām kiyā. (*vah)
3SG.OBL-ERG work.M do.PFV.M.SG 3SG.M/F.NOM
'He/she did the work.'
(adapted from Pandharipande 1981: 168)

(9) वह काम कर गया। (*उस ने)
vah kām kar gayā. (*usne)
3SG.DIR work.M do go.PFV.M.SG 3SG.OBL-ERG
'He did the work unintentionally.'
(adapted from Pandharipande 1981: 169)

As seen in these two constructions, there are two candidates to be the agent-like and the object-like arguments, respectively; however, they are different in terms of their case-marking system and transitivity. This is due to the fact that in (9) *jānā* is the intransitive vector verb of *karnā*. An important question remains; that is, whether *jānā* in (9) conveys different semantic and pragmatic features to (8). I will introduce this topic in the next section by reviewing some scholars' opinions.

3 Transitive verbs + *jānā* and the lack of the agent-like argument's volitionality: some scholars' view

It is difficult to understand the principles governing the use of a vector intransitive verb with transitive polar verb. This is because, first of all, there are different opinions about the number, status, meanings, and typology of Hindi vector verbs. The two intransitive vector verbs most commonly compounded with transitive polar verbs are *jānā* and *bɛṭhnā*. Due to a lack of research, it remains unclear whether these vectors can occur with every transitive vector verb; this question is beyond the scope of the present paper. Consequently, after a short general introduction about the use of *jānā* with transitive polar verbs, I will focus on *khā jānā* and *pī jānā*. I will discuss them in detail in the following sections, where I will point out that according to the majority of scholars, the intransitive vector *jānā*, when compounded with + *ne* polar verbs, signals a lack of volitionality of the agent-like argument (cf. Pandharipande 1981, Kachru 1981). For example, Kachru (1981: 185) asserts that: "Compounding with *jānā* 'to go' or *bɛṭhnā* 'to sit' negates the volitionality of the main verb, [...]". This seems to be especially true with verbs such as *jānnā* 'to know', *samajhnā* 'to understand', *pahčānnā* 'to recognize', which are neither clearly volitional, nor non-volitional. Indeed Kachru (1981) exemplifies her position by giving the following two examples, with English translations, where the polar verb *samajhnā* 'to understand' is compounded with the vector verbs *lenā* 'to take' and *jānā* 'to go', respectively:

(10) मैंने समझाया तो उस ने सवाल अच्छी तरह से समझ लिया।

mẽ-ne	*samjhāyā*	*to*	*us-ne*	*savāl*
1SG.DIR-ERG	explain.PFV.M.SG	then	3SG.OBL-ERG	question.M

aččhī	*tarah*	*se*	*samajh*	*liyā.*
well	manner	with	understand	take.PFV.M.SG

'I explained and he understood the question well.'
(adapted from Kachru 1981: 187)

(11) उनके बिना कहे ही वह समझ गया कि उन्हें उस की बातें अच्छी नहीं लग रही हैं।

un-ke	*binā*	*kahe*	*hī*
3pl.OBL-GEN.OBL	without	say.PFV	EMPH

vah	*samajh*	*gayā*	*ki*	*unhẽ*	*us*
3SG.dir	understand	go.PFV.M.SG	that	3PL.OBL-DAT	3SG.OBL

kī	*bātẽ*	*aččhī*	*nahī*	*lag*	*rahī*	*hẽ.*
GEN.F	speech.F.PL.DIR	good	neg	like	PROG.F	be.AUX.PRS.3PL

'Without their saying anything, he knew that they did not like what he was saying.' (adapted from Kachru 1981: 187)

Nespital (1997: 557) seems to agree with Kachru's position. He clearly states that in respect to polar verbs denoting the acquisition of knowledge, information etc. the intransitive vector verb *jānā* (as in 11) conveys that the agent-like argument acquired something without any great effort and that the acquisition is/was only superficial. The fact that *jānā* conveys a lack of volitionality of the agent-like argument is also true according to Mohanan (1994). However, this scholar, addressing the idea of conscious choice as the semantic factor conditioning the ergative case on the agent-like argument of a perfective transitive sentence, quotes the following example where *jānā* is compounded with *pīnā* 'to drink'. As we can see, this is unlike *samajhnā* etc.

(12) रवि दवाई पी गया।
ravi *davāī* *pī* *gayā.*
Ravi.M medicine.F drink go.PFV.M.SG
'Ravi (impulsively) drank up the medicine.'
(adapted from Mohanan 2004: 74)

However, is it true that 'volitionality' is the only semantic property of the construction governing the choice of *jānā* as an intransitive vector verb with + *ne* polar verbs, in particular polar verbs that do not denote the acquisition of knowledge, information, etc.? In respect to these polar verbs, is an original transitive construction made intransitive through the use of *jānā* only in those cases where there is a lack of agentivity and thus transitivity? Or, are there other factors involved in this choice? I will try to answer these questions in the following two sections.

4 Transitive verbs + *jānā* and the lack of the agent-like argument's volitionality: testing the validity of the correlation

Transitivity is one of the syntactic phenomena which most directly affects the grammatical encoding of participant roles (cf. Hock 1985: 247); indeed, several syntactic as well as semantic aspects of transitivity have been discussed in the context of language typology, ergativity, relational grammar and causativity (cf. Pandharipande 1981: 161). The large number of studies devoted to this issue illustrates not only that transitivity is a fundamental notion, but also, and perhaps most importantly, that is a very complex category, just like the notions of 'subject' and 'object' inherited from the Western grammatical tradition, which are often problematic when extended to more 'exotic' languages (cf. Lazard 2002, Kittilä 2002, 2006).[4]

4 The complexity of the transitivity notion is raised by Lazard (2002: 150), who explicitly asks in the first page of his work, "What is transitivity?". Furthermore, the complexity of the same notion, especially when used to establish the theoretical framework underpinning various

In order to understand the essential nature of transitivity, some authors have pointed out that if it is true that transitivity was traditionally (and for the most part still is) considered a binary property of a verb (or a sentence), it is also true that, starting from and following the well-known paper of Hopper & Thompson (1980) and others (cf. Tsunoda 1985, Lazard 2002, and also papers included in Hopper & Thompson (eds.) 1982), there is a good amount of evidence suggesting that transitivity is not a simple, discrete phenomenon which is either present or absent. On the contrary, the notion of transitivity must be analyzed as a scalar notion composed of different parameters, rather than a clear-cut dichotomy. Lazard (2002) spoke of 'restricted transitivity' vs. 'generalized transitivity' and proposed a transitivity gradient.[5]

The fluidity of the transitivity category must be adopted for Hindi as well.[6] This has already been demonstrated in the not very recent publications of Bhatia,

---

alignment systems, is also examined in the recent papers of Haspelmath (1993, 2011), Geoffrey Haig (2008, 2009), and Shibatani (1999; cf. also Shibatani & Pardeshi 2001).

5 Lazard (2002) also adds that the typical morphosyntactic encoding of a prototypical transitive construction – prototypical in the sense of the (semantic) parameters advanced by Hopper & Thompson (1980) – is widely used in sentences expressing processes or situations other than prototypical actions, but that this extension is not the same in all languages. The result is that in all languages there is a class of bi-actant constructions which deviate from the prototypical transitive construction in respect to their morphosyntactic encoding. This deviation reflects a difference in semantic transitivity and these constructions are considered morpho-syntactically as 'intermediate constructions'. In the framework of 'restricted transitivity', the intermediate constructions are considered 'intransitive', whereas in the framework of 'generalized transitivity', they are characterized as 'less transitive'. Starting from the fact that example (12), according to the definition given above, is an authentic sentence with a compound verb, I would like to continue my analysis by postulating that this particular type of construction is an 'intermediate construction', which could certainly be characterized as 'intransitive' in the framework of 'restricted transitivity'. Moreover, the same sentence could also be characterized as 'less transitive' in the framework of 'generalized transitivity'. In particular I would like to examine if its status as an 'intermediate construction' reflects a non-prototypical process or action.

6 In the Hindi grammatical tradition, the notion of transitivity has not only a central, but also a special role, because, according to the majority of Hindi grammarians, the difference between transitive and intransitive clauses directly affects, for example, the grammatical encoding of participant roles. As pointed out by Bhatia (1981), the distinct syntactic behavior of transitive and intransitive verbs in perfective sentences was noted for the first time in the Hindi grammar of John Gilchrist (1796). After its publication, the majority of Hindi grammars which distinguished between transitive and intransitive sentences usually give, as a valid criteria, the fact that Hindi (at least Modern Standard Hindi) only marks the "subject" of transitive clauses (in this paper the 'agent-like argument') with the postposition *ne*, now generally classified and glossed as the ergative case-marker. Within this framework a verb is considered transitive if, in the perfective aspect, the agent-like argument is followed by *ne*. According to some linguists, this approach of

Kachru and Pandharipande, which appeared in the Fall 1981 issue of *Studies in the Linguistics Sciences*. Some years later, in 1985, a paper of Hock also appeared.[7] These scholars, discussing the various ways of encoding different grades of transitivity in Hindi when it is treated as a scalar notion or as a gradient feature, have concluded that, as in all languages, transitivity in Hindi cannot be defined in terms of only one feature, but rather, as an amalgam of several features. In particular, Pandharipande (1981: 164–165) added that the concomitance of all these features is essential for transitivity in Hindi; consequently, the absence of any one of these can be enough to mark a verb/sentence as intransitive. With reference to the examples given above, this may seem to precisely reflect Hindi constructions with *jānā* as an intransitive vector verb of + *ne* polar verbs if we accept that *jānā* is used to convey a lack of 'volitionality'. That is, in the original transitive construction one feature of transitivity is lacking (i.e. 'volitionality') and thus the sentence is made intransitive through the use of the intransitive vector verb *jānā*. As a result, this particular use of *jānā* seems to be the formal encoding of a process of de-transitivization. Is this a complete answer, or is there something more?

First of all, not all authors agree regarding this connotation of *jānā* as an intransitive vector verb with a transitive polar verb. For example, Nespital (1997: 557), speaking of *khā* + *jānā*, states that this compound verb is, "To emphasize additionally that the action was carried out completely, also in the sense that the object(s) of the action was/were affected/changed/consumed... all (without exception) or entirely, wholly" (cf. also Guru 1978 and McGregor 1977: 100).[8]

Hindi grammars is not entirely correct (cf., for example, Mohanan 1994), since there is not an entirely consistent association between ergative marking and transitivity. Moreover, according to some other authors (cf., for example, Davison 1999), the use of *ne* is conditioned by syntax, not by semantics. In particular, according to Mohanan (2004), this is due to the fact that:
1) there are some verbs that, although transitive, do not employ *ne* after the agent-like argument in perfective sentences (e.g. *lānā* 'to bring', *bhūlnā* 'to forget') and 2) moreover, some intransitive verbs can optionally employ the postposition *ne* (e.g. *nahānā* 'to take a bath', *bolnā* 'to speak', *samajhnā* 'to understand').

7 Kachru's and Pandharipande's papers primarily addressed the pragmatic factors which govern transitivity-sensitive processes; Bhatia concentrated on the ergative; and Hock examined the extent to which lexical features may affect transitivity.

8 Moreover, Nespital adds that *jānā* as a second member with *kahnā* is used "To point out additionally that the actor performed an action, very often a speech act, at the time of going or leaving e.g.: *kah jānā* [...] to say (s.th) (to s.o.) (at the time of going away or leaving)". It is interesting to note that McGregor (1993: 750b) in his entry for the verb *bolnā* defined the compound verb *bol jānā* as 'to leave a word with someone'.

Regarding the hypothetical connection between the lack of the agent's volitionality and the presence of *jānā* as an intransitive vector verb compounded with a polar transitive one, I would like to report, provisionally, the following example analysed with reference to Hopper & Thompson's parameters of transitivity:[9]

(13) राम ने गुलाब-जामुन खाया।
Rām-ne gulāb-jāmun khāyā.
Rām.M-ERG gulab-jamun.M eat.PFV.M.SG
'Rām ate gulab-jamun.'

1. Agent is human (or at least animate).
2. Agent is conscious.
3. Agent has as goal a change in state of patient.
4. Change of state is physical.
5. Agent has ability to effect change in patient.
6. Agent is responsible for the change in patient.
7. Agent is source of energy required.
8. Agent touches patient with self or instrument.
9. Agent succeeds in effecting change in patient.
10. Change of state in patient is perceptible.

Now consider the following variant of (13), where the only difference is that *khānā* is compounded with the intransitive vector verbs *jānā*, which makes the sentence intransitive:

(14) राम गुलाब-जामुन खा गया।
Rām gulāb-jāmun khā gayā.
Rām.M gulab-jamun.M eat go.PFV.M.SG
'Ram ate gulab-jamun.'

The translation, but especially the transitivity score seems to be the same. In fact:

1. Agent is human (or at least animate).
2. Agent is conscious.
3. Agent has as goal a change in state of patient.

9 The following two examples with related explanations were given to me by one anonymous reviewer. His useful comments helped me to go beyond Hopper & Thompson's transitivity parameters.

4. Change of state is physical.
5. Agent has ability to effect change in patient.
6. Agent is responsible for the change in patient.
7. Agent is source of energy required.
8. Agent touches patient with self or instrument.
9. Agent succeeds in effecting change in patient.
10. Change of state in patient is perceptible.

I therefore believe that in this section we have achieved two important results thanks to the analysis adopted. Firstly, it is not always clear if 'volitionality' is the factor determining the use of *jānā* as an intransitive vector verb compounded with a polar transitive one. It seems that even if there is volitionality on the part of the agent-like argument, *jānā* can be used. Secondly, there is some other factor(s) governing this use of *jānā* which is not included in Hopper & Thompson's transitivity parameters. This factor, perhaps, is governed by a Hindi transitivity category.

At this point, I will address these two points by adopting a synchronic perspective of data taken from contemporary Hindi sources (cf. 5).

5 Transitive verbs + *jānā*: in search of a pragmatic approach

Based on Hindi synchronic data and following the remarks of the previous section, we can start our analysis with a question. If the combination of a transitive polar verb with the intransitive vector verb *jānā* is used to signal the lack of the specific semantic parameter of 'volitionality', why, in modern Hindi texts, do constructions like (15) appear? Indeed, in this construction, the transitive vector verb *lenā* is used with the transitive polar verb *pīnā* with an agent-like non-human animate argument, that is, with an argument certainly not high in the hierarchy of animacy.

(15) बिल्ली ने [...] सारा दूध पी लिया।
billī ne [...] *sārā dūdh pī liyā.*
cat.F-ERG all milk.M drink take.PFV.M.SG
'The cat [...] has drunk all the milk.'
(*Jñāna Sarovara* p. 9)

We can suppose that in this construction *billī* (= 'cat'), even if an animate non-human, has some sort of volitionality. But if so, why can we not assume the same sort of volitionality for (16) below?

(16) हलवाई का दूध बिल्ली पी गई। [...]

halvāī	*kā*	*dūdh*	*billī*	*pī*	*gaī.* [...]
sweet-maker	GEN.M.SG	milk.M	cat.F	drink	go.PFV.F.SG

'The cat has drunk the confectioner's milk.'
(adapted from: http://www.svyambanegopal.com/अनुवाद-आजाद-कथा-भाग-3-लेख)

I think the analysis should be more subtle, trying to go beyond a single parameter and in particular beyond the single parameter of volitionality.

As I already mentioned in summary above, this paper will examine the + *ne* polar verbs *khānā* 'to eat' and *pīnā* 'to drink', primarily because the compound verbs *khā jānā* and *pī jānā* appear very frequently in the texts examined. The relatively high frequency of *khā jānā* and *pī jānā* is also evidenced by the fact that Hindi grammars and/or Hindi linguistic studies frequently employ these verbs to exemplify constructions with + *ne* polar verbs compounded with the intransitive vector verb *jānā*. Furthermore, I would like to add that Masica (1976: chapter 5) considers the so-called 'ingestive' verbs (as, for example, to eat and to drink) to be "[...] occupying a halfway station between intransitives and transitives [...]". Can we therefore assume that a possible explanation for the fact that in Hindi *khānā* and *pīnā* are compounded with *jānā* is a result of their intransitive, or less transitive, behavior? Recently Næss (2007: Chapter 4) dedicated an entire chapter of her book on Prototypical Transitivity to analyzing the morpho-syntactic encoding, with related semantic features, of 'eat' and 'drink' expressions, focusing on the notion of 'affected agent'. So, even if *khānā* and *pīnā* and related verbs, when non-compounded, exhibit prototypically transitive patterns, could the notion of 'affected agent' help us to understand the use of *khā jānā* and *pī jānā*? Hook (1985), discussing the meaning of centripetal verbs such as 'eat', 'drink', etc., argued that their compounding with the vector *denā* 'to give' is not possible; *lenā* 'to take', on the other hand, is possible, and is used semantically as a least-marked vector in compounds. According to the same author, *lenā*, when used as vector, conveys the semantic feature of the action being done for the benefit of the agent; this is especially true for verbs like *khānā*, *pīnā*, etc. However, there are many other shades of meaning that these verbs can express. For example, sentences with *khānā* and *pīnā* can express a process or action which is 1) performed 'for the benefit of the agent'; or 2) a performance seen as different from the 'performance for the benefit of the agent'. In greater detail a 'performance' a) that is ‘a bad performance for the benefit of the agent’, b) seen as ‘a bad performance for the benefit of the agent’, but also c) seen as a ‘bad performance from the point of view of the speaker, irrespective of the benefit of the agent’.

Is it in one of these circumstances that *jānā* is used as a vector verb with *khānā* and *pīnā*? First, let’s look at some examples reported by few scholars who have recently examined this type of construction. These authors attempted to go beyond the analysis which only considers the semantic parameter of agent volitionality. However, I want to stress that the majority of the following arguments are the result of examples taken directly from authentic material: Hindi literary texts, newspapers, magazines and blogs found on the Internet.

In the context of the above remarks, let us consider example (17) from Montaut (2004):

(17) मैं ज़रूरत से ज़्यादा खा गया, पेट फूल गया, झपकी लग गई।

mɛ̃	*zarurāt*	*se*	*zyādā*	*khā*	*gayā,*	*peṭ*
1SG.DIR	need	than	more	eat	go.PFV.M.SG	belly

phūl	*gayā,*	*jhapkī*	*lag*	*gaī.*
swell	go.PFV.M.SG	doze	be attached	go.PFV.F

‘I ate (gulped) more than needed, my belly swelled up, I felt sleepy.’
(adapted from Montaut 2004: 126)

In this construction, there is no evidence to suggest the non-volitionality of the agent-like argument, but it is impossible to be certain without context. However, a possible explanation is that, in (17), *jānā* is used because the author, instead of expressing the regular act of eating, wished to emphasize a particular effect of the act on the agent-like argument. With the use of *zarurāt se zyādā*, ‘more than needed’, the action of *khānā* ‘to eat’ results in an unintended, unwanted, unpleasant, unexpected, and irrevocable effect. This result is in fact explicitly mentioned in the same sentence with the expression *peṭ phūl gayā, jhapkī lag gaī* ‘(my) belly swelled up, (I) felt sleepy’. Perhaps, due to this emphasis, and in consideration of the ideas of Masica (1976: chapter 5) and Næss (2007: chapter 4) on ‘ingestive verbs’ discussed above, the agent became an affected agent, a sort of semi-patient. Is the construction made intransitive through *jānā* for this reason? To answer this question, it is necessary to look at other similar sentences in context. First, though, let us consider another example from Montaut (2004):

(18) महिला एक ही साँस में पानी पी गई।

mahilā	*ek*	*hī*	*sā̃s*	*mẽ*	*pānī*	*pī*	*gaī.*
woman.F	one	just	breath	LOC	water.M	drink	go.PFV.F

'The woman gulped all the water in a single breath.'
(adapted from Montaut 2004: 181)

No context is provided for this sentence; however, the use of the expression *ek hī sā̃s mẽ* 'in a single breath' accords with the use of *jānā* as vector for *pīnā*. Moreover, it is worth noting that in (17) the agent-like argument and the speaker are the same, while in (18) they are different. As I will show, this is an important aspect of this analysis.

In order to better understand the features governing the use of *jānā* as vector verb for *khānā* and *pīnā*, it would be useful to examine similar sentences found in authentic Hindi sources; that is, as mentioned above, not only in literary texts, but also in newspapers, magazines and blogs found on the Internet. This will allow for an examination of the sentences in context.

First, let us have a look at (19), which is similar to example (18). This sentence is taken from *Godān*, a well-known novel of Premchand, who is one of the most celebrated Hindi-Urdu writers of the Indian subcontinent.

(19) उन्होंने ग्लास ले लिया और सिर झुकाकर एक साँस में पी गए।

unhõ-ne	*glās*	*le*	*liyā*	*ɔr*	(*ve - zero*)
3pl.OBL-ERG	glass.M	take	take.PFV.M.SG	and	[...]

sir	*jhukā-kar*	*ek*	*sā̃s*	*mẽ*	*pī*	*gae.*
head	bow.CP	one	breath	LOC	drink	go.PFV.M.pl

'He took the glass, bowed (his) head [...] drank down (the liquor) in one breath [...]' (Premchand, *Godān*, chapter 6)

In order to understand why *pī gae* is used in sentence (19), it is important to note the use of the expression *sā̃s mẽ* 'in (one) breath', as in the previous example. Unlike the previous example, we are able to consider the sentence's context. In (19) the referent of the agent-like argument (*unhõne*, ve) is Paṇḍit Oṃkārnāth, who, on account of his religious views, generally abstains from alcohol, but in these particular circumstances he finds himself unable to refuse. In the context of chapter 6 of *Godān*, where the sentence is found, the agent-like action can be said to lack complete volition. However, I would like to advance another hypothesis. Perhaps in (19) the use of *jānā* as the vector verb for *pīnā* is attributable to the speaker's attitude, who in the context of the sentence is the narrator. Is the vector verb used to express the narrator's negative feelings toward the action done by the agent-like argument? I think this is the case. In fact, the majority of examples I have found share this pragmatic feature and, moreover, in each of them the semantic features of the sentence are less important. In some cases, the speaker and the patient-like argument are the same because a 1st personal pronoun as in the following example:

(20) चूहे ने सोचा मैं बाहर निकला तो बिल्ली मुझे खा जाएगी।
čūhe-ne sočā mẽ bāhar
mouse.M-ERG think.PFV.M.SG 1SG.DIR outside
nikl-ā to billī mujhe khā jāegī.
come out.PFV.M.SG then cat.F. 1SG.OBL.ACC eat go.3SG.FUT.F
The mouse thought: "If I come out, the cat will eat me."
(http://www.nyu.edu/gsas/dept/mideast/hindi/stories/mouse.html)

In (20), *jānā* again expresses a negative attitude toward the act of eating from the point of view of the speaker, who, as the patient-like argument, is certainly not interested in 'the performance for the benefit of the agent', in this case, 'the cat'. I argue that what was suggested above is further strengthened by the analysis of analogous constructions taken from on-line newspapers and magazines. Let's consider some examples.

(21) चीन के एक अजीबोगरीब मामला सामने आया है। चीन के शेंगडॉन्ग प्रांत में एक शख्स अपनी पत्नी की नाक काटकर सिर्फ इसलिए खा गया, क्योंकि उस की पत्नी ने उस का फोन नहीं उठाया।
čīn mẽ ek ajībogarīb māmlā sāmne āyā
China LOC one bizarre case in front come.PFV.M.SG
hɛ. čīn k-e śẽgḍāng prānt mẽ
AUX.be.PRS.3SG China GEN.M.OBL Shandong province LOC
ek śakhs apn-ī patnī kī nāk kāṭ-kar sīrph
one man refl.F wife.F. GEN.F nose cut-cp only
islie khā gayā, kyõki us kī patnī ne
for this eat go.PFV.M.SG because 3SG.OBL GEN.F wife.F. ERG
us kā phon nahī̃ uṭhāyā.
3SG.OBL GEN.DIR.M.SG phone.M NEG pick up.PFV.M.SG
'A bizarre case came from China. In the Chinese province of Shandong one man cut and ate his wife's nose only because she did not pick up phone.'
(adapted from: http://www.livehindustan.com/news/international/article1-Man-In-China-Bites-Off-Wife-Nose-Eats-It-For-Not-Answering-Calls-494076.html)

(22) मगरमच्छों का एक खौफनाक विडियो सामने आया है, जिसमें एक मगरमच्छ चिड़ियाघर में एक दूसरे मगरमच्छ का पैर खा गया।

magarmaččh-õ *kā* *ek* *khɔphanāk* *viḍiyo*
crocodile.M.OBL.pl GEN.M.SG one creepy video.M
sāmne *āyā* *hɛ,* *jis-mẽ*
in front come.PFV.M.SG AUX.PRS.3SG rel.OBL.LOC
ek *magarmaččh* *čiṛiyāghar* *mẽ* *ek* *dūsre*
one crocodile.M. zoo LOC one other
magarmaččh *kā* *pɛr* *khā* *gayā.*
crocodile.M GEN.M.SG foot eat go.PFV.M.SG
'A creepy video of crocodiles arrived where one crocodile in the zoo ate a foot of another crocodile.'
(adapted from: http://hindi.news24online.com/huge-crocodile-rips-eats-playmate-arm-1/)

(23) अपने पार्टनर की सहमति से यह व्यक्ति उसे खा गया।

apn-e *pārṭnar* *kī* *sahmati* *se*
rifl.M.OBL partner.M GEN.F agreement with
yah *vyakti* *use* *khā* *gayā.*
3SG.dir man.M 3SG.OBL-ACC eat go.PFV.M.SG
'This man had eaten his partner with his consent.'
(adapted from: http://www.gazabpost.com/cannibal-from-germany/)

In the above examples, and in many others found on the Internet, the use of *jānā* as an intransitive vector verb is, again, the formal encoding of the negative attitude (astonishment, shock, etc.) of the speaker or narrator toward the action expressed by *khānā*. Similar examples are found with *pīnā*. In addition to the particular pragmatic circumstances just mentioned, it is interesting to note that, in many examples found in newspapers and magazines, the use of *jānā* as a vector for *khānā* and *pīnā* polar verbs is found in the headings of articles with the agent-like argument positioned as the last word after the verb. Constructions (24) and (25) are typical examples:

(24) माँ का गला काट खून पी गया बेटा।
mā̃ kā galā kāṭ khūn
mother.F. GEN.M.SG.DIR throat cut blood
pī gayā beṭā.
drink go.PFV.M.SG son.M.
'A son having decapitated his mother drank her blood.'
(adapted from: http://www.livehindustan.com/news/national/article1-Odisha-Nabarangpur-boy-murder-mother-Rabi-Jani-slit-his-mother-throat-493560.html)

(25) मछली पकड़ रहे युवक को ज़िंदा खा गया मगरमच्छ।
mačhlī pakaṛ rah-e yuvak ko
fish catch stay.PROG.OBL youth ACC
zindā khā gayā magarmaččh.
alive eat go.PFV.M.SG crocodile.M.
'A crocodile devoured a young man alive while he was fishing.'
(adapted from: http://khabar.ibnlive.com/news/city-khabrain/crocodile-ate-young-man-in-indore-377047.html)

I argue that these two features validate my hypothesis. In fact, the use of this atypical construction in the headings of articles demonstrates a feeling of shock or astonishment. The use of the agent-like argument in the last position of the sentence is another proof of the departure from the quintessential features of a typical transitive sentence.

6 Conclusion

In conclusion, the preceding data support the argument that Hindi *jānā*, as a vector intransitive verb with polar + *ne* verbs, formally encodes reduced transitivity and intransitivity, the latter depending more on pragmatic than semantic factors. Previous studies have suggested that *jānā*, as a de-transitivisation device used with *khānā* and *pīnā* as simple main verbs, is contingent upon the lack of one important feature of the agent-like argument; that is, volitionality. Other studies have speculated that *jānā* is used with the same transitive polar verbs to emphasize what was actually realized by an act in contrast to what was ideally realizable. However, my analysis has shown that *jānā* is used to formally encode the attitude of the speaker or narrator toward the action and its effect. This is the case even when the action is performed deliberately by the agent.

References

Bhatia, T. K. 1981. 'The treatment of transitivity in the Hindi grammatical tradition', *Studies in the Linguistic Sciences*, 11:2. 195–208.

Butt, Miriam. 2010. 'The Light Verb Jungle: Still Hacking Away'. In Mengistu Amberber, Brett Baker & Mark Harvey (eds.), *Complex predicates in cross-linguistic perspective*, 48–78. Cambridge: Cambridge University Press.

Butt, Miriam. 1995. *The structure of complex predicates in Urdu*. Stanford, CA: CSLI.

Butt, Miriam & Wilhelm Geuder. 2001. 'On the (Semi-)Lexical Status of Light Verbs'. In Norbert Corver & Henk van Riemsdijk (eds.), *Semi-Lexical Categories*, 323–370. Berlin & New York: Mouton de Gruyter.

Butt, Miriam and Gillian Ramchand. 2005. 'Complex Aspectual Structure in Hindi/Urdu'. In N. Ertischik-Shir and T. Rapoport (eds.) *The Syntax of Aspect*. Oxford: Oxford University Press, 117–153.

Caracchi, P. 2002. *Grammatica Hindi*. Torino: Magnanelli. (4th edition).

Davison, A. 1999. 'Ergative case licensing in a split ergative language', in Singh, R. (ed.), 1999. *The Yearbook of South Asian Languages and Linguistics*, Tokyo Symposium on South Asian Languages. Contact, Convergence and Typology. New Delhi/Thousand Oaks/London: Sage Publications, pp. 291–307.

Gilchrist, J. B. 1796. *A Grammar of the Hindustani Language*. Menston: The Scholar Press Ltd. (1970 Reprint).

Guru, K.P. 1978. *Hindi vyākaraṇa*. Vārāṇasī: Nāgarīpracāriṇī Sabhā. (XII ed.).

Hacker, P. 1961. 'On the problem of a method for treating the compound and conjunct verbs in Hindi', *Bulletin of the School of Oriental and African Studies* 24.484–516.

Haig, G. 2008. Alignment change in Iranian languages: a construction grammar approach. Berlin/New York: Mouton de Gruyter.

Haig, G. 2009. 'Non-canonical subjects and alignment change – where's the connection?'. Lecture at the Workshop: Reconstructing Alignment Systems. University of Bergen, Norway, May 14–15, 2009.

Haspelmath, M. 1993. *A grammar of Lezgian*. (Mouton Grammar Library, 9). Berlin: Mouton de Gruyter.

Haspelmath, M. 2011. 'On S, A, P, T and R as comparative concepts for alignment typology', *Linguistic Typology* 15. pp. 535–567.

Hock, H. H. 1985. 'Transitivity as a gradient feature? Evidence from Indo-Aryan, especially Sanskrit and Hindi'. In Zide, A. R. K., D. Magier, and E. Schiller. (eds.). 1985. *Proceedings of the conference on participant roles: South Asia and adjacent areas*. Bloomington: Indiana University Linguistics Club, pp. 247–263.

Hook, P. E. 1974. *The compound verb in Hindi*. The University of Michigan: Center for South and Southeast Asian Studies.

Hook, P. E. 1976. 'Some syntactic reflexes of subcategories of agent in Hindi'. In Verma, M. K. (ed.), 65–78.

Hook, P. E. 1978. 'The Hindi compound verb: What it is and what it does'. In Singh, K. S. (ed.), *Readings in Hindi-Urdu linguistics*. Delhi: National Publishing House. pp. 130–157.

Hook, P. E. 1985. 'Coexistent analyses and participant roles in Indo-Aryan'. In Zide, A. R. K., D. Magier, and E. Schiller (eds.). 1985. *Proceedings of the conference on participant roles:*

South Asia and adjacent areas. Bloomington: Indiana University Linguistics Club, pp. 264–285.
Hook, P. E. 1991. 'The Emergence of Perfective Aspect in Indo-Aryan Languages'. In Traugott, E. C. & B. Heine (eds.), *Approaches to Grammaticalization*, Vols. I–II. Amsterdam: John Benjamins, pp. 59–89.
Hook, P. E. 2001. 'Where do Compound Verbs Come From? (And Where are They Going?)'. In Singh, R. (ed.), *The Yearbook of South Asian Languages and Linguistics*, Tokyo Symposium on South Asian Languages. Contact, Convergence and Typology. New Delhi/Thousand Oaks/London: Sage Publications, pp. 101–131.
Hopper, P. J. & S. A. Thompson. 1980. 'Transitivity in grammar and discourse', *Language* 56. pp. 251–299.
Hopper, P. J. & S. A. Thompson (eds.). 1982. *Studies in transitivity*. (Syntax and Semantics 15). New York: Academic Press.
Kachru, Y. 1981. 'Transitivity and volitionality in Hindi-Urdu', *Studies in the Linguistic Sciences* 11:2. Pp. 181–193.
Kachru, Y. 2006. *Hindi*. Amsterdam/Philadelphia: John Benjamins Publishing Company.
Kittilä, S. 2002. 'Remarks on the basic transitive sentence', *Language Sciences* 24. Pp. 107–130.
Kittilä, S. 2006. 'The anomaly of the verb "give" explained by its high (formal and semantic) transitivity', *Linguistics* 44:3. Pp. 569–612.
Lazard, G. 2002.'Transitivity revisited as an example of a more strict approach in typological research', *Folia Linguistica* 36. Pp. 140–190.
Mahajan, A. 2012. 'Ergatives, antipassives and the overt light v in Hindi', *Lingua* 122:3. Pp. 204–214.
Masica, Colin P. 1976. *Defining a Linguistic Area. South Asia*. Chicago: University of Chicago Press.
Masica, Colin P. 1991. *The Indo-Aryan Languages*. Cambridge: Cambridge University Press.
McGregor, R. S. 1977. *Outline of Hindi Grammar, with exercises*. Delhi: Oxford University Press.
McGregor, R. S. 1993. *The Oxford Hindi-English dictionary*. Delhi: Oxford University Press.
Mohanan, T. 2004. *Argument structure in Hindi*. Stanford, CA: Center for the Study of Language and Information, Stanford University.
Montaut, A. 1991. *Aspects, voix et diathèses en hindi moderne*. Louvain-Paris : Éditions Peeters.
Montaut, A. 2004. *A Grammar of Hindi*. Munich: Lincom Europa.
Næss, Å. 2007. *Prototypical transitivity*. Amsterdam: John Benjamins.
Nespital, H. 1997. *Dictionary of Hindi Verbs*. Allahabad: Lokbharti Prakashan.
Newman, J. (ed.). 2009. *The linguistics of eating and drinking*. Amsterdam & Philadelphia: John Benjamins.
Pandharipande, R. 1981. 'Transitivity in Hindi', *Studies in the Linguistic Sciences* 11:2. Pp. 161–179.
Premachanda. 1966. [1936] *Godāna*. Ilāhābāda: Sarasvatī Press.
Shibatani, M. 1999.'Dative subject constructions twenty-two years later', *Studies in the Linguistic Sciences* 29:2, Pp. 45–76.
Shibatani, M. & P. Pardeshi. 2001.'Dative Subject Constructions in South Asian Languages'. In Singh, Rajendra (ed.), *The Yearbook of South Asian Languages and Linguistics*, Tokyo Symposium on South Asian Languages. Contact, Convergence and Typology, New Delhi/ Thousand Oaks/ London: Sage Publications, pp. 311–347.

Snell, R. & S. Weightman. 2010. *Teach Yourself. Complete Hindi*. London: Hodder Education.
Tsunoda, T. 1985. 'Remarks on transitivity', *Journal of Linguistics* 21. Pp. 385–396.
Verma, M. K. (ed.). 1976. *The notion of subject in South-Asian languages*. Madison, WI: South Asian Studies Publications, University of Wisconsin.

Liudmila Khokhlova

Syntactic constraints in modern Hindi

Abstract: The purpose of this paper is to show that some of the Hindi word order rules and controlling properties of arguments described by some authors [T. Mohanan 1990; 1994; Butt 1995] may be applied to prose, but not to poetry. The paper establishes that out of five main constraints on scrambling possibilities in Hindi proposed by Mohanan, only one can be claimed to be universal, i.e. the auxiliary verb in a CP cannot be separated from the main one. One of the constraints suggested by T. Mohanan seems not to be a constraint at all: the nominal component within the CP is free to scramble both in prose and poetry. Three constraints are valid for prose texts, but not for poetry: in poetry the separation of parts of noun phrase does not obligatorily imply the initial position; scrambling of the main and light verbs is allowed; the negative particle may be separated from the verbal predicate. In comparison with prose, poetry allows more NPs to control conjunctive participles. Hence, the important task would be to investigate the reasons why a reader/listener considers certain sentences grammatical in poetry but ungrammatical in prose.

Keywords: Syntactic constraints, scrambling; controlling properties

1 Introduction

The issue of word order and word order flexibility within the basic pattern form the basis for traditional typology. The relative order of the sentential elements (S, O, V), the ordering of noun and adjective, and so on. underlie many language universals (Greenberg 1966).

The basic syntactic structures of simple sentences in modern South Asian languages, as well as case marking and agreement, have been thoroughly described by C. Masica (1991). Most comparative syntactic studies of Western NIA languages have either focused on Hindi/Urdu or used Hindi/Urdu data. Works by Yamuna Kachru, Braj B. Kachru, Tej K. Bhatia (1976), Alice Davison (2004), Miriam H. Klaiman (1979), Annie Montaut (1994, 2004), Peter Hook (1976), and

Liudmila Khokhlova, Institute of Asian and African Studies, Moscow State University, Russia.
Email: khokhl@iaas.msu.ru

https://doi.org/10.1515/9783110610796-012

Liudmila V. Khokhlova (1989), amongst others, are dedicated to understanding the properties of arguments in Hindi/Urdu.

The purpose of this paper is to analyze word order rules and the properties of arguments described by Miriam Butt (1995), Alice Davison (2004), Annie Montaut (2004, 2004a), Tara Mohanan (1990; 1994) and other scholars in order to reveal universal syntactic rules that are valid in all styles of Modern Hindi and 're-stricted' rules that may be applied only to a particular register.

It has been shown by many linguists that Hindi, along with the majority of other South Asian languages, occupies an intermediate position on the continuum of word order freedom (T. Mohanan 1990; 1994), (Butt 1995) etc. The prototypical (canonical, unmarked) word order is SOV. Though the language belongs to the analytic type (the index of synthesis is 1,74–1,82 (Zakharyin 1965)), its word order is considered relatively free (T. Mohanan 1994).

Arguing that the terms 'free' and 'fixed' word order are relative since 'fixed' word order usually exhibits a certain degree of freedom, while 'free' word order usually implies certain restrictions, K.P. Mohanan and T. Mohanan (1994: 158–159) try to give an accurate definition of both terms. They argue that when we exchange the position of two NPs in the English sentence in (1), there is a corresponding switch in the interpretation of theta roles:

(1a) John pinched Bill.
(1b) Bill pinched John.

In Malayalam the same exchange in position does not cause a corresponding switch in the interpretation of theta roles:

(2a) *John* *billine* *ṉuḷḷi*
John-N Bill-A pinched
(2b) *billine* *John* *ṉuḷḷi*
Bill-A John-N pinched
'John pinched Bill.'

The authors suggest using the term 'free word order' to refer to the phenomenon illustrated by Malayalam (2), which contrasts with the term 'fixed word order' illustrated by English (1). However, it is easy to find examples like English (1) in a typical free word order language like Russian:

(3a) *mat'* *l'ubit* *doč.*
mother -NOM=ACC love.PRS.3SG daughter-ACC=NOM
'Mother loves daughter'

(3b) *doč* *l'ubit* *mat'.*
daughter-NOM=ACC love-PRS.3SG mother -ACC=NOM
'Daughter loves mother'

In other paradigms, Nominative and Accusative will have different markings, therefore a change in their positions will not cause a corresponding switch in the interpretation of theta roles, but will be used only for topic-focus change:

(4a) *babuška* *l'ubit* *vnuka.*
grandmother-NOM love-PRS.3SG grandson-ACC
'Grandmother loves (her) grandson.'

(4b) *vnuka* *l'ubit* *babuška.*
grandson-ACC love-PRS.3SG grandmother-NOM
'It is grandmother who loves (her) grandson' or (depending upon intonation) 'It is grandson whom grandmother loves'.

This means that the same device (exchange in NP position) may be used for both the different interpretation of theta roles and topicalization.

K. P. Mohanan and T. Mohanan's definition of fixed contrary to free word order may be made more accurate by saying that in fixed word order languages *all* nominal paradigms belong to the English sentence type (1), while in free word order languages there must exist paradigms of the Russian type (4).

Both free and fixed word order languages have common features concerning the placement of definite and indefinite NPs in a sentence. For example, there exists a strong tendency for indefinite nominals to occur in non-initial position (Clark 1978), while definites have a strong tendency to occur in sentence-initial position (Mona Singh 1994: 230).

In free word order languages, definiteness of a bare NP may be related to its scrambled position. Mona Singh (1994: 217–235) has shown that in Hindi a patient is definite in all scrambled positions, i.e. in all cases where it does not immediately precede the verb.

The degree of word order freedom in a particular language may be determined on the basis of different criteria: the amount of scrambling constraints within a clause, possibility of scrambling across clauses etc.

K.P. Mohanan & T. Mohanan described a wide range of scrambling possibilities both across nonfinite clauses which are arguments of the matrix predicate and also across nonfinite adjunct clauses (T. Mohanan 1990: 11), (K.P. Mohanan & T. Mohanan 1994: 159–160).

I consulted 10 native speakers of Hindi in order to check K.P. Mohanan & T. Mohanan's sentences demonstrating scrambling rules both across clauses and within a clause. Six informants were students of Jawaharlal Nehru University (Delhi), three of them were educated in Hindi-medium schools whereas the other three were educated in English medium schools. Four out of the six native speakers were professional translators from Russian into Hindi whose initial education was Hindi-medium, followed by studies in two languages, namely English and Russian.

2 Scrambling constraints across clauses

2.1 Non-finite clause is the argument of the matrix predicate:

In case of prototypical word order, a non-finite clause being the argument of the matrix predicate usually precedes the latter: in (5a) the non-finite clause *kitāb paṛhne-ko* is placed before the matrix predicate *kahā*:

(5a) आज माँ ने बच्चे से किताब पढ़ने को कहा।
āj *mā̃-ne* *bačče-se* ***kitāb paṛhne-ko*** *kahā.*
today mother-ERG child-ABL book read.INF.OBL-ACC tell.PST.M.SG
'Today the mother told the child to read the book.'
(T. Mohanan 1994: 159–160)

T. Mohanan argues that according to the information structure content, parts of the non-finite clause may be separated and scrambled against the arguments of the matrix predicate. However my informants, even those who were teachers and translators with very good command of Hindi, could find an intonation pattern easily only for 5(b) below, where the direct object of the non-finite clause is placed immediately after the subject and before the adverb of the main clause.

(5b) माँ ने किताब आज बच्चे से पढ़ने को कहा।
mā̃-ne ***kitāb āj*** *bačče-se* ***paṛhne-ko*** *kahā.*
mother-ERG book today child-ABL read.INF.OBL-ACC tell.PST.M.SG
'Today the mother told the child to read the book.'

Sentences (5c) and (5d) below were considered as 'ungrammatical' by four and as 'unnatural' by six informants:

(5c) आज किताब माँ ने बच्चे से पढ़ने को कहा।।
āj ***kitāb*** *mā̃-ne* *bačče-se* ***paṛhne-ko*** *kahā.*
today book mother-ERG child-ABL read.INF.OBL-ACC tell.PST.M.SG

(5d) बच्चे से किताब माँ ने पढ़ने को आज कहा ।।
bačče-se ***kitab*** *mā̃-ne* ***paṛhne-ko*** *āj* *kahā.*
child-ABL book mother-ERG read.INF.OBL-ACC today tell.PST.M.SG

Sentence (5e) was defined as 'artificial' by 6 out of 10 native speakers:

(5e) आज बच्चे से किताब माँ ने पढ़ने को कहा।
āj *bačče-se* ***kitāb*** *mā̃-ne* ***paṛhne-ko*** *kahā.*
today child-ABL book mother-ERG read.INF.OBL-ACC tell.PST.M.SG

My preliminary results show that only one deviation from the prototypical word order is accepted by all Hindi speakers, i.e. the one where the direct object of the non-finite clause is placed immediately after the subject and before the adverb of the main clause, other possibilities of scrambling across Hindi clauses need thorough investigation.

2.2 Non-finite adjunct clause:

In the case of prototypical word order, parts of the adjunct clause are not separated:

(6a) आज बच्चे ने माँ को फूल देकर अपना काम किया।
āj *bačče-ne* ***mā̃-ko*** ***phūl*** ***dekar*** *apnā*
today child-ERG mother-DAT flower give.CONV self's
kām *kiyā.*
work do.PST.M.SG
'Today, after giving the flower to her mother, the child did her own work.'

Out of three scrambling possibilities suggested in (Mohanan 1994: 159–160), all ten informants could easily find intonation patterns to provide cues for parsing in (6b) and (6c):

(6b) आज माँ को बच्चे ने फूल देकर अपना काम किया।
āj ***mā̃-ko*** *bačče-ne* ***phūl*** ***dekar*** *apnā*
today mother-DAT child-ERG flower give-CONV self's
kām *kiyā.*
work do.PST.M.SG

(6c) आज फूल बच्चे ने माँ को देकर अपना काम किया।
āj ***phūl*** *bačče-ne* ***mā̃-ko*** *dekar* *apnā*
today flower child-ERG mother-DAT give.CONV self's
kām *kiyā.*
work do.PST.M.SG

However (6d) was considered 'unnatural' by 8 out of 10 native speakers (despite all attempts to find intonation clues).

(6d) आज माँ को फूल बच्चे ने देकर अपना काम किया।
āj ***mā̃-ko*** ***phūl*** *bačče-ne* ***dekar*** *apnā*
today mother-DAT flower child-ERG give.CONV self's
kām *kiyā.*
work do.PST.M.SG

The reasons for the acceptance hierarchy in (5) and (6) are yet to be investigated using more data. A preliminary conclusion is that scrambling possibilities constraints exist both in sentences where the non-finite clause is the argument of the matrix predicate and in non-finite adjunct clauses.

3 Scrambling possibilities inside a clause

3.1 The prototypical word order rules imply the final position of the constituent N+light verb as in (7a):

(7a) राम ने मोहन पर भरोसा किया।
Rām-ne *Mohan-par* ***bharosā*** ***kiyā.***
Ram-ERG Mohan-on faith.M.SG do.PST.M.SG
'Ram relied on Mohan.' (Mohanan 1994 : 202–203)

According to T. Mohanan, the N in a CP is not a direct daughter of S, but forms a constituent with the light verb and cannot be separated from it. This is why (7b)–

(7d), where parts of the CP change their position in a sentence but are not separated, are grammatical:

(7b) मोहन पर राम ने भरोसा किया।
Mohan-par Rām-ne ***bharosā*** ***kiyā.***
Mohan-on Ram-ERG faith.M.SG do.PST.M.SG

(7c) राम ने भरोसा किया मोहन पर।
Rām-ne ***bharosā*** ***kiyā*** *Mohan-par.*
Ram-ERG faith.M.SG do.PST.M.SG Mohan-on

(7d) मोहन पर भरोसा किया राम ने।
Mohan-par ***bharosā*** ***kiyā*** *Rām-ne.*
Mohan-on faith.M.SG do.PST.M.SG Ram-ERG

According to T. Mohanan, all types of separation of N and light verb make the sentence ungrammatical (7e)–(7i):

(7e) *राम ने भरोसा मोहन पर किया।
Rām-ne* ***bharosā* *Mohan-par* ***kiyā.***
Ram-ERG faith.M.SG Mohan-on do.PST.M.SG

(7f) *भरोसा राम ने मोहन पर किया।
****bharosā*** *Rām-ne* *Mohan-par* ***kiyā.***
faith.M.SG Ram-ERG Mohan-on do.PST.M.SG

(7g) *मोहन पर भरोसा राम ने किया।
Mohan-par* ***bharosā* *Rām-ne* ***kiyā.***
Mohan-on faith.M.SG Ram-ERG do.PST.M.SG

(7h) *मोहन पर राम ने किया भरोसा।
Mohan-par Rām-ne* ***kiyā* ***bharosā.***
Mohan-on Ram-ERG do.PST.M.SG faith-M.SG

(7i) *राम ने मोहन पर भरोसा किया।
Mohanpar* ***kiyā* *Rām-ne* ***bharosā.***
Mohan-on do.PST.M.SG Ram-ERG faith.M.SG

The only possibility for scrambling is topicalization, when the light verb in a CP may be displaced from the CP to the clause initial position for special discourse effects:

(7j) किया राम ने मोहन पर भरोसा।
kiyā *Rām-ne* *Mohan-par* ***bharosā.***
do.PST.M.SG Ram-ERG Mohan-on faith.M.SG
'It was Ram who relied upon Mohan.' (Mohanan 1994: 201)

However, all native speakers I consulted accepted (7e)–(7i). Contrary to (5b)–(5d) above, they easily found intonation clues in (7e)–(7i) that corresponded to topic-focus changes. Some suggested adding the focus marking particle *to* to make the sentence clearer in writing, while all informants considered the intonation correct enough to understand the meaning in oral presentation (7k):

(7k) मोहन पर भरोसा राम ने तो किया।
Mohan-par ***bharosā*** *Rām-ne* *to* ***kiyā.***
Mohan-on faith.M.SG Ram-ERG EMPH do.PST.M.SG
'It was Ram who relied upon Mohan.'

In poetry, scrambling of the nominal component within the CP is very common:

(8) सभी मुझे करेंगे दो, चार को छोड़ कभी-न-कभी प्यार।
sabhī *mujhe* ***karẽge*** *do* *čār* *ko* *čhoṛ*
everybody I.ACC do.FUT.3.PL two four ACC leave.ABS
kabhī-na-kabhī ***pyār.***
sometimes love
'Everybody–with the exception of two-four people–will once love me.' (Raghuvīr Sahay 'Merā jīvan', kavitakosh.org)

The three constraints on scrambling possibilities inside a clause described by T. Mohanan (1990, 1994) and M. Butt (1995) proved to be not universal. It will be shown below that they are valid only for prose texts and may be violated in poetry.

3.2 Scrambling of direct daughters of S

In prose, only direct daughters of S may scramble, while parts of a noun phrase may not. (9a) demonstrates the basic word order adjectives *Anū-kī* and *purānī* which are not separated from the noun *kitāb:*

(9a) इला ने राम से अनु की पुरानी किताब खरीदी।
Ilā-ne Rām-se ***Anū-kī purānī kitāb*** *kharīdī.*
Ila-ERG Ram-ABL Anu-GEN old book.F buy.PST.F
'Ila bought Anu's old book from Ram.'

All deviations from that prototypical word order are ungrammatical in prose:

(9b) *इला ने अनु की राम से पुरानी किताब खरीदी।
Ilā-ne* ***Anū-kī* *Rām-se* ***purānī kitāb*** *kharīdī.*
Ila-ERG Anu-GEN Ram-ABL old book buy.PST.F
(9c) *राम से अनु की पुरानी इला ने किताब खरीदी।
Rām-se* ***Anū-kī purānī* *Ilā-ne* ***kitāb*** *kharīdī.*
Ram-ABL Anu-GEN old Ila-ERG book buy.PST.F
(9d) *इला ने अनु की राम से पुरानी किताब खरीदी।
Ilā-ne* ***Anū-kī* *Rām-se* ***purānī kitāb*** *kharīdī.*
Ila-ERG Anu-GEN Ram-ABL old book buy.PST.F
(9e) *राम से अनु की पुरानी इला ने किताब खरीदी।
*Rām-se ***Anū-kī purānī*** Ilā-ne ***kitāb*** kharīdī.
Ram-ABL Anu-GEN old Ila-ERG book buy.PST.F

According to T. Mohanan, the only possibility to separate a genitive modifier of a noun phrase from its head is to put this modifier clause initially (in the case of topicalization):

(10a) मोहन की आज रात राम किताब पढ़ेगा।
Mohan-kī *āj rāt Rām* ***kitāb*** *paṛhegā.*
Mohan-GEN today night Ram book read.FUT.M.SG

Any other separation of the genitive modifier is ungrammatical (10b)

(10b) *आज रात मोहन की राम किताब पढ़ेगा।
āj rāt* ***Mohan-kī* *Rām* ***kitāb*** *paṛhegā.*
today night Mohan-GEN Ram book read.FUT.M.SG
(T. Mohanan 1990: 202)

However, in poetry the separation of parts of noun phrase does not obligatorily imply the initial position: in (11) below the genitive modifier *jīvan-kī* is separated from the noun *madhuśālā,* but the sentence remains grammatical:

(11) व्यर्थ सुखा डाली जीवन की उसने मधुमय मधुशाला।
vyarth sukhā ḍālī ***jīvan-kī***
invain dry throw-PST.F life-GEN
us-ne ***madhumay madhuśālā.***
he-ERG honeyed Madhushala.F
'In vain he dried honeyed Madhushala'

3.3 Scrambling of main and light verbs

In prose, the order of main and light verbs cannot be scrambled. The prototypical word order in (12a) with the main and light verbs in the final position may be changed for special discourse effects, placing the whole predicate in initial (12b) or medial position (12c).

(12a) अंजुम को गुस्सा आ गया।
Anjum-ko gussā ***ā gayā.***
Anjum.F-DAT anger come go.PST.M.SG
'Anjum became angry.'

(12b) आ गया अंजुम को गुस्सा।
ā gayā *Anjum-ko gussā.*
come go.PST.M.SG Anjum.F-DAT anger
'Anjum became angry.'

(12c) गुस्सा आ गया अंजुम को।
gussā ***ā gayā*** *Anjum-ko.*
anger come go.PST.M.SG. Anjum.F-DAT
'Anjum became angry.'

However, any scrambling of the main and light verbs is impossible in prose: (12d)–(12e):

(12d) *गया अंजुम को गुस्सा आ।
****gayā*** *Anjum-ko gussā* ***ā.***
go.PST.M.SG Anjum.F-DAT anger come

(12e) *गुस्सा आ अंजुम को गया।
gussā* ***ā* *Anjum-ko* ***gayā.***
anger come Anjum.F-DAT go.PST.M.SG. (Butt 1995)

In poetry, scrambling of the main and light verbs is allowed. In (13) the main (*bujh*) and light (*gaye*) verbs are scrambled:

(13) गये बुझ दीप भी सारे।
gaye bujh dīp bhī sāre.
go.PST.M.PL go out light also all.M.PL
'All lights went out.' (Raghuvīr Sahay *Merā jīvan*)

3.4 Positioning of negative particle

In prose, the negative particle always appears to the left within the verbal predicate in sentential negation (Butt 1995).

(14) राम ने मोहन पर भरोसा नहीं किया।
Rām-ne Mohan-par bharosā ***nahī̃ kiyā.***
Ram-ERG Mohan-on faith NEG do.PST.M.SG
'Ram did not rely on Mohan.'

In poetry, the negative particle may be separated from the verbal predicate:

(15) किंतु नहीं फिर राजा ने सुख जाना।
kintu ***nahī̃*** *phir Rājā-ne sukh* ***jānā.***
but NEG again Raja-ERG joy know.PST.M.SG
'But Raja was never happy again.' (Bhawani Prasad Mishra, *Sannata*)

3.5 Scrambling of verbal constituents

The only universal constraint on scrambling possibilities that exists both in prose and in poetry is that the verbal constituents of a CP cannot be scrambled among one another (Butt 1995: 98). The analytic form of the verbal predicate that prototypically occupies the final position in the sentence (16a) may be placed in initial (16b) or medial position (16c):

(16a) अंजुम ने ख़त लिखा है।
Anjum-ne xat ***likhā hɛ.***
Anjum.F-ERG letter.M.NOM write.PFV.M.SG AUX.PRS.3.SG
'Anjum has written a letter.'

(16b) अंजुम ने लिखा है ख़त।
Anjum-ne **likhā** **hɛ** xat.
Anjum.F-ERG write.PFV.M.SG AUX.PRS.3.SG letter.M.NOM
'Anjum has written a letter.'

(16c) लिखा है ख़त अंजुम ने।
likhā **hɛ** *xat* *Anjum-ne.*
write.PFV.M.SG AUX.PRS.3.SG letter.M.NOM Anjum.F-ERG
'Anjum has written a letter.'

However, parts of the verbal predicate cannot be separated (16d)–(16f):

(16d) * अंजुम ने लिखा ख़त है।
* *Anjum-ne* **likhā** *xat* **hɛ.**
Anjum.F-ERG write.PFV.M.SG letter.M.NOM AUX.PRS.3.SG

(16e) * अंजुम ने है ख़त लिखा।
* *Anjum-ne* **hɛ** *xat* **likhā.**
Anjum-ERG AUX.PRS.3.SG letter.M.NOM write.PFV.M.SG

(16f) * अंजुम ने ख़त है लिखा।
* *Anjum-ne* *xat* **hɛ** **likhā.**
Anjum-ERG letter.M.NOM AUX.PRS.3.SG write.PFV.M.SG

4 Controlling properties of NPs

Hindi, like other Western NIA languages, demonstrates role-oriented controlling properties of NPs (Montaut 2004, Khokhlova 2016). Conjunctive participles in Hindi are controlled by Agent, Experiencer and Possessor (Kachru et al 1976; Klaiman 1979; Khokhlova 1989):

4.1 Agent

(17) घर आकर उसने रोशनी जलाई।
ghar ākar us-ne rośnī jalāī.
home come.ABS he-ERG light turn on.PST.F.SG
'Having come home he turned on the light.'

4.2 Passive Agent

(18) घर पर बैठकर उससे खाना नहीं बनाया जाता।
ghar-par bɛṭhkar us-se khānā nahī̃ banāyā jātā.
home-at sit.ABS he-ABL food NEG prepare.PRS.PASS.M.SG
'Sitting at home he does not feel like preparing food.'

4.3 Experiencer

(19) यह कहानी सुनकर दूसरी पसंद नहीं आएगी।
yah kahānī sunkar dūsrī pasand nahī̃ āegī.
this story hear.ABS another taste NEG come.FUT.F.SG.
'Having heard this story another story will not please him.'

4.4 In rare cases it may be controlled by the Agent of the embedded clause predicate

(20) डाकू महल में घुसा ... घोड़ा चुराकर निकलते समय राजा वहाँ आ पहुँचा।
ḍākū mahal-mẽ ghusā... ghoṛā čurākar.
robber palace -in penetrated... horse steal.CONV
nikalte samay Rājā vahā̃ ā pahũčā
go out.IMPFV.OBL time Raja there come arrive.PST.M.SG
'The robber penetrated into the palace...Having stolen the horse, at the time of coming out the king... arrived there.'

Some informants expressed doubts about the acceptability of (20), but these doubts must be groundless as the text was included in a Hindi manual prepared by the Central Hindi Directorate (Reading Script of Hindi Records/ Cassettes 1981: 45).

4.5 Possessor

(A) Alienable possession:

(21) लगान चुकाकर उसके पास इतना तो बच ही जाएगा कि भूख से न मरे।
lagān čukākar uske pās itnā to bač hī
tax pay.CONV he-near so much EMPH remain EMPH
jāegā ki bhūkh se na mare.
go.FUT.M.SG that hunger of NEG die.SUBJ.3SG
'Having paid off the tax, (there) will remain so much to him that he would not die of hunger.'

(B) Inalienable possession - 'possessor' marked by *kā* postposition and 'possessed' are always connected by 'whole-part' relations (Khokhlova 2016):

(22) उस लड़के को देखकर शिला का दिल तड़पने लगा।
us laṛke-ko dekhkar śIlā-kā dil taṛapne lagā.
that boy.ACC see.CONV Shila-GEN heart palpitate start.PST.M.SG
'Having seen that boy, Shila's heart started palpitating.'

In verse, 'possessor' marked by *kā* postposition and 'possessed' are not necessarily in 'whole-part' relations:

(23) रानी का हँसकर सुन पड़ता था ताना।
Rānī-kā hãskar sun paṛtā thā tānā.
Rani-GEN smile.CONV hear fall.PST.IND mockery
'Smiling rani's mockery was heard.' (Bhavani Prasad Mishra, *Sannātā*)

5 Conclusion

Out of five main constraints on scrambling possibilities in Hindi described by T. Mohanan only one proved to be universal: the verbal constituents of a CP (i.e. participle and auxiliary verb) can never be scrambled among one another.

One of the constraints suggested by T. Mohanan seems not to be a constraint at all: the nominal component within the CP is free to scramble both in prose and poetry. Three constraints are valid for prose texts, but not for poetry: in poetry the separation of parts of noun phrase does not obligatorily imply the initial position; scrambling of the main and light verbs is allowed; the negative particle may be separated from the verbal predicate. In comparison with prose, poetry allows more NPs to control conjunctive participles.

The crucial question to be answered is: what makes the readers/listeners of poetry accept and consider grammatical sentences they would have rejected as ungrammatical in prose? The syntactic analysis given above demonstrates that studies of word order, NP's controlling properties and of syntax in general demand consideration of a broad corpus of text types, including poetic ones, in order to discover the entire range of syntactic possibilities. Poetic texts have their own specificity in ergative alignment, case marking, usage of tense forms, etc. that are yet to be investigated thoroughly.

References

Butt, Miriam. 1995. *The Structure of Complex Predicates in Urdu*. CSLI Publications. Stanford, California.

Clark, Eve. 1978. Locationals: Existential, locative and possessive constructions. In J. H. Greenberg (ed.), *Universals of human language*, vol. 4. Stanford, CA: Stanford University Press.

Davison, Alice. 2004. Non-nominative subjects. In P. Bhaskararao & K. V. Subbarao (eds.) *Hindi-Urdu. VP structure and case parameters* Vol.1, 141–168. Amsterdam/Philadelphia: John Benjamins Publishing Company.

Hook, Peter. 1976. Some Syntactic Reflexes of Sub-Categories of Agent in Hindi. In M. K. Verma (ed.), *The Notion of Subject in South Asian Languages*, 65–78. Wisconsin: University of Wisconsin, Department of South Asian Studies Publication Series.

Greenberg, John. 1966. Some Universals of Language with Particular Reference to the Order of Meaningful Elements. In J. H. Greenberg (ed.), *Language Universals, with Special Reference to Feature Hierarchies*, 73–113. The Hague: Mouton.

Kachru, Braj, Yamuna Kachru & Tej K. Bhatia. 1976. The Notion <Subject>. A Note on Hindi-Urdu, Kashmiri and Punjabi. In M. K. Verma (ed.), *The Notion of Subject in South Asian Languages*. Wisconsin: University of Wisconsin, Department of South Asian Studies Publication Series.

Khokhlova, Luidmila.V. 1989. Subject properties of NPs in Western NIA languages. *Papers of Moscow State University*, Series 13, N 4: 34–45. (in Russian)

Khokhlova, Liudmila V. 2016. Ergative alignment in Western New Indo-Aryan languages from a historical perspective. In E. Dahl & K. Stronsky (eds.), *Indo-Aryan Ergativity in Typological and Diachronic perspective*, 165–200. Amsterdam/Philadelphia: John Benjamins Publishing Company.

Klaiman, Miriam. 1979. On the Status of the Subjecthood Hierarchy in Hindi. *IJDL*, vol.8, N 1: 15–31

Masica, Colin. A. 1991. *The Indo-Aryan Languages*. Cambridge: Cambridge University Press.

Mohanan, Tara. 1990. *Argument Structure in Hindi*. Stanford: CSLI Publications. Dissertations in Linguistics Series.

Mohanan, Karuvannur. P. & Tara Mohanan. 1994. Issues in Word Order in South Asian Languages: Enriched Phrase Structure or Multidimensionality. In Miriam Butt, Trasy Holloway

King & Gillian Ramchand (eds.) *Theoretical perspectives on Word Order in South Asian Languages*, 153–183. Stanford: CSLI Publications.

Mohanan, Tara. 1994. Case OCP: A Constraint on Word Order in Hindi. In Miriam Butt, Trasy Holloway King & Gillian Ramchand (eds.) *Theoretical perspectives on Word Order in South Asian Languages*, 185–215. Stanford: CSLI Publications.

Montaut, Annie. 2004. *A Grammar of Hindi*. Lincom Europa.

Montaut, Annie. 2004a. Oblique main predicates in Hindi as localizing predication. In P. Bhaskararao & K. V. Subbarao (eds.) *Hindi-Urdu. VP structure and case parameters* Vol.1, 141–168. Amsterdam/Philadelphia: John Benjamins Publishing Company.

Singh, Mona. 1994. Thematic Roles, Word Order, and Definiteness. In Miriam Butt, Trasy Holloway King & Gillian Ramchand (eds.) *Theoretical perspectives on Word Order in South Asian Languages*, 217–235. Stanford: CSLI Publications.

Zakharyin, B. 1965. Hindi typology. In *Narody Azii I Afriki*, N5: 127–134. (in Russian)

Ghanshyam Sharma

A pragmatic account of directive strategies in Hindi

Abstract: The paper presents a pragmatic account of different directive strategies a speaker adopts when issuing commands in Hindi. It takes a pragmatic approach to analyze not only the canonical form of the Hindi imperative but also other sentence types which are employed to express directive illocutions. Furthermore, in analyzing the data to establish links between a linguistic unit and the illocution thereby conveyed, the paper takes a 'form-to-illocution' viewpoint rather than adopting the opposite entrenched 'illocution-to-form' approach. It does this by investigating various Hindi sentence types which are employed in diverse directive strategies to convey deontic modal meaning. The paper presents a modal account of various directive strategies in Hindi.

Keywords: Directive strategies, Hindi imperatives, obligation, deontic modality

1 Preliminaries

Although the imperative has been a topic of grammatical investigation for millennia, some recent trends in linguistics and philosophy have given it further dimensions, thus making it a part of an all-inclusive term – namely, the directive. Such a term is meant to cover a wide variety of commands issued by the speaker (hereafter S, wherever possible) to make the hearer or the addressee (hereafter H, wherever possible) carry out a desired action (hereafter X, wherever possible). The paper analyzes not only the canonical form of the imperative in Hindi but also some other sentence types which are typically employed by S to issue different types of commands and to make requests, pleas and suggestions.

Before analyzing various Hindi sentence types and making an attempt at uncovering their modal meaning according to their role in diverse directive strategies, it would be appropriate, however, to limit our scope and define some of the terms employed in the present study. Put more succinctly, by canonical imperative we mean a sentence in what we are accustomed to call the imperative mood

Ghanshyam Sharma, Institut national des langues et civilisations orientales, 65 rue des Grands Moulins, Paris, France. Email: hindi.paris@gmail.com

https://doi.org/10.1515/9783110610796-013

(Palmer 2001: 80), loaded with S's command directed to a second person H (Aikhenvald 2010: 18; Birjulin & Xrakovskij 2001: 5). In this study, all other Hindi sentence types lacking the imperative mood used by the S to issue commands are classified as 'non-canonical imperatives', even if they are directed to a second person addressee and carry to varying degree elements of deontic necessity or deontic possibility. Hence, a Hindi command containing an infinitive falls under the 'non-canonical imperative' class, even though – similar to a canonical imperative – it carries the deontic necessity element, albeit with a deferred time reference. Likewise, other commands containing either a subjunctive or imperfective verb form are classified as 'non-canonical imperative' since they lack imperative mood marking. In addition, some other sentence types through which S reminds H of her/his obligations are also analyzed for their role in directive strategies.

Given that the aim of this study is to describe modal meaning of selected Hindi sentence types for their standard use in diverse directive strategies, no attempt thus will be made to describe either third person-oriented commands (i.e. jussives) or first person-oriented commands (i.e. hortatives). In addition, the paper does not aim to present an exhaustive list of all Hindi sentence types which can be employed to issue directives nor does it intend to uncover different types of directives such as willful and non-willful directives, commissive directives, expressive directives, etc. as investigated in Van Olmen (2011: 41–50).

Furthermore, for a pragmatic analysis of Hindi directive strategies, the paper intends to adopt a 'form-to-illocution' approach rather than the opposite 'illocution-to-form' approach developed by a number of scholars.[1] In other words, rather than conducting an empirical survey of the frequency of their uses, the paper instead intends to investigate major Hindi sentence types which typically express directive illocution, theorizing certain elements of an ideal conversational setting in which they are supposed to be employed. The term 'modal meaning' is treated

1 De Clerck (2006) and Van Olmen (2011) meticulously put forward a theory which can roughly be termed as 'illocution-to-form theory' which requires serious consideration in any typological research on imperatives. However, for various reasons, a slightly different approach is attempted in this study. Firstly, there is a shortage of a wide all-representative Hindi corpus to test any scientific hypothesis with. Secondly, there are some inconsistencies in the speech act terminology which does not help dredge up essential semantic elements of utterance meaning: for example, 'I'm hungry' (an assertion), 'I will never forget your help' (commissive), 'May God bless you!' (expressive), etc. may all be employed by S to issue the same directive illocution. Thirdly, it is believed that by strictly adopting illocution-to-form approach, one must consider not only the imperatives, but all sentences types which can be employed by S to convey a directive illocution: assertive (i.e. I'm hungry!), interrogatives (i.e., Could you open the door?), expressive (Oh, it is too hot in here!), etc.

here as that part of utterance meaning which S – either overtly or covertly – necessarily attaches to its inherent proposition in any normal conversational setting. Thus, in making an assertion such as "John lives in Paris", S attaches to its propositional content the following meaning: "for all I know I communicate to you that it is necessarily true" that "John lives in Paris", or to put it symbolically, $K_s\Box P$[2] (P = John lives in Paris). Similarly, in issuing a command through a canonical imperative such as "Read it!", S attaches to its propositional content a directive modal meaning such as the following: "for all I want I tell you/ demand" that "You necessarily do X": $W_s\Box!X$ (i.e. You necessarily accomplish X). Hence, to some extent, modal meaning is comparable to the concept of illocution – as conceived in the speech act theory – but at the same time quite different from it: illocution is an overlay which may contain numerous sentences whereas modal meaning is S's meaning assigned to each and every sentences. Finally, although a number of interesting studies have developed a parallel line of research in illocutionary logic[3] as well as in formal semantics,[4] the paper seeks to develop a different formal-functional line of research focusing mainly on the linguistic forms employed in different directive strategies by Hindi speakers.

2 Elements of directive strategies in Hindi

2.1 Pronominal reference

Most Hindi grammar texts provide a sketchy discussion of the distribution of the second person pronoun in the imperative (Kellogg 1875: 229; Sharma 1958: 82; McGregor 1972: 43; Montaut 2004: 114; Kachru 2006: 78; Koul 2008: 116) as they do not make any distinction between one addressee and more than one addressee. For the purpose of the present paper, it can be stated that depending on the type of relationship S has with H, s/he can choose from three pronominal

2 Symbols used: K_s = 'speaker knows'; K_h = hearer knows; B_s = 'speaker believes'; B_h = 'hearer believes'; $\Box$ = 'necessarily', 'it is necessary that'; $\Diamond$ = 'possibly', 'it is possible that';, !X = 'do X'; $\neg\Box$= negation; ∴ therefore; W = want.

3 Unlike Searle & Vanderveken (1985) who have developed illocutionary logic to study speech acts, it is believed here that illocutions do not tantamount to a sentence, nor even to an utterance of it.

4 The present author considers Huntley's (1984) truth-conditional account of imperative incongruous since the scope of veracity in formal semantic analysis is rather fuzzy: Is it the veracity (i.e. truth-conditions) of the utterance one is making or that of the action yet to be carried out by the addressee?

forms of reference to H to express commands through a canonical imperative, namely: *tū* ('you', intimate) which is a second-person singular), *tum* ('you', familiar or friendly) which is a second-person plural, and *āp* ('you', polite, respectful or formal) which is a second-person plural and has its own distinct plural imperative form. However, if H is treated equally as a single person or more, the following six possibilities – i.e. (i) through (vi) – of the second person Hindi pronoun can be envisaged in natural communication:

(1) Hindi pronouns

	H (one person)	H (more than one person)
Intimate	(i) *tū* 'you'	(iv) *tum* (*log*) 'you all'
Familiar or friendly	(ii) *tum* 'you'	(v) *tum* (*log*) 'you all'
Polite or formal	(iii) *āp* 'you'	(vi) *āp* (*log*) 'you all'

The canonical Hindi imperative marks person and number and consequently the addressee can have all the above mentioned six second person pronominal references, but, as can be seen in the following example, at the level of verbal inflection Hindi exhibits three canonical imperative forms only. For example, in (2), the verb *jānā* 'to go' shows three forms in the imperative mood, namely, *jā* 'go!' (with second person singular *tū*), *jāo* 'go!' (with second person plural and friendly *tum*) and *jāie* 'go!' (with second person plural, formal or polite *āp*).

(2a) ~~तू~~ बाजार जा।
(~~*tū*~~)(i) *bāzār* *jā*
you.2SG.INTI bazaar go.IMP.2SG[5]
'Go to the bazaar [right away]!'

(2b) ~~तुम~~ बाजार जाओ।
(~~*tum*~~)(ii)/ (~~*tum log*~~)(iv), (v) *bāzār* *jāo*
you.2PL.FAM you.2PL.FAM bazaar go.IMP.2PL.FAM
'Go to the bazaar [right away]!'

5 Abbreviations: ACC= accusative; DAT= dative; DIFF= differential; FAM= familiar; FUT= future; IMP= imperative; IPFV= imperfective; INF= infinitive; INTI= intimate; OBL= oblique; PFV= perfective; PL= plural; POL= polite; SBJV= subjunctive; SG= singular; 2PL= second person plural; 2SG= second person singular; 3PL= third person plural.

(2c) ~~आप~~ बाज़ार जाइए।
(~~*āp*~~)(iii)/ (~~*āp log*~~)(vi) *bāzār* *jāie*
you.2PL.POL you.2PL.POL bazaar go.IMP.2PL.POL
'Please go to the bazaar [right away]!'

2.2 Degree of strength of deontic modality

In almost all directive illocutions through which S expresses her/his desire or wishes for the referred agent to perform X, deontic modality is employed. As stated above, the person(s) by whom such a desired action is to be carried out can be any of the following: second person(s) – the imperative; third person(s) – the jussive; or, in monologues, even first person(s) – the hortative. The following taxonomy will show the degree of strength of the deontic modality involved in the various cases:

(3) Conversational settings

	Speaker	Addressee(s)	Referred Agent	Strength of The directive
Situation 1	I (we)	you [SG/PL]	you [SG/PL]	Strongest ↑
Situation 2	I (we)	you [SG/PL]	s/he/they	
Situation 3	I (we)	you [SG/PL]	I/we	
Situation 4	I (we)	I	I/we	
Situation 5	I (we)	I	a/he/they	
Situation 6	I (we)	You [SG/PL]	[none]	
Situation 7	I (we)	I	[none]	↓ Weakest

As discussed elsewhere (Sharma, G. 2000), in situation 1, S wants the addressee(s) to perform X because the addressee in this case is also the intended agent of X. In situation 2, it is the third person(s) who should carry out X, while in situations 3 and 4 the first person(s) should accomplish it. Situations 4, 5 and 7 are monologues (in which S is also the addressee) while their respective referred agents differ in having in 4 a self-reference (possibly including others), in 5 a third-person referred agent and in 7 no referred agent at all. Situation 6 has an addressee other than S, but also has no referred agent. For example, a speaker may mutter to her/himself (or enunciate someone else) a sentence such as 'It must rain tomorrow' or 'It should be a hot day tomorrow', without a referred agent existing to carry out any supposed action.

Thus, whether an imperative sentence is an order, request, plea, exhortation or permission depends not only on the pronominal form of reference used to refer to H but also on the conversational setting. Although the pronominal forms of reference are indicators of the kind of relationship between S and H, they are believed to indicate the illocutionary flexibility of the utterance as well; i.e. the selection itself of one of the pronominal forms of reference can render an imperative sentence to exist as an order, request, demand or permission.

3 The first directive strategy: The canonical imperative

The most frequent way of issuing commands in Hindi is to use the canonical imperative, termed also as present imperatives (Sharma, A. 1958: 83), immediate or direct imperatives in the literature. By employing a canonical Hindi imperative, S asks H to accomplish or begin accomplishing a particular act X at the moment of utterance t_n. As explained in (2), this form of Hindi imperative exhibits three distinct verb forms corresponding to the six pronominal forms of reference in the second person described in (1).

3.1 Preparing illocutionary grounds for making a command through the canonical imperative

S issues a command through the canonical imperative – otherwise known as direct or immediate imperative in the literature – at time t_n under any of the following conditions:

(4) a. S wants H to carry out X.
b. S thinks that H is able to produce X.
c. At the moment of utterance, S believes that it is necessary for H to produce X,
i.e. $B_s \Box !X$, and
either $B_s \neg K_h \Box !X$ or $\neg B_s K_h \Box !X$ (i.e. $\Diamond K_h \Box !X$; $\Diamond \neg K_h \Box !X$).
d. S imagines that H's action in carrying out X will either be in H's, or in S's interest, or in the interest of a third party (hereafter TP).
e. At the moment of utterance, t_n, S either knows or believes that either

e'. H has not started action X, and thus S asks H to carry out X at t_n, or
e''. H has already initiated action X at a time t_{n-1}, but the task is still incomplete and so the aim of S's order is to ensure H completes the task at t_{n+1}.
f. At the time of utterance S either knows or believes either that
f'. At the time t_n H is engaged in carrying out action Y that would prevent him from fulfilling X at t_{n+1}, or
f''. At the time in question, H is not engaged in some other activity that would prevent him from immediately undertaking X.
g. If f' is the case, then S asks H to abandon Y and to start carrying out X. Thus, S does not allow H to carry out any action other than X before it is completed.
h. It is necessary for S to carry out the action X:
$\Box !X$ (= H necessarily does X)
$\therefore \neg\Diamond \neg!X$
i.e., it is obligatory that H performs X, and, therefore, it is not possible that H chooses not to undertake X.
i. The possible time lag between t_{n-1} and t_n and t_{n+1} is arbitrary and will depend on some mutual knowledge between S and H; it might be an instant or even a period lasting longer than a year. The accomplishment of the desired action may vary according to the type of verb used. Some verbs (e.g. jump etc.) will of course require only a few seconds for the action to be completed, whereas other verbs (e.g. learn etc.) may last as long as the agent's lifetime.
j. When S issues a command using a direct imperative, S wants H to know that S has a set of beliefs about the addressee and that s/he is interested in seeing the outcome and completion of the desired action.

This is the most common and frequent imperative type in Hindi which, as mentioned above, is employed by S to convey to H commands relating to an action X to be carried out immediately, without any other action Y being allowed before X. In (5a) through (5c), the same directive illocution is evoked to H according to three pronominal references to H.

(5a) (तू) इसे पढ़।
(*tū*) *ise paṛh*
you.2SG.INTI it read.IMP.2SG
'Read it [right away]!'

(5b) (~~तुम~~) (~~तुम लोग~~) इसे पढ़ो।
(~~tum~~)/(~~tum log~~) *ise paṛho*
you.2PL.FAM it read.IMP.2PL.FAM
'Read it [right away]!'

(5c) (~~आप~~) (~~आप लोग~~) इसे पढ़िए।
(~~āp~~)/ (~~āplog~~) *ise paṛhie*
you.2PL.POL it read.IMP.2PL.POL
'Please read it [right away]!'

3.2 The question of a special form of ĀP-class imperative

In addition to the three forms mentioned in (5a)–(5c), the canonical Hindi imperative exhibits yet another imperative form, as in (5d), which is used exclusively with the second person plural – formal, polite or respectful – form of pronoun *āp*.

(5d) (~~आप~~) इसे पढ़िएगा।
(~~āp~~) *ise paṛhiegā*
you.2PL.POL it read.IMP.2PL.POL
'Please read it [right away], will/won't you?!'

This deferential form of imperative (Shapiro 1989 : 89; Shapiro 2003; 268) is in frequent use – more particularly in the eastern variety of Hindi – and is considered as the most polite form of imperative as it indicates an even greater degree of politeness. Some scholars have classified it either as a future imperative (Sharma 1958: 84) or as an imperative which require H to accomplish X at a future point in time (Shapiro 1989: 89; Kachru 1980: 119) – keeping in mind its *-gā* suffix which morphologically marks future tense in the Hindi verb formation. In the present analysis, however, this form of imperative belongs to the class of immediate or direct command – albeit to the class of most polite imperatives – but not necessarily to the class of deferred commands to which we will get in 4. As the acceptability of (5e) and the anomaly in (5f) show, by using this form of imperative S may ask H to accomplish the task immediately rather than at a future point in time:

(5e) (~~आप~~) यहाँ बैठिएगा।
(~~āp~~) *yahā̃ bɛṭhiegā*
you.2PL.POL here sit.IMP.2PL.POL
'Please sit down here [now], will/won't you?!'

(5f) ?? (~~आप~~) यहाँ कल बैठिएगा।
??(~~āp~~) *yahā̃ kal* *bɛṭhiegā*
you.2PL.POL here tomorrow sit.IMP.2PL.POL
'Please sit down here tomorrow, will/won't you?!'

It is worth pointing out that, although by issuing a command through canonical or direct imperatives S is demanding H to perform the task immediately, the accomplishment of it as required by S depends on the type of verb in imperative since the duration of action may vary with respect to the lexical aspect (i.e. Aktionsarten) of the verb employed.

4 The second directive strategy: Deferred imperatives

By issuing a command through deferred imperative, termed by some authors as future imperative (Sharma A. 1958: 84), S asks H to perform X not immediately, but at a future point in time, t_{n+1}. For McGregor (1972: 45), it implies less of an immediate specific request and more to impending events not directly visualized, generalized situations, and precepts, etc. In the present analysis, however, S issues such deferred commands bearing in mind that the location and the point in time at which X has to be carried or both might be different from the location or the point in time of the utterance. Thus, the action required by this imperative is in general performed subsequent to some other actions, whether these actions are a part of the entire process concluding with the required action X, or to any other unrelated actions Y which appear to be independent of action X. However, in some circumstances S may ask H to carry out X at the same place and time. In such cases S will require H to suspend any other actions or tasks (Y, Z), so as to be entirely free to carry out X.

4.1 Preparing illocutionary grounds for making a command through the deferred imperative

While issuing such commands, S will be in one of the following discourse situations:

(6) a. S believes that H can carry out X, and either knows or believes that at the time of utterance is engaged in carrying out some other action Y:

a' H is involved in completing Y, and therefore S believes that it would not be possible for H to bring about X before having accomplished Y. S thus asks H to perform the task immediately after the completion of Y.

a'' H is involved in carrying out Y, and S wants H to interrupt this task and undertake X even before s/he has accomplished Y. S will in such circumstances add certain terms to show politeness, or to express concern that H is already occupied. S may either ask H to try to make an extra effort, or do something special as a favor for S, i.e. using a particle such as *zarā* (just: would you mind ...), etc.

b. S either knows or believes that H is not busy doing anything which may prevent H from carrying out X, but,

c. Whether or not H is involved in any task other than X, S wants H to carry out X at some future moment in time:

c'. Though H is not carrying out an act deemed by S as preventing the completion of X by H, X will still occur either at a different location from the place of utterance or at a distant point in time in the future. H will therefore only be able to carry out X at a future time, and S will not force him to perform it immediately following the issue of the order.

c''. The action will be performed at a different location and S will not be present to check if the task has been fulfilled or not. Thus, H will not be required by S to be responsive, or to report back on the completion of the activity. Any actions will be permissible for H from the time that the command was issued to the moment of the accomplishment of the task.

d. By issuing a command through the 'indirect imperative' S intends for H to know one of the following: (1) that S is not interested in seeing the outcome of the action and leaves it to H to decide whether to accomplish the action or not; (2) in cases where S wants H to abandon the action Y to carry out X, s/he may want to communicate that s/he is interested in seeing the outcome and completion of the desired action.

Thus, the main distinguishing characteristic between the first strategy (i.e. an immediate command through canonical imperative) and the second strategy (i.e. a deferred command expressed through an infinitival verb form) results in the type of world in which H is required to perform X. In fact, in the case of the former S asks H to carry out the action immediately (i.e. in the world in which S has issued a command) whereas in the latter S issues a command to be fulfilled in a deferred world, and this deferred world might be in a different action place or a different point in time. The required action X may even be undertaken at the place of utterance, but in such cases X is going to be subsequent to some other action, say

Y. In all the cases of deferred imperative, the action is deferred to a point in time beyond the time of utterance.

(7a) (तुम) इसे पढ़ो।
(*~~tum~~*) *ise paṛho*
you.2PL.FAM it read.IMP.2PL.FAM
'Read it (right away)!'

(7b) (तुम) इसे पढ़ना।
(*~~tum~~*) *ise paṛhnā*
you.2PL.FAM it read.INF
'You read it (as and when the moment occurs)!'

(7c) (तुम) ज़रा इसे पढ़ना।
(*~~tum~~*) *zarā ise paṛhnā*
you.2PL.FAM just it read.INF
'Would you read it (just now)?!'

Whereas in (7a) – an example of an immediate command – the action desired by S has to be carried out by H at the same place and point in time, in (7b) – which is an example of a deferred command – the actions requested by S must be carried out either at a future time or at a different spot from that where the command is issued. As mentioned above, by selecting this kind of imperative S communicates to H that s/he recognizes that either the task has to be done at a different place or at a later moment (and hence deferred) or is subsequent to some other action Y, which is necessary before X can be undertaken. The concept of different worlds therefore seems to be useful here because in all the cases of deferred imperative the required action has to be carried out in a world which, for various reasons, is different from the world in which the command has been issued. Furthermore, S seems to suggest that since the world in which s/he is present is different from the world in which the action will take place, it will not be possible for her/him to see the outcome of the action. Therefore, it is up to H to complete the undertaking or not.

There are, however, cases where this imperative may be employed by S to ask H to carry out the task in the same world as that in which both S and H find themselves. In (7c), for instance, S invites H to abandon action Y (signaled by the Hindi particle *zarā*) in order to accomplish the task X at the time of utterance. In such cases, the meaning of the imperative derives from S's recognition of H's being busy in some other task. S is well aware of the fact that H is engaged in performing and therefore asks H to interrupt Y and begin X by using the deferred command. The deferment of the action by H in this case is not evident from any situational element and can be understood only in terms of the interruption in the action in which H is engaged.

4.2 Revisiting the difference between the first strategy (immediate command) and the second strategy (deferred command)

As explained above, in addition to differences in preparatory grounds of the two types of imperatives in question, the main distinguishing feature between them is that while in the first type of command S wants to see the outcome of H's undertaking the required task in the case of the second type of command S leaves it to H to carry out the task in a world which may or may not be different from the world in which the command has been issued. Some examples will follow to illustrate the above:

(8a) (तुम) अब मेरे साथ बाजार चलो।
(~~*tum*~~) *ab mere sāth bāzār čalo*
you.2PL.FAM now with me bazaar come.IMP.2PL.FAM
'Come to the bazaar with me [right now]!

(8b) (तुम) *अब/ कल मेरे साथ बाजार चलना।
(~~*tum*~~) **ab/kal mere sāth bāzār čalnā*
you.2PL.FAM now/ tomorrow with me bazaar come.INF
'Come to the bazaar *now/tomorrow with me!'

(8c) (तुम) अब/ *कल यहाँ बैठो।
(~~*tum*~~) *ab/*kal yahā̃ bɛṭho*
you.2PL.FAM now/tomorrow here sit.IMP.2PL.FAM

As can be seen, the presence of a Hindi adverbial *ab* 'now' and *kal* 'tomorrow' makes the deferred commands in (8b) and (8c) anomalous. Both (8b) and (8c) are pragmatically unacceptable in the presence of adverbials *ab* 'now' and *kal* 'tomorrow' since in (8b) the required task has to be completed at a deferred point in time rather than immediately whereas in (8c) it has to carried out immediately.

5 The third directive strategy: Commands through the subjunctive

A very polite way of issuing commands or making pleas in Hindi is to employ a non-canonical imperative which is obtained through the use of the subjunctive or optative (Kachru 2004: 78, 178). With the absence of any imperative mood in it, some authors prefer to call it an 'indirect' command (Sharma 1958: 107). However, such commands are limited to two (out of three) forms of the second person pronoun only – *tum* ('you' familiar or friendly) and *āp* ('you', polite, respectful or formal) – as only the person referred to with one of these two forms is given the possibility of refusing to comply with the command. The person referred to with the singular second person pronoun form – namely *tū* ('you', intimate or subordinate) – is not allowed the right of non-compliance and thus there is no form of command through subjunctive which may refer to this person. The overall picture of the distribution of subjunctive forms can be presented as follows:

(9)

PRONOUN	IMP	SUBJ	COMMAND IN SUBJ
i *tū* 2.SG	*paṛh*	*paṛhe*	----
ii *tum* 2.PL	*paṛho*	*paṛho*	*paṛho*
iii *āp* 2.PL	*paṛhie*	*paṛhẽ*	*paṛhẽ*

It is evident from (9) that as the third strategy to issue commands, H uses a sentence which has a subjunctive verb form and the person referred to with the pronominal form *tū* (intimate or subordinate) is given the possibility of non-compliance of the command. Furthermore, it is apparent that this type of imperatives is always elliptical since either a clause containing speaker's wish, an *if*-clause or even a *then*-clause is missing from it. Such a form can be joined to another clause through a conjunction that, 'I want that ...' as in (10) where to obtain its full meaning the subjunctive form of the clause requires another clause (in brackets) which expresses S's desire that the action referred be carried out by the agent:

(10) (मैं चाहता हूँ कि आप) यहाँ आएँ।
(*mɛ̃ čāhtā hũ ki āp*) *yahā̃ āẽ*
I want aux that you.2PL.POL here come.SBJV.2PL.POL
'(I want that (you)) come here, will/won't you?!'

Other kinds of bracketed elements may comprise those expressing possibility, desirability etc. in a conditional sentence form. In general, the bracketed elements are in the form of an if-clause which is not pronounced, but inferred, though they can also be in a 'then-clause' form. The imperative-in-subjunctive in (11a), for example, can take any of the supplementary elements from (11b) – 'If you wish..', (11c) – 'If it is possible ...' or (11d) – 'It would be nice...'.

(11a) यहाँ आएँ।
yahā̃ āẽ
here come.SBJV.2PL.POL
'Please come here!'
'Please come here if you wish!'
'If it is possible, please come here.'
'It would be nice if you came.'

(11b) अगर चाहते हैं तो ...
agar čāhte hɛ̃ to
if want.IPFV.M.PL aux.PL then
'If you want/wish ...'

(11c) अगर हो सके तो ...
agar ho sake to
if become possible.SBJV.SG then
'If it is possible ...'

(11d) ... तो अच्छा हो/ होगा
... (*to aččhā ho/hogā*)
... then good be.SBJV.SG/be.FUT.M.SG
'It would be nice...'

When S issues commands through the subjunctive, s/he asks H to perform X in the same way as direct commands. Both types share the same preparatory grounds, although in the case of command-through-subjunctive – after providing good reasons for the execution of the action – S still eventually gives H the possible choice whether to perform the action or not. This kind of verbal encoding with the option for H to refuse to undertake act X derives from the understood element (either 'then-clause' or 'if-clause') of the conditional imperative. This attached element is the sole factor that adds an air of politeness to such commands, transforming them from orders into requests. S seems to suggest that it is not obligatory for H to undertake X; nonetheless, it would be nice if H decides to do it:

(12a) $\Box$!X ('obligatorily do X' or 'it is obligatory for you (H) to do X')
(12b) $\neg\Box$!X ('not obligatorily do X' or 'it is not obligatory for you (H) to do X'), i.e.

(12c) $\Diamond X \rightarrow \Diamond !X$, (if it is possible for you (H) to accomplish X, then possibly bring about X), or

(12d) $\neg\Diamond X \rightarrow \Diamond\neg !X$ (if it is not possible for you (H) to accomplish X, then it is possible for you not to do X)[6]

While the immediate commands (discussed in 3) and deferred commands (discussed in 4) are of type (12a), the imperative-through-subjunctive is of type (12b). Thus through a conditional imperative made up of a subjunctive form of the verb, S communicates both (12b1) and (12b2) at the same time. It is this underlying pragmatic string that makes this command special. The pragmatic strings are of two types: one contains an element expressing S's desires that can be joined though the conjunction *ki* (that) to the imperative, as in (13a), and the second is similar to a pure conditional utterance as seen in (13b):

(13a) I want that if P, then Q(!X) at time t_{n+1}.
= 'I want that if it is possible for you to do/ if you like it etc., then do X.'

(13b) If P, then Q(!X) at time t_{n+1}.
= 'If it is possible/ If you like/ etc., then do X.'

To sum up then, the imperative-through-subjunctive in Hindi can have either the if-clause or the then-clause of a conditional sentence.

6 The fourth directive strategy: S's reproach

To express commands through another kind of non-canonical imperative, Hindi employs the imperfective participle of the verb or labeled by some authors as contingent (Kachru 1980: 119). This is a very special way of issuing commands in Hindi in that, similar to the imperative with the subjunctive, it appears to be a residue if-clause of a complete conditional sentence in which the consequent '... *to aččhā hogā* ...' ('... then it would be/would have been nice.') is dropped and the antecedent if-clause '*agar khiṛkī band kar dete* ...' ('if you could/could have closed the window ...') is retained. The full meaning of such counterfactual commands presupposes that H should have already undertaken a required action prior to the utterance, but so far he has not fulfilled the task. S therefore believes that H will

6 Note, however, that only (b1) is deontic. (b2) is permission rather than a command and is essential for (b1)'s realization.

deduce from the utterance that he is still under the obligation to accomplish the task and will possibly carry it out. The pragmatic constraints on this kind of imperative can be summarized in the following way:

(14) a. S believes that H was under the obligation to carry out an action X at a time t_{n-1} (i.e. prior to the time of utterance t_n).
b. S either knows or believes that, by the time of utterance, H has not carried out X.
c. S knows or believes that H either knows or believes that S knows that H has not carried out X, i.e., $B_s/K_s\,B_h/K_h\,K_s\,P$ (where P stands for the proposition 'H has not yet carried out X').
d. S believes that from her/his utterance H will be able to deduce that s/he is still possibly required to carry out X at time t_{n+1}, t_{n+2} or t_{nn}.
e. S believes that by uttering the imperative with an imperfective participle s/he can still persuade H to execute the task.

The imperative with a subjunctive verb form can also be used in conditional senses, though it does not entail the information regarding H's unfulfilled obligation, as is the case of the imperative with imperfective participle or contingent. In fact, in the commands with the subjunctive, S does not intend to inform the addressee that he has not accomplished action X. An imperative of this form follows:

(15) ~~आप~~ खिड़की तो बंद कर देते।
(~~āp~~) *khiṛkī* *to* *band* *kar* *dete*
you.2PL.POL window.F.SG at least closed do.root give.IPFV.M.PL
'If only you had closed the window, at least!'
['you haven't done that'; 'you were and still are obliged to do it'; possibly do it; at time t_{n+1}; in w_1]

This variant of command is dependent upon different types of shared knowledge between S and H, and the actual form expressed will have a different meaning for the person involved. For example, it may be expressed by S as irritation, disappointment, or a rebuke; though at the end of the dialogue S may have modified her/his initial mood towards her/his addressee by conceding something more desired by H.

(16a) (~~कम से कम~~ ~~तुम~~) चाय तो पी लेते।
(~~*kam-se-kam*~~ ~~*tum*~~) *čāy to* *pī* *lete*
at least you tea at least drink.root take.IPFV.PL
'If only you had drunk some tea at least!'
'If only you {would /were to} drink some tea!'
['you haven't carried out X yet'; 'it was required of you';
'you are still obliged to do it'; 'I want you to do it at time t_{n+1} in w_1]

(16b) (~~अच्छा होता~~ ~~तुम~~) चाय पी लेते।
(~~*aččhā*~~ ~~*hotā*~~ ~~*tum*~~) *čāy pī* *lete*
good be.IPFV.M.SG you.2PL.FAM tea drink.root take.IPFV.M.PL
'It would have been nice if you had drunk some tea!'
'If only you had drunk some tea!'
'If only you {would /were to} drink some tea.'
['you haven't accomplished X yet', 'it was required of you', 'I want you to do it'; possibly do it; at time t_{n+1}; in w_1]

Similar to the imperative with subjunctive form of the verb, the imperative with imperfective participle can also have a reading which can express S's desire for H's action.

7 Other verbal strategies

7.1 Directive strategy: Referred agent's obligations

As has been mentioned elsewhere (Sharma 2000: 185–202), in addition to the above mentioned canonical and non-canonical types of imperatives and other constructions employed by S to issue commands, Hindi also allows S to employ three other constructions to express obligations of the agent referred to (AGREF), namely, *ČAHIE* constructions, *PAṚNĀ* constructions and *HONĀ* constructions. At the surface-structure level, the three constructions under discussion are syntactically parallels, inasmuch as all of them demand an agent NP in a dative construction signaled by the postposition *ko* and a VP which includes a verb in the infinitive plus one of the three verbal markers. However, differences can be found with respect to the verbal agreement as each construction shows with the object of the verb.

7.1.1 ČĀHIE constructions: S's advice to H

Through this construction, S after assessing X's utility gives advice to H to accomplish the task X. Its preparatory conditions should be the following ones:

(17) – S wants H to carry out X at time t_n.
– To this end, S utters a sentence containing ČĀHIE
– S does so because s/he believes that for all s/he knows that AGREF 's doing X would be useful/ helpful/ beneficial/ advantageous or even necessary for AGREF or would be in the interest of either addressee, speaker or a TP, or
– On the basis of all what S knows, s/he believes that AGREF 's carrying out X would be an appropriate deed based on the moral obligations required of AGREF.

7.1.2 PAṚNĀ constructions: contra agent's desire

Through this construction S, on the other hand, tells H to accomplish X even though s/he recognizes H's unwillingness to carry out the task. Its preparatory conditions can be summarized in the following manner:

(18a) S desires that H carries out X at time t_n).
(18b) To this end, S utters a sentence involving PAṚNĀ.
(18c) There may or may not be an addressee, and the reference to AGREF may be either the addressee, a TP, or S itself.
(18d) S performs under one of the following conditions:
(i) S/he believes that AGREF will not willingly carry out X.
(ii) S/he believes that AGREF will have difficulties in or will feel uneasy about performing X.

7.1.3 HONĀ constructions: neutral obligations

Through the use of this modal verb, the speaker intends to remind AGREF about her/his intention (or a normal obligation he is under) to carry out action X:

(19) a. S desires H to carry out X at time t_n).
b. S does so under any of the following conditions:
i S is not quite sure whether AGREF still remembers his duty to carry out the action X or s/he is under the impression that AGREF may possibly

have forgotten an action already planned by her/himself or required by some internal or external authority.

ii On the basis of all S knows, s/he believes that AGREF's accomplishing X would be a correct act under moral or other kind of obligations on AGREF.

Examples in (20) illustrate the above mentioned constructions. In (20a), for example, S considers it beneficial for H to carry out X, in (20b) S recognizes H's unwillingness. (20c) carries neutral obligation in that it contains neither S's advice to H for accomplishing X nor S's recognition of H's unwillingness to carry out X.

(20a) तुम्हें तीन केले खाने चाहिए।
tumhẽ tīn kele khāne čāhie
you.DAT three banana.M.PL eat.INF.M.PL is advisable
'You should eat three bananas.'

(20b) तुम्हें तीन केले खाने पड़ेंगे।
tumhẽ tīn kele khāne paṛẽge
you.DAT three banana.M.PL eat.INF.M.PL fall.M.PL.FUT
'You will have to eat three bananas.'

(20c) तुम्हें तीन केले खाने हैं/ होंगे।
tumhẽ tīn kele khāne hẽ/hõge
you.DAT three banana.M.PL eat.INF.M.PL be.PL.PRES/M.PL.FUT
'You got/are/supposed to eat three bananas.'

8 The LET-construction in Hindi

In his detailed analysis of imperative and other directive strategies in English and Dutch, Van Olmen (2011: 23) establishes nine distinguishing criteria – the LET-criterion the first, which he considers fundamental for separating canonical imperatives from non-canonical ones. However, the Hindi construction which is equivalent to the English LET-construction seems to pose a problem for Van Olmen's generalization in that both the canonical and non-canonical Hindi imperative forms equally exhibit the equivalent of the English LET-construction. In Hindi, when S asks H to let her/him or a third party (i.e. TP) undertake X, say 'read', S does not issue a command asking H to carry out X, but on the contrary S asks H not to put obstacles to S's or a TP's in accomplishing it. One ought to notice here that the imperative mood is not on the verb 'read', but on the verb 'let'. In other words, S asks H to permit or allow (i.e. X) S or TP to carry out Y. The LET-construction is unique since through an imperative construction S asks H to carry out X whereas through an imperative form of let S asks H to allow her/him or a TP to carry out Y. In this kind of deontic modality, the imperative mood is placed on the Hindi verb *denā* 'give' which collocates with preceding oblique case infinitives expressing the granting of permission, and containing pronouns or nouns in oblique case with a dative case marker *ko* (McGregor 1972: 146), preceded by an oblique infinitive which indicates the action the speaker or a TP (and not H,) wishes to perform. An imperative which is directed at H can be represented by an imperative sign placed before the content of the utterance, i.e. !X, whereas the imperative with let verb requires another element placed before the content of an imperative as in (21b):

(21a) !X (i.e. (You) carry out X)
i.e., (You) Read it.
(21b) !LET/X/ (You) let S or a TP carry out X.
i.e., (You) let S or a TP read it.

As the example in (21b) demonstrates, the S's command in the let-construction is directed at the let verb rather than at the real action mentioned by X, 'read'. The let-construction in Hindi thus exhibits all types of imperatives discussed in the previous sections, both canonical and non-canonical. The following sections provide a detailed analysis of the Hindi let-construction.

8.1 The Hindi LET-construction through an immediate imperative

In this kind of imperative S tells H to obligatorily let a TP carry out the task mentioned by the verb without delay. Since the action mentioned by the verb in such an imperative is to be carried out either by S or a TP rather than by H, H's role in this imperative, therefore, is simply to allow or permit the accomplishment of X.

(22) उसे इसे पढ़ने दो।

use	*ise*	*paṛhne*	*do*
s/he.DAT	it	read.INF.OBL	give.IMP.2PL

'Let her/him read it, [right away]!'

8.2 The Hindi LET-construction through a deferred imperative

In this kind of imperative S tells H to obligatorily let a TP carry out the action mentioned by the verb at a future point in time. Both S and H share knowledge of or beliefs regarding the TP's intention of carrying out the action. S leaves it to H to fulfill the obligation by not obstructing TP, and in doing so, it implies that s/he is not going to check whether H will indeed fulfill the obligation.

(23) उसे इसे पढ़ने देना।
use *ise* *paṛhne* *denā*
s/he.DAT it read.INF.OBL give.INF
'Let her/him read it [as and when the moment occurs]!'

8.3 The Hindi LET-construction through a subjunctive imperative

By uttering this imperative sentence S invites H to possibly fulfill the obligation by not obstructing a TP in carrying out an action mentioned by the verb at a point in time subsequent to the utterance. As is common with all the cases of the imperative with a subjunctive verb form, this type also gives H the choice or possibility not to fulfill the task. This means that H is free to obstruct TP in carrying out the task if H desires or has reason to.

(24) (~~आप~~) उसे इसे पढ़ने दें।
(~~*āp*~~) *use* *ise* *paṛhne* *dẽ*
you.2PL.POL s/he.DAT it read.INF.OBL give.SBJV.PL
'If possible, please let her/him read it [right away]!'

8.4 The Hindi LET-construction through an imperfective imperative

In this circumstance, S simply reminds H of the unfulfilled obligation to let a TP take up a task at a time prior to the time of utterance. S believes that H should have allowed or let a TP carry out the task mentioned by the verb. The utterance of this imperative, therefore, should be treated as a reproach rather than an example of deontic modality. However, in some cases this utterance might mean that it is still possible for H to fulfill the obligation by allowing a TP to carry out the task. It is only in this last sense that the imperative becomes deontic.

(25) उसे इसे पढ़ने देते।
use ise paṛhne dete
s/he.DAT it read.INF.OBL give.IPFV.M.PL
'If only you would let her/him read it!'

8.5 The Hindi LET US-constructions

When S has to request H to perform a joint action, S makes use of the imperative which exhibits the subjunctive verb form. Such commands are issued as an invitation to H to join with or work together with S in accomplishing X. It is to be noted, however, that the Hindi verb *ānā* 'to come' exhibits three imperative verb forms according to three forms of second person pronoun, whereas the Hindi verb *pīnā* 'to drink' is in the first person plural subjunctive form. Such forms are polite requests or proposals rather than orders.

(26a) (~~तू~~) उसे इसे पढ़ने दो।
(~~*tū*~~) *ā čāy piyẽ*
you.SG.INTI come.IMP.2SG tea drink.SBJV.PL
'Come on, let us have some tea!'

(26b) (~~तुम~~) आओ, चाय पिएँ।
(~~*tum*~~) *āo čāy piyẽ*
you.PL.FAM come.IMP.2PL tea drink.SBJV.PL
'Come on, let us have some tea!'

(26c) (~~आप~~) आइए, चाय पिएँ।
(~~*āp*~~) *āie čāy piyẽ*
you.2PL.POL come.IMP.2PL.POL tea drink.SBJV.PL
'Please come on, let us have some tea!'

9 Negative commands through imperatives: Prohibitives

In Hindi all the above mentioned imperative types are negated exactly in the same way as non-imperative sentences. However, the distribution of three negative markers (or negative particles) shows some constraints. Hindi is one of those languages which utilize different negative particles to express different types of modality (van der Auwera 2001). In fact, Hindi possesses three negative markers to express epistemic and deontic modalities: *nahī̃*, *mat*, and *na*. Although exceptions to the rules are attested in the spoken variety of Hindi, the distribution of negative markers in the modern standard Hindi sentences is not an arbitrary one, but is governed both by the type of sentence they are employed in and by some pragmatic constraints. As discussed elsewhere (Sharma 2001), the distribution of negative markers can be summarized in the following way:

(27) Negative Modalities in Hindi
  a. Modal necessity
    a1. Epistemic necessity $\Box\neg P$ *nahī̃* (necessarily not P)
    a2. Deontic necessity $\Box\neg !X$ *mat* (necessarily don't do !X)
  b. Modal possibility
    b1. Epistemic possibility $\Diamond\neg P$ *na* (possibly not P)
    b2. Deontic possibility $\Diamond\neg !X$ *na* (if it is possible, don't do !X)

Since imperative utterances are concerned with deontic necessity and possibility, only two negative markers can be found in Hindi imperatives: *mat* and *na*.[7]

9.1 Immediate negative imperative (or prohibitive)

By attaching a negative marker to a direct imperative S prohibits H from taking up a task that H is set to carry out. S thus imposes a command on H with regard to H's planned action.

(28) (~~तुम~~) इसे मत पढ़ो।
  (~~tum~~) *ise mat paṛho*
  you.2PL.FAM it don't read.IMP.2PL
  'Don't read it!'

7 Some languages do not possess negative markers to show the distinction between epistemic negation and deontic negation. In English, for example, both 'It is not good' showing the epistemic negation and 'Do not eat it!' showing the deontic negation have the same negative marker 'not'. It does not make any distinction even between negative necessity and negative possibility: both 'It is not necessarily good' (i.e. epistemic negative necessity) and 'It is possibly not good' (i.e. epistemic negative possibility) carry the negative marker 'not'. Likewise, both 'Necessarily don't eat it!' (i.e. deontic negative necessity) and 'Possibly don't eat it!' (i.e. deontic negative possibility) carry the same negative marker 'not'. Hindi shows differences in all the negation types. The role of Hindi negative markers in expressing modality, however, is supplementary and determined primarily by the modality of the main verb or the auxiliary.

The example in (28) requires an immediate response by H. This involves forbidding action already in process or about to be commenced. They all presuppose that S has some knowledge or beliefs that H is already involved in an task which in future will be forbidden. They all stress the suspension of that action already begun or is about to begin, and they all presuppose that S believes or knows that H is already carrying out the action which is forbidden. It is also possible that H is about to undertake such action immediately following the order, and thus S feels it necessary to tell H not to carry it out.

9.2 Deferred negative imperative

To ask H not to carry out a task through indirect imperative is to forbid her/him to take it up at a future point in time. On the basis of existing knowledge and beliefs, S foresees that H will take up the task and wants to inform H that taking up the task would not be acceptable in S's opinion. Since in the indirect imperatives S will not be in a position to check H's fulfilling the command, it is up to H to decide whether to obey or ignore it.

(29) (~~तुम~~) इसे मत पढ़ना।
(~~*tum*~~) *ise mat paṛhnā*
you.2PL.FAM it don't read.INF
'Don't read it (as and when you happen to do)!'

There seems to be no difference in meaning between the three action types used in this kind of imperative as none of the actions presupposes its beginning at the time of utterance. The prohibition of H's activities is based on S's assessment of the likelihood of H's taking up the tasks habitually at a place and time different from that of the utterance. S may or may not know or believe that H has indeed been involved in carrying out the tasks regularly prior to the time of utterance.

9.3 Negative command through subjunctive

In issuing a negative command through an imperative with the subjunctive form of the verb, S does not oblige H to refrain from carrying out the action. S intends to communicate that it is up to H to take up the task or not, although S would prefer her/him to perform and complete it rather than ignoring it. The negative marker in this kind of imperative is *na*, rather than *mat*, as *na* carries a deontic possibility whereas *mat* expresses deontic necessity.

(30) (आप) नदी में न कूदें।
(~~*āp*~~) *nadī mẽ na kūdẽ*
you.2PL.POL river in not jump.SBJV.2PL.POL
'Would you please not jump into the river (now)!'

In (30), the pronominal form of reference is *āp* only and hence the deontic possibility only is expressed.

9.4 Negative command through imperfective participle

While issuing a command consisting of an imperative sentence with an imperfective participle, S implies that H has not, at the time of S's utterance, carried out or taken up the task. In issuing negative commands comprising the imperfective participle of the verb S implies that H has already carried out and concluded the task or is in the process of taking it up. Thus, this is a statement denoting a fact rather than a command carrying deontic modality. S is aware that there is nothing H can do about it. It is therefore a sort of complaint.

(31) (आप) इसे न पढ़ते।
(~~*āp*~~) *ise na paṛhte*
you.2PL.POL it not read.IPFV.M.PL
'If only you didn't read it (now), (will you/won't you?)!' [Although I see that you are planning to.]

9.5 Negative commands with 'let-a-TP-not-do-X'

Whereas the negative markers in imperative sentences are directed at H's carrying out an action X and, therefore, both the negation and deontic modalities (deontic necessity and deontic possibility) have as their scope exclusively H's action; in the case of an imperative with a 'let-a-TP-do-X' construction, instead, they show different applications. The negative markers in a 'let-a-TP-do-X' imperative cover both the let verb (demanding H's action or inaction) as well as the real action which is to be carried out by a TP. Likewise, although both the deontic necessity and the deontic possibility are directed at H (it is H on which deontic modalities are imposed), they seem to be related to TP as well (since it is the TP's action which will show if H has fulfilled his task according to the type of modality s/he was under). The negative marker in Hindi shows differences according to the kind of deontic modality it is to carry: *mat* ('don't') carries deontic necessity and *na* ('don't') in contrast carries deontic possibility.

10 Imperatives and verbal aspect

It is generally believed that as compared to other sentence types imperatives are not rich enough in marking aspectual distinctions (Aikhenvald 2010: 125). In contrast to the widely held belief, however, the Hindi data show that all types of Hindi imperatives discussed in the previous sections (i.e. immediate, deferred, polite and reproachful, etc.) can morphologically mark almost all the types of verbs (simple, causative, conjunct and compound, etc.) with different verbal aspects. Without presenting a detailed analysis of the phenomenon, however, the following discussion of immediate imperative with different verbal aspect marker will suffice to substantiate our claim.

Hindi morphologically marks at least three verbal aspects in the verbal conjugation of an imperative sentence: the iterative habitual, the iterative continuous (or iterative progressive), and the perfective. (32a) is a case of an imperative without any aspect linked to the verb, whereas (32b), (32c) and (32d) are examples of the imperative with aspectual element linked to the verb. While habitual and progressive aspects are evidenced in a word or grammatical item, as seen in (32b) and (32c) respectively, the perfective aspect is observed through a compound verb construction in an imperative mood, as in (32d). In the latter case S's command aims to make H bring the action to completion, reaching the final desired outcome X.

(32a) (तुम) अख़बार पढ़ो।
(*~~tum~~*) *axbār* *paṛho*
you.2PL.FAM newspaper read.IMP.2PL
'Read the newspaper [now]!'

(32b) (तुम) अख़बार पढ़ा करो।
(*~~tum~~*) *axbār* *paṛhā* *karo*
you.2PL.FAM newspaper(s) read.PFV do.IMP.2PL
'Read newspapers every day [from now on]!'
'Make it a habit to read newspapers every day!'
[obligatorily and habitually do x] or

(32c) (तुम) अख़बार पढ़ते रहो।
(*~~tum~~*) *axbār* *paṛhte* *raho*
you.2PL.FAM newspaper(s) read.IPFV.MPL stay.IMP.2PL
'Continue reading/to read the newspaper!'
'Continue reading/ to read newspapers!'
'Keep on reading newspapers!'

(32d) (तुम) इस अख़बार को पढ़ डालो।
(*~~tum~~*) *is* *axbār* *ko* *paṛh* *ḍālo*
you.2PL.FAM this.OBL newspaper acc read.ROOT put.IMP.2PL
'Read this paper through [now]!' put.IMP.2PL

11 Summary

The detailed discussion in previous sections demonstrates that S has a number of directive strategies to choose from to convey commands in Hindi. First and foremost, it is the canonical form of the Hindi imperative through which S issues a command carrying an immediate deontic necessity, viz. □!X *at time t*. Additionally, in view of H's engagement with some other action Y or just being aware of the fact that X is scheduled to take place after Y, S can also issue a command asking H to obligatorily carry out action X at a later point in time, viz. □!X *at time t+1*. This type of command is issued through the Hindi infinitive. Secondly, S has at his/her disposal another type of sentences (in subjunctive mood) to ask H to possibly carry out action X at will, viz. ◊!X *at time t*. As demonstrated above (see (9)), this type of polite command can be issued only to the agent referred to by two out of three pronominal forms, namely, *tum* 'friendly You' and *āp* 'honorific/formal-You'. In other words, it is not employed to issue commands to the agent referred to by the Hindi pronoun *tū* 'intimate-You'. This is one of the most important types of non-canonical imperatives in Hindi. Thirdly, S can also have recourse to sentences in the imperfective to express his/her reproach, asking H to carry out action X. In other words, you should have carried out the action X – yet you have not – there is still time for you to accomplish it. As we have seen, the above mentioned forms of non-canonical imperative are generally of conditional types, but they may also be phrases dependent on a principle clause containing S's wish or desire. Furthermore, in its directive strategy reserve, Hindi has three more constructions to express an agent's obligations carrying S's different attitudes towards the action X, namely, INF + *cāhie* 'S's advice to H to carry out X', INF + *honā* 'S's reminder to H to carry out X' and INF + *paṛnā* 'H is forced against her will to carry out X'.

References

Aikhenvald, Alexandra Y. 2010. *Imperatives and Commands* [Oxford Studies in Typology and Linguistic Theory]. Oxford: Oxford University Press.

Birjulin, L. A. & Xrakovskij, V. S. 2001. Imperative sentences: theoretical problems. In *Typology of Imperative Constructions* [LINCOM Studies in Theoretical Linguistics 09], Victor S. Xrakovskij, 3–50, Muenchen: Lincom Europa.

De Clerck, Bernard. 2006. The imperative in English: A corpus-based, pragmatic analysis. PhD dissertation, University of Ghent.

Guru, Kamta Prasad. 1919. *Hindi Vyakaran* (21st edition 2000). Varanasi: Nagri Pracharini Sabha.

Huntley, Martin. 1984. The semantics of English imperatives. *Linguistics and Philosophy* 7: 103–133.

Jary, Mark & Kissine, Mikhail. 2014. *Imperatives*. Cambridge: Cambridge University Press.

Kachru, Yamuna. 1980. *Aspects of Hindi Grammar*. New Delhi: Manohar Publications.

Kachru, Yamuna. 2006. *Hindi* [London Oriental and African Language Library]. Amsterdam: John Benjamins Publishing Company.

Kellogg, S. H. 1875. *A Grammar of the Hindí Language* (3rd edition 1938, reprinted 1965). London: Routledge & Kegan Paul.

Koul, O. N. 2008. *Modern Hindi Grammar*. Springfield: Dunwoody Press.

McGregor, Ronald S. 1972. *Outline of Hindi Grammar* (3rd revised and enlarged edition 1995). Oxford: Clarendon Press.

Montaut, Annie. 2004. *A Grammar of Hindi* [LINCOM Studies in Indo-European Linguistics]. Munich: Lincom Europa.

Palmer, Ralph. 2001. *Mood and Modality*. Cambridge: Cambridge University Press.

Searle, John & Vanderveken, Daniel. 1985. *Foundations of Illocutionary Logic*. Cambridge: Cambridge University Press.

Searle, John. 1979. A taxonomy of illocutionary acts. In *Expression and Meaning*, John R. Searle (ed), 1–29. Cambridge: Cambridge University Press.

Shapiro, Michael C. 1989. *A Primer of Modern Standard Hindi*. Delhi: Motilal Banarsidass Publishers.

Shapiro, Michael C. 2003. Hindi. In *The Indo-Aryan Languages* [Routledge Language Family Series], George Cardona & Dhanesh Jain (eds), 250–285. London: Routledge.

Sharma, Aryendra. 1958. *A Basic Grammar of Modern Hindi* (4th edition 1983). New Delhi: Central Hindi Directorate, Ministry of Education and Culture.

Sharma, Ghanshyam. 2000. Pragmatic explanations for expressing obligations of the agent referred to in Hindi. In *The Yearbook of South Asian Languages and Linguistics*, Rajendra Singh (ed), 185–202. New Delhi: Sage Publications.

Sharma, Ghanshyam. 2001. The negative modality in Hindi. *Annali di Ca' Foscari, XL*: 131–149.

van der Auwera, Johan, Dobrushina, N. & Goussev, V. (2005) Imperative-hortative systems. In *The World Atlas of Language Structures*, Haspelmath, Martin, Dryer, Matthew S., Gil, David & Comrie, Bernard (eds), 296–299. Oxford: Oxford University Press.

van der Auwera, Johan. 2006. Imperatives. In *Encyclopedia of Language and Linguistic*, Keith Brown (ed), 565–567. Amsterdam: Elsevier.

van der Auwera. Johan. 2001. Negating dynamic and deontic modality in Hindi-Urdu and Bangla. In *Linguistic Structure and Language Dynamics in South Asia*. [Papers from the

proceedings of SALA XVIIII Roundtable] A. Abbi, R. S. Gupta & A. Kidwai (eds), 327–347. Delhi: Motilal Banarasidass.
Van Olmen, Daniël. 2011. The Imperative in English and Dutch: A Functional Analysis in Comparable and Parallel Corpora. PhD dissertation, University of Antwerp.

Tej Krishan Bhatia

Discovering the Hindi grammatical tradition: Historicity and second language acquisition

Abstract: The main objective of this paper is to examine the oldest grammar of Hindi from two perspectives – historical and second language acquisition. In order to achieve these goals, the discovery and analysis of Ketelaar's Dutch manuscript found in the National Archives, The Hague (MS: C-76) has been carried out (see Bhatia and Machida 2008). The paper comprises two parts: the first part briefly presents a biography of Ketelaar in order to shed light on input type(s) and input condition(s) responsible for the makeup of his grammar. The second part analyzes the key characteristics of the gram-mar together with the pattern of second language acquisition of the pioneering grammarian. Finally, the conclusions are presented.

Keywords: Second language acquisition, Critical Period Hypothesis, cross-cultural encounters

1 Ketelaar: Biography and Grammar

The oldest grammar of Hindi was written in 1698 by Jean Josua Ketelaar in Dutch. Ketelaar was not a run-of-the-mill type of grammarian. He had an interesting life in terms of the array of trading, diplomatic, and linguistic journeys he undertook in India and in Arabia. His real family name was spelled as Kettler. He was a German, born at Elbing on the Baltic Sea, on 25 December 1659; he was the eldest son of a bookbinder who started his career as a bookbinder's apprentice but often got into trouble, robbing and even trying to poison his master! Fired from his job, he went to Danzig (now Gdansk), where he committed yet another theft, eventually leaving for Stockholm in 1680. Two years later he joined the East India Company and sailed for India; that is where his last name was changed to Ketelaar.

The East India Company in those days hired a large number of "its lower personnel from Germany" (Vogel 1935 [1964 reprint]: 817) perhaps due to military and economic ambitions of the East Indian Company, particularly the East India

Tej Krishan Bhatia, Syracuse University, USA. Email: tkbhatia@syr.edu

https://doi.org/10.1515/9783110610796-014

Company's joint collaboration with the Dutch United East India Company to attack Portuguese and Spanish ships off the coast of China in order to secure trading posts in China. On his arrival at Surat in 1683, he was appointed as a "pennist", a clerk. He rose to the position of "assistant" in four years. Between 1705 and 1708 he successfully completed two Arabian missions of purchasing coffee. By 1708 he was appointed as "senior merchant" because of his expertise in the "Moorish" language and customs. Later he was accredited to the Moghul emperors, Shāh Bahādur Shāh (1708–1712) and Jahāndār Shāh (1712), as Dutch envoy. In 1711, he was also appointed the company's "director of trade" at Surat (see Vogel 1935 [1964 reprint] for more on Ketelaar's biography). The term "Moorish", meant "Muslims" in European languages of the time but in the context of India, Ketelaar and others refers specifically to the Arabic-Persian mixed variety of Hindī-Hindustānī.

As an ambassador of the Dutch Embassy, he accompanied Jahāndār Shāh to Delhi during the summer and rainy season of 1712 to negotiate official *firmāns* 'edicts decrees, or a royal letters'. From the official documents, it is clear that Ketelaar took an active role in diplomatic and business negotiations. However, a series of troubles were brewing for him. On the way to Delhi, he took a short detour through Rajasthan. This, in turn, unleashed a series of unfortunate events for him., most important of which were the following three: First, he had to pay a considerable toll tax, *rāhdārī*, to chief Churāman while passing through the Jat territory, which took an economic toll on the Company; the toll tax became the subject of controversy for his employer. Second, in October, on his return to Surat via Agra, Gwalior, Narwar, Sironj, Sarangpur, Ujjain, Dohad, and Godhra, he encountered even more problems such as peasant revolts and a run-in with fearsome tribes such as the Bhils and Kolies. The bright side of this (mis)adventurous trip was his contact with a wide variety of diverse ethnic groups and language varieties. Third, once back in Surat, more bad news was waiting for him. The emperor Jahāndār Shāh was overthrown by his nephew, Farruksiyār. Consequently, he could not reap the benefits of his cumbersome travels and business negotiations. However, these did not deter him from his professional and linguistic goals.

In 1715, Ketelaar was appointed Dutch envoy to Persia. His mission to Persia mirrors his visit to Delhi: full of adventures and diplomatic activities. On 12 May 1718 he died of fever at Gombroon (now Bandar Abbas) on the Persian Gulf while returning from Isfahan; the fever may have been contracted during a two-day stay in the local jail occasioned by his refusal to order a Dutch ship to act, under the Persian governor's orders, against Arab invaders (see Vogel 1935). Perhaps it was not in the interest of trade policies of the Dutch East India Company to side with Persia against Arabia.

1.1 Discovery of the Hindi grammatical tradition: Three manuscripts

Until the 1930's the oldest grammar of Hindi was considered to be extinct. Naturally, then, the authorship, dating and authenticity of the grammar were shrouded in mystery. The discovery of the oldest grammar has its own interesting history. A series of historical accidents and intermittent exchanges of information among a handful of scholars saved the grammar from being extinct. The key researchers who uncovered the first grammar of Hindī are Sir George Grierson, Emilio Teza, Prof. Suniti Kumar Chatterji and Dr. J. Ph. Vogel. (For a more detailed historical account of the discovery of the Ketelaar's grammar, see Bhatia 2001.)

In July 1981, I visited various archives in the Netherlands including the Utrecht University Library. The only manuscript I found in the Hague, National Archives was then considered "original and only surviving" manuscript (see Bhatia 2008, volume 1, page 17 on the discovery of the Hague, National Archives (dated 1698; see Figure 1)). It turns out that in addition to the Hague National Archives, two other manuscripts of the oldest grammar exist – The Utrecht University Library (Ms. Number 1478; See Figure 2) and the Paris Manuscript (Paris, Hôtel Turgot, Fundation Custodia library, Institut Néerlandais, Inv. no. 1991-A615 (183 p.)). For the detailed discussion of the Hague and the Paris manuscripts, see Bhatia and Machida 2016. As McGregor (2001: 20) points that the Utrecht manuscript may have been copied from Ketelaar's original material for private use by someone already having some acquaintance with Hindī-Hindustānī, but less familiar with its vocabulary than its grammar. In other words, the Utrecht University manuscript constitutes a variant and is driven by The Hague manuscript. Therefore, The Hague manuscript serves as a basis for the analysis of Ketelaar's language acquisition of Hindi as a second and/or foreign language.

The complete Dutch title of the Hague manuscript and its English translation of Ketelaar's work is as follows.

> Instructie off Onderwijsinge Der Hindoustanse en Persiaanse talen, nevens hare declinatie en Conjugatie, als mede vergeleijkinge, der hindoustanse med de hollandse maat en gewighten mitsgaders beduijdingh eenieger moorse namen etc.
>
> — Jean Josua Ketelaar, Elbingensum engecopieert door Jsaacq van der Hoeve, van Uijtreght Tot Leckenauw AD. 1698
>
> 'Instruction or teaching of the Hindustānī and Persian languages, including their declension and conjugation also comparison of the Hindustānī with the Dutch measure and weights and the meaning of some Moorish names etc.'
>
> — Jean Josua Ketelaar of Elbing Copied by Jsaacq van der Hoeve, of Utrecht at Lucknow A.D. 1698.'

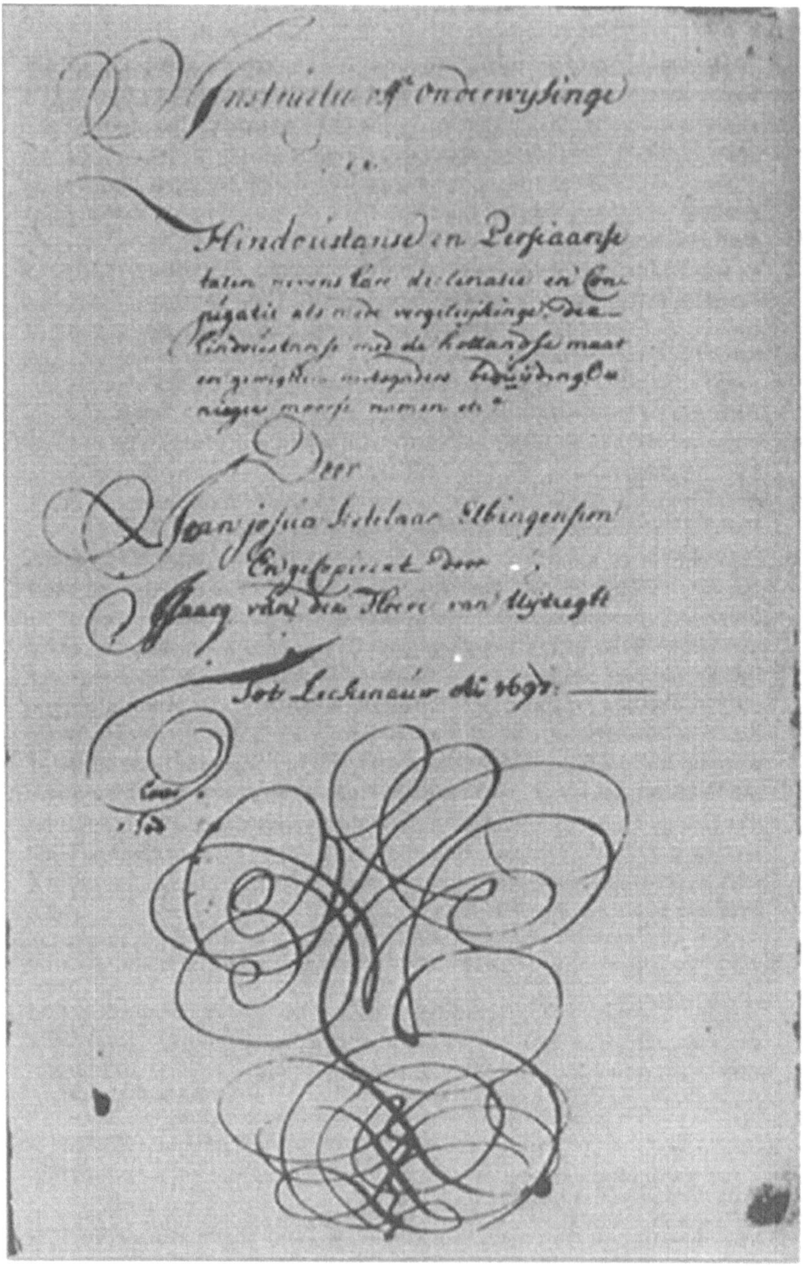

Fig. 1: Title Page of the Hague Manuscript: Ketelaar's Grammar (1698)

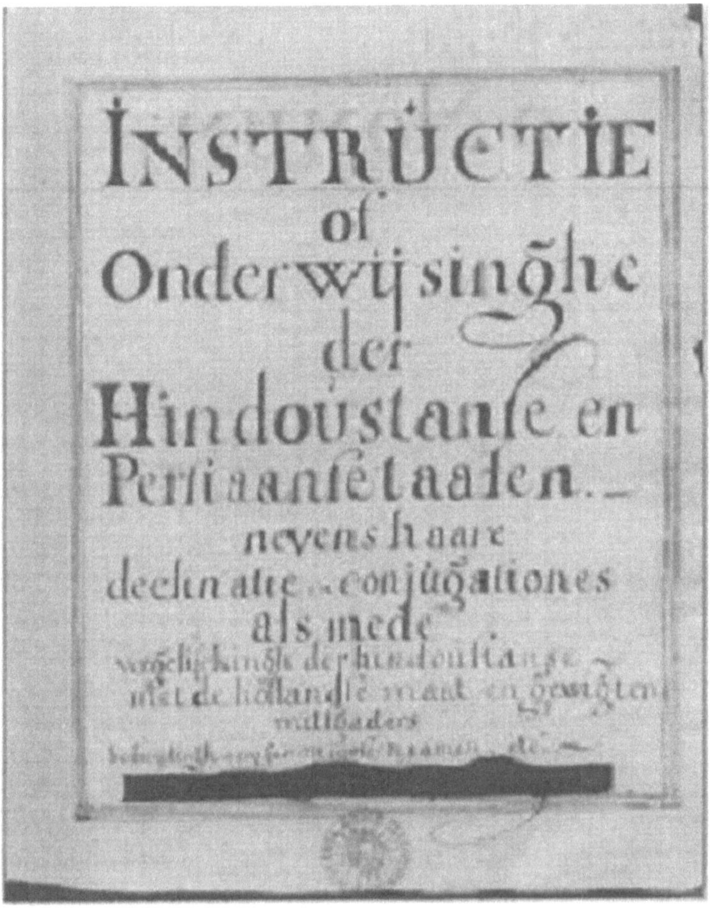

Fig. 2: Title Page of The Utrecht Manuscript: Ketelaar's Grammar

1.2 The grammar: Organization and salient features

Ketelaar's grammar has the general organization of: the title page, a foreword by the copyist (Ad Lectorem Benevolum "to the kind reader"), a brief introduction to the Hindī language by Ketelaar (voor Reeden "Preface"), a table of contents, the main body of the work consisting of two components – lexicon and grammar – followed by a Hindī translation of some Christian texts. It ends with an index of Dutch words with page numbers indicating where the Hindī/Persian words are in the text.

The table of contents of Ketelaar's grammar reveals other key goals – pragmatic (e.g. commercial, military, among others) and religious goals – that were left unaccounted for by Jsaacq van der Hoeve. Whether the pragmatic and religious objectives reflect the personal identity of Ketelaar or the language policies of the Dutch East India Company requires further research. For details, see Bhatia and Machida (2008: 33–36; see Appendix 1).

The main body of Ketelaar's grammar consists of two components – a lexicon and a grammar. The grammar component is sandwiched between the two main parts of the lexicon. The first portion of the lexicon (Ketelaar's sections 1–44) constitutes nearly half of the work and is organized into forty-one semantic and three grammatical classes. The second part of the lexical component (sections 50–52) is devoted to teaching the meaning of "Moorish" names, of phonetically similar words or expressions (homonyms and near homonyms), and of culturally sensitive Hindī words. An alphabetic index is provided at the end of the grammar.

Three noteworthy properties of the work emerge at first glance. First, it is primarily data-oriented. Contrary to the underlying generic nature of Indic language grammars, it places heavy emphasis on presenting raw Hindī data (e.g., nominal, verbal paradigms etc.) rather than on formulating rules and capturing generalizations based on the presented data. Rule formulation is not lacking though. Second, the grammar is developed in the lexicographic tradition. More emphasis is given to the dictionary of Hindī than to the grammatical sketch of the language. This property distinguishes it from both the preceding Indian grammatical tradition and the succeeding Hindī one, in which lexicography was seen as an independent component of language pedagogy and was rarely mingled with the grammatical component. The third notable feature of Ketelaar's work is its bilingual approach, which surfaces in both the grammatical and the lexical components. The grammar was intended as a two-language grammar, that is, of Hindī and Persian, an attempt to write a conjoined two-language grammar. Perhaps the dual grammar attempt was motivated by the similarity between the two languages and Ketelaar's interest in comparative methods. For details, see Bhatia and Machida (2008: 43–44). Similarly, Ketelaar attempted to provide a bilingual lexicon by presenting Persian equivalents of the Hindī lexical items but, unfortunately, could not complete the Persian section; a significant portion of it was left blank. Nevertheless, this approach can be very rewarding since it can provide to researchers an empirical basis for distinguishing between Hindī and Persian. Consider, for example, Ketelaar's listing of Persian and Hindī words for 'snow.' He assigns the word *baraf* to Persian but not to Hindī. Surprisingly, the Persian word is an integral part of modern-day Hindī.

Other distinctive characteristics of the work emerge when one glances through the dictionary section. A set of three criteria went into his overall classification of lexicon – semantics, grammar, and acquisition. Ketelaar divided the Hindī lexicon into forty-one semantic (sections 1–41), three grammatical (42–44), and three pedagogically-motivated (51–53) classes (see Table 3 for Ketelaar's terminology). Although some of the semantic classes, such as the family, numerals, names of days, months, and humans and parts of the body, overlap with those in traditional grammars, most of them fall in the domain of grammars for "special purposes." The inclusion of classes of vocabulary dealing with high offices, despised and dishonest professions, military offices, jewels, money, ship and its equipment, and the like must have been inspired by, but not restricted to, the European and lexicographic and phrase book tradition as evidenced in the merchant and marine dictionary of Berlaimont and others. (See Herren and Brown 1988; Osselton 1973). Nevertheless, special purpose grammars involving professional lexicon mark a point of departure from the usual trend in the development of the grammatical tradition of a language, since they are generally viewed as late developments in such traditions. Lexicon is the main strength and salient feature of his work. The merit of this approach is valid for language learning and communication.

Although Ketelaar's grammar was a pioneering work, it did not develop in a linguistically and grammatically impoverished environment. It is worth noting that when Ketelaar was engaged in writing his grammar, a new research paradigm was also emerging, prompted by the 'Age of Discovery'. A multitude of motivations such as the consideration of civilizing the old world (e.g. the spread of Christianity), and trade, and epistemology among others, set the stage for linguistic and cross-cultural endeavors. While Ketelaar was in Surat, Gujarat, the presence of Catholic and Jesuit missionaries was quite pronounced in South India in addition to the presence of Capuchin friar of Surat. The explosive issue of Malabar rites – the adaptation of local rituals into Christianity in the Catholic Church – also had its own linguistic dimension, which favored vernacular languages (i.e. Hindī-Hindustānī and other local languages) over prestige languages such as Persian and Sanskrit. Hindī-Hindustānī was, by then, considered the most widely spoken language in the Mughal courts, namely in the court of Akbar (1556–1605) and Jahangir (1605–1727). Hindustani was deemed a critical language for the pursuit of a long-term religious and intellectual exchange between the Jesuits and the Indians. In a Jesuit report of 1649, Francesco Morando was credited as a "great master of Parthian and the Hindī-Hindustānī language". (See Aranha 2015: 344 for more details). Against this background, it is hard to conceive of the possibility that Ketelaar was totally unaware of such cross-cultural dimensions of Hindī-

Hindustānī and the contact between the two classical grammatical traditions, namely Sanskrit and Latin. In spite of this, the Ketelaar grammar did not follow the classical model(s) of grammar.

2 Ketelaar's grammar: A second language acquisition perspective

Ketelaar developed an in-depth field knowledge of India by interacting with different strata of the society and while marching with armies and dealing with diplomats in royal courts. He was quite well-versed in the areas of business, diplomacy, and military. His grammar is a collection of his field notes. The form of Hindi he heard at various settings (natural settings), he recorded his data. From his work it becomes clear that in addition to Surat and Delhi, Agra and Lucknow also played an important role in Ketelaar's linguistic life. In addition to Gujarat, his affiliation with the Hindī-Hindustānī and Rajasthānī-speaking areas was quite strong. From the perspective of theory of second language acquisition, multivariant Hindī constituted the input type and his learning in field situations marked input condition. The underlying nature of his input type(s) and input condition(s) went into the making of his grammar. This explains the reason for the distinct nature of the Hindī grammar that Ketelaar wrote.

Ketelaar was an adult learner. His language learning began after the Critical Period. The Critical Period Hypothesis by Lenneberg (1967) is sensitive to age, i.e. the age of language acquisition. Research on grammatical errors of second language shows that L2 learners transfer the grammatical rules – phonetic, phonological, morphological, and syntactic rules – of L1 to their second language (L2).[1] Therefore, it is predictable that an English/Dutch-speaking learner of Hindi is

1 This hypothesis attempts to explain the qualitative difference(s) between adult language learning and children language acquisition. For instance, children are better equipped than adults to acquire languages completely (with native competence) without much effort and without any formal instructions between the age of 2 and 5 years. Such an ease of language acquisition is credited to their brain 'plasticity' before puberty. Afterwards, the Critical Period Hypothesis notes language learning requires more effort and motivation because of a loss of brain plasticity resulting in the completion of the lateralization of the language function in the left hemisphere of the brain. Unlike children, adults rarely achieve native-like competency in their second language (L2). An important way in which second language learning (L2) is different from first language (L1) learning is the influence of the mother tongue (L1) on second-language (L2) learning. For details, see Bhatia (2011).

likely to experience difficulties in hearing, producing and acquiring a four-way contrast between Hindi aspiration and voicing contrast (i.e. unvoiced unaspirates, unvoiced aspirates, voiced unaspirates, and voiced aspirates). This prediction can be attested by the pattern of Ketelaar's acquisition of Hindi phonetics summed up below in Table 1.

Tab. 1: Ketelaar's Acquisition of Hindi Consonants

Target Consonant	Consonants as Perceived and Transcribed by Ketelaar				Ketelaar's Examples	Hindī Target and Meaning
	Common	Frequent	Rare	Exception		
k क, [q] क़	k	Kk	--	--	*kaam* *akkla*	*kām* 'work' *akelā* 'alone'
k^h ख, [x] ख़	k, [gh]	kk, ch	kgh	g	*rak* *sukkā* *sichija* *kghatte* *rag* *[ghoda]*	*rak*^{h} 'put' *sūk*^{h}*ā* 'dry' *sik*^{h}*āyā* 'taught' *k*^{h}*ātā* 'eat' *rak*^{h} 'put' [*xudā* 'God']
g ग, ğ [ग़]	g	gh	--	--	*girre* *ghin*	*girā* 'fell' *gin* 'count'
g^h घ	g	--	--	--	*gora*	*g*^{h}*oṛā* 'horse'
c च	tsj, sj	ts, tsch	sch	s	*tsjok* *sjora* *tsitter* *miritsch* *kenschte*	*cauk* 'crossing' *caurā* 'wide' *citra* 'picture' *mirca* 'pepper' *k*^{h}*īctā* 'pull'
c^h छ	tsj	ts	s		*tsjorre* *poetste*	*c*^{h}*orā* 'boy' *pūc*^{h}*tā* 'ask'
j ज, [z] ज़	dsj, j, [s]	sj, ds	dz, dj		*dsjate* *dsante* *sjawaab* *[saer]*	*jātā* 'go' *jāntā* 'know' *javāb* 'answer' [*zahar*] 'poison'
j^h झ	dsj	sj	s		*dsjot* *samsje* *toesjre* *boos*	*jhūṭ*^{h} 'lie' *samajhe* 'understand' *tujhe* 'to you' *bojh* 'burden'
ṭa ट	t, th	--	--	--	*rootie* *beetha*	*roṭī* 'bread' *beṭā* 'son'

Tab. 1 (continued)

Target Consonant	Consonants as Perceived and Transcribed by Ketelaar				Ketelaar's Examples	Hindī Target and Meaning
	Common	Frequent	Rare	Exception		
ṭ^{h}a ठ	t, th	th			*dsjot* *beth, betth*	*j^{h}ūṭ^h* 'lie' *baiṭ^h* 'sit'
ḍa ड	d, dh	--	--	--	*der* *dhoeba*	*ḍar* 'fear' *ḍūbā* 'drowned'
ḍ^{h}a ढ	d	dh			*dounte* *dheela*	*ḍ^{h}ūḍ^{h}tā* 'search' *ḍ^{h}īlā* 'loose'
t त	t	th	--	--	*tom* *koetha*	*tum* 'you' *kuttā* 'dog'
t^h थ	t	th	--	--	*haat* *the*	*hāt^h* 'hand' *t^{h}ā* 'was'
d द	d	dh	--	--	*deeta* *koedhe*	*detā* 'give' *kūde* 'jumped'
d^h ध	d, dh	--	--	--	*dhoobi* *ander*	*d^{h}obī* 'washerman' *and^{h}erā* 'dark'
n न	n	--	--	--	*ander*	*and^{h}erā* 'dark'
p प	p, ph	b	--	--	*bāb*	*bāp* 'father'
p^h फ, [f] फ़	P				*pal*	*p^{h}al* 'fruit'
b ब	bh				*bhel*	*bail* 'ox'
b^h भ	b				*baloe*	*b^{h}ālū* 'bear'
m म	m				*tamboe*	*tambū* 'tent'
y य	j, ij	Js			*dhaaijn*	*ḍāyan* 'witch'
r र	r				*tsjeer*	*sher* 'lion'
l ल	l				*laal*	*lāl* 'red'
v व	w				*sjawaab*	*javāb* 'reply'
sh श	tsj				*tsjasada*	*shahzādā* 'prince'
s स	s, c				*samsje* *ceu*	*samj^{h}e* 'understand' *sev* 'apple'
h ह	h	zero			*sijaah* *hadjm*	*syāh* 'black' *hajjām* 'barber'
ṛa ड़	r	d			*badaa*	*baṛā* 'big'
ṛ^{h}a ढ़	d	r			*boedia*	*buṛ^{h}iyā* 'old women'

Ketelaar failed to recognize three underlying reasons for the problem at hand: (1) the phonetic and phonological differences between Dutch and Hindī, namely the absence of features such as aspiration and retroflexion in Dutch; (2) the inadequacy of the Dutch writing system to capture the specific phonetic/phonological properties of Hindī; and (3) human limitations in transcribing naturally spoken, real-time speech in the absence of such modern recording instruments as tape recorders. Instead, he holds the habits of native speakers of Hindī responsible for the problem. He complains, for example, that many Hindī words are "half-pronounced and mumbled." This explanation is clearly a reflection of his linguistic prejudices and attitudes, which are responsible for his conclusion that the learning of Hindī requires a great deal of attention on the part of its learners. Most importantly, he inadvertently adds yet another myth to language learning, namely the role of native speaker to speak clearly, enunciating each sound properly in order to facilitate second language learning.

Ketelaar was self-taught adult learner and often made predictable and systematic errors at the level of phonetics and phonology pertaining to Hindi aspiration and retroflexion due to interference from Dutch and German. His transcriptional system was influenced as well by Dutch-German. Table 1 above and Table 2 below give more details about his transcriptional system.

Tab. 2: Ketelaar's Acquisition of Hindi Vowels

Target Vowel	Vowels as Perceived and Transcribed by Ketelaar			Ketelaar's Examples		Hindī Target and Meaning
	Common	Frequent	Rare	Exception		
a अ	a	e	o	ae	*karta*	*karta* 'does'
					gea	*gayā* 'went'
					somsje	*samj*^{h}*e* 'understand'
					haeddi	*haḍḍī* 'bone'
ā आ	aa	a, e	o	ao	*maa*	*mā* 'mother'
					puchte	*pūc*^{h}*tā* 'ask'
					karro-mat	*karāmāt* 'magic'
					naom	*nām* 'name'
i इ	i	--	ei, ie	u	*gin*	*gin* 'count'
					dein	*din* 'day'
					duwana	*divānā* 'crazy'
					giere	*girī* 'fell'

Tab. 2 (continued)

Target Vowel	Vowels as Perceived and Transcribed by Ketelaar				Ketelaar's Examples	Hindī Target and Meaning
	Common	Frequent	Rare	Exception		
ī ई	ie	i, ij	e	--	*tier*	*tīr* 'arrow'
					teeri	*terī* 'your'
					baij	*b^hāī* 'brother'
					giere	*girī* 'fell'
u उ	u	o	oe	a	*pukar*	*pukār* 'call'
					moft	*mufta* 'free'
ū ऊ	oe	u	--	--	*poeroeb*	*pūrab* 'east'
e ए	ee	e	ae	a	*beeth*	*beṭā* 'son'
					tsjije	*cāhiye* 'want'
ai [ae] ऐ	ai [ae]	e	eij	a	*baith*	*baeṭ^h* 'sit'
					sethan	*shaitān* 'satan'
					peijssa	*paesā* 'money'
o ओ	oo	o	--	--	*dhoobi*	*d^hobī* 'washerman'
au औ	au	oo	ou	a	*kon*	*kaun* 'who'
					oor	*aur* 'and'
					doure	*dauṛe* 'ran'

Ketelaar places more emphasis on communicative competence than on grammatical competence. His communicative approach is grounded in culture-based language teaching. This approach is self-evident from his rather detailed treatment of "Moorish" names and similar (homophonous or semi-homophonous) words, and his definition/explanation of culture-specific words given in sections (50)–(52) of his work. Even the title of his work emphasizes the pragmatic and pedagogical aspects of his work.

The grammar component gives a barebones outline of Hindī grammar. The grammatical categories postulated for Hindī and their treatment are similar to those of traditional grammars: nominal, adjectival, pronominal, adverbial, and verbal categories.

Hindī nouns are marked by number, gender, and case: two numbers (singular and plural), two genders (masculine and feminine), and six cases (nominative, genitive, dative, accusative, vocative and ablative). Therefore, Ketelaar does not seem to have followed the Latin model in toto. In fact his grammatical model is not strictly Latin, as is evident from the arrangement of cases – the vocative case precedes the ablative case in Ketelaar's grammar. The four conjugational patterns of Hindī nouns show that Ketelaar intended to develop a purely phonetically based classification of nouns. According to this classification, Hindī nouns may end in any of the four phonetic segments, *a*, *i u*, or a consonant. These four types take a regular set of inflections and postpositions.

Pronouns are classified into four classes: personal, demonstrative, relative, and interrogative. Of these four types, only personal pronouns are presented with complete paradigms. The second-person pronouns follow the paradigm of the first person. It is noteworthy that in the paradigms of the second-person pronouns there is a complete omission of the honorific pronoun *āp*. The paradigm of the third person is full of errors and fails to distinguish between the paradigms of the proximate demonstrative pronoun *yah* (this) and the third-person pronoun *vah* (he/she).

Ketelaar does not give complete paradigms for the three other pronominal types (demonstratives, interrogatives, and relatives), but only a partial listing plus a few sample sentences illustrating their use. Particularly noteworthy is the fact that he does not even list relative pronouns such as *jo* 'who' but instead uses interrogative pronouns such as *kon* 'who'. While other forms of interrogative pronouns such as *kja 'what,' kjon 'why,' kon 'who'* are listed, their corresponding relative pronouns are omitted. Evidently Ketelaar's own linguistic background, which permits the use of interrogatives as relatives (in certain contexts), is responsible for his failure to recognize the difference.

The motivation for postulating a separate class of possessive pronouns from genitive pronouns seems to be that they are marked for the number and gender of the following nouns and hence have the three distinct phonetic shapes of every possessive pronoun.

Two important features of Ketelaar's analysis of pronouns are the discussion of negative particles and the sociolinguistic constraints on Hindī pronominal usage. Since the treatment of negative particles is also provided under the section on pronouns, it gives the impression that Ketelaar favored the treatment of negative particles as pronouns. The three particles identified by Ketelaar are *na*, *ney*, and *mat*. As far as the position of the negative particles in a sentence, the only observation made is that *mat* can appear either preverbally or post-verbally, implying that the other two negative markers have a fixed word order (i.e., preverbal position). It is also noted that honorific forms are always expressed by employing the plural forms of pronouns; however, the singular forms are used to address people younger than the speaker (Ketelaar manuscript page 83; Mills 462–463). Under the titles "substantive" and "adjective," Ketelaar addresses the derivation of nouns from adjectives and vice versa. Primarily, three processes are discussed. The first deals with the derivation of nouns from adjectives by the addition of *ī*. The second concerns the description of agentive nouns by the addition of *cī*, *wālā*, and *dās*. The last process permits the derivation of adjectives from a noun by the addition of two morphemes, *gār* and *dār*. The formation of comparative and superlative adjectives received considerable attention in the discussion of adjectives. The honorific particle *jī* and the feminine suffix –*in* also receive attention under adjectives.

In regard to the tense system, Ketelaar points out that Hindī has eight tenses – present, imperfect, perfect, future, second future, imperative (a mood rather than a tense category), infinitive (which is an odd tense category), and pluperfect. Needless to say, his discussion of tenses is in a premature stage as he seems not to differentiate between a tense category and a mood. Similarly, he fails to include the subjunctive mood in his table of tenses and does not analyze counterfactuals. In addition, the data presented in the conjugations are not free from errors. These inaccuracies notwithstanding, it seems from the conjugations patterns presented and the discussion thereof that Ketelaar only had the following six tense scheme in mind: (1) present, (2) perfect, (3) imperative, (4) imperfect, (5) infinitive, and (6) future. In order to present a complete tense scheme for Hindī, Ketelaar adds two more subcategories, namely pluperfect and, what he calls, second future. In fact, in his tense scheme, the perfect and future were further subdivided into perfect and pluperfect, future and second future, respectively. The following Table summarizes the first person conjugational forms of verb *honā* 'to be' in the eight tenses, as posited by Ketelaar. For the entire paradigms and their critical evaluation, see Bhatia and Machida (2008: 117–143).

Tab. 3: Hindi tenses as perceived by Ketelaar

Tenses (Ketelaar 1698)	Dutch	Ketelaar Hindi	Modern Hindi Target
Present	ick ben	*me he*	मैं है **'I am'**
Imperfect	Ick	*me hoea*	मैं हुआ **'I was'**
Perfect	Ick	*me hoeetha*	मैं हुए था **'I have been'**
Future	ick zal zijn	*me hunga*	मैं हुँगा **'I shall be'**
Second Future	ik wil zijn	*me hoonga*	मैं होगा **'I will have been'**
Imperative	blijft ghij	*toe roo*	तू रह **'(you) be'**
"Infinitive"	zijn	*hoea*	होआ **'to be'**
Pluperfect	ick zal zijn	*me hougea*	मैं होगा **'I have been'**

Similarly, Ketelaar did not distinguish between the simple and compound verbs (e.g., *cuknā* 'to complete'). Consequently, he treats the past tense of simple verbs and compound verbs with *cuknā* as two distinct past tense forms. According to

Ketelaaar, when one wants to say 'if one will have eaten' is not much in use with the Moors, the words were as follows:

Tab. 4: The Hindi compound verbs as perceived by Ketelaar

Dutch	English	Ketelaar	Hindi Transcription	Hindi Target
indien ik sal gegeten hebben	if I had eaten	tad me kaijtsjka	tada mãĩ k^hāi cukā	तद मैं खाइ [खा] चुका

The same tendency is witnessed in the case of complex verbs with *karnā* 'to do' and *honā* 'to be'.

The classification schemes of tenses have several shortcomings. The most serious is that Ketelaar failed to distinguish among tenses (present, perfect, and future), moods (imperative, etc.), and participles (imperfect, etc.). Also, it seems that variations and exceptions motivate his subclassification of perfect and future tense. He was a structuralist in his orientation: he had neither a conceptual sociolinguistic framework nor the analytical tools to analyze free variation. For every distinct form encountered, he posited a subcategory of the tense. A case in point is his classification of first future and second future, see Chatterji 1933 and Vogel 1941 for a detailed analysis of Ketelaar's grammar section. In spite of these shortcomings, one must give credit to Ketelaar that he never failed in his observation about the SOV word order of Hindi.

An overview of the grammatical component shows that Ketelaar's treatment of Hindī grammar is quite rudimentary and does not have much depth from the point of view of current developments in Hindī grammar. This is not unexpected when we consider that it is a pioneer work which came into being under severe handicaps. Several topics of Hindī grammar, such as its writing system, phonetics, and phonology, received either little or no attention.

The omission of the writing system provides further insights into Ketelaar's unconventional approach to language pedagogy. The history of the Indic grammatical tradition is testimony to the fact that Indic scripts held a special fascination for nonnative grammarians. Ketelaar's departure from this traditional approach by nonnative grammarians cannot be overlooked. Throughout the grammar Ketelaar employed the Roman script in the transcription of his Hindī data.

Inclusion of the Hindī translation of the Lord's Prayer, the Ten Commandments, and some beliefs about moral conduct is another important feature of Ketelaar's grammar.

3 A Reassessment of Ketelaar's Grammar

Our new findings based on direct evidence call for a reassessment of earlier reports of Ketelaar's grammar. The grammar is not free from shortcomings. Ketelaar naturally committed linguistic errors, both transcriptional and factual, at all linguistic levels: phonetics/phonology, morphology, and syntax. But one must remember that grammar was not written in a prescriptive framework. Prescriptive grammarians may decry his errors, but they are a gold mine for researchers in (real-time-) language processing, second-language acquisition, sociolinguistics, language variation, language methodology, and language modeling, particularly for linguistic ecology and language evolution (see Mufwene 2001).

Most importantly, the grammar is a time capsule and provides a window through which to view perspectives on the nature of bilingualism/ multilingualism and the society in seventeenth-century India. It is capable of shedding light on contemporary issues ranging from globalization and business models of communication to the invisible history behind the history of the emergence of comparative and historical methods in linguistics, for more details, see Bhatia and Machida 2008.

4 Conclusions

The pioneering tradition of the Hindi grammatical tradition was non-native in origin. Contrary to the widely held belief by historians of Hindī grammar, the first grammar of Hindī was written neither in English nor in one of the other Indian languages. Its creator was neither an Englishman nor an Indian. The first grammar of Hindi was written in Dutch using Dutch-German transcription system.

Unlike missionaries, Ketelaar neither consulted with Pundits nor did he ask them to edit his grammar. Thus, his grammar is a gold mine for second language acquisition research and presents a raw acquisition data of his second language learning and language variation in Hindī. Furthermore, it opens new frontiers in the study of the evolution of scientific thought in the linguistic sciences.

References

Aranha, Paolo. 2015. Vulgaris seu Universalis: Early Modern Missionary Representations of an Indian Cosmopolitan Space. Cosmopolitismes en Asie du Sud: Sources, itinéraires, langues (XVIe-XVIIIe siècles), eds. Corinne Lefèvre, Ines G. Županov, Jorge Flores, Collection *Puruṣārtha* 33. Paris: Éditions de l'École des hautes études en sciences sociales, 331–360.

Bhatia, Tej K. 1987. *A History of the Hindī grammatical tradition: Hindī-Hindustānī grammar, grammarians, history and problems*. Leiden: E. J. Brill.

Bhatia, Tej K. 2001. Grammatical traditions in contact: The case of India. *Indigenous grammar across cultures*, ed. by Hannes Kniffka, 89–115. New York: Peter Lang.

Bhatia, Tej K. 2011. Teaching language. In: *The Cambridge encyclopedia of languages and linguistics*, pp. 842–845. Cambridge: Cambridge University Press.

Bhatia, Tej K. and K. Machida. 2008. *The oldest [European] grammar of Hindustani: language, contact and colonial legacy*. Tokyo, Japan (3 volumes). Tokyo: Tokyo University.

Bhatia, Tej K. and K. Machida. 2016. Pioneering Dutch scholarship on historical Indology and linguistic sciences. *Histoire, épistémologie, langage* 38/1, pp. 39–62.

Chatterji, S. K. 1933. The oldest grammar of Hindustānī. *Indian Linguistics* [1965 Reprint] II. 68–83.

Lenneberg, E. 1967. *Biological foundations of language*. New York: Wiley Press.

Herren M. W and S. A. Brown. 1988. *The sacred nectar of the Greeks: The study of Greek in the West in the early Middle Ages*. London: University of London King's College.

McGregor, S. 2001. *The formation of modern Hindi as demonstrated in early 'Hindi' dictionaries*. Amsterdam: Royal Netherlands Academy of Arts and Sciences, pp. 1–31.

Mufwene, S. 2001. *The ecology of language evolution*. Cambridge: Cambridge University Press.

Osselton, N. E. 1973. *The dumb linguists: A study of the earliest English and Dutch dictionaries*. Leiden: Publications of the Sir Thomas Browne Institute, Special series.

Vogel, J. Ph. 1935. Jean Josua Ketelaar of Elbing, author of the first Hindustānī grammar. *Bulletin of the School of African and Oriental Studies* VIII. 817–822. University of London [reprint 1964].

Appendix 1
Register der Capitulen
(Table of Contents)

Ketelaar's Section	Dutch	English
1	van God	of God
2	van de wereld	of the world
3 n	van de lughts vertoogen n	of the air n
4	van de winden	of the winds
5	van de gewesten der wereld en elementen	of the parts of the world and elements
6	van de mensch en sijn deelen	of human and his body parts
7	van de familien	of the family
8	van de hooge ampten	of high offices
9	van de kunst ambaght en kleine ampten	of the arts and lower offices
10	van de militaire ampten	of the military offices
11	van verscheijde natien	of the different nations
12	van de veraghte en oneerleu ampten	of the despised and dishonorable occupations
13	van viervoetige land gediertens	of the quadruped land animals
[14]	van't gevogelte	of the birds
[15]	van't bloeijeloose gedierte	of bloodless creatures [insects]
[16]	van de feneijnige gediertens	of poisonous animals
17	van de vischen	of the fishes
18	van de eetwaaren	of the foods
19	van de dranken	of the beverages
20	van de kleederen	of the clothes
[21]	van't huij en sijn deelen	of the house and its parts
22	van't huijsraed en gereetschappen	of the furniture and tools
23	van de oorlogs behoeften	of the war materials
24	van den boom en sijn vrughten	of trees and their fruits
25	van de thuijn en veld vrughten	of the garden and field fruits [crops]
26	van de specereijen	of the spices
27	van de juwelen	of the jewels
28	van de boegh giften	of the minerals
29	van't geld	of the money
30	van de landschappen	of the landscapes
31	van't schip en toebehooren	of the ship and its equipment

Appendix 1 (continued)

Ketelaar's Section	Dutch	English
32	van de verruwen	of the colors
33	van de tijden	of the times
34	van de maanden	of the months
35	van de dagen	of the days
36	van't getal	of the numbers
37	van't order getal	of ordinal numbers
38	van't gebrooken getal	of fractional numbers
39	van de vijf sinnen	of the five senses
40	van verscheijde siecktens	of the different illnesses
41	van verscheijde oliteijtan	of different oils
42	van de substantiva en adjectiva	of diverse nouns and adjectives
43	van de adverbia	of adverbs
44	van de verba	of verbs
45	verba der eerste conjugatie	verbs of the first conjugation
46	declinatie der Persiaanse taale	declension of the Persian language
47	conjugatie der Moorse+ taale	conjugation of the Moorish language
[48]	declinatie der Moorse++ taale	declension of the Moorish language
49	conjugatie der Moorse++ taale	conjugation of the Moorish language
50	beduijding eeniger Moorse namen	meaning of some Moorish names
51	naast gelijckende woorden	homonymous and semi-homophonous words
52	explicatie eeniger hindoustanse woorden	explanation of some Hindustānī words
[53]	reductie van caren en ponden	deduction of caren and pounds...

[ ] left blank in the original; our numbering.
+ copyist's error; the intended word was 'Persian'
++ The title in the main text uses the word Hindustānī instead of Moorish

There is also a "mystery" page (untitled page) preceding the title page. At first glance, it appears to be an irrelevant page for the work and to give the impression of a scribble aimed at pen tuning. But the page is neatly boxed and is retained in the manuscript along with other important pages. Although some parts of the page give an appearance of the early Indic writing system, I am not certain. Was it an attempt to record some letters of business script? However, one thing that is somewhat clearer is Ketelaar's attempt to record Indic/Hindī numerals; although they were not used in the official documents since Persian was the official language, they were quite prevalent at the time in the daily business activities of the Hindus.

There is a discrepancy between the table of content and the number/content presented in the main body of the grammar. An all-inclusive list of table of contents is given below.

Appendix 2
A complete Table of Contents based on the body of the manuscript

Ketelaar's section	Dutch	English	Manuscript pages
* [A]		untitled ("mystery") page	
* [B]	instructie off	instruction or...	
* [C]	Ad Lectorem Benevo-lum	to the kind reader	
* [D]	voor Reeden	preface	
* [E]	Register der Capitulen	Table of Contents	
1	van God	of God	1
2	van de wereld	of the world	1
3	van de lughts ver-toogen	of the air	1
4	van de winden	of the winds	1
5	van de gewesten der wereld	of the parts of the world	2
6	van de mensch en sijn deelen	of the human and his body parts	2–4
7	van de elementen+	of the element	4–6
[7a]	van de familien	of the family	
8	van de hooge ampten	of the high offices	6–8
9	van de kunst ambaght en kleine ampten	of the arts and lower occupations	8–10
10	van de militairen	of the military offices	10–11
11	van verscheijde natien	of the different nations	11–12
12	van de veraghte en oneerlijke ampten	of the despised and dishonorable occupations	12–13
13	van viervoetige land gediertens	of the quadruped land animals	13–14
14	van't gevogelte	of the birds	14–15

Appendix 2 (continued)

Ketelaar's section	Dutch	English	Manuscript pages
15	van de bloeijeloose beeskens	of the bloodless creatures	15–16
16	van de feneijnige gediertens	of the poisonous animals	16
17	van de vischen	of the fish	16–17
18	van de eetwaaren	of the foods	17–18
19	van de drank	of the beverages	18–19
20	van de kleeden	of the clothes	19–20
[21]	van't huij en sijn deelen	of the house and its parts	20–21
22	van't huijsraed en reetschappen	of the furniture and tools	21–26
23	van de oorlogs behoeften	of the war materials	27–28
24	van den boomen ende sijn vrughten	of the trees and their fruits	28–29
[25]	van de thuijn en veld vrughten++	of the garden and field fruits [crops]	28–29
26	van de specereijen	of the spices	29–30
27	van de juweelen	of the jewels	30
28	van de bergiften	of the minerals	31
29	van't geld	of the money	31–32
30	van de landschappen	of the landscapes	32–33
31	van't schip en toebehooren	of the ship and its equipment	33–34
32	van de verruwen	of the colors	34–35
33	van de tijden	of the times	35–36
34	van de maanden	of the months	36
35	van de dagen	of the days	37
36	van't getal	of the numbers	37–38
37	van't order getal	of the ordinal numbers	38–39
38	van't gebrooken getal	of the fractional numbers	40
39	van de vijv sinnen	of the five senses	40
40	van verscheijde siecktens	of different illnesses	41
41	van verscheijde oliteijten	of different oils	41
42	van devirse substantiva ende adjectiva	of diverse nouns and adjectives	42–52
43	van de adverbia	of adverbs	52–56
44	verba	verbs	57–66
[45]	verba der eerste conjugatie	verbs of the first conjugation	66–71

Appendix 2 (continued)

Ketelaar's section	Dutch	English	Manu-script pages
46	van de declinatie der Persiaanse taale	of the declension of the Persian language	72–73
47	van de conjugatie der Persiaanse +++ taale	of the conjugation of the Persian language	74–78
[48]	declinatie der Hindoustanse ++++ taale	declension of the Hindustānī language	79–85
49	conjugatie der Hindoustanse ++++ taale	conjugation of the Hindustānī language	86–92
50	beduijding eeniger Moorse namen	meaning of some Moorish names	93–94
51	naast gelijckende woorden	homonymous and semi-homophonous words	94–97
52	explicatie van verscheijde soo persiaans als Hindoustanse woorden bij mooren gebruijkelijk	explanation of several Persian and Hindustānī words used by the Moors	98–106 [106–107 blank]
[53]	Tein Giboden; de twaelf artijkulen onses algemeenen endo ongetwijgfled en christal geloofd; Tonse Vader +++++	Lord's Prayers; The Twelve Christian Beliefs; Our Father	108–111 [112–117 blank]
[54]	instructie tot gebruijck der volgende taefel ++++++	instruction to the use of following tables	118–123
[55]	index... +++++++	index...	124–144

[ ] our insertion or numbering; sections [A], [B], [C], [D], [E] are not included in Ketelaar's Register der Capitulen (Table of Contents).

+ Although Ketelaar's table of contents give the following title "van de gewesten der wereld en elementen," the element portion is actually covered in section 7 of the main body.

++ Section 25 "van de thuijn en veld vrughten" 'of the garden and its field fruits [crops]' of Ketelaar's table of contents is merged into section 24.

+++ Ketelaar's table of contents: 'Moorse' instead of "Persiaanse"

++++ Ketelaar's table of contents: 'Moorse' instead of "Hindoustanse"

+++++ Ketelaar's table of contents: "reductie van caren en ponden" 'deduction of caren and pounds' instead of "Tein Giboden..."

++++++ Ketelaar's table of contents lack the title: "explicatie van verscheijde soo persiaans als Hindoustanse woorden bij mooren gebruijkelijk"

+++++++ Ketelaar's table of contents the title: "index..."

List of contributors

Tej Krihsan Bhatia is a Professor of Linguistics & Cognitive Sciences and Director of South Asian Languages at Syracuse University. He is also a Fellow of the Forensic Sciences and National Security Institute, and is affiliated with the Information and Technology Group at the Maxwell School of Citizenship and Public Affairs, the Cognitive Sciences Program, and the International Relations program at the Maxwell School. He teaches classes on forensic linguistics, sociolinguistics, and bilingualism. He has published 16 books and numerous articles on bilingualism, multiculturalism, media and advertising, socio- and psycho-linguistics, and English and South Asian languages. He is a recipient of the Chancellor's Citation Award for Excellence in Research, and has received grants from the National Science Foundation, U.S. Department of Education, Mellon Foundation, The Smithsonian Institution, and the Linguistic Society of America, among others. Professor Bhatia has been named President of the International Association of World Englishes in 2018.

Rajesh Bhatt is a professor of linguistics at the University of Massachusetts at Amherst. After receiving his PhD from the University of Pennsylvania in 1999, he taught linguistics at the University of Texas in Austin for five years. He has also been a visiting Professor at MIT and taught at a number of international summer schools such as LSA summer institute (MIT/Harvard 2005, University of Colorado 2011, University of Chicago 2015), the LOT winter school, LISSIM, the EGG summer school, the NYI summer school and Crete-Ling. His research interests lie in the field of comparative syntax of Modern Indo-Aryan languages as well as the syntax-semantics interface. Professor Bhatt has published widely on different topics in Indo-Aryan linguistics and was part of NSF funded Hindi-UrduTreebank project at IIT in Hyderabad, India.

Pradeep Kumar Das is a Professor of linguistics at JNU, New Delhi. He has done research in the field of morpho-syntax for the last 24 years. He has published papers in both national and international journals. He worked in the Department of Linguistics at the University of Delhi for thirteen years before joining the faculty at the prestigious Jawaharlal Nehru University in New Delhi. His work on Grammatical agreement in Hindi-Urdu and its major varieties is considered a major contribution in the field of language typology and received praise from none other than Bernard Comrie: "It is a pleasure and a privilege for me to introduce the first monograph of a promising young Indian scholar to the linguistic community."

Veneeta Dayal is Professor of Linguistics at Rutgers University, where she has taught semantics since 1990. She studies the semantics of natural language and its interface with syntax, typically from a cross-linguistic perspective, with particular focus on WH-constructions, bare nominals, (in)definiteness, genericity, word order, and free choice items. Her work has appeared in Linguistic Inquiry, Natural Language and Linguistic Theory, and Natural Language Semantics, and she is the author of Locality in Wh Quantification (Kluwer, 1996), Questions (OUP, 2016) and co-editor of Clause Structure in South Asian Languages (Kluwer 2004).

Andrea Drocco is a Fixed-term Researcher in the Department of Asian and North-African Studies at Ca' Foscari University of Venice where he teaches Indo-Aryan linguistics and the Hindi language. After receiving a PhD in Indological Studies in 2005 from the University of Turin, he has taught Indo-Aryan linguistics at the same University. His main area of research is the development of the alignment system of New Indo-Aryan languages, in particular in the period preceding the 19th century. He has published research papers not only on the morphosyntactic alignment of Braj-bhasha, Hindi and Bangani, but also on the interpretation of the technical terms *tatsama*, *tadbhava* and *deśī* in the context of the Prakrit grammatical tradition.

Shamim Fatma is an Associate Professor of computational linguistics at the Mahatma Gandhi International Hindi University at Wardha in India, where in addition to teaching the Hindi language, she carries out research in the field of Hindi computational linguistics.

Vincent Homer is an assistant professor of linguistics at the University of Massachusetts at Amherst and a researcher at CNRS in Paris. After receiving his PhD from the University of California Los Angeles in 2011, Professor Homer has taught at different international summer events such as the EGG Summer School and the Generative Grammar summer school in Tbilisi, Georgia. He is a formal semanticist with a keen interest in the areas of polarity, negation, presupposition, modality and aspect. His work has a strongly cross-linguistic bent with papers that examine Haitian Creole, Italian Sign Language, Hindi-Urdu in addition to English and French.

Peter Edwin Hook is Emeritus at the Universities of Michigan and Virginia. His academic interest has been in the linguistic description of languages belonging to the Indo-Aryan family in South Asia, and more broadly in their place in Masica's Indo-Turanian linguistic area. He taught linguistics, South Asian languages and literature at the University of Michigan for three and a half decades, and published on both Indo-Aryan languages and linguistics. His chief contributions are The Compound Verb in Hindi and numerous articles on the compound verb and other syntactic and semantic phenomena in western Indo-Aryan languages and dialects spoken in North India, West India, and Pakistan: Kashmiri, Marathi, Gujarati, Rajasthani, Shina, and Sanskrit. After Jules Bloch, Hook was the first to realize that Kashmiri, not unlike German, has V2 word order. More recent publications have refined the notion of South Asia as a linguistic area as first adumbrated by Murray Emeneau and – with the addition of Central Asia and Eastern Asia – expanded by Colin Masica.

Luidmila Khokhlova is Associate Professor of Philology at Moscow State University, where she teaches Hindi, Urdu and Punjabi, General Linguistics and courses like the Historical Development of Western New Indo-Aryan languages in the 14-20th centuries, the Syntactic Typology of the New Indo-Aryan languages, the Grammatical and Semantic Structures of Hindi/Urdu. The main spheres of her interest are the historical syntax of Western Indo-Aryan, the semantic structure of Hindi, the sociolinguistic problems of South Asia and Sikh studies. Her work has appeared in Papers of Moscow State University, Berliner Indologische Studien, Lingua Posnaniensis, Language Documentation & Conservation (University of Hawai'i Press), Indian linguistics, Osmania papers in Linguistics, etc. She is also one of the authors of a number of Hindi manuals for Russian students.

Ekaterina Kostina has taught Hindi, Bengali, Sanskrit – both languages and literatures – at St. Petersburg State University for over 13 years now. After her graduation in 2004 from the same University, she joined the department of Indian Philology where, in addition to her teaching activities, she actively pursues a great research interest in the field of Indo-Aryan languages, History of Indian studies in Russia, Indian cinema, Indian diaspora as well as the use of new technologies in Hindi language teaching. She has published numerous research papers on topics such as the use of Vyākhyā method in Hindi teaching, Hindi personal pronouns, oblique case and tense and aspect in Hindi.

Omkar N. Koul (Indian Institute of Language Studies, New Delhi) – a famous Indian linguist – held several academic as well as administrative positions for four decades. In particular, he was a professor at the LBS National Academy of Administration, Mussoorie, India, and a professor at the Central Institute of Indian Languages, Mysore. Koul also served as Acting Director of the Central Institute of Indian Languages from 1999 to 2000. He founded and for many years edited the Kashmiri literary journal वाख. As a researcher, his interests included the areas of linguistics, language education, communications management, and comparative literature.

Anoop Mahajan is a Professor in the Department of Linguistics at UCLA. He received his PhD in Linguistics from MIT in 1990 and has taught at UCLA since 1992. His research includes work in formal generative syntax with a special emphasis on how to account for typological variation across languages. He has published research on various topics in syntax that include word order and scrambling, agreement and case, ergativity, partial wh-movement and relative clauses.

Emily Manetta is a formal theoretical syntactician of Indic languages, with a particular interest in wh-questions and A-bar movement, ellipsis phenomena, and the verbal domain. She earned her PhD in linguistics at University of California Santa Cruz in 2006; her dissertation examined wh-questions in Hindi-Urdu and Kashmiri. She is an Associate Professor at the University of Vermont and is currently serving as chair of the Anthropology Department. Professor Manetta's most recent project investigates resumptive pronouns in Romani and returns to issues of wh-scope marking and relative clauses.

Annie Montaut is Emeritus professor at INALCO, where she taught Hindi and Indian linguistics for several decades until her retirement in 2013. She also taught at Ecole Normale Supérieure, University of Paris X and was a Fellow at the Institut d'Etudes avancées de Nantes in 2016. She has authored Le Hindi, Société de Linguistique de Paris (2012), Hindi Grammar Lincom Europa (2004) and co-edited Les mots du discours, Cahiers de l'INALCO (2003), La Saillance, Faits de langue 39 (2012). She has published numerous papers in Hindi Semantics and Syntax and recently contributed to diachronic studies (in Indo-Aryan Ergativity in Typological and Diachronic Perspective Dahl & Stronski (eds.), Benjamins, TSL 112, 2016; Diachronic Typology of non-canonical Subjects, Kulikov & Serzants (eds.), Benjamins, 2013) and grammaticalization (in Unity and diversity in Grammaticalization Scenarios, Malchukov & Bisang (ed.), Benjamins, 2017). She is also a literary translator from Hindi to French and has translated about 16 books.

Ghanshyam Sharma is Professor of Hindi at INALCO, Paris. He received a PhD in Hindi form Agra University, India and a PhD in semiotics from the University of Bologna, Italy. Before coming to Italy for post-doctoral research with Umberto Eco in Bologna, he was a Research Assistant at the Central Institute of Hindi, Agra. He has taught at the University of Venice and the University of Bologna. He is a semiotician with a keen interest in pragmatic aspects of Hindi grammar and Conditionals in Indo-Aryan languages. He has published numerous articles on topics in Hindi grammar and compiled the first-ever commissioned Italian-Hindi-Italian dictionary. He has also translated novels, from Italian into Hindi as well as from Hindi into Italian.

Boris Zakharyin is Professor of Indian Philology at the Institute of Asian and African Studies, Moscow State University. He is now the head of the Department of Indian Philology and has taught for over 40 years different Indian languages such as Hindi, Urdu, Kashmiri, Sanskrit, Pali and Telugu as well as topics such as 'Classical Indian Linguistic Tradition (Vyaakaraṇa)', 'Grammatical Structure of New Indo-Aryan languages', 'History of Indo-Aryan' and 'Linguistic Typology'. He has authored 13 books and 75 articles, mainly in Russian, and participated in various linguistic conferences in Russia and abroad. Popular among Indologists, he is a well-known scholar and widely cited author of some major works on Indology in general and Indian grammatical tradition in particular.

Index

ability 147, 148, 149, 150, 151, 152, 154, 155, 156, 157, 166, 174, 175, 178, 181
abstract nouns 193
accusative 197, 198, 199, 200, 202, 203, 206, 207, 208, 209, 210, 212, 289
acquisitive 177
Adger 63, 79
adjectival 108
adjective ontology 224
Aelbrecht 52, 68, 72, 79
afflictives 252
Agnihotri 121, 145
agreement 107, 108, 110, 111, 112, 187, 188, 201, 203, 213, 214, 215
Ahmed 47, 66, 79, 80
Aikhenvald 304, 328, 330
aktionsart 62, 74, 311
Alsina 48, 78, 79
Amarkānt 166, 183
Amberer 48
A-movement 105
anaphora 47, 53, 59, 82
anaphoricity 4
anaphorized 127, 129, 133
anumati 152, 153
aorist 108
Apabhraṃśa 123, 164, 183
Aranha 339, 349
articles 1, 2, 3, 6, 7, 8, 16, 21, 22, 23, 24
Ashokean Prakrit 124
aspirates 341
Assamese 120
attributive 107

Bahasa Indonesia 192
Bahl 187, 196, 197, 209, 213
Bailyn 72
Baker 48, 75, 78, 79, 80
Balti 258, 263
bare nominal 1, 2, 4, 6, 8, 10, 11, 12, 13, 16, 18, 20, 21, 22, 23, 24
bare nominals 24
Bashir 48
Beames 119
Begum 218, 243
benefactor 194
Bengali 116, 120, 144, 148, 180
Benveniste 140, 144, 145
Bhaṇḍārī 153, 154, 155, 156, 157, 183
Bhatia 273, 274, 283, 287, 301, 333, 335, 338, 340, 346, 348, 349
Bhatt 27, 30, 32, 46, 47, 51, 54, 58, 63, 67, 69, 70, 80, 126, 131, 144, 148, 160, 167, 183
Bhattacharya T., 19
Bhattacharyya, P. 195, 213, 218, 243
binding 99
Birjulin 304, 330
Bloch 120, 123, 124, 144
blocking 18
Brahmānand 150, 183
Brajbhasha 121, 141, 145
Bresnan 48, 78, 79
Brown 339, 349
Bubenik 120, 123, 144, 164, 171, 183
Bundeli 122, 145
Burton-Page 218, 243
Burushaski 258, 259, 263
Butt 47, 119, 126, 144, 190, 191, 213, 218, 243, 266, 283, 287, 288, 294, 296, 297, 301, 302

čāhie 153, 319, 320, 321
canonical 204, 205, 206, 207, 208, 209, 210, 211, 212, 213
canonical argument 204
canonical imperative 303, 305, 306, 308, 312, 315, 317
canonical imperatives 329
canonical marking 204
Caracchi 265, 269, 283
Cardona 119, 144, 165, 167, 183, 185
Carlson 9
case licensing 85, 89, 92, 93, 95, 96, 105
case markers 194, 209
case position 93, 97, 104

https://doi.org/10.1515/9783110610796-015

Caṭṭopādhyāẏ 174, 183
Caudharī 154, 168, 183
causativity 272
Chakrabarti 195, 196, 213
Chatak 120, 144
Chatterji 124, 335, 347, 349
Chierchia 14, 16, 18, 19, 21, 25
Chinese 49
Chomsky 93, 106, 187, 206, 207, 213
Choudhury 47, 53, 83
Cinque 96
Cinque's universal template 103
Clark 289, 301
commissive 304
comparatives 27
complex predicate 47, 188, 190, 191, 192, 193, 194, 195, 204, 217
compound verbs 217, 218, 265, 266, 268, 277
Comrie 96, 187, 204, 205, 207, 214, 215
conjunct verb 187, 188, 190, 191, 192, 193, 194, 195, 196, 197, 198, 199, 200, 201, 203, 206, 207, 208, 209, 210, 211, 212, 218
Conjunct verb 217, 221, 225, 226, 227, 230, 234
conjunctive 155
constraints 287, 289, 290, 292, 294, 300
controlling properties 287, 298, 300
converb 147, 163, 164, 165, 166, 167, 170, 172, 174, 175, 176, 182

Das 187, 191, 199, 214, 219, 243
Daschenko 148, 183
dative 174, 194, 199, 200, 203, 206, 208, 209, 211, 212
Davison 47, 49, 50, 52, 53, 62, 79, 80, 81, 287, 288, 301
Dayal 1, 4, 5, 14, 16, 17, 19, 21, 22, 25, 126, 131, 195, 214
De Clerck 304, 330
De Vogüé 128, 130, 144
deferred imperative 311, 326
definite 1, 2, 3, 4, 5, 6, 7, 8, 13, 14, 16, 17, 18, 19, 20, 21, 22, 23, 24, 289
demand 308, 319
demonstratives 345
deontic modality 303, 307, 322, 323, 327, 328, 330
deontic necessity 325
deontic possibility 325
Depiante 68, 81
derivation 107
determiner phrase 85
de-transitivisation 282
differential object marking 94
differential verbal comparatives 27
direct daughters 294
direct object 151, 153, 154, 166, 172, 173, 192, 205, 207, 209, 210, 211
directive illocutions 303, 307
directive strategies 303, 304, 305, 321, 329
ditransitive 194, 199, 200, 207, 208, 212
Dixon 204, 213, 214
Doron 49
Dravidian 107, 112
Drocco 121
Duroiselle 174, 183
Dutch 333, 334, 335, 337, 338, 340, 342, 343, 346, 347, 348, 349, 350, 351, 352, 353, 354
Dymshits 171, 177, 178, 183

Eastern languages 123, 124, 139
Eaton 141, 144
ellipsis 47, 48, 49, 51, 52, 53, 54, 55, 56, 58, 59, 60, 61, 64, 68, 70, 71, 72, 74, 78, 79, 81, 82, 83
Emonds 72, 81
English 27, 29, 30, 31, 32, 44, 45, 288, 289
Enç 6
epistemic necessity 325
epistemic possibility 325
ergative 86, 113, 198, 199, 200, 208, 209, 210, 212, 214
ergativity 272
Ernoult 140, 144
excorporation 75
experiencer 247, 248, 249, 250, 252
expressive directives 304

Farkas 7, 25
Fiengo 48
finite verb 154

finiteness 206
Fodor 6, 25
Folli 50, 64, 76, 77, 81
Frankel 128
Funakoshi 49, 53, 57, 58, 81
future 346, 347

genitive 151, 152, 197, 202, 209, 211
German 333, 343, 348
gerund 115, 116, 117, 119, 120, 121, 122, 124, 133, 139, 140, 141, 144
Geuder 49, 62, 80, 266, 283
Gilchrist 273, 283
Godān 279
Goldberg 47, 49, 53, 55, 68, 69, 81
Gopāl 154, 183
grammaticalization 190, 193, 214
Greaves 164, 168, 171, 174, 179, 180, 183
Greenberg 287, 301
Gribanova 47, 49, 52, 53, 54, 57, 59, 60, 68, 69, 72, 81
Grierson 115, 116, 144, 146
Grimshaw 73
Gruber 194
Gujarati 116, 119, 121, 139, 140, 141, 142, 144, 145, 146
Guru 169, 183, 191

Hacker 266, 283
Haig 273, 283
Hankamer 48, 59, 82, 83
Hardt 48
Harvey 48
Haspelmath 119, 141, 144
head movement 50
headlessness 245
Hebrew 49, 53, 55, 81
Heim 2, 3, 25
Heine 124, 144
Herren 339, 349
Hock 195, 214, 272, 274, 283
Hoekstra 75
Hoernle 116, 119, 145
Hoji 49
Homer 27, 30, 32, 46
honā 151, 153, 319, 320
Hook 47, 48, 49, 62, 82, 86, 106, 148, 167, 178, 183, 191, 214, 218, 243, 245, 246, 250, 253, 259, 263, 265, 266, 267, 268, 277, 283, 284, 287, 301
Hopper 266, 273, 275, 276, 284
hortatives 304, 307, 330

idiom chunks 102
imperatives 303, 304, 308, 310, 311, 314, 315, 319, 321, 322, 324, 325, 326, 328, 329, 330, 346, 347
imperfect 346, 347
inability 157, 176
incorporation 195, 196, 197, 200, 214, 215
indefinite 1, 2, 3, 4, 5, 6, 7, 8, 9, 10, 11, 12, 13, 15, 16, 17, 18, 19, 20, 21, 22, 23, 24
Indo-Aryan 115, 120, 122, 139, 140, 141, 144, 145, 146, 161, 163, 164, 165, 167, 174, 183, 184, 185, 186, 245, 247, 250, 255, 259, 263
infinitive 115, 116, 117, 118, 119, 120, 121, 122, 125, 126, 127, 128, 129, 132, 133, 134, 138, 139, 140, 141, 142, 143, 145, 346
ingestive verbs 278
instrumental 197, 202
interrogatives 345
Intrinsic agreement-pattern 187
Ionin 24
Irish 49
island 47
islandhood 61
islands 59, 60
Italian 126

Jain 155, 173, 183, 185
Japanese 192
Jayaseelan 48
Jespersen 62, 82
Jha 164, 184
Johansson 163, 183
Johnson 48
jussives 304

Kachru B., 287, 301
Kachru, Y. 109, 155, 167, 168, 176, 183, 191, 204, 213, 214, 215, 268, 269, 271, 274,

284, 287, 298, 301, 305, 310, 315, 317, 330
Kalasha 258, 263
Kale 162, 163, 183
Kamaleśvar 152, 156, 158, 159, 161, 169, 180, 183
kāraka theory 207
Kashmiri 245, 249, 250, 251, 252, 253, 254, 255, 259, 261, 262, 263
Katenina 169, 175, 183
Kayne 75, 104, 106
Keenan 86, 96, 106
Kellogg 191, 215, 305, 330
Kennedy 48
Ketelaar 333, 334, 335, 336, 337, 338, 339, 340, 341, 342, 343, 344, 345, 346, 347, 348, 349, 350, 351, 352, 353, 354
Keyser 50
Khatrī 158, 183
Khokhlova 123, 142, 145, 287, 288, 298, 300, 301
Kidwai 4, 26, 47, 57, 58
King 49
Klaiman 195, 215, 287, 298, 301
Ko, 24
Kohlī 151, 153, 157, 158, 166, 183
Koizumi 68, 82
Korean 192
Koul 86, 106, 245, 249, 250, 253, 255, 305, 330
Kratzer 93, 106
Kumar 51, 52, 67, 70, 82
Kurylowicz 140
Kuteva 124, 144
Kuznetsov 165, 184

Lahiri 49
Latin 118, 124, 140, 141, 144, 340, 344
Lazard 272, 273, 284
Levin 219, 243
Li 27, 28, 45, 46
light verb 159, 168, 187, 190, 191, 193, 194, 195, 196, 197, 198, 199, 200, 201, 202, 203, 204, 208, 209, 210, 211, 212, 218, 219, 222, 243
Liperovskiy 109, 110, 114
Lobeck 48
Löbner 2, 5, 26
locative 194, 197, 202
long distance agreement 126, 127, 128, 129, 130, 131, 132, 134, 138, 140, 141, 142
Longobardi 19, 26

Machida 333, 335, 338, 346, 348, 349
machine translation 218, 219, 222
Mahābhāratam 162
Mahajan 47, 48, 49, 62, 63, 70, 72, 73, 82, 85, 89, 90, 91, 92, 93, 94, 95, 96, 104, 106, 126, 145, 268, 284
Mahrotrā 150, 184
Maithili 120, 145
Malayalam 288
Malchukov 250, 258, 263
Manetta 47, 66, 67, 68, 70, 73, 77, 79, 82
Marathi 116, 118, 123, 139, 144, 145, 146, 255, 258, 261, 263
Martins 49, 82
Masica 4, 166, 167, 174, 176, 184, 191, 215, 255, 263, 266, 277, 278, 284, 287, 301
matrix subject 100
Matthews 169, 171, 172, 184
May 48
McCloskey 47, 49, 55, 58, 68, 69, 82
McGregor 167, 171, 175, 184, 267, 268, 269, 274, 284, 305, 311, 322, 330, 335, 349
Medieval Hindi 165
Megerdoomian 50, 76, 77, 83
Mel'čuk 250, 263
Menon 47, 49, 53, 83
Merchant 52, 68, 72, 83
Mīcū 154, 184
Middle Indo-Aryan 108, 165
Mills 345
Minimalist 75
Mitr 181, 184
modals 147, 148, 160, 174
Modern Braj 165
Modern Kangri 141
Mohanan 126, 191, 194, 211, 215, 274
Mohanan, K.P. 215, 288, 289, 290
Mohanan, T. 47, 48, 49, 62, 79, 83, 191, 194, 195, 196, 197, 201, 202, 203, 215, 218, 243, 271, 272, 284, 287, 288, 289, 290, 292, 293, 294, 295, 300, 301

Molesworth 261, 263
Mona Singh 289
Montaut 150, 155, 159, 167, 171, 172, 173, 176, 184, 268, 269, 278, 279, 284, 287, 288, 298, 301, 302, 305, 330
Moulton 68
Mufwene 348, 349

Næss 277
Nāgar 151, 153, 155, 184
Nandan 181, 184
Nāth 161, 184
Neo-Carlsonian approach 1
Nepali 180
Nespital 156, 165, 167, 169, 172, 176, 184, 267, 271, 274, 284
New Indo-Aryan 108
New Testament 165, 179, 180, 184
Nishioka 38
nominal category 344
nominal host 187, 190, 191, 193, 195, 197, 198, 199, 200, 201, 202, 203, 204, 208, 209, 210, 211, 212
nominal paradigm 338
nominative 197, 198, 199, 202, 204, 206, 207, 208, 209, 210, 211, 212, 213, 246, 249, 250, 261, 289
non-canonical argument 204
non-canonical imperative 315
non-canonical imperatives 304, 317, 319, 321, 322, 329
non-canonical marking 204, 207
noun ontology 222
null object pronominal 49
null pronominals 51, 52, 54, 59

Oberlies 164, 184
obligation 303, 318, 320, 321, 323
oblique infinitive 147, 150, 155, 160, 174, 176
Ogawa 250, 263
Oku 53
Old Hindi 164, 174, 180
Old Marathi 123
Old Rajasthani 122, 123
Onishi 204, 213
ontological features 217, 222, 227
ontology 217, 222
Oranskaya 155, 184
Osselton 339, 349
Otani 49, 68, 83

Pā̃ḍe 155, 169, 184
Paillard 128
Pal 218
Pali 163, 164, 174, 183, 184
Palmer 304, 330
pānā 147, 148, 156, 158, 159, 160, 161, 172, 173, 174, 175, 176, 179, 182
Pandharipande 267, 268, 269, 270, 271, 272, 274, 284
Pāṇini 207
Pāṇinian hypothesis 207
Pardeshi 273, 284
paṛnā 153, 319, 320
participial modifiers 109, 112, 113
passivization 268, 269
Payne 54, 83
perfect 346, 347
permission 147, 148, 149, 153, 156, 174, 177, 178, 179, 181, 308, 317, 322
permissive 152, 156, 160, 174, 175, 176, 177, 178, 182
Persian 47, 50, 52, 56, 63, 64, 70, 75, 76, 77, 78, 81, 82, 83, 239, 240, 241
phantom valents 245, 261
phi-features 206, 208, 209, 210, 211, 212
Pischel 164, 184
pluperfect 346
Pollock 68
polysemy 40, 46
Pompur 253, 263
Poornima 148, 167, 170, 184
Portuguese 49
possibility 147, 148, 149, 152, 155, 156, 162, 165, 169, 181
potential mood 155
potentials 179, 181, 182
pragmatic approach 276
Prakrit 164, 172, 184
Prasād 151, 175, 185
Premchand 151, 173, 177, 178, 183, 185, 279
Premdās 150, 185
prenominal relative clause 85
prenominal relatives clause 85

present 346, 347
presumptive 155
preterit tense 108
preterite tense 245, 246
preverbial 250, 257, 258
prohibitives 324
pronominal binding 100

Rajasthānī 340
Ramchand 47, 48, 49, 50, 62, 63, 67, 72, 73, 74, 75, 78, 80, 83, 266, 283
ranking 16, 18, 21
Rasekhi 56
reciprocal 97
reconstruction 100
reduced transitivity 265, 282
relative clauses 85
relatives 345
relativization 90
relativizer 107, 108
reproach 317, 323, 329
request 308, 311, 324
Rett 40
Robinson 21
Ross 47
Russian 49, 288, 289, 290, 301, 302

Sag 6, 25, 48, 59, 82, 83
Saito 49
saknā 147, 148, 152, 156, 158, 159, 160, 161, 165, 166, 167, 168, 169, 170, 171, 172, 174, 175, 179, 180, 181, 182
Saksena 189, 195, 196, 202, 205, 210, 215
sambhāvanā 152, 153
Sanskrit 115, 116, 118, 119, 120, 121, 122, 124, 139, 140, 145, 339
Śarmā 150, 154, 184, 185
Schachter 102
Schmidt 167, 171, 178, 185
Schönenberger 24, 26
Schwartzschild 120
Schwarzschild 42
scrambling 287, 289, 290, 291, 292, 293, 294, 296, 297, 300
second future 346, 347
Sells 48, 78, 79
semantic bleaching 193
semantic bonding 195, 201, 212
semantic field 194
semantic pattern 229
Shapiro 167, 170, 185
Sharma, A. 191, 215, 305, 308, 310, 311, 315, 330
Sharma, G. 307, 319, 325, 330
Shibatani 273, 284
Shina 258, 259, 263
Shlomper 148, 156, 185
Siewierska 258, 263
Simpson 47, 49, 53, 68, 83
Singh, A.K. 152, 185
Singh, B. 159, 173, 178, 185
Singh, D. 218, 243
Singh, M. 289
Singh, R. 121, 145
Singh, Rājnāth 161, 185
Singh, S.B. 160, 185
Snell 121, 145
Southworth 115, 116, 119, 120, 121, 139, 146
speech act 114
Speijer 161
Spejer 171, 185
Strnad 164, 170, 172, 174, 185
structural case 187
Subbarao 109, 112, 113, 114
subjecthood 204
Sulger 79
Suthar 119, 144
Śyāmsundardās 172, 175, 185
Syed 68, 83

Tada 104
Tagare 120, 146
Takahashi 30, 46, 53, 57, 83
tatsama 150
Telugu 107, 109, 112
Tessitori 122, 146
Thakur 4, 26
Thomas 140, 144
Thompson 273, 275, 276, 284
Thomson 266
Tikkanen 165, 171, 172, 185
Toosarvandani 47, 52, 57, 63, 64, 70, 75, 76, 77, 78, 83
topichood 22

Touratier 140, 146
transitivity 265, 266, 270, 272, 273, 274, 275, 276, 283, 284, 285
Tripāṭhī 151, 154, 160, 162, 184, 185
Tsunoda 273, 285

Uchida 219, 243
Ultsiferov 170, 171, 177, 185
unaccusative 27, 110, 131
unaspirates 341
underlying clauses 113
unergatives 33
Upādhyāy 181, 185

Vaidya 79
valency 248, 256
valency difference 248
Vālmīki Rāmāyanam 163
van der Auwera 324, 330
Van Olmen 304, 321, 331
Van Olphen 155, 159, 185
Varmā 154, 157, 177, 185
vector verb 265, 266, 267, 268, 269, 270, 271, 272, 274, 275, 276, 277, 278, 279, 281
verbal noun 115, 116, 120, 122, 124, 132, 133, 134, 140, 141
verbal paradigm 338
verbalizer 225, 228, 229, 231, 232, 238
Verbeke 195, 215, 253, 255, 263
Verma 4, 26, 109, 114, 191, 211, 215
Vincente 68
Vogel 333, 334, 335, 347, 349
volitionality 266, 270, 271, 272, 274, 275, 276, 277, 278, 282, 284

Wali 123, 144, 146
Wei-Te Chen 218, 243
Whitman 49, 68, 83
Whitney 171, 185
Williams 48
Winter 54, 84
Wurmbrand 104
Wurmland 126

Xrakovskij 304, 330

Yādav 160, 171, 172, 185
Yaśpāl 169, 173, 180, 186
Yates 179, 186

Zakharyin 288, 302
Zia 259, 263
Zograf 165, 167, 170, 175, 186
Zwart 75

www.ingramcontent.com/pod-product-compliance
Lightning Source LLC
Chambersburg PA
CBHW031421230426
43668CB00007B/382
* 9 7 8 3 1 1 0 7 0 8 0 5 9 *